ACTION RESEARCH for Teachers
Traveling the Yellow Brick Road

Mary Louise Holly
Kent State University

Joanne M. Arhar
Kent State University

Wendy C. Kasten
Kent State University

Third Edition

Allyn & Bacon
is an imprint of

Boston   New York   San Francisco
Mexico City   Montreal   Toronto   London   Madrid   Munich   Paris
Hong Kong   Singapore   Tokyo   Cape Town   Sydney

Vice President and Editor in Chief: Paul A. Smith
Senior Editor: Linda Ashe Bishop
Senior Managing Editor: Pamela D. Bennett
Senior Project Manager: Mary M. Irvin
Editorial Assistant: Demetrius Hall
Senior Art Director: Diane C. Lorenzo
Cover Designer: Brian Huber
Cover Image: Elisa Rogers
Operations Specialist: Matthew Ottenweller
Director of Marketing: Quinn Perkson
Marketing Manager: Krista Clark
Marketing Coordinator: Brian Mounts

Photo Credits: "Shawn," Prentice Hall School Division; "Jon," Frank LaBua/PH College; "Terry," Michael Littlejohn/PH College; "Roberto," Prentice Hall School Division; "Ruby," PH College

For related titles and support materials, visit our online catalog at www.pearsonhighered.com

Library of Congress Cataloging-in-Publication Data
Holly, Mary Louise.
  Action research for teachers: traveling the yellow brick road/Mary Louise Holly,
Joanne M. Arhar, Wendy C. Kasten.—3rd ed.
    p. cm.
  Includes bibliographical references and index.
  ISBN-13: 978-0-13-515761-9
  ISBN-10: 0-13-515761-7
  1. Action research in education. I. Arhar, Joanne M. II. Kasten, Wendy C. III. Title.
  LB1028.24.A75 2009
  370.7'2—dc22   2008002780

Printed in the United States of America
10 9 8 7 6 5 4 3 2 1   [RRD-VA]   12 11 10 09 08

**Allyn & Bacon
is an imprint of**

Invitation and Road Map for the Journey to Oz

More than one hundred years ago, Dorothy, in the *Wizard of Oz*, found herself in a strange land and started an adventure that would change her life and enable her to see her everyday surroundings with new eyes. The Yellow Brick Road, circuitous and enchanting, *was* easy to miss—as it did not lead Dorothy on the most direct route to the end of her journey. But, it was intriguing and engaging, allowing her to challenge herself in new mysteries and delights.

The challenges of the twentieth century were no less daunting to Dorothy than challenges and opportunities are to twenty-first century teachers. We invite you as a twenty-first century educator to join us as we journey on our own Yellow Brick Road, allowing you to critically reflect upon your own teaching and learning. Even as the journey can be arduous, the travel is worth it, paved with new understandings and enlightened viewpoints. Come with us now on the surprising and intriguing adventures of an action research journey.

What is the action research journey? In fact, what is action research?

Action research (AR) in the context of teaching is a form of inquiry designed to improve our teaching by using professional (informed) eyes to observe our own practice. We collaborate with others to enhance the power of our learning and we face the challenges we meet with action and analysis, sharing the results with others for critique. According to noted scholar John Elliott (1991), "Action research might be defined as the study of a social situation with a view to improving the quality of action within it."

David Tripp (1990) and his Australian colleagues describe AR as "a family of activities in curriculum development, professional development, school improvement programs, and systems planning and policy development. These activities have in common the identification of strategies and planned action which are implemented, and then systematically submitted to observation, reflection, and change" (p. 159).

Wilford Carr (2003) describes AR's essence: "The choice of action research is based on your educational beliefs, something for which you are morally responsible . . . . Action Research is not a thing. It is not a method. *It is an Aspiration*, and how you reach that aspiration in a practical context." The action research journey, then, is a process and structure for realizing educational aspirations. Can you recall what drew you to teaching? What were your aspirations? What are they now?

Why *This* Narrated Expedition?

As teacher-educators, we wanted to find a way to explain and facilitate action research as the journey that it is, not as a set of methods and techniques, a way to get from A to B by the shortest possible trip. Trips are fast and easily forgotten, but a *journey*? That's an entirely different way to move and be, filled with exploration, mystery, and challenge.

Our preservice and graduate students wanted a clearly narrated expedition that made practical sense, a grounded how-to guide with many examples. We wanted a book that would enable and support teachers to become experts in their own practice, as well as articulate spokespersons, critics, and colleagues able to communicate their appreciations and understandings to others. We wanted a book that made use of *all* the colors of the rainbow. We wanted AR in technicolor and motion, where curiosity, play, imagination, and creativity, as well as informed and disciplined method, were used in the service of social and educational aims.

This book is intended for educators committed to improving life through education. Although most examples in this book are drawn from classroom teachers, the processes we advocate are equally relevant to all who teach: parents, administrators, supervisors, college teachers, community and agency people, those in the helping professions such as theologians and nurses, professional organizations, and business people.

This book is designed to make conducting action research a natural part of teaching, because teaching well is a scholarly process, linking together practical aspects of how to conduct action research with scholarly tools that support the cycle of reflective practice. You will find out how you come to different understandings, and how you and your colleagues can become more articulate spokespersons for educating young people and adults. You will find illustrations of how other teachers have become researchers, and how they have learned to focus selectively, take action, document, analyze, and come to better understand some of the day-to-day and recurrent challenges of teaching.

Our journey through *Action Research for Teachers* provides us with a framework for problem solving in collaborative contexts. In collaborative problem posing and problem solving, we find that action research is a powerful method for documenting, developing, and evaluating the curriculum. Simultaneously, AR is a formidable process for evaluation and assessment as well as for professional growth.

How often have we looked to wizards for answers we could have found within ourselves? And, much to the point of AR, answers we can find with the help of our colleagues. So, while we are off to see the wizard on what might seem to be a perilous adventure, we are in good company. We will soon find ourselves, along with Dorothy and her friends, traveling the Yellow Brick Road. We will follow our hunches and discover that by sticking together, putting our *minds* and *hearts* and *courage* to the task, not only will we feel success along the way, but we will become wizards in our own lands of Oz.

Road Map of the Journey

Now that we have discussed some of the reasons for the journey, here is a road map for the organization of this book. The title of this book, *Action Research for Teachers*, directly and simply catches the main thrust of the book. It also forms the acronym ART, which aptly expresses our belief in the creative artistry of teaching and learning. Good teaching, learning, and research, by their very natures, are forms of action that are distinguished by what John Dewey termed an attitude of scientific inquiry. And this inquiry, we find, is a creative process.

You are the architect of your actions and your action research. You create your research path by deciding to make the journey, making—or creating—your Yellow Brick Road as you go.

As you travel through *Action Research for Teachers*, you will find several features that are designed to empower you—to develop the tools, powers of critical thought, creativity, and insights that you will use to create your own Yellow Brick Road—long after Dorothy is safely, if considerably wiser, back in Kansas.

- **Bookends**: A beginning and an ending to our journey
    1. *Invitation and Road Map for the Journey to Oz* that you are reading right now.
    2. *Lessons from Oz* for standing back and learning from where we've been.
- **Seven Sections**: Each complete with excerpts from *The Wonderful Wizard of Oz* (Baum, 1900) to set the tone of the section.
    - I. *The Scholar's Journey*
    - II. *Defining and Putting Action Research in Context*
    - III. *Exploring Researcher Selves and the Profession*
    - IV. *Developing an Inquiring Mind*
    - V. *Designing and Planning an Action Research Study*
    - VI. *Analyzing and Interpreting Data*
    - VII. *Writing and Sharing the Research Story*
- **Exploring the Forest**: At the conclusion of each section you will find a workshop of explorations and exercises that will enable you to develop tools for the journey, as well as to carry out an action research project as we progress through the book. These workshops will help you to keep a researcher's journal and to develop and collect artifacts that will provide materials from

which you can develop a mini-portfolio to present your study findings and illustrations of how you came to them.

- **Stepping Stones**: Within many chapters you will find Stepping Stones that will enable you to quickly gain insights and tips into processes such as Getting Organized, and Knowing What Documents and Artifacts to Save, and what URLs and technologies might be useful.
- **Case Studies**: Examples and excerpts from case studies and from other researchers' data collection will enable you to quickly grasp ideas described in the text. Five teachers accompany us on our journey, sharing their studies with us as we work through the book. Shawn is a young second-grade teacher helping a student from Korea learn English. Jon and Terry are veteran teachers focused on improving the reading of fifth graders through a literature-based program. Roberto, a veteran middle school special education teacher, creates a more inclusive school environment. Ruby, a middle-aged student teacher, emphasizes democratic processes for ninth graders studying U.S. government in a civics class.
- **Travelers' Notes**: In these appendices, fellow scholars provide notes of their projects: how they analyzed their data, told their research stories, and organized and displayed their data. A proposal and full-length action research study are included.
- **Glossary**: In order to join the conversation (and to leave your own notes and stories for the next travelers) you need to understand the terms. For quick reference, find these at the back of the book.

Although we have designed this book for a straightforward journey, we realize that there are many roads to Oz; some shorter than others, and that, depending on your experience and purposes you may want to take the superhighway. If so, read Section I, The Scholar's Journey, and then jump ahead to Section V, Designing and Planning an Action Research Study. You might choose the superhighway and later go back to visit missed sections. We think Sections II, III, and IV are important. They have to do with putting one's study into context, a key consideration in action research. Section II places action research into the larger context of paradigms, theories, and research, and provides discussion of orientations to knowledge and a brief history of how AR has developed. Section III explores and takes into account a key element—the selves who make and narrate the journey. We begin by taking ourselves into account, in a process called *autobiographical inquiry*. (Although this process forms an important basis for all aspects of the journey, it is linked quite closely with the narrative process that is the focus of Section VII.) Section IV, Developing an Inquiring Mind, addresses how to take a curiosity or problem and develop it into an action research study.

Sections V and VI take us through three of the four phases of the action research process, including planning and designing action research projects, and making sense out of the data we collect by analyzing, synthesizing, and interpreting it.

Section VII focuses on portraying and sharing the story with a variety of other people and finding media and methods appropriate for different audiences.

We conclude our journey by looking back at where we began and how we put it all together. We derive lessons from Oz—what we have learned from our journey and what it means for us as professionals.

Acknowledgments

We would like to acknowledge the many students, teachers, and other colleagues who have contributed to our growing understanding of teaching and learning and action research. Through them we are made aware of the challenges and triumphs possible for those who persist in pursuing questions and matters of consequence. We include examples from their studies in this text. Beyond their immediate work, however, is the power of their message: that through heart, mind, courage, and action, teaching and learning can be transformed. Not, however, without the company of our friends, those critical colleagues who, in the spirit of collegiality on this journey we call teaching and learning, have challenged our thinking. They are the wizards we celebrate throughout this book.

Our four case studies are drawn from the work of Jill Zuckerman Braun, Janice Schelat, Teresa Sopko, Rosemary Rudesal, and Angela Langstaff. We thank them in particular, for their willingness and courage to share some of their personal insights AND frustrations. The full-length action research study included in Travelers' Notes G is written by Rebecca Wiehe and Martha Pero.

From Joanne Arhar's action research classes over the years, she would like to thank the Master's in Arts of Teaching (MAT) students and classroom teachers whose work she has included in this book: Angela Langstaff, Pam Donaldson, Rosemary Rudesal, Deb Friesen, Antoinette Hampton-Wheeler, Tracy Kilfoil, Erika Weliczko, Gayle Buck, Darlene Mitroff, Andrea Nixon, Meridith Niecamp, Andrew Glasier, Trish Yakovich, Lorinda Koss, Matt Naska, Mary Schwartz, Rebecca Wiehe, Martha Pero, and many others who are not mentioned here.

From Wendy Kasten's action research classes over the years, she would like to thank the following graduate students whose work she has included in this book: Kathleen Ruttan, Bonnie Hood, Kelly McDougal, Kelly Chaboudy, Kim Gerdes, Patricia Whittaker, Cheryl Goldstein, Lisa Wood, Leann Laure, Lore Hawkins, Misse Farinacci, Brenda Greene, Perrine Robinson Geller, Jodi Dodds Kinner, Lynda Cornett, Nancy Dunker, Maureen Coe, Victoria Tapp, Vickie Greguric, Meredith Maurer, Tina Seese, Christine Crosslands, Mary Kirt, JoAnn Carter, Marjorie Braddix, Mark Tanski, Allyson Meyer, Vicki Kendra, Lisa Leone, Pam Russomanno, Pam Vanaags, Maren Koepf, Sandra Gardner, Karen Taylor, Suzanne Burkhardt, Georgia Darrah, Melisa Carlson, Joan Diamond, Jennifer Kadilak, Carol McIntosh, Diane Ingersoll, Barbara Martanovic, Debora Austin, Beth Souers, Carol Young, Kathleen Miller, Ann Ritchie, Sandra Hartman, Kelly DiThomas, Debra Lipnos, Christine Barkhurst . . . and all of the others whose work contributed in many ways to the writing of this book.

Mary Louise Holly would like to thank students and teachers over the years who have taught her about action research. Chuck Coleman, in 1969, at age 6, in a rural Michigan primary school classroom, taught a young teacher the need for humility, empirical evidence, and collaboration. Martha MacLure, a 6-year-old 20-odd years later in Norwich England, taught lessons of imagination and the will to create, and their power in any learning experience. Maggie MacLure brought substantive critique of action research. John Elliott's passion, commitment, and action on behalf of students and teachers to furthering the profession through Action Research have long been contagious. The Collaborative Action Research Network (CARN) which he founded, and people associated with it, Marion Dadds, Christine O'Hanlon, Bridget Somekh, Chris Day, Jack Whitehead, Richard Winter, Stephen Rolland, Pam Lomax, the late Kathe Greene, and colleagues Rob Walker and Michael Schratz and their work on qualitative methodology for social change as well as colleagues from Deakin University including Collin Henry, Helen Henry, Richard Davis, and Helen Modra deserve special note. Bev Timmons, Rich Ambrose, Beth Swadener, and the Master's Cohort teachers in Early Childhood Education at Kent State University, especially Cathy Reiner, Gwendolyn Bryant, Carol Law, and Becky Miller, who contributed to the manuscript, thank you. Helen Hulbert, thank you.

We would like to thank the reviewers of our manuscript for their insight and comments: Virginia A. Batchelor, Medaille College; Karen Ford, Ball State University; Leanna Manna, Villa Maria College; and Nancy Williams, University of South Florida.

Chrys Bouffler, from Queensland, Australia, suggested we journey to Oz in this book. Thank you.

Although there are many contributors to our thinking, what we have made of their contributions remains solely our responsibility.

The Yellow Brick Road beckons.

Contents

SECTION III   Exploring Researcher Selves and the Profession   57

SECTION IV   Developing an Inquiring Mind   79

SECTION VI Analyzing and Interpreting Data 185

I

The Scholar's Journey

"... **Y**ou must go to the City of Emeralds. Perhaps Oz will help you."

"Where is this City?" asked Dorothy.

"It is exactly in the center of the country, and is ruled by Oz, the Great Wizard I told you of."

"Is he a good man?" enquired the girl, anxiously.

"He is a good Wizard. Whether he is a man or not I cannot tell, for I have never seen him."

"How can I get there?" asked Dorothy.

"You must walk. It is a long journey, through a country that is sometimes pleasant and sometimes dark and terrible. However, I will use all the magic arts I know of to keep you from harm."

The Wonderful Wizard of Oz
L. Frank Baum (1900)

We invite you to begin the scholar's journey in Chapter 1 with reasons for the journey and a call to meet the challenges you will face as you learn to engage in your own action research. In Chapter 2 you will step into the forest to find, explore, and learn to use a few of the scholar's tools, including a journal to record your adventure.

CHAPTER 1

Somewhere Over the Rainbow . . .

Action research is a special kind of research that relies on a journey filled with action, reflection, and critique. Each step is intentional though our intentions aren't always conscious. Sometimes we have to trust our intuitions, and take steps to find out what we know but don't know we know, and to find out what we don't know and need to know.

Action research is a journey of *transformation*. Unlike previous efforts, we won't try to fix us—to make us "do more," "move faster," or "do better." In fact, we start from the premise that we are fine just as we are, that we have a great sense of the future, and that this journey will help us to bring today in line with that future. That means we will focus on our aspirations—on what our beliefs and values commit us to—on what we most want to bring about for students. We will develop a language of inquiry that will enable us to find the emeralds in our actions, to learn from our experience. The action research journey will enable us to live our aspirations even if it's hard to think about aspirations when we live in a world of unprecedented change, with demands increasing at an alarming rate. How do we keep our lives in balance? How do we decide what is worthy of our attention and energy?

A Time for Transformation If Ever a Time There Was

Between the years 1999 and 2002 the total number of publications in the history of publishing doubled. And the rate of change is accelerating: it doubles within 1 1/2 years as of this writing. Once people actually thought they could keep up with it all—and often they could! Not any more.

The so-called Millennial student, for example, is living in a world that was beyond the imaginations of all but the most clairvoyant teachers and faculty members when they themselves were students. What does this suggest for learning and for teaching in schools today? What experiences, minds, and hearts do students bring with them into the classroom? What do we envision for our students? What futures are we teaching toward and into?

We need to conceptualize and do our work *differently*. Teacher as conveyer of information has severely limited benefits. In the words of Robert Barr and John Tagg (Barr & Tagg, 1995) the instructional paradigm has far outreached its usefulness: it's time to move to the *learning paradigm*. As Robert Ornstein and Paul Ehrlich put it in *New World, New Mind* (1989), we need to change the way we think about the future, about teaching and learning. Action research is a structure for thinking about and navigating in this new world—and for bringing this new world into being. We need a critically transformative pedagogy that enables us to grow in ways that are creative, collaborative, and generative toward futures we create rather than inherit.

So how do we become critically reflective and generative in our educational practices? In *Becoming a Critically Reflective Teacher*, Stephen Brookfield (1995) notes that there are four lenses through which one can learn to be critically reflective: autobiography, colleagues, students, and literature. We add a fifth, one that is informed by and makes use of the first four; that is, action research, learning from our own and others' experience.

Action Research Defined: Doing It Differently

According to John Elliott (2003), action research starts with a feeling—a sense of frustration, or, better yet, a sense of creative possibilities for action, and the pronounced commitment to "do it differently," to bring one's practice in line with one's values and aspirations. Action research involves the continuous modification of a situation and theorizing from the standpoint of action. The action in action research is a special kind of generative action. Drawing on the work of philosopher Hannah Arendt (1958), Elliott suggests that action is one of the three basic modes of human activity: labor, work, and action. *Labor* is what one does to sustain life and comprises repetitious activity. *Work* involves projects and the creation of enduring objects or artifacts for use rather than to satisfy basic needs (as in labor). But *action* is an activity that changes a human situation by initiating something new.

> [H]uman beings learn who they are from their actions in the human world . . . action is always carried out in the company of others conceived as free and equal individuals who possess the exercising agency. . . . In action the agent takes into account the unique points of view that others hold toward the situation in question . . . the agent reveals his or her own distinctive view of the situation, but has developed it in communication

with others and accommodates . . . their own distinctive outlooks . . . for Arendt, the self only exists in action. (2003, pp. 24–25)

Action is distinguished from "activity" when that activity doesn't involve human intent and agency. For example, one can engage in mindless activity—such as on an assembly line—and need not take into account anyone else's perspective. Action research, on the other hand, implies consciousness and intention in taking the viewpoints of those in the study into account.

Research, as we discuss in Section II, consists of action that is systematic, self-critical inquiry made public (Stenhouse, 1975). For educators, action research offers a powerful tool for transforming the educational environment and what takes place under the auspices of the school.

The action research journey is

- a powerful process and structure for *professional growth and development* and lifelong learning;
- a structure that supports *critically reflective practice* that can become a natural part of teaching and learning;
- a process made possible by *intentional and conscious learning from experience*;
- *continuing staff development, cultural transformation*, and *educational change*; and
- *research-enabled curriculum and program development*.

The action research journey enables us to focus on what we value most, prioritize, and seek to achieve, thereby *living more effectively*.

New Worlds–New Challenges–New Minds

The long era of certainty is over. The modern era, "based on the premise that the world is objectively knowable, and that knowledge so obtained can be absolutely generalized" (Havel, 1992), has overextended its shelf life. We have begun to accept that our perspectives will always be partial. We are coming to understand the truth of what many Native Americans and poets have long known: we must learn to love the journey more than the destination. Life is a process; it is all journey. Destinations are not separate from the journey, they are markings—small and large—within the journey.

Not long ago, lifelong learning was something noted in reports and curriculum documents as something to reach for. Now we realize that it is a fact of life. We know much more about how people learn; "the (90s) decade of the brain" (1990s) brought us greater understanding of how the brain works, of how we come to develop the kinds of minds that "are us" (LeDoux, 2003; Ornstein, 1995).

The end of the modern era has enormous implications for education, not the least of which is the need for an educational system that is structured based on our aspirations for the future, not the past. As a noted scholar once said: "Our eyes are in the front of our heads—not in the back! They are designed to look forwards not backwards! Too much attention to the past can weigh us down!" Fixing what is wrong in the past will never bring us our imagined future; doing today differently can; envisioning that future and building structures to live it will.

The educational scholar's life is one of commitment to realizing one's aspirations, and thus to continual inquiry and growth. That is what this book is about. Action research enables us to see into the darkness created by previous levels of awareness and development. The imbalance of the world's resources and wealth and its effects on the environment and people's lives, and the misunderstanding and poverty of sensitivity and imagination to see below the surface of our social worlds, continues to build until, in an event like September 11, 2001, in New York City, it erupts and captures our attention, or a film such as Al Gore's *Inconvenient Truth* enables us to see what we'd rather not see.

Human Understanding and Community

We need different ways of thinking, different kinds of education and scholarship. We need, as Havel (1992) says, to *"try harder to understand than to explain."* Although much more is known about the world and its peoples, making sense of it is problematic. Mostly, we need *human understanding* and *connection*. We need to see and be in relationship—with the land, with ourselves, and with others. Although we may not be able to control the future in the ways we once thought we could, the good news is that with historical consciousness, sensitivity, and social purpose, together we *can* influence and help to shape new futures.

By the late nineteenth century, John Dewey had called for the creation of democratic communities where learning, individually and collectively, would be everyone's responsibility. For most of the twentieth century we focused on the individual. The democratic societies we sought would be comprised of informed, caring, and thoughtful citizens. Although the individual was key to social development, we didn't fully understand the importance of Dewey's concept of community.

The concept of community—holding values, beliefs, and aspirations in common—and its basis on the premise that all who belong contribute to the good of the community, is foundational for a democratic society. Communication is central to relationship and to community. We live and breathe shared social practices, beliefs, and values. We bring our worlds into existence through language and create and sustain community through networks of conversation.

We are social beings, related in ways that we only rarely appreciate. The importance of social context and communication to understanding was the major theme of scholar Erik Erikson, a contemporary of John Dewey and Jean Piaget. As a social scientist, he developed the concept of identity and a theory of psychosocial development, central to which is the idea that social contexts shape the human beings we become—as individuals and as groups. We will return to the work of these three scholars in Section III. Their work provides foundational theories that will inform our educational experiences—how we understand our students, our colleagues, and ourselves.

Challenges to Educators

Are we committed to a world of abundance for all? Do our aspirations include each student living to her or his potential on an earth where communities are stewards of the planet and its resources? Do our aspirations include community, literacy, and lifelong learning? If so, each presents challenges and opportunities.

Community. Given the diversity of students, the complexity of school curricula, and the demands of postmodern life, not the least of which are the challenges of communication between and among people from the equivalent of different planets, how do teachers cultivate environments that call forth the riches that such diversity affords? How do teachers learn to provide evolving structures within which communication, connections, and community can develop?

Information, human, and environmental literacy. In what areas will students have the opportunity to become literate? What kinds of minds will children have the opportunity to develop? In what subject areas will schools provide foundations for further learning? What, as Elliot Eisner (2001) suggests, will be the explicit curriculum (what we say we are teaching), the implicit curriculum (what we don't say but is implicit in what we do: hall passes, seats facing front, art time on Friday afternoons), and the null curriculum (what we do not give students an opportunity to learn)?

A fast-moving society where students have access to the world's greatest literature, science, and arts, as well as to the worst in opinion and misguided thinking, from editorials to cartoons to pornography, creates a need to help students develop skills in discrimination. What is worth knowing and how do we know? How do we find credible information? These questions involve *technological information, and at more foundational levels, human and environmental* literacy.

Lifelong learning and transformation. Given the increasing complexity and amount of knowledge, and expanding capacities to deal with this knowledge, there are challenges for the teacher, not the least of which is discovering what students bring with them into classrooms. What are, for example, their experiences and dreams? Although some students have access to the latest computer equipment and are facile with Web-searching electronic environments, other students have little access outside of—or even within—school. How to navigate the information world has become part of the curriculum that teachers must learn as well as teach.

The emphasis shifts from learning bodies of knowledge to learning ways of knowing within different subjects and languages: thinking like a mechanic or an architect, developing the presence of a poet, the ear of a musician. The teacher's challenge is in developing structures within which all students can learn. As Robert Kegan notes in *In Over Our Heads* (1994), the challenge involves not only changes in students' behavior or feelings, but in their consciousness, not only in *what* they know, but in *how* they know. This is true for us as well.

These kinds of changes in consciousness call for different kinds of teaching and documentation of learning over time. To capture these kinds of learning, standardized tests are not adequate. We need to use new kinds of conversations and tools when lifelong learning, literacy, and community are educational aspirations. Evaluation and assessment methods become more complex as documentation of learning over time enables educators to converse at new levels. For these more complex forms of documentation, and the conversations that they make possible, action research can provide a structure. Together we can *create new possibilities for action* (Elliott, 2003).

CHAPTER SUMMARY

In this chapter we explored why it is important to take the action research journey in this time of accelerating change. We described action research as a way of doing work differently and learning from this experience. We highlighted three challenges that face educators at all levels: community, human literacy, and lifelong learning and transformation. We concluded with challenges to educators. And just how do we meet the challenges? With professional tools that enable us to keep track of our experiences and to learn from testing out our ideas in practice. That is the topic of the next chapter.

CHAPTER 2

Learning: Creating New Possibilities for Action

Teaching is a learning profession in which we aspire to be as wizards who create new possibilities. Inquiry with others (community) is the fuel that keeps us wizards. In this chapter, we address professional learning and community, and we introduce a series of workshops, *Exploring the Forest*, that will help us to develop the scholar's tools for completing an action research project as we travel through the chapters of this book. In this first workshop we discuss two basic tools of the educational scholar—the professional journal (documentation) and the portfolio (the illustrated journey to share with others)—that we will use on our journey to Oz.

Professional Learning, Scholarship, and Community

Professional learning involves critically reflective practice in which we question our assumptions and personal experiences, and we inquire into the perspectives of students, colleagues, the social context, and the literature. The subject matter of learning includes learning itself: What is worth knowing? How do we decide? Who decides? What do we know about how people learn and grow? What do we know about effective teaching? What do we know about our students and what they bring into the classroom? How can we provide environments that help students to develop their capacities and interests for further learning?

John Dewey (1916) makes the point that all learning is not equal: *Noneducational learning* doesn't change anything; a few days after the test, what was learned either is gathering dust in the mind's recesses or has departed. *Miseducational learning* means that deeper learning on the topic is either sidetracked or subverted; picking apart poems for parts of speech can extinguish the desire to read poetry. *Educational learning* increases the capacity for further learning toward socially worthwhile goals, starting from the learner's experience.

The importance of learning from experience has been known since the profession began. From the early days of in-service training institutes, to more recent workshops and grant activities, the goal has been to improve learning and what happens in classrooms. What has changed is the complexity of learning and the tools we have, individually and collectively, to learn. We have moved into a larger arena, that of scholarship.

Over the years, educators have become a larger and more diversified group. Our roles and responsibilities have increased and expanded; the students we teach and the subject matter, like their contexts, have grown in complexity. Although we have attempted to work with others in more collaborative and participatory ways, until recently there have been few sustained collaborative efforts from which to learn, and more than a few organizational constraints to doing so. Narrow, rigid, and linear uses of space, time, and scheduling, for example, have mitigated against the very collaborative relationships that might help us to meet the demands of social and environmental changes, but also to create visions and structures for possible futures.

Not long ago, scholarship was considered to be the sole purview of specialists located at universities and research organizations. Classroom teachers had few opportunities for "research" as it was defined. There was a general view that researchers should be removed from the "real world" of practice. Many researchers prided themselves on self-imposed isolation and the *objectivity* that could attend their removal from the daily world. More recently, in the social sciences and education in particular, the number of researchers choosing to enter the real world of practice, where they embrace their own senses and *subjectivity*, has grown. Slowly, subjectivity has become, if not always seen as desirable, at least not seen as antithetical to the research process. There are several other changes taking place, including:

- A growing realization that objectivity is a myth, that we each see and interpret from a point of view and live in language communities that shape us as much as we shape them
- A growing number and diversity of people conducting research, including learning communities (and communities of practice) where multiple perspectives contribute richness to the inquiry
- Researchers straying into more complex and "messier" questions, topics, and terrains, taking on social issues
- Research conducted closer to the subject of inquiry (such as in classrooms as well as laboratories)

Traditionally, scholars in education were people outside the schools. They conducted research in schools on teaching and learning, curriculum, administration, and organizational and professional development. But these scholars were not answering the pressing questions posed by teachers. Teachers, unlike many other workers, are by profession committed to results that benefit *these* students, not only those in the future. See Stepping Stones 2.1.

In 1975, British scholar Lawrence Stenhouse published a book titled *An Introduction to Curriculum Research and Development* in which a central chapter, and indeed the theme of the book, was the "teacher as researcher" and the genesis of a new professional. The same year, *School Teacher*, a sociological study by a U.S. sociologist, Dan C. Lortie (1975), brought another major contribution to the discussion. From his book, we learned more about who we were as teachers, why we decided to become teachers, and how we developed as a profession. These two key works enable us to better understand the roots and profile of the profession. These works and others offer a foundation for charting the future of an evolving profession, one which is directed as much by its *internal* (professional teachers) as by its *external* influences and environments (business community, legislatures, and

STEPPING STONES 2.1

What's the Difference Between a Job and a Profession?

Teachers make a commitment to enter teaching, a profession, which is different from a job. So, what are some of the things that make a profession different from a job?

- A profession requires a higher level of education for entry-level positions. A bachelor's degree or the equivalent is generally needed, and a master's degree or other post-baccalaureate education might be required.
- The *classic* professions are education, medicine, and law. Today there are others as well.
- A profession implies a scholarly pursuit. That means that on-the-job actions and decisions/policies are guided by research, evidence, or theory.
- Those in a profession have a commitment to learning, to update current knowledge and continue professional development.
- Professions have learned societies, conferences, and journals that assist in the professional development process.
- A professional is entrusted to make judgments in the workplace. A paraprofessional in a workplace takes direction from a professional (such as a teacher's aide or a paralegal).
- A profession deals with a *service* and leadership as opposed to a *product*.
- A profession's society or governmental affiliates develop, publish, and maintain relevant professional standards.

others). Since the time of those works, we have seen a flurry of activity related to teachers and to research:

- *from research* on *teachers* →
    - *to research* in the company of *teachers* →
        - *to research* with *teachers* →
            - *finally to research* by *teachers*,
                with teachers, students, and others.

This book supports that last group, a fast-growing group of practitioner researchers who practice *action research* (AR). A key ingredient to the growth of AR is the community with which one connects, locally and in larger contexts. Much of educational change has failed to make a difference, not because it didn't work, but because there was not a structure to sustain it. The same elements that kept old practices in place continue to mitigate against change, almost no matter how effective the change. What gives action research the power for cultural transformation is the structure that keeps the conversation in existence: the cyclical nature of AR including *action, reflection, observations*. Finally, the match that lights the fire (Scarecrow) is the aspiration—the educational promise—that drives the inquiry and sustains it into new territory.

Action Research and Educational Promise

As we have suggested, action research implies an orientation to research, a form of professional practice, a research process, and, for teachers, a reflective way of teaching. Teachers who ask questions of their practice such as, How can I bring my practice more in line with my aspirations for these students? and, How can I improve my practice? (Whitehead, 1996); who try out ideas in response to those questions; who systematically observe and collect evidence related to their actions; and who then analyze and talk with others about it—these teachers are engaging in reflective practice. They are following the same kind of cyclical process that characterizes action research. They are using professional (informed) eyes to observe their own practice, facing challenges with action and analysis, and sharing the results with others—perhaps their students, their colleagues, parents, the larger community of the school, and the discipline. What makes action research a form of scholarship is the tenaciously inquisitive, purposeful, systematic, critical, self-critical, and collaborative ways one explores and changes one's practice.

Not only can teaching and learning be characterized by an attitude of scientific inquiry, but they can be conceptualized as a moral craft that demands action on behalf of students whose education we shape. Educational scholar Alan Tom (1997) refers to teaching as a moral craft, while British colleague John Elliott (1991) emphasizes the moral nature of our professional commitment to all our students' learning. They refer to the democratic ideals of a profession whose purpose is to educate for freedom and an informed citizenry. What could be more important (and integral) to a democratic society than consciously shaping environments that influence the development of the hearts and minds of our students?

The curriculum is the vehicle for opening, creating, building, and bringing life to educational topics and space; learning is the process through which the curriculum is made manifest. Opportunities and tools to learn can shape their—and our—worlds. This is reason enough for us to develop the tools of scholarship through action research.

We believe, along with the late Lawrence Stenhouse, that "It is teachers who, in the end, will change the world of the school by understanding it." This understanding will come from doing things differently—and observing the consequences. Simply put: *Teaching well is inquiring well.* As agents of change, we commit ourselves to this. In the *Exploring the Forest* section of this chapter, two major tools for capturing and making sense of inquiry are presented.

CHAPTER SUMMARY

We started this chapter with the realization that to be educational wizards, we would need to engage in a special kind of learning—critically reflective practice. We emphasized the key elements of AR that provide a structure for sustaining the AR conversation long enough for cultural transformation: the cycle of reflective practice, dialog, and focusing on our aspirations. We traced the development of research *on* teachers and teaching to research *by* teachers on teaching and noted the importance of community. Action research, we found, is both a process and an orientation to research; it is moral action. And, like any sustained moral action, it takes learning and using tools of the trade. In the following pages we lay the foundation for our wizardry with tools for documentation and learning with the professional journal and portfolio. We will come back to these tools and further develop our scholarship at the conclusions to each section of the book.

SECTION SUMMARY

We began our journey by identifying teaching as a learning profession, and teachers as scholars who aspire to help each student reach her or his potential through community, literacy, and lifelong learning.

With challenges enough to fill the rainbow, and tools for the journey, let's find out more about action research and how it came into being. For those of you taking the Superhighway—move on to Section IV where you will meet Jon and Terry, Shawn, Ruby, and Roberto, five teachers, who, along with our Oz companions, will join the AR journey.

Exploring the Forest

Developing Tools for the Journey

Welcome to the forest!

We will stop at the conclusion of each section of our journey to explore where we have been and to develop the scholar's tools for inqury. Each *Exploring the Forest* might be thought of as a workshop. It is designed to make this journey *ours*—not as spectators but as explorers. This engagement can be facilitated by the journal, an important personal and professional tool for scholarship and research. A journal is a place in which to document and describe experience, to explore, to gather insights, and to give voice to our developing professional hunches and repertoires. Each journal is unique.

In this first *Exploring the Forest*, you will find general information about *journals* and *portfolios*, a way to conceptualize and relate these two tools, and ways to write about and make sense of your work as you document and reflect on it. There are many excellent books and articles on these subjects, and many different ways that journals and portfolios are defined and used. We present some definitions here and discuss how we will use the journal and portfolio in this book. Later, in Section V, we expand the contents you may find useful to include in your journal and portfolio. In this chapter, and in each of the chapters that follow, explorations and exercises are designed and numbered to help develop research tools over the length of our journey. Try them out and feel your capacity for scholarship expand. You will need the following:

- *A loose-leaf binder, bound journal, and/or computer or other electronic device to house your writing* (with a loose-leaf binder you can add, subtract, and move materials around) and a box or other case for objects that do not fit into the binder, journal, or computer. Many objects can be scanned into a computer.
- *Writing tools*: pens, markers, pencils, and/or technological or electronic devices such as tape recorders, notepads, electronic journals, computers.

- *A computer, scanner, and printer.* These are not essential but *highly* recommended. There are distinct advantages to having an electronic journal, not necessarily to replace a paper journal, but to work with it. You can transfer important notes on paper to your computer via typing or scanning— or you can talk into your computer or upload notes. With an electronic journal you can add, copy, subtract, and move around parts of your journal whenever you decide to. You can develop an idea over time, use online resources, and quickly move information into your journal. You can also move things out of your journal to other places, such as a report.
- *Scissors, glue, tape, paints,* and whatever you may wish to use in some of the nonword exercises.
- *Creativity, energy, enthusiasm,* and whatever else you want to use.

There are many ways to plan, document, and learn from experience. We will house and cultivate the fruits of our study in the professional journal. The scholar's tools for our journey are many (they include methods of data collection such as observing, interviewing, and collecting artifacts, as well as methods for analysis and interpretation). We will explore these in subsequent chapters.

The *professional journal* is a rich, evolving database within which the scholar can converse with herself or himself. It is a private document "owned" by the scholar and used to inform practice. It is also a rich source to draw upon for constructing a *purpose-specific portfolio,* which is intended to be a public document used to communicate professional practice to others through narrated illustration.

The Professional Journal

The *professional journal* is a living document we distinguish from other kinds of journals (calendar and chronological elaboration, dialog, reader response, buddy, and content journals used in science, mathematics, and other disciplines) as a working document to which we return to reflect. You can also incorporate writing contained in other types of journals including diaries and logs (which we will soon define). It is a powerful tool for scholarly reflection and professional development, and for collecting, analyzing, synthesizing, interpreting, and extending data. Although most journals are written documents, they can also contain artifacts, drawings, and other forms of documentation and expression such as pictures, charts, diagrams, lists, and excerpts from other materials, reports, pamphlets, videos, compact disks (CDs), and audiotapes. You can organize your journal to suit your needs and purposes. When we refer to journals in this book, we are referring to professional journals as described here, unless otherwise indicated.

If you are going to use a journal on this journey, you may want to start it now. We'll start with some reflection (and gather baseline data).

1. Make two drawings, one of your thoughts and feelings about *research* before you picked up this book and one after you read the first two chapters. After

each drawing, write freely to explain in words what the drawings might say if they could talk. Date these and place them in your journal.

2. Make two more drawings, this time one about your thoughts and feelings about *action research* before you picked up this book and one after you read this chapter. After each drawing, write freely to explain in words what the drawings might say if they could talk. Date these and place them in your journal.

We will find many different kinds of writing useful, among them, log and diary-type writing.

Log sheets are descriptive and objective types of writing in the sense that more than one person could record and understand what is entered (logged). For example, a log might be used to record the questions asked by students during a discussion. Who is speaking? What kinds of questions are they asking? Who is not speaking? You may find it useful to keep a researcher log to record events as they occur, to keep a running record that you can return to for analysis.

Diary-type entries are often written as stream of consciousness. The authors normally hold no illusions of objectivity. As many journal keepers find, diary writing is a good way to "let it all hang out." These entries are often filled with emotion. Diary writing can be quite therapeutic as well as a good source to return to and locate oneself (if rather vividly at times) in the circumstance.

Journals contain these kinds of entries and many others. They can be used to record observations, describe events and experiences, write creatively, make sketches, and to analyze and synthesize. Writing can be objective, subjective, creative, and expressive. All these kinds of information are important to the action researcher. As researchers, we can return to our entries often and make new connections, thinking further about what they contain. For now, try these exercises and invitations to reflect.

3. Keep a *log* of something that would be interesting or useful for you to focus on over the next week (hour, day). Examples might be every time you see a lightbulb go off in a student's mind (when, who, what are the circumstances?); each time the telephone rings (when, who, why); each time your studies are interrupted (when, who, and why); or each time you find yourself automatically winding your way to the refrigerator (time and object sought?). When the designated time is over, sit down and read all that you have written. Think about what happened over that time period. What can you learn?

4. Write a *diary* entry about a recent event that didn't seem fair to you and about which you are critical. It could be a policy or piece of legislation, something that happened to you or to someone around you. Let your thoughts and feelings out. You may find that after your emotions are addressed, your thoughts will become clearer.

5. Write freely and quickly about something meaningful that you recently learned on your own. Don't think too much or edit as you write. Give it a title. Describe it. Now list all the benefits to you from that learning (now and potentially). Next, write about how you learned it. Why is it important to you? Can you learn anything from it about how you learn? If so, write this as a summary statement.

6. Do the same thing as in number 5 for something you learned in a group of other people. What similarities and differences between learning on your own and learning with others do you find? As you process your writing, it becomes a *journal*.

In numbers 5 and 6 you were engaged in what is called *free-writing*; it simply means writing freely. Peter Elbow (1973), a scholar on writing, distinguishes two processes of writing: *growing* and *cooking*. Once you grow your writing, you shape it into something. This process is much like growing tomatoes and lettuce and making them into a salad. Much diary-type writing is of this growing sort. Don't mentally process it. Instead, let your fingers write or type as fast as they can, and don't hinder them by talking to them as they go. Let them talk to you. You have probably heard the statement "How do I know what I think until I see what I say?" Say it on paper, and then look to see what you said. Set a time limit and write until you reach it. You may want to start with 5 or 10 minutes and expand to 15 or 20, 30, or more. We will provide a few ideas to get started with free-writing.

As with quick sketches (with words), you will find some terrific writing and some that isn't so great; it does not matter. The important part is to be in action, to get the creative juices flowing and ideas percolating. Most people we know who have tried this find the process to be enjoyable and productive. If you do, there are some good books to spark more ideas and deepen your writing and thinking. Natalie Goldberg, author of *Writing Down the Bones* (1986) and *Wild Mind: Living the Writer's Life* (1990)—fear-busting, seed-planting, humorous books about writing with lots of ideas for free-writing—says that there are seven rules of writing practice. They happen to be useful for reflective writing (and getting ideas for proposal development):

- Keep your hand moving.
- Lose control (Say what you want to say. Don't worry if it's correct).
- Be specific. Not a *car*, but a *Cadillac*.
- Don't think.
- Don't worry about punctuation, spelling, grammar.
- You are free to write the worst junk in America.
- Go for the jugular. If something scary comes up, go for it. (That's where the energy is.) (1990, pp. 3–4)

Although it may seem strange, free-writing, with as little thinking as possible, is an excellent way to learn to think beyond the surface. We will be talking more in the next few chapters about a very important process that some people call "problematizing our practice." Free-writing is especially good for doing this. When we free-write, we pass right over the heads of our editors, the monitors that keep us on our path. The trouble with editors is they often keep us on a path that can be too straight and narrow. Although it is important to be heading in a direction, we need to have the freedom to let our thoughts and imaginations range more freely than the straight and narrow permits. Free-writing lets us do this. It gives us access to parts of ourselves that can usefully be employed and questioned, parts of ourselves that run for cover when the monitors look in.

7. Do a 10-minute free-write on an idea triggered by something in this chapter.

Portfolio

In eighteenth-century Italy, the portfolio was described as a *porto folio*, coming from *portare*, meaning "to carry", and *fogli*, meaning "leaves" or "sheets of paper." According to the *Oxford English Dictionary* (1979), it has a long history and can be defined as

> A receptacle or case for keeping loose sheets of paper, prints, drawings, maps, music, or the like; usually in the form of a large book-cover, and sometimes having sheets of paper fixed in it, between which specimens are placed. (p. 2245)

The portfolio, as we now refer to it, has its roots in these early uses, which included collections of drawings and art, legal and official documents of an agency or government, and financial holdings. Today, the portfolio is used in all these ways and takes on a professional orientation in educational settings. It is more (and less) than an archive or general collection of items. It is a composition—*a carefully selected, constructed, and narrated collection of work pertaining to a special topic*. Some schools use portfolios to present professional development for review by professional development councils. In an increasing number of school districts in Ohio, for example, local professional development committees use portfolios for licensing review. In these cases, the portfolio is a tool for educational learning, development, and evaluation.

The kinds of portfolios we create depend on our purposes. For example, we might want to create a portfolio to illustrate our work in a course we teach. This is called a *course portfolio*, and it is becoming an important way to study one's course and to share it with others. As the *scholarship of teaching and learning* evolves over time, we will see more and more of this type of portfolio. We study a specific course or topic (What are the topic and area of study? My aims, goals, and/or objectives? What did I do and how did it work? What were student roles, responsibilities, actions, and reactions? What did I learn? So, what does this mean for the future of my teaching this course?), and we present the results of our study in an illustrated document for others. We might develop a portfolio to document and highlight important aspects of teaching over a term or a year or to document benchmarks in a career. These are often referred to as *teaching portfolios*. We would include our aims, documentation of our teaching in different areas over time, and commentary including our interpretations and future directions that follow from the work we illustrate. The portfolio can serve as an illustrated résumé, an evaluation tool, a promotion document, or a story of progress and completion of an action research project.

An *electronic portfolio*, also known as an e-portfolio or digital portfolio, is a collection of electronic evidence assembled and managed by its author(s), usually on the Web. E-portfolio has become popular with the development of new media and technology. It allows the users or owners to record and update information easily; to present themselves with multiple methods including texts, multimedia, and hyperlinks; to organize and reorganize their files easily; and to determine varying degrees of audience access so that the same portfolio can be used for multiple purposes. The e-portfolio complements or replaces a traditional portfolio.

An e-portfolio can be developmental, reflective, or representational. A developmental e-portfolio reports things that the owner has done over a period of time. A reflective e-portfolio focuses on personal reflection on the content and what it means for the writer. A representational e-portfolio shows the writer's achievements in relation to particular work or developmental goals and is therefore selective. The three types are often mixed to achieve different personal, working, or learning outcomes with the e-portfolio owner determining access levels for his or her audience.

Some Popular E-portfolio Systems

- Avenet eFolio: http://www.avenetefolio.com/
- Chalk and Wire: http://www.chalkandwire.com/
- Dot folio: http://www.dotfolio.org/ (Open Source ePortfolio software)
- ePortfolio: http://www.eportfolio.org/
- LiveText: http://college.livetext.com/ (ePortfolio and Accreditation Management System)
- OSP: http://www.osportfolio.org/ (part of the Sakai project)
- rCampus: http://www.rcampus.com/ (Free ePortfolios)
- TaskStream: https://www.taskstream.com/ (ePortfolio and Assessment Management Platform)

E-portfolio Organizations and International Conference Presentations

- Europortfolio: http://www.europortfolio.org/
- ePortConsortium: http://www.eportconsortium.org/

You need not think too much about a portfolio yet; we will collect and construct materials for it in our journals over time. Then we will construct portfolios of the action research process as we near the end of our journey. For now, we explore how others define and use portfolios, and we collect some data to put into our journals.

8. Ask four people for their thoughts on portfolios, electronic or otherwise, and how they use, or might use, them.
9. Free-write about possible purposes you might have for a portfolio. Think about potential benefits of developing a portfolio that tells a story and illustrates key points in your action research project.

SECTION II

Defining and Putting Action Research in Context

"*A*h. *My party's just beginning!*" said the Wicked Witch of the West.

The Wonderful Wizard of Oz
L. Frank Baum (1900)

In this section we will discuss some general terms, concepts, and kinds of study associated with knowledge and research, which will provide a larger context from which to understand action research. We will further define AR, its characteristics and its history, and we will close with exploring the parts of the forest through which we have just traveled. We will begin to find our way within the forest . . . and to identify companions for the journey.

CHAPTER 3

The Bigger Picture: Paradigms, Theories, and Research

In Section I we talked about current challenges facing educators and directions for the future of the profession. We mentioned modern and postmodern worlds, and the end of the modern age as we knew it. Today we are caught between (and living in) modern and postmodern paradigms, or world views, each of which is vying for our attention. According to David Elkind (1997), these two paradigms characterize two distinct periods and can each be described by three different, general beliefs:

Modernity	Postmodernity
Progress	Difference
Universality	Particularity
Regularity	Irregularity

Although there are many different ways to characterize the two paradigms, Elkind provides a general and clear description of each. He notes that Dewey ushered in the modern era in education with his argument that educational progress was developmental. Dewey argued that a progressive educational pedagogy was called for in which students were viewed as active participants, rather than the passive participation that characterized most school activity and curricula of the late nineteenth and early twentieth centuries. The curriculum was organized so that there was a *progression* from simpler concepts to more complex concepts. Dewey's suggestion that students of any age learned best by doing was a *universal* belief—we learn better by doing than by being "done to."

Finally, Dewey also believed that education was *regular* in that there was a "predictable sequence in the acquisition of skills, values, and knowledge" (Elkind, 1997, p. 29). While many of Dewey's early ideas lead into the postmodern era (e.g., in addition to progress, he stressed *difference*), it may make the case more clearly to turn to the work of Jean Piaget, who worked in the modern era but, while doing so, heralded in the postmodern era for education (Elkind, 1997). Not all children, Piaget showed, progress at the same time and in the same way. *Particularity* and *difference* are more the rule than the exception. Each individual has a unique biological endowment and circumstances that interact to make experiences unique—*not* "regular." In schools, postmodern beliefs have been translated to attention to individual differences, diversity, multiple intelligences, multiple ways of knowing, children's rights, and fewer boundaries between public and private life, children and adults, and other forms that make schooling more complex than it was in modern times.

In general, scientists and artists come from different paradigms. There are world views that people develop when they learn within a discipline. People in a scientific discipline hold many things in common and can be said to come from a scientific paradigm. We will talk more about these and other world views later in this chapter. From the scientific paradigm we learn to observe very carefully and analytically. From the artistic paradigm we construct meaning, drawing intentionally from the interaction of inner as well as outer landscapes. Artists interpret and portray their work in creative ways—some mention artistic vision—that enables others to derive insights from their portrayals. We will be developing both of these abilities, observation and portrayal, throughout this book.

In this chapter we started out with *paradigms*. Next, we will look at *theories* and *research*. A scholar generally functions from a frame of reference, or *paradigm*, within a larger group whose perspective the scholar shares. Within this larger group there may be several *theories*, each focusing on a specific phenomenon, be it broadly focused (e.g., psychosocial development) or narrowly focused (e.g., bee pollination in southwest Georgia). The *research* that takes place within this frame of reference and in conjunction with a theory, whether implicit or explicit, in turn can inform both the theory and the paradigm.

Paradigm: A world view or model ascribed to a group of people who hold certain beliefs, knowledge, and understandings in common.

Theory: A systematically organized explanation of a phenomenon.

Research: Systematic self-critical inquiry made public (after Lawrence Stenhouse, 1975).

In general, *we are concerned with the utility of a paradigm and the quality of the explanation generated from a theory and the research that informs it.* Implicit in paradigms are values, whereas the theories that researchers construct may come from their value orientations and a particular paradigm (which may motivate them to raise issues and investigate them using specific methods), but the theories themselves are articulated as a carefully constructed set of principles that hold true no matter what the reader's values.

As we defined *log* in Chapter 2, readers of a ship's log can understand the principles regardless of their points of view. One can also understand elements of a theory no matter the point of view. However, we interpret the *meaning* and possible *application* or *implications* of the theory according to our values. Theories can bring new meanings and coherence to our understanding of a phenomenon, and they help us to interpret what we see and wonder about.

Theorizing is part of the process of forming a *theory*. Today we use the word more generally to mean conjecturing, or speculating. It is what researchers do. In fact, action researchers spend a great deal of time speculating and trying things out. They make their best guesses (hypotheses), and then they test them to see what happens.

Theories provide frames of reference. "Whatever problem we face, the most useful frame of reference will be the one that most adequately helps us to understand and use all of the facts before us" (Combs and Snygg, 1959, pp. 8–9). Scientists in the physical sciences and the human, or social, sciences use theories to explain phenomena as diverse as the origin of the universe, motivation, and school change. We will focus here on a few theories that help us to better understand the complexity of teaching and learning and how we can study it.

We will look at two theories that are particularly important to educators. According to Robert Kegan, these theories have shaped and "influenced nearly every aspect of intellectual life in the last hundred years" (Kegan, 1982, p. 8). One big idea—or theory—is *constructivism*. The other is *developmentalism*. Both have influenced our understanding of how people learn.

Constructivism. The name most often associated with this theory of cognitive development is that of the Swiss genetic epistemologist (a person who studies the nature of knowledge) Jean Piaget. He developed a comprehensive theory of cognitive development based on lifelong research in this area. There are other theories of cognitive development, many of which (including Robert Kegan's theory) are built on Piaget's constructivist theory. In essence, constructivism means that persons (and systems) constitute and construct their own reality. We are meaning-making beings. And what do we make meaning from? Our experiences. And how do we make sense of those experiences? By reflecting on them and making new connections. We do this all the time. People who develop public theories, some of which are referred to as *grand* theories because their scope is broad, do so by careful and systematic study that they make understandable to others. Piaget's theory of cognitive development is one such public, or grand, theory. We each have our own theories about life. Because we do not study and organize them into theories for public use and scrutiny, they are referred to as *personal* theories. Through the action research process we become aware of tacit elements of our personal theories.

According to Piaget, we function and make meaning using a fundamental process that is part of life from our earliest to our final days. Throughout a lifetime, we *assimilate* information that fits into existing ideas, and we *accommodate* information for which we have to amend existing ideas or develop new ones. Assimilation and accommodation are processes that involve multiple ways of knowing. For example, a baby might use a wall to pull herself up. One day she tries this and the wall moves! This seemingly familiar object becomes something it wasn't—a door. Now she can push it at will and learns that this door makes a certain sound when it swings open. It also looks different when it moves. Very quickly she has come to know this object in multiple ways: through sight, touch, and sound. Life itself is a continuous process of bringing assimilation and accommodation into equilibrium. Too much assimilation would be boring; too much accommodation, frustrating.

Piaget used careful observation and analysis. He observed infants discover new things. He actually started out studying insect and plant life in ponds and then used some of his skillful methods of observation and question-posing to study children— his own and other children. He developed a method of questioning children that went beyond prevalent methods used by researchers of his time. This process of gathering data is termed the *clinical method*. With this method, he took children very seriously, asking them open-ended questions. Instead of categorizing their responses as right or wrong, he paid careful attention to the reasoning behind their responses. The answer itself, he found, was only a small part of their reasoning.

Children's art provides a good example of this. Watch a 4-year-old child paint. If you are lucky, you will hear the child talk about what he is doing and you will discover a story. What may look like a muddy or scribbled mess to an unskilled eye may be a wonderful imaginary adventure to the child. Let's take a real example. Martha created this picture (Figure 3.1) and talked about it as she drew. Here is how Martha's observant mother, Maggie, described the picture:

> This is Disneyland. If you look closely (or imaginatively), you will see
> Princess Jasmine in the castle, Aladdin, the monkey, and the magic carpet.
> Also a rainbow. And see your name on the back?

FIGURE 3.1

If we see only scribbles, we miss so much, and it was the "much" that interested Piaget. We do not want to go into depth regarding constructivism or Piaget's theory here—there are many books that do that. We want only to point out that through careful and systematic study, a new theory evolved that changed how we look at child development, schooling, teaching, learning, and curriculum development. Understanding constructivism can make a significant difference in our work. Whether we view Martha as a passive *tabula rasa* (blank slate) on which we write what we want her to learn, or whether we view her as a dynamic, sense-making being makes a considerable difference in our approach to her. Piaget would say that we have a lot to learn from her, and as teachers we can always learn from our students. Yetta Goodman (1991) calls observing children "kid-watching." Martha is a dynamic child who constructs her own knowledge from the environment and her interactions in it.

Piaget discovered that humans change considerably over time, and he called that change *development*, which brings us to the other *big* idea and related theory.

Developmentalism.   On the most fundamental level, life consists of entities in motion over time. *Development* is defined as change over time. As Kegan explains, "Organic systems evolve through qualitatively different eras according to regular principles of stability and change" (1982, pp. 13–14). Once we know a little about this theory, we can see examples of it all around us.

Action Research in the Context of Research

Since action research is a special kind of research, a look at research in general may provide a basis from which to understand its special qualities. *Action* is central. We note three general types of research for the context they provide.

Basic research.   Basic research is usually conceived of in relation to the physical (sometimes referred to as the *hard*) sciences from which it draws its ideas about the nature of knowledge. Knowledge is conceived of as separate from practice; and knowledge can be discovered through the application of rigorous, experimental research methods that include sampling, controls, and manipulation of variables. The goal of this type of research is the development of theories through the discovery of broad generalizations or principles. Basic research advances the frontiers of knowledge; it is less concerned with the application of ideas to the concerns of people. A prime example of the fruits of basic research is Einstein's theory of relativity. While most teachers are familiar with Einstein's equation $E = MC^2$, few understand the implications of its meaning for everyday life. Nor was this potential "use value" likely on Einstein's mind as he unraveled the fundamental mysteries of the laws of physics.

Applied research.   In contrast, applied researchers can use principles and theories but supplement them with informal discovery methods to generate practical results. *Applied research* is more concerned with a direct application of its findings to the concerns of real people and their planet. Leonardo da Vinci did applied research, although he would not have called it that. In fact, he was one of the most notable applied researchers of all time. His notebooks contain countless examples of diagrams and plans for things that can be constructed for real-world use. For example, he created the flintlock, a mechanism for generating the spark for gunpowder. His design was used until the mid-1800s!

Action research.   Action research is a type of applied research that has as its primary goal to improve practice. AR often contributes to the generation of principles and theories while it enhances the professional development of its proponents. Thus, knowledge, practice, and development are connected. It uses a problem-solving approach to improve social conditions and processes of living in the real world. Action research involves an ethical commitment to improving society (to make it more just), improving ourselves (that we may become more conscious members of a democratic society), and ultimately improving our lives together (building community).

There is no attempt on the part of the action researcher to maintain an illusion of objectivity or to remain value-neutral. Rather, an action researcher's job is to bring to light assumptions, beliefs, and actions; to examine them; and to bring their actions into closer alignment with their values and aspirations.

In collaboration with one another and their students, action researchers develop and test theories about their work in a continuing cycle of action, observation, and reflection on the consequences of action. Theorizing includes self-critique: Action researchers constantly examine their actions in light of both their values and an ethical commitment to improving the lives of others.

We will meet many action researchers in the following chapters. They are creating classrooms that are responsive to students' needs for belonging, academic achievement, language acquisition, responsibility, and participation in democratic life. Action researchers demonstrate their increasing awareness of the roles they play in the learning environment.

AR is distinct from basic and other forms of applied research in several ways: (1) AR is conducted mainly by insiders (practitioners) rather than outsiders. (2) AR has an explicit value orientation and doesn't espouse "objectivity" in the traditional sense. (3) AR is geared toward the improvement of the practitioner-researcher as well as practice. (4) It is self-critical inquiry shared with others.

There are many reasons for engaging in educational action research, not the least of which is to enable the profession, and the professionals who comprise it, to establish methods for continuous growth toward socially constructive ends. Sharing one's research, as we will discuss later, can take many forms, including scholarly journals (see Stepping Stones 3.1). From their earliest participation as students in schools that are collaborative, inquisitive, and reflective communities, to engaging in teacher preparation and continuing education institutions and

STEPPING STONES 3.1

Distinguishing Between a Scholarly Journal and a Popular Press Journal

Numerous printed and online serials are available. For the purposes of doing research, scholarly journals are considered to be the most respected, credible sources. Differences between scholarly and popular press journals include:

- Popular press journals are a business designed to make a profit. They are run by a paid staff who must turn a profit to stay in business.
- Scholarly journals are typically run, to varying extents, by scholars in the field. Editors or writers are rarely paid, but the company or agency who publishes it has paid staff and gets paid. Few scholarly journals attempt to and are successful at making a profit to support the organization. The main purpose of a scholarly journal is the dissemination of knowledge.
- Popular press journals generally print with color, more advertising, more eye-catching formats. Scholarly journals have little or no advertising and rarely use color printing.
- Contributions to popular press journals are generally decided by a paid editorial staff. Circulation and profit are primary considerations.
- Contributions to scholarly journals are "blind reviewed." Editorial staff remove author names and references before sending manuscripts to credentialed experts on the topic for feedback. Feedback is taken seriously, and decisions are made related to knowledge and the field rather than economic considerations.
- The "front matter" in all journals gives information about who publishes the magazine. A scholarly journal will acknowledge the journal's mission, audience, and affiliation. Instructions will be included as to how to contribute. Terms like *refereed* and *blind review* indicate a scholarly contribution process. Generally a learned society, institution, or its affiliate sponsor the journal.

Most journals, whether scholarly or popular press, can be downloaded or accessed as e-journals with online subscriptions by individuals or affiliated associations, institutions, or libraries.

Through a search engine such as Google (http://www.google.com), one can usually find some basic information about a journal, including subscription, editorial, and submission. Yet, one usually needs access to a subscription to access individual articles of particular issues. Sometimes that "subscription" can be accessed by owning a library card. Library patrons have access to journals that libraries subscribe to.

schools, teachers can cultivate and support constructive change. Action research is a tool to do so.

CHAPTER SUMMARY

We began this chapter by discussing the bigger picture, the move from modern to postmodern times, and some of the paradigms, theories, and research that provide a context for action research. We looked at constructivist and developmental theories that have been, for good and ill, highly influential to intellectual life during the past century. Action research necessitates theorizing, speculating, and acting. We placed AR in relationship to basic research and applied research, and we noted its distinction in four areas: It is conducted by insiders, it has an explicit value orientation, it is geared toward improvement of the researcher as well as the practice, and it is self-critical inquiry. In the next chapter, we will continue to develop the context of AR with three orientations to knowledge and the methods used by researchers within these orientations.

CHAPTER 4

Three Orientations to Knowledge and Methods of Research

Action research (AR) is a process of theorizing and testing our own, as well as other people's, ideas and theories in practice. It is grounded in ideas about how knowledge is generated and in the relationship between the knower and what is known. The researcher and what is being studied are connected in an interactive way—the values of the researcher influence what is learned.

Thomas Kuhn, a well-respected scientist, wrote a fascinating (and now classic) book about paradigm shifts and changes titled *The Structure of Scientific Revolutions* (1970). In this book he describes how we need to think "outside of the box" (theory and/or paradigm) when a system of thinking no longer works and there is an anomaly that cannot be explained by the current theory or paradigm. When this happens in our teaching, it can lead to AR.

While the contemplation of competing paradigms and theories can absorb (and waste) a considerable amount of energy, this can be a catalyst to further develop our perspectives. Open discussions and debate can enrich us with multiple perspectives. However, as Dewey (1916) pointed out, arguing against another's perspective can also narrow our thinking; reacting against any *ism*, he taught, is a trap that restricts our options. The three orientations to knowledge that we discuss here have their own paradigms, theories, and methods of scholarship.

The world view of the knower is rarely made explicit, even to the knower; but it is of no small consequence, for such paradigms determine how knowledge is approached and defined. It is a model of sorts, a description of how a system works. It is a way of organizing one's thinking and making sense of the world. A paradigm is broader than a theory; it is a birthplace for theories. In the pages that follow, we will discuss a few dominant paradigms and ways of knowing within each. Like any way of categorizing experience and ways of understanding, the paradigm is not static. Paradigms evolve and change over time, as we can see with the modern and postmodern eras.

Now, let's go to another level of discussion and explore some ideas about how knowledge is constructed and acquired. We will find that different views of knowledge construction and discovery result in different purposes and methods for conducting action research.

Orientations

According to Jurgen Habermas, a noted philosopher, knowledge is related to the way people orient themselves to the world (Habermas, 1972). He offered a succinct framework outlining three basic orientations to the world and to knowledge, each of which has a particular interest in mind.

Habermas's Three Basic Orientations to Knowledge

Orientation:	Material well-being	Communication	Freedom
Governed by:	Technical interest	Practical interest in understanding	Emancipatory interest, liberation from oppression
Produces:	Empirical knowing	Situational knowing	Critical reflective knowing

The first orientation, toward material well-being, is "governed by a technical interest in acting on the world. This produces an empirical knowing in the form of facts and generalizations" (Carson, 1990, p. 168). The next orientation, toward communication, "is governed by a practical interest in understanding others. . . . [It] is situational and interpretive, rather than generalizable and empirical" (Carson, 1990, p. 168). The third of Habermas's orientations is toward freedom and the liberation of those who are oppressed. Paulo Freire (1970) is a good example of this, as he taught people in a small South American village to read with materials that enabled them to become conscious of the ways in which they were oppressed. This third orientation "produces a critically reflective knowledge" (Carson, 1990, p. 168). In the United States, Miles Horton (1993) used a similar method of education in the civil rights and labor union movement to empower persons who would not otherwise have had access to educational opportunities. A fascinating account of education and social change from this critical perspective is found in a book of conversations between Miles Horton and Paulo Freire called, aptly, *We Make the Road by Walking* (Bell et al., 1990).

Each of these orientations to the world—*technical, practical,* and *emancipatory*—can be seen in the ways in which practitioners approach improving themselves, their work, and their work lives. Using the ubiquitous example of how we use time in classrooms, we can illustrate these three orientations.

- Those with a *technical orientation* toward time might ask, How can I use my time more efficiently so that my students will have maximum learning time, which may result in increased achievement on standardized tests?
- Those with a *practical orientation* toward time might ask, How do my students think about the time they spend on testing?
- Those with an *emancipatory interest* might ask, How just is the expenditure of time used in preparation for tests that will disenfranchise some students (by not allowing them to graduate if they do not pass the test) and some teachers (by withholding monetary rewards when their students do not pass the test)?

Not only are these distinctions important in terms of understanding the orientations and questions asked by practitioners, but these orientations and ways of knowing also determine to a large extent the research methods that are used in conducting an inquiry. These methods have been termed *empirical analytic* (for those whose interests are technical), *naturalistic* (for those whose interests are interpretive and practical), and *critical* (for those whose interests are emancipatory). Let's look more closely at the methods associated with these orientations.

Methods of Research

Experimental methods.   Experimental methods are normally associated with a technical and empirical orientation to research. Researchers from this orientation use various methods for experimentation and observation of the empirical world—the world that can be seen, heard, touched, tasted, and felt. Hypotheses are tested for verification (can they be verified?) and variables are manipulated (which of these competing explanations of the phenomena under study can be eliminated?). Experimental methods are used to understand a phenomenon that is relatively simple—an atom, for example—in which limited variables must be taken into account as alternative explanations for a change in the atom.

The research setting, often a laboratory, is contrived, and the conditions can be controlled to the extent that it is possible to avoid the influence of variables that are not part of the study. The purpose of the research is to generalize, predict, form laws, and derive cause-and-effect explanations for how and why this thing happens the way it does. This is accomplished by taking things apart to see how the parts fit together, which explains why this method is also referred to as *analytic.*

Because the researcher manipulates variables to determine causal relationships, the outcomes have been manipulated as well. Reality exists in the behavior or appearance that can be experienced; a person using the experimental method seeks to study this reality. Experimental methods have often been used in classrooms to study the effects of different treatments (e.g., sometimes curriculum and teaching techniques). Pretesting and posttesting students who have been assigned to a treatment group (a new method of teaching mathematics), to a nontreatment group (continuing with the same mathematics program), or to various kinds of treatment groups (divided into groups, each using a different mathematics program) provides evidence (or doesn't!) of learning and/or change between or among treatment groups.

Experimental studies (or, as some would say, "quasi-experimental"—acknowledging that true experiments cannot be conducted with human beings) of teaching conducted in the 1960s, 1970s, and 1980s, called *process-product research*, have contributed to understanding specific ways in which basic skills can be taught (e.g., through the use of direct instruction), ways to develop orderly classrooms (e.g., through the use of rewards for positive academic and social behavior), and ways to encourage higher levels of thinking (e.g., through the use of open-ended questions).

Naturalistic methods.   Methods are considered naturalistic when they occur in natural settings (such as classrooms, as opposed to laboratories) where there is relatively little intervention to the normal flow of events. For the most part they are nonexperimental. That is, naturalistic researchers are not interested in manipulating or controlling the situation, and they are not interested in studying interventions in the traditional sense of experimental study. When the purpose of research is to understand *what is* rather than to study that which has been manipulated and controlled, naturalistic research methods are appropriate. In naturalistic research, questions are developed in a cyclical, repetitive process of interaction between the researcher and the researched. Results are compared and contrasted to arrive at understandings that are more sophisticated than those at the outset of the study and result in generating new questions or hypotheses. When the researcher wants to understand something that is complex, socially influenced, dynamic, and interactive with many variables, naturalistic approaches are more appropriate because they enable the researcher to look more contextually and comprehensively (some would call this holistically) at what is occurring.

Understanding how students learn, for example, is an entirely different matter from understanding how the atoms of which students are comprised operate. Given that classrooms are socially complex places, naturalistic approaches are often useful. Reality as we know it is not just what appears on the surface of behavior (or even in the movement of atoms!). Reality is seen in the complex dance of beings in relationships on multiple levels, and it is, in part, created by people. Naturalistic methods enable researchers to seek meaning to enhance human interactions in complex social settings.

For example, one might set out to study how teachers grow. That is a pretty broad question! One of us designed a study to explore that territory. She did not expect to find an answer to that question, but she did expect to gain insights into the nature of professional growth and the conditions that seem to support it. Her study was phenomenological. She wanted to find out how seven teachers perceived their own development, and those aspects of their practice that constrained, supported, or had little effect on their development. She was particularly interested not in other people's views of the teachers, but in their own views—how teachers' worlds felt to them and how they interpreted their experiences (their phenomenal worlds).

The study began in 1980 and lasted well over a year. The researcher participated with and observed the teachers in their classrooms, analyzed their journals, collected and analyzed artifacts, and held weekly seminars during which the teachers talked about their teaching lives and experiences. As in many naturalistic studies, there were mountains of data. An unexpected finding was that writing about practice was a powerful tool for professional development. The power of writing as a tool for professional development is now well known, but at the time it had been used by many qualitative researchers as a way to peer into another's world (Holly, 1989).

Although the study was designed from a naturalistic perspective with the intent to intervene as little as possible in the participants' lives, the unintended consequences of the data-gathering tools (journals and discussion groups in particular) were considerable and contributed valuable means for critique and for professional development. During this same period, researchers in the field of English were exploring the power of writing as a cognitive process (Flower, 1981; Flower and Hayes, 1980, 1981; Perl, 1981). We now have a rich base of studies that illustrate the many benefits of writing about practice.

Critical methods.   Critical theorists claim that the quality of interaction that is sought by those whose orientation is practical cannot be reached without emancipating people who have been constrained from pursuing a better life by one or more of the following: race, class, gender, ability, and age.

The purpose of socially critical research is to improve the lives and environments of those who have been disenfranchised or marginalized, those whose voices are not heard. A teacher, for example, who wonders why the out-of-school suspension list is filled with students of color and the gifted and talented program is filled with white students may be critiquing current practices that value and privilege contributions of a dominant culture over those of nondominant cultures.

Improvement, according to critical theorists, is accomplished by examining our own *false consciousness* (the inability to see the constraints that have shaped us and have been placed on us by dominant forces of oppression); by exposing inequalities in relationships, social structures, and practices such as female subordination, authoritarian power relations between teachers and students and between administrators and teachers, and ability grouping; and by seeking change in those conditions to improve the quality of life for those who have been oppressed.

According to critical theorists, reality is created over time by social, historical, political, cultural, psychological, economic, ethnic, and gender factors. Giroux and McLaren (1986) and other critical researchers have documented that the dominant professional orientation in education has been and still is *technical*. This dominant view is challenged by the critical. Figure 4.1 outlines this discussion of the three orientations to research.

	Experimental	Naturalistic	Critical
Philosophical foundations	*Logical positivism*: concerned with facts or causes of phenomenon rather than the perspective of those involved with the phenomenon.	*Phenomenology*: concerned with understanding human behavior from the perspective of the participants.	*Social critical theory*: concerned with emancipatory political interests, i.e., empowering human beings to transcend the constraints placed by race, class, gender, etc.
Interests served	Technical	Practical	Emancipatory
What is the nature of reality?	Reality exists and can be studied by trying to discover the laws that govern it.	Reality is what individual people or groups of people experience, think it is, and agree that it is.	Reality is created over time by social, political, cultural, economic, ethnic, and gender factors so that what is now considered real was not always so.
What is the relationship between the knower and what can be known?	The researcher and the object of the investigation are considered independent so that the researcher does not influence the object of study.	The researcher and the object of study are interactively linked so that the finding (reality) is created as the research process unfolds.	The researcher and the object of study are interactively linked. The values of the researcher influence what is learned.
What is the purpose of research?	Generalize, predict, form causal explanations.	Contextualize, interpret, and understand perspective of the participant.	Critique the social injustices in society to improve the lives of those who have been disenfranchised.
What are the methods used by the researcher to find what she or he wants to know?	*Quantitative*: Questions and/or hypotheses are empirically tested to verify them, by manipulating the variables so that competing explanations can be eliminated.	*Qualitative*: Questions are answered in a cyclical, iterative process of interaction between the researcher and the researched. Constructions are compared and contrasted to arrive at understanding that is more sophisticated than at the outset of the study.	*Critical*: The researcher and the participants in the inquiry engage in dialog in which the goal is transforming consciousness from one of ignorance of the impact of race, class, gender, etc. toward informed consciousness, with the understanding that oppressive structures can be changed.

The purposes of action research emerge from the purposes of research in general. As action researchers, we come to our practice with *technical, practical*, and *emancipatory* purposes. Many teachers and students begin with questions of a technical or practical nature: improving classroom discipline, student skills in cooperation, effective use of time, or trying to apply the theory of multiple intelligences. As we and our students reflect openly on our work, we can begin to ask ourselves questions of a more critical and social nature, especially if we are challenged to do so (by a reading or colleague who poses questions). The more we critique our work, the more we can come to see injustices done in the name of helping. We can begin to understand the ways in which we are implicated in perpetuating these injustices. And, as we grow in our abilities to entertain more complex perspectives on our own actions, there are reverberations in social and psychological domains also. We address these in Section III.

As we examine underlying assumptions about learning and teaching (both our own assumptions and those of the institutions in which we work), we often find ourselves critiquing the beliefs, structures, and practices that get in the way of creating the quality of classroom life that we seek. If we keep in mind the ethical, moral, and democratic commitments we make when we decide to become educators, we will begin our action research from a more critical stance.

With this critical stance and the questions that follow from it, we find ourselves continuing to ask technical and practical questions, but we put them in the service of new understandings. For example, we may still want to find ways to use time more efficiently, but *what we consider to be efficient* may have changed. Giving young children precut papers instead of encouraging them to cut their own papers may "get the project completed faster," but it also becomes more the teacher's project than the children's, and it does nothing to help children develop skills that will help them to become independent. Most importantly, it sends the child clear—if implicit—messages about power and what is valued.

Images of Teacher Learning: Three Ways to Consider the Relationship Between Knowledge and Practice

Over the past 20 years, there has been general agreement on a new approach to teacher learning and development grounded in constructivism; learners construct or make sense of experience, connecting the new to the known, and as such, are in control of their own learning. Habermas's (1972) three orientations to knowledge help us see that underneath the basic similarity, there are real differences in how knowledge of teaching and the practice of teaching are conceptualized. Exploring the relationships between knowledge and practice illustrates the different images of teaching, teacher learning, and the role of teachers in the change process. This exploration also shows action research to be a transformative process.

Figure 4.2 shows that action research emerges from the critical orientation to knowledge, in which knowledge and practice are united in a praxis aimed to

FIGURE 4.2 *Three images of teacher learning*

Relationship Between Knowledge and Practice	Technical Orientation to Teacher Learning	Practical Orientation to Teacher Learning	Critical Orientation to Teacher Learning
Images of Knowledge	Formal knowledge base of teaching is generated by university researchers.	Practical knowledge of teaching is generated by teachers in their specific contexts.	Knowledge is constructed in communities through systematic inquiries for the purpose of transforming schools.
Images of Teaching	Quality teaching is mastering the formal knowledge base and applying it to practice.	Quality teaching is wise action in the midst of uncertain and changing conditions.	Teaching is a complex activity that occurs within a social, historical, cultural, and political context. Teachers are theorists, activists, and school leaders. The work of teaching is critical, political, and intellectual.
Images of Teacher Learning	Teacher learning focuses on developing deep understanding of subject matter and "best" practice.	Teachers learn by reflecting on their own actions.	Teachers learn collaboratively (whether novice, expert, teacher educator) by making problematic their assumptions of teaching/learning/schooling. They generate local knowledge for public purposes.
Role of Teacher in Educational Change	Teachers individually solve problems using practices consistent with the formal knowledge base.	Teachers reflect with colleagues to improve individual practice.	Teachers try to understand, make explicit, and transform schools and society to make them more democratic and socially just.
Current Initiatives in Teacher Learning	Development of knowledge base; coaching/evaluating teacher education programs and teachers based on their adherence to the knowledge base.	Mentoring/coaching reflective practitioners who examine their own assumptions and use artistry in exploring problems of practice (not measured against a knowledge base).	Action research in inquiry communities; critical reflections, oral inquiries, self-studies.

transform. According to Cochran-Smith and Lytle (1999), "The knowledge teachers need to teach well emanates from systematic inquiries about teaching, learners and learning, subject matter and curriculum, and schools and schooling. This knowledge is constructed collectively within local and broader communities . . . [and] connected to the larger political and social agendas" (p. 274).

The image of teacher is as change agent within the classroom and broader community rather than as implementer of others' knowledge. In this view, teachers learn together by "challenging their own assumptions; identifying salient issues of practice; posing problems; studying their own students, classrooms, and schools; constructing and reconstructing curriculum; and taking on roles of leadership and activism in efforts to transform classrooms, schools, and societies" (Cochran-Smith & Lytle, p. 278) rather than learning individually from experts. Teachers work together to generate local knowledge about teaching and link that knowledge to broader political and social agendas. These views of knowledge, teaching, and teacher learning live side by side with the technical and practical images. That is the nature of life in a postmodern world.

Characteristics of Action Research

Four elements characterize action research: ethical commitment, cycle of reflective practice, public character, and collaboration.

Ethical commitment. The foundation for any action research project is commitment to professional practice and to the democratic principles that undergird it. How best can I serve the students I teach? How can I improve my practice? a teacher-researcher may ask. Does this curriculum privilege a few at the expense of others? and, Whose needs are *not* being met? Whatever the question, the researcher is motivated by a concern for examining the social consequences of teaching practice.

For the action researcher, improvement means moving toward a more democratic learning community. This entails creating conditions that ensure the participation and development of individuals within the community. Students and teachers develop toward common understandings of what it means to be a valued member of a community.

If these are the goals and values that action researchers hold as they work to improve their teaching, what are the working principles that guide their actions? Stringer (1996) provides some useful guidelines that also characterize successful learning communities:

- Relationships are equal, not hierarchical. Leadership shifts and depends upon expertise and the challenge at hand, rather than by position.
- Communication is authentic, sincere, and open.
- Participation is focused, active, and supportive of group aims and direction.
- All participants are involved and function in cooperative and inclusionary ways. (p. 38)

The promise of power and control that undergirds hierarchical and bureaucratic ways of organizing schools makes the enactment of these principles difficult to achieve. Traditionally, schools have been organized in ways that allow those "on top" (superintendents, supervisors, and principals) to control those "on the bottom" (teachers and students) so that schools run "efficiently" and so that students and teachers are accountable to state and national standards.

Anyone who is familiar with what actually happens in schools (or any social organization for that matter) knows that human beings are relatively unpredictable, and that attempts to control them meet with little success. The consequence of being controlled (for those on the bottom) is increased frustration and alienation as they try to produce outcomes within the restrictive environment of policy and procedures. The consequence for those on top is increased stress as they try to follow the mandates from "above" and deal with the resistance from "below," trying to solve complex problems associated with education (Stringer, 1996). Without the active support of school administrators, community members, and government officials, these democratic values will be difficult to achieve.

Cycle of reflective practice.   According to Stenhouse (1975), the impulse behind research is *curiosity*. For those of us who teach, this means taking a look at something in our practice that intrigues us. We follow this curiosity, preferably with some ferocity, into its den in the forest and abide there until we can begin to formulate potentially useful ways of engaging with it and learning about it. We plan our path (which becomes our design and "proposal") to find out more about this curiosity, and we consider how we can protect our inquiry from the myriad of distractions that invite themselves into our teaching days. So, we start out with curiosity, we stick with it until we can describe it as *inquiry*, and we plan how we can conduct our studies.

In many forms of research we follow the plan (design), collect information (which we sort out as our data), analyze it, and write up our findings. Generally, the project is complete after we have written and presented the report. In action research, the process proceeds somewhat differently. It includes trying out our ideas, observing, and documenting our actions and the consequences of these actions. As the process continues, we try out other ideas and continue the cycle of *acting, observing,* and *reflecting*, which ultimately takes us to other questions and new cycles. In a sense, AR is less linear, less tidy, and messier than what we normally think of as research. Action researchers can begin anywhere in the cycle depicted in Figure 4.3, and they can proceed in a number of ways. They revisit parts of the cycle as the study evolves.

The research cycle includes acting and finding the consequences intriguing, observing (looking at) something that begs attention, and reflecting (thinking) on teaching. One part of the cycle can lead into any other. The process itself is *educational*. To be a professional educator, Stenhouse (1975) said that *teachers must inevitably be intimately involved in the research process*, which, when used, becomes educational.

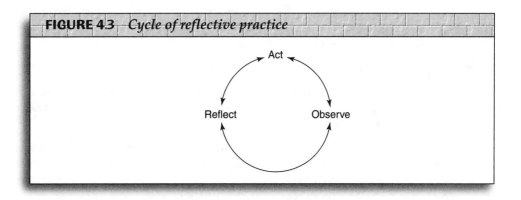

FIGURE 4.3   *Cycle of reflective practice*

The cycle of reflective practice that characterizes action research becomes the process teachers use to generate knowledge of teaching. In an interactive and simultaneous way, we *reflect* on our values and how we hope to carry them out in our teaching. These reflections guide the plans we make to improve our practice. We *act* out our values with our students in our classrooms and schools. We *observe* the consequences of our actions through the systematic creation of "data," continuously interpreting these data in light of our collective pursuit of a more just and democratic life. The cycle continues as we consider new ways to bring teaching more closely in line with our values. At the same time, we develop professionally into more complex ways of thinking; greater moral, ethical, and social responsibility; and psychological and emotional maturity. Figure 4.3 illustrates the nature of these action research processes.

Action researchers design their watching into their work, not only as an afterthought, such as an epilogue or "reflections on the process," but also as a documented reflective process throughout. As the philosopher Sartre put it, research is undertaken by intellectuals, persons whose "minds watch themselves." This is the important *self-critical* part of Lawrence Stenhouse's definition.

Public character.   For it to be research, Stenhouse (1975) says that it must be shared with others. Research is systematic and sustained inquiry. It is planned and self-critical, and it is subjected to public criticism and to empirical tests where they are appropriate. His shortened version is *systematic self-critical inquiry made public*. Making inquiry public enables the researcher to learn from putting the inquiry into public form as well as from the responses of others, and importantly, to have a record that contributes to an ongoing network of professional conversations— sometimes referred to as a knowledge base for practice. With growing networks of conversation taking place on-line, it is necessary to be able to distinguish reliable sources of information (see Stepping Stones 4.1). Through public critique and conversation, multiple perspectives are brought together to enrich the potential uses of the inquiry not only for the immediate researchers, but for others as well. This brings us to the last key component of AR: collaboration.

STEPPING STONES 4.1

When Is a Web Site a Reliable Source?

With so much information readily available at our fingertips, how does one separate reliable information on the Internet from that which is inappropriate to use? Here are some tips:

- Web sites that end in .com are commercial and therefore related to a business. It is less likely you would find a scholarly reference on a business Web site.
- Web sites that end in .org are sponsored by organizations and are generally nonprofit. Not all organizations are scholarly ones or reliable sources.
- Web sites ending in .gov are government affiliated, including K–12 schools.
- Web sites that end in .edu are educational institutions, such as K–12 schools, colleges, and graduate schools.
- Web sites that end in .net are network organizations affiliated with an association, institution, or organization.
- Get to know the learned societies that govern various subject areas, such as the National Council of Teacher's of English (for English language arts) or the National Council of Social Studies (for social studies).
- Get to know other organizations and their Web sites that have to do with schools, such as the American Library Association, the National Parent Teacher's Organization, and the National Education Association. All these organizations have Web sites that may be helpful to find statistics, trends, and current events related to education.
- Many college faculty have Web sites. These sources are intended for particular uses and may not be reliable sources to cite in scholarly work.
- When evaluating Web sites, consider the following points:
  - Authority—Do the creators have expertise, experience, credentials, and institutional affiliation?
  - Organizational Information—What is the organization, and who runs it and pays for it? What type of organization is it?
  - Objectivity—Is the purpose of the Web site made clear? Is there an obvious bias or viewpoint? Is the sponsorship fully disclosed?
  - Does the URL suggest a reputable agency or institution?
  - Accuracy—Is the information presented current? Are facts cited? Is the information in line with similar Web sites?
  - Usability—Is the site easy to maneuver? Written appropriately for the intended audience? Well presented? Adequately edited? Is there a link back to the homepage?

Information based on Kent State University Library Web site evaluation authored by Barbara Scholman, Reference Librarian, 2003.

Collaboration.   Although it is satisfying, and indeed necessary, for the teacher-scholar to have inner conversations about one's research, it is also essential to have the perspectives of others. With Arendt's emphasis on the importance of action in human intent and agency, the power of change comes only when purposes intersect, when action meets conditions of accord with others (Arendt, 1958).

The beginning of this journey has to do with listening to those around you (especially students and colleagues) in seeking different perspectives and kinds of information (data) and support (collaboration). Involving others can take many forms—from asking students for their perceptions and opinions to full-blown community development projects in which all members participate in a research process that is mutually beneficial. To put this into action and to start down the Yellow Brick Road takes initiative.

Action research is a process of democratizing research and educational practice. It is a democratic orientation to professional practice, a way of learning and improving oneself and one's practice. It is a process that employs systematic and sustained inquiry, and it is made public. It is a self-directed journey, guided by a commitment to building a democratic learning community; and it leads to greater professionalism. Part of this professionalism is because it is action in collaboration with students and/or colleagues.

CHAPTER SUMMARY

This chapter provides a framework and context for action research as a form of knowledge and research method. With a commitment to social change, action researchers engage in a cycle of reflective practice, public discussion, and collaboration.

CHAPTER 5

From a Meandering Path to the Yellow Brick Road: A Brief History of Action Research

Our road began long before it was paved. In fact, you might as well call it a dirt path for most of its history. You are about to meet quite an interesting group of people, whose work as thinkers and researchers paved the way for early teacher research and eventually action research. You will notice how researchers often go against the grain of what is common knowledge. Through careful observation, data collection, analysis, and interpretations that they discuss publicly, they make possible new ways of seeing and understanding.

Against the Tides: Trailblazers

Being skeptical enables new ways of seeing and understanding. These are our new eyes. Remember Galileo? Just think how much courage Galileo needed. Galileo's careful research provided concrete (observable) evidence and provided the basis for laws that would change our understanding of the cosmos and earth's place in it. Unfortunately, this ran against the beliefs of the time and ran contrary to the beliefs held in the Roman Catholic Church, so he faced ridicule and was threatened with death for his "grounded theories." His published work *Dialogue Concerning the Two Chief World Systems* was an attempt to deal with official resistance to his ideas and factual observations.

He recognized that doing the research wasn't the hardest part—getting people to consider his ideas was.

For Galileo to do research that supported Copernicus's theory that the sun (not the earth) was the center of the universe was to take a radically different point of view from the prevailing views of his time. Never mind that it took 300 years for others to recognize his brilliant contributions! (Better late than never.)

And besides, we can learn from his mistakes—the one most pertinent to us here is that the researcher (like Copernicus) cannot expect the research to speak for itself. As researchers, we have to make the results and implications of our research understandable to others.

Galileo was just one of the trailblazers who prepared the way for teacher research and eventually action research. Thinkers such as Aristotle, Copernicus, Galileo, and Newton went against the grain of accepted beliefs of their time. Newton, for example, was so upset with the lack of acknowledgment of his book *Principia Mathematica* that he simply stopped publishing his work at all for a long time. He *delayed* publication of the law of gravity for 20 years!

Other thinkers went against the grain of accepted research methods. Whereas naturalistic methods of research were used primarily in studying the natural world, Comenius, Rousseau, Pestalozzi, Montessori, and Ashton-Warner applied naturalistic methods to the study of children. And they used their observations to study the consequences of their actions on the children they taught. It is easy to see why it took such courage for these teachers to become researchers. By observing children and developing teaching strategies based on these observations, these thinkers and teacher-researchers were challenging the accepted tradition that research be conducted by trained outsiders and under controlled conditions.

Teacher research.   Let's look at how action research can be connected to a broader, more inclusive type of research: *teacher research*. AR is a type of teachers' research. Some people use the two terms interchangeably, but we think that it is worth making a distinction between them. *Teacher research* is a broader term and incorporates research that does not satisfy (nor would its researcher normally want it to) the four criteria we set forth in Chapter 4. For example, it need not be a cyclical kind of research nor conducted in collaboration with anyone. It can be individual or group research, and it can include all kinds of systematic inquiries conducted by teachers. Many, though not all, people agree with Stenhouse (1975) that for it to be research, it must be made public.

Action research, on the other hand, is carried out by teachers who have an explicit agenda based on the four characteristics we outlined earlier. We don't want to muddy the already murky waters here, but perhaps a chart would help. See Figure 5.1.

John Dewey holds a special place in the development of teacher research and action research. A progressive educational philosopher, he was critical of the traditional separation of knowledge and action. Dewey applied the scientific method of problem solving to education. He believed that teachers needed to test their ideas in action—while they were teaching. He believed that by bringing a healthy

FIGURE 5.1 *Types of research teachers do*

Teacher Research

Any kind of research undertaken by a teacher or a group of teachers and others.

Classroom Research

Any kind of research undertaken by a teacher or teachers, or others, in and about classrooms.

Action Research

Research undertaken by individuals or groups that is founded on an active ethical commitment to improve the quality of life of others, is critically reflective in nature and outcome, is collaborative with those to be affected by actions undertaken, and is made public.

Teacher Action Research

Action research conducted by a teacher or teachers.

Classroom Action Research

Action research that takes place within and is focused on life and practices (teaching and learning) within classrooms and schools.

Collaborative Action Research

Action research undertaken by individuals or groups who share a common focus.

skepticism to their teaching, rather than jumping uncritically from one technique to another, teachers were better able to reflect on their practice. He was critical of education that simply taught students to fit in. He believed that it was our duty to help students become increasingly more complex, socially aware, and responsible citizens, and active participants in a democratic society. To Dewey, the classroom was a democratic community. His thinking was considered revolutionary because he integrated child development, the social and democratic ideals of schooling, and the curriculum. He exalted experience itself as a teacher and deepened the teachers' role to include study of the child as a foundational element for curriculum development, teaching, and evaluation. Figure 5.2 outlines the development of the teacher-researcher.

Action research: Constructing the Yellow Brick Road.   Kurt Lewin, a social psychologist and a contemporary of John Dewey, developed the methods and principles to enable any social organization, including schools, to act as an agent for democratic change. Constructing the Yellow Brick Road formally began with Lewin's work in the 1930s and 1940s when he was a consultant for various groups. He developed experiments that compared the products of groups working under different degrees of participation in decision making (Adelman, 1993).

Scientist/Thinker	Contribution to Research	What We Derive for Teacher Research
Aristotle (384–322 B.C.)	Valued observer's role in constructing reality; morally informed action clarifies belief and deepens understanding.	Importance of observation for learning; importance of basing our action on a morally grounded belief system.
Copernicus (1473–1543)	Went against common thought and created a firestorm; replaced the earth with the sun as the center of the cosmos.	Simplicity, harmony, and order are aesthetic goals.
Galileo (1564–1642)	Investigated physical causes and established celestial physics on firmer ground; careful observation and documentation.	Follow your instincts, collect documentation, use diplomacy, and do question the powers that be!
Newton (1642–1727)	Developed the law of gravity.	We cannot be deterred from making public what we learn, even though others may be critical of our ideas.
Comenius (1592–1670)	Conducted empirical observations of how children learn.	Child-centered observation as a basis for teaching methods; one of the earliest teacher-researchers.
Rousseau (1592–1670)	Applied naturalistic methods of inquiry (which had been used for centuries to observe nature) to the study of children.	Use of naturalistic methods of observation as a basis for forming educational principles.
Pestalozzi (1746–1827)	Tested and applied his ideas of child rearing in educational settings.	Use of inquiry method of observation to address needs of students.
Montessori (1870–1952)	Conducted naturalistic methods of observation with teachers and students. Trained teachers to be observers of the effects of their teaching on students.	Use of observation to help us understand the effect of our actions on students.
Ashton-Warner (1908–1984)	Saw teaching as an art form. Role of the teacher as calling on children's resources and having the patience to listen, watch, and wait; harnessing of creative energies as the agent of change.	Use of diary to record observations of students as a way of understanding the resources they bring to their own learning.

One of Lewin's greatest contributions to social change was his use of action research (a term coined by a man named Collier just a few years before Lewin started his experiments) to help participants "learn to become detached and objective in examining the foundations of their biases" (Ebbutt, 1985, p. 154). For example, Lewin helped a group of managers at a new factory to examine their belief that newly hired, unskilled female trainees would not be able to perform their tasks as efficiently as already skilled men. Lewin helped us to see the importance of recognizing the biases, opinions, and prejudices we all have that, when they go unexamined, impede us from seeing ourselves and our situations in new ways.

At the same time as Lewin was conducting his research, other people in psychology and psychiatry were trying to find ways of communicating more adequately. Part of their efforts were aimed at helping people to "see gaps and discrepancies between their perceptions and actions in their relationships with others" (Holly, 1989, p. 152). They were trying to uncover problems in personal and interpersonal communication that prevented them from recognizing and challenging their own biases and distorted perceptions (Lippitt, 1949). So, instead of continuing the tradition of focusing on changing *others*, research was turned toward changing one's *own behavior* and understanding. The research itself was empowering to the person and group conducting it, and it contributed to knowledge about social relations and change.

Today's action research, sometimes referred to as *educational action research*, grew from these earlier forms of inquiry and AR in the social and psychological professions. It pertains to individuals trying to monitor and learn from reflection on action and trying to become aware of discrepancies among perceptions, values, and actions. It contains elements of individual and group self-study, and social action.

Today, there are networks and AR groups that provide forums for discussion, support, and collaboration all over the world. There are core groups in Bath, England, associated with Jack Whitehead, and at Deakin University in Australia, where Stephen Kemmis, Robin McTaggart, and Collin Henry have been instrumental in the growth of AR. The network that we are most familiar with is that which has been developed from the works of British action researchers Lawrence Stenhouse and his colleague John Elliott. John Elliott founded the *Collaborative Action Research Network (CARN)*, which, since 1967, has been comprised of an international group of teachers, administrators, and teacher educators involved in AR.

In Lawrence Stenhouse's 1975 book, *An Introduction to Curriculum Research and Development*, he traced the development of research in classrooms and research on teaching, including interaction analysis and what has been called *social anthropology*, among other areas of inquiry. Although AR had its origins in the experimental, psychological studies of Kurt Lewin, most action research studies developed from a more qualitative orientation and employ both naturalistic and experimental methods. As we reflect on the purposes of action research and observe its evolution over time, this makes sense. Inquiry that focuses on self-study, social improvement, and collaborative action naturally lends itself to a mode of inquiry that values individual and social interpretation as a basis for developing knowledge. The most important factor to remember is that *the context, questions, purposes, and participants* drive the appropriateness of methods.

In Figure 5.3 we provide a few brief portraits of some notable contributors and groups that illustrate some of the breadth and depth of the AR process as it evolved in the twentieth century. We call these the pavers of the action research road.

FIGURE 5.3 *Pavers of the action research road*

Noteable Contributor	Noted Position	Contribution to Action Research
John Dewey American	Educational philosopher; progressivism	Connected theory and practice through critical reflection—teachers must study the consequences of their actions. Conceived of teaching as an ethical and moral enterprise in which teachers educate students for responsible citizenship.
Kurt Lewin American	Social psychologist	Conceived of *action research* as research conducted by scholar-practitioners who improve their social situations; participants must become objective in examining their own biases; saw AR as a way of describing professional development in social situations.
Stephen Corey American	Curriculum theorist	Applied AR to education as a means of reconceptualizing curriculum from an efficiency model (belief that top-down is the most efficient way to achieve outcomes) to a curriculum developed by teachers with the goal of promoting a critical social consciousness of the impact of power in society.
Joseph Schwab American	Curriculum theorist	Emphasized the importance of group practical deliberation in curriculum development by teachers; based on the idea that the process of education is more important than the outcomes and the possibilities that curriculum action can make things "right."
Lawrence Stenhouse British	Director of the Humanities Curriculum Project	Stressed that teaching should be based on research carried out by teachers rather than by specialists; teaching is improved by teachers studying the effects of their actions.
John Elliott British	Director of the Ford Teaching Project and founder of Collaborative Action Research Network (CARN)	Believed that educational research is a moral endeavor in its attempt to realize values in practice; teachers develop theories as they teach. Developed a model of the action research process that includes a sequential cycle of action and reflection.

Today: AR as Critical Reflection

The brief history we recounted in this chapter brings us to modern and postmodern times in which change and complexity are recognized as inevitable and constant. We are moving away from the *modern* world where life was thought to be a bit more manageable than we now know it to be. We thought we could straightforwardly attack and solve many of our problems. Researchers from outside our schools could do research and curriculum development for us. The best disciplinary minds could together produce excellent curricula.

Unfortunately these curricula didn't work in many classrooms. For example, "Man: A Course of Study" was one of the most professionally staffed and creative curriculum design projects in recent history. It was more consistent with constructivist and developmental theories than most other curricula. Historians, scientists, artists, and others were involved in designing this innovative and integrated social studies curriculum. The materials included excellent suggestions for highly active and creative student and teacher participation. Unfortunately, the materials were out of step with the people they were to benefit. Had teachers been involved in the design and development process, the story would likely have been entirely different.

Ours is a time in which teachers and researchers expose multiple dimensions of a "problem," where one "solution" leads to other "problems." The world that most of us grew up in is different from the world in which we are called to teach. Simple reflection won't do.

Critical reflection means looking beneath surfaces, asking questions, raising issues, exercising and judging merit. Whose interests *are* being served by this approach to teaching science, art, or literature? How did this happen? Does this curriculum serve all the children? Whose needs *are not* being met? This is what Wilf Carr and Steven Kemmis mean by *critical reflection* in their book *Becoming Critical* (1986). Critical reflection can be defined as "being able to understand, analyze, pose questions, and affect and effect the socio-political label and economic realities that shape our lives" (Leistyna et al., 1996, p. 334).

We become critical as we move beyond "surviving." Francis Fuller (1969), through her research on teacher professional development, was able to document what happened to teachers' concerns over time. She developed a theory that described three phases of a teacher's growth over time. In the first phase the teacher was concerned with survival: What do I do on Monday? How can I plan enough to fill the day? In the second phase the teacher focused on curriculum development and learning to teach more knowledgeably, efficiently, and effectively. In the third and last phase, the teacher focus was So what? What are the social, political, economic, and educational consequences of what I do?

This last phase is more typical of the critical theorist orientation. The teacher at this point is concerned with larger social issues and long-term consequences. Teachers do not automatically go through these phases during the course of their careers. Some teachers *begin* their teaching careers with a socially critical eye toward practice, especially if they have colleagues who support a questioning stance. These teachers may walk a very different path in their development.

CHAPTER SUMMARY

After discussing several types of research that teachers do in schools today, we made an excursion into the past. We saw the seeds of teacher research in the relentless quest for learning exhibited by scholars from Aristotle to Galileo to Newton. Empirical investigation was conducted at great cost to the researchers who went against common knowledge and blind adherence to professed certainty that ruled across the Dark Ages.

From dirt path to John Dewey and Kurt Lewin and to the paving of the Yellow Brick Road, scholars have challenged current thinking. With Kurt Lewin's research, AR had a start with an overtly social purpose: The people affected by research were to have a say in the conduct of that research. Discrimination in the workplace was fought with empirical evidence. Stephen Corey worked to demonstrate to educators the power of AR to improve education. The movement in education gathered momentum when Lawrence Stenhouse, John Elliott, and others in the United Kingdom worked with teachers in growing numbers and built networks for AR. Today those networks continue to grow. Critical AR is no longer the purview of the few, but the calling of many! While new teachers were characterized not so very long ago by survival, critical reflection and inquiry take practice to a new level, one where social change is not only possible, but probable, even for those entering the profession.

SECTION SUMMARY

Action research is an orientation to and a form of professional development. In many respects AR is a logical outgrowth of humankind's inquisitive constitution. Over the ages, from long before Aristotle to postmodernity and beyond, humankind has asked fundamental questions and sought ways to make life better. Action research is one way we can collectively do so. As a systematic, sustained, and publicly shared way of learning and improving oneself and one's practice, AR has the power to perpetuate continuous renewal and creative experience. As a self-directed *and* collaborative journey, AR leads inexorably toward greater professionalism both within ourselves and for shaping the conditions of our profession. This development in our professional lives and work is guided by critical reflection as we examine ourselves and our practice with an eye toward improving the social consequences of what we do. Teachers are agents of change.

Exploring the Forest

Finding Our Way

Contexts and Companions

We have covered considerable ground in this section. We have briefly investigated some of the people and contexts that surround and shape action research, because we think this knowledge gives us a clearer picture of AR, its roots, and its uses. Whole books have been written on this subject, and we urge you to peruse some of them. Robin McTaggert provides two sources: *Action Research: A Short Modern History* (1991) and an edited volume, *Participatory Action Research: International Contexts and Consequences* (1997). For now, let us reflect on some of the ideas presented in this chapter.

1. *Research experience.* What are your experiences with research? How could your experiences with research hinder and help you in pursuing your area of interest?
2. *Definitions of research terms.* Set aside a section of your journal for definitions related to research. Using the text, define the following, and include any other terms that occur to you:
   - Theory, theorize, theoretical
   - Paradigm
   - Naturalistic research
   - Experimental research
   - Basic research
   - Applied research
   - Action research
   - Research methods

3. *Theories.*   Many theories will be useful to you as a professional educator during your career. These theories inform the development of the most important theory—your own. Three salient theories to us in this book are *constructivism, developmentalism,* and *critical theory.* As a supersleuth researcher, do the following two things. Do the first before you read the second.
   - Draw a symbol and do a free-write for each theory.
   - Now write a brief definition of each. Give an example of each. Use your free-write for ideas, and consult this text and any other sources you might find useful.

4. *Critical colleagues.*   As we discussed, professionals engage in critical reflection. Collaboration is a defining aspect of our professional lives. With whom (and how) do we form working relationships? *Critical colleague* is the term we will use to describe a person or persons with whom to share, discuss, and give and receive critical feedback. By *critical* we mean feedback that is challenging, collegial, respectful, and useful. Talk with another person, preferably a critical colleague, about these three theories and your current understanding of them. What are her or his thoughts? What place do any of the theories have in your teaching? Do you find any relationships between and among them? These theories give us a language to talk about experience, and if we hold on too tightly—as we can to our own theories—they narrow rather than open our perspectives. If we only understand the mechanics, we won't grasp enough to enrich our perspective.

   These theories describe, in a systematic way, many things that we observe and relate to in everyday life. What do we do in schools that has a developmental basis? We don't expect a 6-year-old to have the same experiences in school as a 12-year-old. What do we do in school that is *constructivist* in orientation?

5. *Three purposes of AR.*   Material well-being, communication, and freedom are the three ways of knowing described in this chapter. We have used these ways of knowing as a means to frame three purposes of action research. Each is necessary to our personal and collaborative well-being and to our professionalism. While research is certainly possible without the primary goal of creating more just, equitable, democratic classrooms, professional practice is not. Referring to the discussion of these three purposes in the text, use your journal to jot down a few ideas and an example of when each is important to you. Are there times when your primary concern is with acting in such a way as to maintain your (and your students') material well-being? Are there times when the efficiency and effectiveness of your practice are of utmost importance? Are there other times when your primary concern is with a practical interest in understanding? And are there times when your primary concern lies in understanding the relationship between your goals and values and what your students are learning, with educational goals, activities, and experiences that lead to a more just, equitable, democratic classroom? Are there times when your goal is to liberate your students

(and perhaps yourself) from oppressive situations? Use these jottings to start a conversation with your critical colleague(s). When you have finished this conversation, spend 15 minutes recording key ideas generated from it in your journal. What ideas, questions, or thoughts do you have as a result of this conversation? Highlight one or two that you might want to revisit.

The final exercises for Section II are designed to explore the historical and current contexts of your professional work.

6. *Journals.*   What are the key journals in your area? *Childhood Education* (for teachers of young children), *Middle School Journal* (for middle school teachers), and the *Language Arts* and *The Reading Teacher* (for teachers of literacy) are a few examples to get you started. Search your library for a list of relevant journals. Select one that seems most relevant to your work and, starting with the earliest issue in your library, scan the tables of contents and articles to see how it has developed over time. What were the topics in the earliest journals? What research methods, if any, were referred to in early articles? What topics are addressed today? What research methods are used for what types of research? Do you find AR among them? Are the topics and issues different in the later journal issues? If so, in what ways? Why might this be so? If not, why not theorize?

7. *Influential or significant people.*   What people have influenced you most in your education? In what ways have they been influential or significant? You may feel a kinship or connection to someone from your past or present. Write a portrait for your journal of that person, and use stories to illustrate the ways in which they have affected you. Write as many portraits as you wish. Write about one in depth or several in less depth. Might it be worthwhile to share this with the person portrayed or with another colleague?

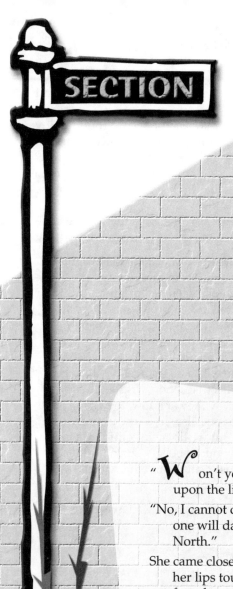

III

Exploring Researcher Selves and the Profession

" W on't you go with me?" pleaded the girl, who had begun to look upon the little old woman as her only friend.

"No, I cannot do that," she replied; "but I will give you my kiss, and no one will dare injure a person who has been kissed by the Witch of the North."

She came close to Dorothy and kissed her gently on the forehead. Where her lips touched the girl they left a round, shining mark, as Dorothy found out soon after.

"The road to the City of Emeralds is paved with yellow brick," said the Witch; "so you cannot miss it. When you get to Oz do not be afraid of him, but tell your story and ask him to help you. Goodbye, my dear."

The Wonderful Wizard of Oz
L. Frank Baum (1900)

Who am I? Where did I come from? Where am I going? In this section we address some of these questions and others related to professional development with the aid of autobiographical writing. In the first sections of this book, we explored the contexts of action research. Now it is time to focus on the person who conducts action research. We will see how the professional and political spheres interact with and shape the personal domain, which in turn influences professional and political life.

How can I return home to Kansas? you ask. We each have a "round shiny mark" inside, and it will help us to navigate. Returning home is a powerful incentive, one that will lead us on a journey that is sometimes frightening, sometimes difficult. During this journey we meet new people; explore our roots, human nature, and life; and gain insights we never could have predicted at the start of the journey.

Stephen Brookfield (1984), a specialist in adult learning, says that asking challenging questions is important, *especially* when they take us into unknown territory.

> Taking the risk to think critically, and to realize in our actions the insights we gain through this, is one of the most powerful activities of adult life. The reason we persist in doing this, even when it seems to produce only frustration, perplexity, and anxiety, are the rewards it produces . . . we are engaged in a continual process of creating and re-creating our personal, work, and political lives. We do not take our identities as settled; rather, we are aware of the scope for development in all areas of life. We see the future as open to our influence [and] . . . the world as changeable through our own individual actions and through collective action. . . . We do not accept the idea that because things are the way they are now, they must always be this way . . . [Nor] that we (or anyone else) have the ultimate answer to life's ambiguities and problems. But we do have confidence in knowing that . . . the actions we take arising out of beliefs, spring from a process of careful analysis and testing against reality—in other words, from critical thinking. (Brookfield, 1984, p. 254)

Our journey begins at home, with who we are and how we have gotten to be who we are. As Socrates put it, "Know thyself."

CHAPTER 6

Journey of the Self: There's No Place Like Home

There is no place like home, and we take home with us wherever we go. Early in Dorothy's journey, she examines the importance of home, a place she has taken for granted. Our journey, too, entails an examination of our roots, of what we value, believe, and hope to accomplish. In this chapter our work includes discussion of the multiple selves who inhabit us and find their way into our teaching, and of ideas for autobiographical explorations.

Home is a place inside of us, our base, a security we feel, and a nest from which to reflect, act, and observe. Although we take home with us, and feel confident and secure with its familiar wisdom, we also challenge its certainty and introduce new ways of being. This stretches us in sometimes uncomfortable ways. We learn about ourselves when our assumptions and beliefs are challenged. So, as we speak about the roles and responsibilities of our professional selves (teacher, colleague, student, decision maker, etc.), we will keep in the back of our minds the compass that guides us.

What is the *self*? This is not easy to answer, and although we explore the topic here, we don't have the answer. We do know that the self starts at home, in our biology and our experiences. We know that while the self is relatively stable over time, it is also dynamic, resisting growth and seeking it, offering security. We become frustrated with its guarded traditions. We know that the self evolves through learning and that learning is physical; that as we grow and learn, new connections are made in the brain and new dimensions of the self come into being. Although we may not be able to erase previous connections, we can form new ones and strengthen these (Zull, 2002). This is how we grow as people and as teachers.

Beyond that, what you find depends on whom you ask. Ask a poet or a painter, a philosopher, a biologist, a psychologist, or a sociologist, and in fact, ask different members of these communities and you will get different responses. The behaviorist takes a view of the self that colors what can be seen; the psychoanalyst stands on different foundations, studying who is "at home" and who operates underground (unconsciously). Neural scientist Joseph LeDoux (1996, 2002) and biologist-educator James Zull (2002) emphasize the importance of the brain's biology to learning, and of emotion as the "mortar that holds things together" (2002, p. 8). For LeDoux (2002), the self is synaptic, only a tiny portion of which is conscious.

Each scholar has multiple points of view. We won't step into their debates here but since the self is the chief architect guiding our actions in research, it is important that we step into the subject of the self from a perspective that is useful to AR. As Hannah Arendt (1958) points out, we learn about the self through action. *Who is the self that researches? What do we see and where are we standing when we observe? Simply put, whose eyes can see what? What informs our vision, and our actions? What do we make of our actions?*

Ways to Explore Our Teaching Selves

There are many ways to gain self-knowledge. In the following pages we explore a few of these ways that can be useful for action researchers.

Doing self-talk.   Have you ever noticed any private conversations taking place inside your head? Although these inside characters rarely rest, we aren't usually conscious of their debates. When we listen carefully, however, particularly at times when we are making decisions, we can tune into revealing conversations. Let's listen in on one such conversation. We will give each of the *selves* a different number (Self 1, etc.). The problem under consideration is "I'm hungry!"

Self 1: Let's go and get a hot fudge sundae with lots of nuts and whipped cream! (A more health-conscious self counters with this idea.)
Self 2: It would be better if I had a salad with tofu and bean sprouts.
Self 1: Oh, yuck! (Another more mediating voice offers a compromise.)
Self 3: (eagerly): How about a lowfat, fruit-flavored frozen yogurt?
Self 1 and **Self 2**, while not exactly jubilant, react with relief and go along with the compromise.

We often have these kinds of inside self-talk sessions concerning our teaching lives. Joanne recently engaged in self-talk about a student who was upset that "rules were being changed" midstream on an assignment. During a class discussion several students brainstormed possible ways to do the assignment. When Joanne encouraged them to use these new insights in their work, one student objected, saying, "I have already done the assignment, and now you are asking

this is an idiotic example

me to change my writing! I am extremely busy and finished it early so I wouldn't have to deal with it again!"

One voice told Joanne: Being a teacher means being flexible and adapting to new ideas—a lesson the student could better learn now than later. Another voice said: This student needs to read her syllabus more carefully and stop whining! Another voice said: I want to be an understanding teacher. This student is under a great deal of stress. And yet another thought occurred to Joanne: As a teacher, have I provided adequate structure and still allowed for flexibility in my assignments?

All this internal talk can influence our behavior. If we become aware of the chorus within, and hear what it says, we have the possibility of taking a new and possibly more insightful perspective. In this case, Joanne chose to react to the student in a way that minimized the student's stress *and* to examine the manner in which she presented assignments.

Critical reflection on her identity as a constructivist teacher helped Joanne recall the frustration she (and her colleagues) often felt in similar situations. As a teacher, she wants to provide sufficient structure to help students grow, without stifling their creativity and sense of responsibility with too many required rules and procedures. Many students resist this approach, wanting more specific guidelines. Thus, committing herself to a constructivist approach to teaching—and *living it*—will continue to be a challenging journey.

Interviewing others.   In exploring our roots, we can interview mothers, fathers, older siblings, extended family, friends, and colleagues. Often the comments of these others will spur memories of particular events or patterns and add multiple perspectives to emerging self-understanding. For example, as one part of her educational autobiography, Wendy interviewed her mother. Her mother shared stories of how Wendy liked to "organize her work space" prior to beginning a project and recalled her excitement at learning to read. This information helped her make sense of her career choices and her ways of operating as a teacher.

Examining personal artifacts.   In sharing the development of herself as a teacher, Margo, a preservice teacher, created an album of photographs. She traced the multiple identities she explored during adolescence. From a shy, overweight kid, to a prom queen, to a mother, she demonstrated how her multiple selves and the pain of making transitions from one to another would ultimately lead her to become a more sensitive and empathic teacher of young adolescents. The seeds of our emerging selves can be found in report cards, letters, photographs, program notices, and dried flowers—musty reminders of our formative experiences and the persons we are becoming as teachers.

Recalling significant others.   Uri Bronfenbrenner, a noted child development specialist, once said that the one thing that every child needs for healthy development is at least one person who is crazy about her or him. That one crazy-about-you person becomes a significant other. Pamela Donaldson, a preservice teacher, wrote a poem that illustrates the power of a significant other in shaping her life.

Pam: I did terrible things, starting in first grade, when I decided to hide between two closets for four hours. Not only did the fire department and police come, thinking I was kidnapped, but they called my mom from work. I did it for attention—the same reason I did every other terrorizing thing that I decided to do. Then, in first grade, after being kicked out of my assigned classroom by the teacher, I was sent to Mrs. Harvey's class. Her beautiful and nurturing personality changed my behavior, and I decided I wanted to be the same kind of influence on children that she was on me.

Soo Badd

I was soo badd
So bad, teachers feared me,
I was the one they sent to someone else's class,
The desk always next to the teacher's,
The one who placed tacks on your chair,
Who put paint in your hair,
I was soo badd.

Soo badd, they knew my mother by her first name,
"Mary, Mary, why is your daughter so scary!
Maybe she should go to a special school,
Go learn with the other fools,
She's just soo badd!"

One day, they sent me to Mrs. Harvey's class
Once again, there were tacks on someone else's chair,
As (usual) I thought, boy am I in trouble again,
Instead she said, "Why don't you grin?"

She said, "You're smart, and beautiful, why don't you show it?"
She said, "You're not that bad and I do know it."

She made a difference in my life the first day I met her,
And I can promise you I won't forget her,
But instead remember her always! Thank you, Mrs. Harvey, for all my good days!!!!!!!

People teach by example, by the ideas they explore with us, by their insights, by their expectations, by the questions they ask, and by the ways they come to know. Teachers influence our thinking not only directly through the courses they teach, but indirectly through sharing themselves and how they see the world. Friends, family, teachers, students, and strangers can help.

Using metaphors. Metaphor is a form of symbolic language in which one thing is used to describe another. The AR journey, for example, is a metaphor for the developmental journey of improving ourselves as teachers. Using metaphors can help us gain self-knowledge because metaphors form "the basis of the conceptual systems by means of which we understand and act within our worlds" (Taylor, 1984, p. 5). Metaphors capture images that crystallize meaning. Metaphors of teaching enable us to capture essences of our teaching identities and to observe changes in those identities.

For example, one middle school teacher described different phases of her teaching career by comparing them to other occupations. One year, for example, she termed her *butler* phase because she felt like a servant to institutionalized systems and to her students—"serving knowledge to them on a platter." She referred to another era as her *train conductor* phase, when she was passing out things and collecting them. After reviewing his own long-term journal entries, another teacher realized that his metaphor was that of a *policeman*, leading him to reexamine his commitments and attitudes toward teaching and the conditions in which he found himself functioning.

Evoking metaphors from the arts to describe teaching can bring about surprisingly fresh insights. Letishia, for example, selected jazz as a metaphor for her teaching style. She compared the improvisational nature of jazz to the spontaneity and creativity involved in her teaching. While she was always well prepared for her lessons, she learned to follow the lead of her students and let the lesson take its own natural course. Another teacher reported feeling like a theatrical *stage manager*, responsible for much of what happens in a play but always behind the scenes, supporting actors.

Metaphors that define the self (teacher) also define the *other* (student) in revealing ways. For example, the metaphor of a teacher as policeman could suggest that students are unmanageable. Defining ourselves as train conductors could suggest that students are passengers. Defining teaching as *improvisation* could imply that students are an *ensemble* of creative and not always predictable musicians.

Understanding critical incidents. A critical incident is typically considered to be an event or situation that marks a significant turning point in our lives. Small and seemingly insignificant events can be *made* critical by the way we look at them. By probing and challenging underlying assumptions behind our actions and statements, an incident can become critical.

A recent discussion in a student teaching seminar may help to illustrate this kind of thinking. Into his second week of student teaching, Tom was overwhelmed with discipline problems in his middle school science class. In the seminar he described the students as rude and uncooperative to the point where he felt he was unable to teach science. He described the classroom rules that he made up to ensure a manageable environment and his frustration that students seemed to mock his rules and test him every step of the way. He told of his mentor teacher's reaction: "You waver between being too strict and too easy on the students. They are getting mixed messages and getting confused." Recalling this recurring situation, Tom confessed, "I don't know who I am anymore! I am a nice guy. I hate being mean to them—it does no good anyway!"

Students in the student teaching seminar asked Tom questions about how he started class, his tone of voice, how he gained his students' attention. Many ideas emerged, but none more powerful than the question, Do you feel that this is *your* class—or your *mentor's?* Tom smiled, almost sadly. "Perhaps I am trying to please my mentor more than I am trying to figure out a way to be with my students." This was a critical incident for Tom. It ushered in a new way of thinking about his dilemma. He began to wonder if he was being fair to his students and to himself. It also offered him the potential to "regroup" and to approach this problem from a more authentic self. As critical colleagues, or mentors, we hope that this reflective process leads him to consider *student* roles and responsibilities, in addition to his own. *Whose* class is this? What are each of our roles and responsibilities?

Creating a time line of incidents and people.   By creating a time line of our lives, marking the influence of critical incidents and people, we can coax the emergence and profile of our teaching selves. While some people feel as if they were born to be teachers, for many of us, the journey to teaching has been a circuitous one. Thinking about our lives historically can yield patterns and insight. One teacher who did this exercise discovered how important and influential her family was to her. Another teacher found a pattern of struggle against injustices that he was sure became manifest in his decision to work with children with special needs.

Developing a philosophy of teaching.   Our philosophies evolve as we gain experience and understanding. According to the *Merriam-Webster Dictionary* (1974), philosophy is "a critical study of fundamental beliefs and the grounds for them" (p. 522). So, as we develop professionally as action researchers, we expand the grounds for our beliefs.

While most of us function quite well from our own set of beliefs and hypotheses about what teaching is without a formal philosophy, to be able to articulate our orientation and the assumptions that guide our work is both useful and necessary. When we make a claim, for example, what is our rationale for making it?

Few educators have developed a written philosophy of education similar to John Dewey's philosophical treatise "My Pedagogic Creed," written around the turn of the century when he was a young scholar (Archambault, 1964). Yet it can be quite helpful to our research and development to record our beliefs about the purposes of schooling, how children learn, and the roles and responsibilities of teachers and of students. We, too, can use this as a foundation for our thinking about testing, approaches to discipline, and other issues confronting teachers today. The more we read, study, discuss, and cogitate over educational issues, problems, and dilemmas, the more articulate we can become in putting forth our own evolving points of view. As professionals, we can ask ourselves and our colleagues to articulate the grounds of our beliefs and to make tacit beliefs and assumptions visible.

In Chapter 4 we described Habermas's technical, practical, and critical orientations to the world. Age, motivation, experience, and situations, including school norms and culture, influence how one's orientation and beliefs develop over time. Many teachers, for example, began practice with a technical or practical orientation and did not consciously take on a social advocacy role associated with the critical orientation toward teaching until later in their careers. Because AR is overtly democratic and social change is foundational to it, action research has the potential to enhance social advocacy in our schools and to do so from the beginning of one's career. Along with John Dewey, many prominent scholars, notably Maxine Greene, suggest that philosophy is not an entity; it is not something you *have*—it is a process, something that you *do*. You *live* it.

CHAPTER SUMMARY

The journey of the self begins long before we are aware of it and continues in conscious and unconscious ways. To become aware of the journey and the forces that shape it, is to make possible ways to create the future. Each autobiographical return is a reconstruction, and while we cannot change the past, we can learn from it.

As we explore the people and customs that left lasting impressions on us, and as we integrate past learning and upgrade it to today's world, we can develop our philosophies of teaching in ways that build on our values, beliefs, and aspirations. In the next chapter we extend our autobiographical inquiry with developmental continuums enabling us to look over many years of experience in a short time.

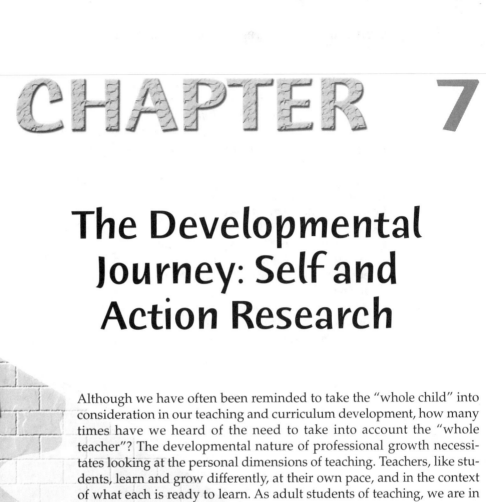

CHAPTER 7

The Developmental Journey: Self and Action Research

Although we have often been reminded to take the "whole child" into consideration in our teaching and curriculum development, how many times have we heard of the need to take into account the "whole teacher"? The developmental nature of professional growth necessitates looking at the personal dimensions of teaching. Teachers, like students, learn and grow differently, at their own pace, and in the context of what each is ready to learn. As adult students of teaching, we are in charge of our own learning.

We learn when people and situations challenge us and provoke us to think. For example, we may see clearly a behavior or practice that is problematic in someone else that we have yet to see in ourselves. Such situations can be gifts to our professional growth.

To take a real-life example, Mary Lou, as a classroom teacher, noticed that Barb, her teaching mate, had a terrible time wrapping up lessons so that the second-grade children in their classroom could be on time for the bus to take them home. Barb was absent one day. Much to her surprise and chagrin, Mary Lou found herself taking more than a few children home after they all missed the bus. Many winding, bumpy country miles later, the realization dawned on her that *she*, too, had "a terrible time wrapping up lessons." Numerous chances to confirm or disconfirm her hypothesis presented themselves: Getting the children ready for lunch and recess provided a wealth of confirmations that, although not comforting, did stimulate useful change!

There are other basic developmental principles that can be useful as we look at our professional lives. The most basic is that *development is movement toward more complex, differentiated, and inclusive perspectives.* As we learn, we become able to see new things in our physical and social worlds. To *differentiate* means to be able to see differences, to discriminate between objects or ideas and thus to see greater complexity. Where we at first saw only green, now we see many shades of verdure: olive, kelly, lime, and some we have yet to name—soft, sharp, dull, and mottled. We learn to discriminate between objects, and between ideas. The last part of the principle, *inclusive*, refers to the ability to become more comprehensive and expansive in our understanding; to bring a diversity of people, ideas, or objects together; and to be more flexible in our intelligence.

We grow in the ability and the capacity to differentiate and to think inclusively. Let's look at embracing diversity, for example. We grow in the ability to understand other people's perspectives, to cherish cultural rituals that are different from our own, while gaining appreciation of similarities and realizing that we must all be stewards of the earth.

This principle applies to all domains of development including the following:

Physical and motor.   We start out tiny and by fits and starts and uneven spurts grow to be large; we learn to walk before skipping; to scribble before drawing.
Social and emotional.   We arrive in the world with reflexes and relatively undifferentiated feelings. We become able to distinguish between tears of laughter and sorrow. From "Mommy and I are one" to "I am a separate person," to ever more sophisticated social relationships, we grow.
Cognitive.   To use language as an example of this domain, we enter the world with a broad array of sounds. Within the first years of life we begin to differentiate sounds and to use some and let some go. We put the sounds we use into shapes called words, and before you know it, we move from sentences to elaborate discourse—all within the early years of childhood!

Development is not a smooth journey although it is predictable in some ways. But an odd thing happens with this process called *growth:* Complex and interconnected processes are taking place that are not easy to see or to understand. For example, when something is learned, much of that learning takes place where we can't see it. Yet, when learning comes to fruition, we know it. As teachers, we don't always see development occurring in others—especially our students. Here's an anecdote to illustrate our point.

A delightful 6 1/2-year-old chap named Chuck was paying attention to a squirrel and some birds outside the back window of his classroom. His frustrated teacher decided to make an example of Chuck for not paying attention to the math lesson she was so painstakingly (and unsuccessfully) teaching: "Chuck? (!) Perhaps you can come finish the numbers on the board for the boys and girls? (!)" Slowly, calmly (as was his modus operandi), Chuck s a u n t e r e d to the board— a l l t h e w a y u p t o t h e f r o n t o f t h e c l a s s r o o m —without saying a word or making eye contact with another human being, but seeming to study with a 60-year-old scientist's eyes several things outside of normal vision along

the way. Picking up the chalk with a purpose and no wasted effort, he completed the math problem, turned around to face the class, and with his eyes meeting theirs, explained in simple, clear, direct, and understandable terms what the teacher had failed to teach.

Chuck's learning of mathematics certainly wasn't visible to his teacher. In fact, the teacher may have assumed he wasn't learning anything at all. Perhaps the main learning here was the teacher's. Learning is usually more complex than meets the eye.

A Developmental Continuum: Learning from the Journey

Our lives, like Chuck's life, are filled with curiosities, with things that attract our attention and energy. Poet Rainer Maria Rilke had wise advice for a young poet seeking answers, that is good advice for action researchers: "learn to love the journey; the questions themselves . . . **Live** the questions . . ." (Rilke, 1984, p. 34). As adults, we can reflect on our lives and make sense of key experiences that continue to shape our professional lives.

To map aspects of our growth visually, from the time we were young to recent years, we might draw a continuum with phases or categories like this:

Developmental Continuum by Age Ranges

1	2	3	4	5	6
0–5 Early Childhood	6–10 Middle Childhood	11–14 Early Adolescence	15–18 Adolescence	19–26 Early Adulthood	27– Adulthood

These categories parallel general periods in development. Depending on the theory studied, categories vary slightly by age. Soon we will describe a continuum and theory that spans the entire life cycle. For now, these general categories serve our purposes. There are many ways to explore our earlier years by using a continuum such as this. What, for example, are your earliest memories? What attracted your attention? What were your curiosities?

Using the same basic continuum, we can chart our formal education:

Return to this continuum later and write about some of your school experiences. Which school experiences can you remember most easily? Which are most difficult to recall? Why? What didn't happen?

We can look at many kinds of growth chronologically. We can describe development by domain: cognitive, social-emotional, psychomotor, physical, and so on. For example, we might chart our development as social beings. Let's take a total life perspective, sometimes referred to as a life span approach, and borrow from Erik Erikson's theory of psychosocial development (Erikson, 1950) to build a continuum. By putting our lives into a broader context, we can take the edge off the stress we face today. What seemed to be the end of the world at age 18 gets a different interpretation at ages 23 and 34 and 56 1/2. We can use this principle when we look at some of today's challenges. A broader perspective enables us to address a phenomenon from multiple perspectives. As action researchers we learn to view phenomena from multiple perspectives. As you read through Erikson's eight stages shown in Figure 7.1, keep in mind that the tensions for each stage are never resolved or completed. We come to terms with them during the time indicated, but we meet them in different circumstances throughout the life cycle. Whenever we find ourselves in a new situation, for example, most of us struggle a bit with trust.

Which of these tensions are most prominent in your life today?

For those of us who have been teaching a while, we can create our own teaching continuums to describe how we've grown and changed, starting with our own teacher preparation and student teaching experiences.

Since action research can be viewed as a developmental process, we can use the same kind of continuum to make sense of it. We can see where AR might start: with a curiosity. The question we form as a result can be developed into an action research project. Dorothy, for example, might start with the comment, "My dog Toto doesn't listen to me very well!" But perhaps the problem lies within her as well: "I wonder how I can improve my communication skills with Toto?"

FIGURE 7.1 *A life span continuum for psychosocial development*

1	2	3	4	5	6	7	8
Birth– 1 Year	2–3 Years	4–5 Years	6–11 Years	12–18 Years	Young Adulthood	Middle Adulthood	Old Age

1. *Basic trust versus mistrust* is the dominant tension negotiated in the first year of life.
   - Consistency, continuity, and sameness of experience provided by the caregiver lead to the infant's first social achievement: congruence of inner certainty and outer reality that needs will be met.

2. *Autonomy versus shame and doubt* are the alternative basic attitudes in tension during these 2 years.
   - The opportunity to try out his or her skills in a secure and supportive environment enables the young child to gain a sense of autonomy, and the ability to hold on and to let go.

3. *Initiative versus guilt* becomes a tension as the young child enjoys new mental and locomotive powers.
   - Pleasure and confidence in the launch and conquest of carrying out her or his activities are the achievements secured by the child whose questions are met with affirming responses.

4. *Industry versus inferiority* becomes the focus as the child moves into the world, production, and education.
   - Being encouraged to make and do things and to be recognized for her or his efforts and accomplishments leads to a sense of industry as the child learns to handle the tools for the "big people."

5. *Identity versus role confusion* is a central tension as the body and mind change rapidly and basic competence with tools and production has been achieved.
   - The adolescent's ability to integrate multiple identifications, aptitudes, and new social roles with confidence, inner stability, and strength leads to a successful transition to career and adulthood.

6. *Intimacy versus isolation* becomes the focus of social development as one attains a more stable sense of self and competence in the adult world.
   - With commitment to others—to love—and to causes beyond one's self—to work—one develops the capacity for intimacy, which results in a stronger and larger sense of self as well.

7. *Generativity versus stagnation* is present when one confronts the future.
   - The achievement here lies in establishing, creating, and supporting others and the environment.

8. *Ego integrity versus despair* is the summing up of someone's one and only life cycle.
   - Acceptance of one's life, love, and work leads to authenticity, congruence, and completeness.

Using the following action research continuum, think through your own interest.

Action Research Continuum

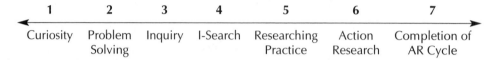

We will start with the simplest process, developing one's curiosity, and progress to a more complex inquiry until we arrive at an AR project as described in number 6.

1. *Curiosity:* Posing questions and musing: "I wonder why I dread Mondays!"
2. *Problem solving:* "Next Monday I'm going to notice what is happening when I feel frustrations, and then maybe I can change it."
3. *An inquiry:* Deciding on a strategy to come to an answer: "I'm going to keep a running record each day for two weeks and see if I can find anything unusual that happens on Mondays."
4. *I-search:* Gathering information (data) and following through to some action is considered to be an I-search: "What do I know about Mondays? In what ways are they different from other days? I wonder if other teachers feel this way. I'll ask my colleagues. Each time I feel dread and am frustrated, I will write about it in two ways: (1) I will describe carefully what is happening; and (2) I will write about my thoughts and feelings and actions. Then I will put all this information together, analyze it, and see what I find."
5. *Researching practice:* "I will take what I have learned in my I-search and design and carry out a study to see if my earlier findings are supported."
6. *Action research:* "I will extend my study to include myself as well as my students. I will proceed systematically, using a variety of data collection methods and analyzing data in a way that will help me verify my findings. I will collaborate and share with others. For example, I am going to work with my students and two of my colleagues to study my teaching with a focus on Mondays. My colleagues will study their classes and involve their students. Then we will meet and compare data. When we find trouble spots, we will discuss them, pool our suggestions, and try doing things differently— documenting them—and see what happens. We will get into a cycle of trying things out to see what works."
7. *Action research* cycle is complete: We have learned from our experiences, reflected on them, and are ready to begin a new cycle or project.

In the next chapters, you will follow along the action research journeys of teachers in a variety of subjects and settings. These teachers and student teachers have been our students, and we have shared parts of their journeys with them.

We want to offer a word of caution here about continuums. Although the modernist notion of development as a general movement toward greater complexity and inclusivity (inclusivity means that we are more open to diversity *and* that each part of the continuum includes previous parts) can be useful, postmodernists caution that this is only a part of the picture, and that we rarely progress evenly or in only one direction. Growing is more complex and multifaceted than that. That's why the term *recursive* is often used to describe AR—not only do we move back and forth along a continuum in our practice, but within action research itself, we move back and forth between and among collecting data, analyzing data, and drawing tentative conclusions.

Learning from the Journey

Because we live in a world of relationships, we are influenced by the actions of others and we influence the actions of others through our actions. In the words of Hannah Arendt (1958), we live in a web of relationships which is "a medium where every reaction becomes a chain reaction and every process is the cause of new processes" (p. 190). Each action is part of a chain. One reason the continuum can be a powerful tool for professional growth and action is that it enables us to see ourselves in a context that is not possible at the time of our actions. We are, at the time of action, caught up in our actions and see our circumstances only from our own point of view. In hindsight, or as Arendt (1958) puts it: "He who acts never quite knows what he is doing." She goes on to explain "the light that illuminates processes of action . . . appears only at the end. . . . Action reveals itself fully only to the storyteller, that is, to the backward glance of the historian, who indeed always knows better what it was all about than the participants . . . What the storyteller narrates must necessarily be hidden from the actor himself, at least as long as he is in the act or caught in its consequences" (p. 201).

Taking time to reflect, especially in a visual form such as writing or drawing, engaging in the kind of developmental continuums we suggest here and in the Exploring the Forest workshops, enables us to gain distance and become, if not a separate person, at least a storyteller that can narrate from a detached perspective. We will come back to the Action Research Storyteller in Chapter 16. We conclude our discussion of development with the lenses of three major domains.

Three Domains of Development

When we conduct action research, we develop simultaneously in three domains. These three domains, adapted from the research on adult and professional development by Sharon Oja (1989), parallel the journey of the Scarecrow, the Tin Man, and the Lion.

Cognitive and conceptual complexity.   As with the bright Scarecrow, the developmental journey starts wherever a person is and moves toward greater complexity and simplicity; creates a larger repertoire from which to draw; and develops problem-solving, research abilities, and reflective processes.

Moral, ethical, and social responsibility.   And as the sensitive Tin Man, in his quest for a heart, the action research journey deepens consciousness and awareness, respect for diversity, and understanding of others. It also promotes collaboration, community, and valuing others.

Psychological and emotional maturity.   Like the courageous journey of the brave Lion, the AR journey can move us from closed, protective, defensive, rigid positions to more open, creative, and inclusive perspectives toward others. The journey is toward higher self-acceptance, self-esteem, and personal agency, and toward increasing the capacity and ability to nurture these characteristics in others.

CHAPTER SUMMARY

Using a continuum to chart development, as we have done in this chapter, enables us to see a phenomenon over time. We can begin to see patterns and how one event can influence and relate to others. We can zoom in on one period in our lives, when we were the age of the people we teach (if they are younger), for example, or chart certain aspects of our lives over the time we have lived so far, our educational experiences, for example. Our professional capabilities and dispositions can be explored; what were our main intellectual achievements of the last 5 years? What were our most important social experiences—those that have had the greatest impact upon us—over the years in which we were preparing to teach? How might those experiences influence the research we develop and conduct today? What educational experiences have had the greatest impact on our assumptions and beliefs about teaching and learning? How might the action research journey influence the complexity we see in teaching and learning? How might it affect our social responsibility to students or colleagues, and our psychological maturity?

We explored Erik Erikson's theory of psychosocial development, and how we might use developmental continuums to appreciate the AR journey as well as to learn from it.

SECTION SUMMARY

We hope that by the end of this section, you have a chance to consider your roots, your experiences, and your beliefs and how these influence your professional life. We hope that you will gain perspective on aspects of your experiences and education that you may not have had the opportunity to expore from a development point of view before. When you began the study of research, you might not have imagined how personal and professional growth might be part of the journey. You might want to return to this section later as you construct your own lessons from Oz at the conclusion of this book.

On the next leg of our journey, we will be your travel guides along with many student-researchers who have generously agreed to share their questions, experiences, anxieties, studies, triumphs, surprises, and reflections about their journeys.

At last, it's time for those ruby slippers.

Exploring the Forest

Finding Our Roots

Personal and Professional Journeys of the Self

We have many possible explorations on this leg of our journey. There are suggestions throughout this section that you might find useful. We will highlight a few here and direct you back into the chapters for other ideas. This is an important part of the journey, as we are making conscious some of the experiences that have shaped and continue to shape us as persons who choose to be professionals. The writings and creations we do in our journals here are foundational to what follows in other chapters. Building on this foundation not only will enhance and make the rest of the journey easier, but also will make our progress visible.

David Tripp uses the word *autopilot* to refer to our often uncritical business-as-usual stance toward our interactions and decision making. This is fine for most of our functioning, but many professional decisions call for a more conscious process. By building a better understanding of who we are and how we got to be this way, we can shift from functioning on autopilot to a state of consciousness, and even to critical consciousness. As Maxine Greene might say, we move toward a state of being *awake* and our life becomes *doing philosophy*. You might even say we can *be our philosophy*. Being fully who we are can only happen when we are awake! Functioning on autopilot often has to do with responding to someone else's agenda. We might agree with what we have been taught to do; then again, we may not. The key is to make *conscious decisions* on matters of consequence. Only then are we free people. And that is what we mean when we talk about being professional: making critical decisions and using our educational imaginations to make learning more worthwhile.

1. *Doing self-talk.* Begin to pay more attention to some of the conversations taking place inside you. Think back to a recent time when you debated with yourself about an action you were contemplating. Record the options you considered. Give these different options tags, such as self 1, self 2, and self 3. Or create names such as Tim(id), Win(Win), Care(less), Ms. Prim, Master Controller, and Wise Guy. What would each of these characters (or personalities) say? What might each be lobbying for and why or toward what ends? What would be the main trait of each? Take these to the extreme. Which personality won? What were the consequences? Now, see if you can pay closer attention to some of the conversations that take place inside you as they happen, and record a few in your journal. How many such discussions do you think take place in a day?

2. *Self-in-a-bag.* Take 10 or 15 minutes to think about who you are. What artifacts and symbols could you put together that would give people a sense of who you are? Now, find a bag that is appropriate to you—plastic, paper, cloth of any kind—and put into it five to seven artifacts, metaphors, or symbols that give a good sense of who you are. After you have done this, do the interviews suggested below. You may wish to add an item or two to the bag.

3. *Interviews.* Who are the people who knew you well when you were a child? List them. Who were the people who knew you best as an adolescent? As a young adult? List them. Select a few from each category (categories may overlap), and write a brief portrait of each person you select; include an example of something you did with this person. Which of these people are still in your life? Select one, two, or three who are and have a conversation with them related to the years in which they knew you. What do they remember about you and about the times? What few words, symbols, or artifacts would they use to describe who you were then? Place them in your bag.

4. *Bag-write.* Now, with these artifacts and symbols all together in your bag, write a brief portrait of yourself using the artifacts. Look back at the personalities you wrote about in self-talk. Do you see any sign of them within the bag? If so, write about them.

5. *Time line of critical incidents and people.* Create a time line of critical incidents and significant people who have influenced your life and your teaching self. Write a paragraph or two about each incident and person and how they influenced you and your teaching. Include the consequences of their influence on you. Keep your writing brief. You can always go back later and elaborate.

6. *Teaching philosophy.* What is your philosophy of teaching? A teaching philosophy can be a set of beliefs about the purposes of schooling, how children learn, or the roles and responsibilities of teachers and students. Theoretically this philosophy guides the actions we take. It can provide a foundation to return to, to reflect upon, and to develop. Write a one-page statement of your teaching philosophy.

7. *Development and learning continuum.* Go back to the continuum presented in Chapter 7, and construct a continuum for your life by age and by level of schooling. For each, begin to do some free-writing about memories related to

each marker. They need not be exhaustive, and you can return to explore different phases later on. Hopefully through these explorations, you have a slightly different perspective on your history and your present selves. To conclude this section and make use of the professional contexts we began to build in Chapter 2 with disciplinary explorations, as well as to lead into the next leg of the journey, think about the last exploration in this section.

8. *Your own action research questions.*   Revisit the last explorations in Chapter 2 about journals and significant people, and generate a few questions related to your own work. If, for example, you were going to publish a paper in the journal you reviewed, what might the title of your paper be? What questions and methods might you employ? At this point, do not be too specific or overly concerned with the *how* of it. Just think about what you are interested in and what you might be able to do in your own practice related to it. In fact, it might be a good idea to limit this exploration to 15 or 20 minutes so that you get fairly spontaneous and creative ideas without getting bogged down. You will not have to *do* any of them if you choose not to. Would any of the influential people you cited earlier have any ideas for you to consider related to the research topic(s)? It might be useful to generate a few topics—maybe more. Perhaps after you have played a bit with possible ways to improve your practice, one will become more feasible or more valuable for you to study at this time.

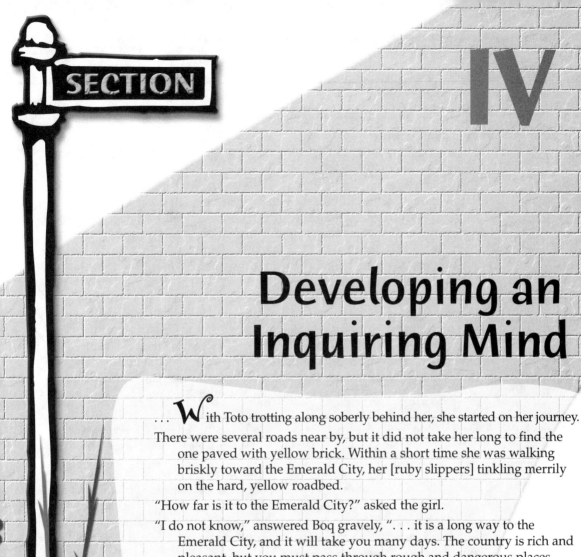

SECTION

IV

Developing an Inquiring Mind

... **W**ith Toto trotting along soberly behind her, she started on her journey.

There were several roads near by, but it did not take her long to find the one paved with yellow brick. Within a short time she was walking briskly toward the Emerald City, her [ruby slippers] tinkling merrily on the hard, yellow roadbed.

"How far is it to the Emerald City?" asked the girl.

"I do not know," answered Boq gravely, ". . . it is a long way to the Emerald City, and it will take you many days. The country is rich and pleasant, but you must pass through rough and dangerous places before you reach the end of your journey."

The Wonderful Wizard of Oz
L. Frank Baum (1900)

The Yellow Brick Road reminds us that we have questions and a topic to pursue. But there are inevitable obstacles we must face. As we focus our energies on specific AR questions, we will be surprised at how rejuvenating the journey will be. As the title of this section suggests, we are going to generate a topic and then explore questions to guide our studies. We will also look at our questions (and our practice) problematically, trying to explore the hidden assumptions and biases that color our thinking. You may want to skip to the "Exploring the Forest" section at the end of this section so that you can work through some of the exercises as we go along. Some of the exercises will help you to identify topics and questions. The questions that underlie our work in this chapter frame the research proposal.

What is my research interest?   To explore that research interest, we offer some additional questions to consider:

- **Why am I interested?** What values and beliefs do I want to live out in my teaching? (Think about the work you began in the last section.) Articulating a philosophy of education is a good starting point for examining our practice. Is our philosophy a living part of what we do? If we claim to be developmentalists or constructivists, are these beliefs enacted in our daily work? If we consider ourselves to be critically oriented, are we aware of the social, cultural, political, and economic contexts that shape our work and the lives of our students?
- **What is my question?** How can I bring my teaching more in line with my values, beliefs, and aspirations?
- **What do I already know?** What do my experiences tell me about this classroom, these students, this school, this curriculum, the politics surrounding decisions that are made?
- **What do others know?** What can I learn from scholars who have explored this topic and whose theories and research have been made public? What can I learn from other colleagues—teachers, school support staff, youth-serving agencies? From families, community members, business people, legislators, lawyers, doctors?
- **What do I expect to find?** In combination with what I know and what I learn from others, what are my informed hunches (and biases) about my topic of interest?

By the end of this section, you will have the opportunity to explore these questions for yourself and to see how the teachers in our case studies explore them. And, in the process, you may find out some important things about yourself and your research interest. "Exploring the Forest" at the end of Section IV will offer additional ways to develop questions.

As you think about a topic, the values and beliefs that shape your interest, and what you and others know about it, the focus of your scholarship becomes clearer. Thinking about what we *expect* to find helps us to be realistic as we define our question(s) and become *aware* of our expectations. By stating what they are, we may bring to the surface hidden biases and challenges in our studies. These expectations are a basis for our personal hunches and hypotheses. When they are combined with what we learn about our topic from others (scholars and practitioner-scholars), we can reformulate these into scholarly hunches and "test" them by looking for "evidence" that either confirms or disconfirms them. As we challenge ourselves by talking and writing about our topics in new ways, we will come to a deeper appreciation of them and will be able to better define our questions. Just as importantly, we will develop courage. Once our intellectual curiosity is working, our fears recede. The further we get into our topics, the more we will *enjoy discussing them with others*. By the time we get to the Emerald City and share our results, we will look back on this part of the journey and smile.

We will begin our journey with *wonder*, with little wonders (I wonder how I could. . . ?) and curiosities (What if. . . ?). The action researchers whose case studies we present here will become travel companions as they share their curiosities and wonders, which, in the next few chapters, we will develop into studies.

Shawn is a young teacher in her fourth year of teaching in a suburban district. The demographics of this district include many non-English speakers who were drawn to this area by a local industry. Shawn loves challenges that keep her learning and was genuinely excited to find that she was getting a student who did not speak English.

Jon and Terry: Jon is a middle-aged teacher who was on leave when he teamed up with his friend Terry to teach in a "low achieving" fifth-grade classroom. Terry, a teacher of 15 years, has always taught in a low-income district near her home. Jon and Terry both felt that ability grouping was unfair to students.

Roberto grew up in a family that knew how it felt to care for someone with a disability. His mother became blind when he was 14 years old. As the oldest of five children, he quickly assumed responsibilities at home. Friends and extended family in the Hispanic community provided a network of support. Roberto's desire to teach students with special needs grew from this experience of a strong and caring community.

Growing up in the South in a family that participated in the civil rights movement, **Ruby** majored in political science and continued her activism in local politics after graduation. However, she decided that teaching was the best way to provide social justice in society. Ruby came to study teaching at the age of 50 when her children were in middle school and her husband's job stability made it feasible for her to enroll in a full-time graduate teacher education program.

CASE STUDIES

Shawn

Helping Jen Learn English as a Second Language

One day, the principal of Shawn's school arrived at the classroom door with an announcement: This second-grade class would be getting a new student. Shawn's newest second grader would be a young girl from Korea who would need to learn English.

Although Shawn was pleased to be getting a new student, she immediately wondered, How can I best teach her? Shawn knew little about English as a Second Language (ESL) issues or strategies, the child, or Korea. No one in the district spoke Korean. Undaunted, Shawn was committed to help each student, including Jen, to succeed.

Shawn accepted the challenge willingly as a valuable learning experience. She knew there would be support from the school ESL teacher and from the research mentor from the university program where she was completing a master's degree in reading. How would this child from a different country, immersed in a new language and culture, fare? She wondered, How can I facilitate Jen's becoming comfortable in the new classroom community? How would Jen learn English, and how would this process proceed? How would Jen's need to learn English have an impact on her growth in other subjects? Shawn's many questions fueled the desire that led to a case study of Jen.

The Literature Circles Study

Jon

Terry

Jon and Terry are veteran teachers who share an interest in improving the teaching of reading with 10- and 11-year-old students. Terry taught in a school that insisted on *tracking* or ability-grouping classes (in spite of considerable research demonstrating the negative effects of tracking—see Oakes, 1985; Slavin, 1988; Wheelock, 1994). She had been given all the lowest-achieving fifth-grade students and least-proficient readers, according to standardized tests. In fact, Terry's school labeled these readers "at-risk," based on below-average reading-level test scores. Since Jon was on sabbatical and did not have his own classroom, the two teachers, both enrolled in a graduate action research class, decided to team up in Terry's classroom. They wondered, "What can we do to improve matters for these children?"

In the past, the readers assigned to Terry's class had received instruction limited to district-adopted basal readers and accompanying workbooks. Terry's concerns about the lack of choice, excitement, and high-quality literature in this program resulted in her seeking alternatives. Terry felt strongly that the monotony of the reading program was failing to enthuse students about reading. Both teachers were committed to their students having exemplary instruction—instruction that would be consistent with the current theory and practice that they were studying in their master's degree program. So, these two teachers asked: Would at-risk readers become excited about reading and improve their abilities if the teachers implemented a literature-based approach with the use of trade books, literature response journals, and meaningful discussions about literature in place of the mundane diet of basal readers and workbooks?

The S.T.A.R. Club Study

Roberto

"I just don't get it!" Roberto exclaimed to his fellow special education teacher. "I know these [regular education] kids have been with our students in *inclusion* classes in the past, but they act like they've never seen a student from special education. I thought inclusion worked well at the elementary school, but it isn't working here in the middle school!" The rationale for including Roberto's students with multiple handicaps in some regular education classes was for these students to gain acceptance from their "typical" peers. But what he observed in the hallways, in the lunchroom, and in classes where his students were integrated with "typical" students was limited conversation, limited interaction, and often shunning of students in special education. Was this because it was not "cool" to hang around with kids who were "different"? With this sense of frustration and desire to understand and change the situation, Roberto, a veteran middle school special educator, wondered what he could do. He looked for insights and solutions to this vexing problem.

The Democratic Classroom Study

Ruby

Ruby was a student teacher in a ninth-grade civics class who thought it ironic, even disturbing, that students were learning about democracy without practicing it in their classrooms. Research on teaching social studies bore out her own observations over the years—that social studies was not living up to its potential as a learning ground for participatory democracy. Mindful of the important role schools can play in developing informed and active citizens, Ruby found that her question revolved around this issue: How can I create a democratic civics classroom? Ruby wanted to transform the course students described as "boring" and "irrelevant" to one in which they would all become immersed participants in the complexities of the democratic process. Ruby's own activist spirit fueled this commitment.

Action research projects can cover a range of interests and settings. In these actual cases, they cover English as a Second Language, reading, special education, and democracy in the classroom. These teachers wish to improve their own practice, school conditions, and their students' learning. We will watch their studies unfold over the next several chapters.

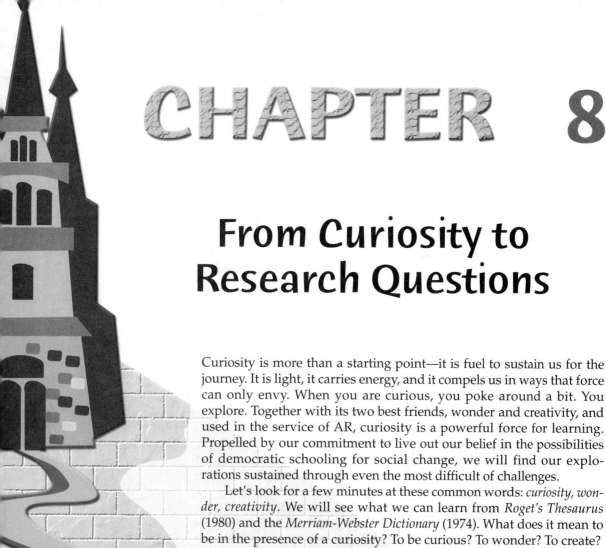

CHAPTER 8

From Curiosity to Research Questions

Curiosity is more than a starting point—it is fuel to sustain us for the journey. It is light, it carries energy, and it compels us in ways that force can only envy. When you are curious, you poke around a bit. You explore. Together with its two best friends, wonder and creativity, and used in the service of AR, curiosity is a powerful force for learning. Propelled by our commitment to live out our belief in the possibilities of democratic schooling for social change, we will find our explorations sustained through even the most difficult of challenges.

Let's look for a few minutes at these common words: *curiosity, wonder, creativity*. We will see what we can learn from *Roget's Thesaurus* (1980) and the *Merriam-Webster Dictionary* (1974). What does it mean to be in the presence of a curiosity? To be curious? To wonder? To create?

Curiosity—Interest, marvel, celebrity, prying, wonder, inquisitiveness, interrogativeness, phenomenon, oddity, rarity (*Roget*, 1980, p. 94).

Curious—Inquisitive, odd, inquiring, recondite, meddling, unique, questioning, scrutinizing, rare, prying, peering, searching, peeping, singular (*Roget*, 1980, p. 94).

Wonder—Miracle, surprise, awe, puzzlement, fascination, phenomenon, admiration, marvel, sign, surprise, prodigy (*Roget*, 1980, p. 488).

Create—To bring into being; to exist; make; produce (*Merriam-Webster*, 1974, p. 176); frame, construct, shape, mold, form (*Roget*, 1980, p. 90).

Sounds like fun, eh? Being curious, wondering, and creating are often pleasant states. There are other reasons to cultivate them during our journey, especially at the start. In addition to providing fuel for our work, they can turn much of our work into play. Yes, *play*. Long disparaged, play is one of the supreme accomplishments in adult life. In fact, at least one notable scholar of human development, Ashley Montagu, in *Growing Young* (1989), writes about this. He points out that adults need to take clues from children and adopt many of the *children's* characteristics and qualities, most notably play, wonder, curiosity, and openness to experience.

When we are able to take what we know, suspend judgment, and enter into a playful state with an idea or object, then new ideas, conceptions, and uses can present themselves. There is room for them. When we stop relentlessly trying too hard, sometimes a magic synthesis takes place. This magic synthesis *is* creativity (Arieti, 1976). When we are crowded with *shoulds* and *oughts* and *rules* and concerned with knowing it all, there is little room for play and the kinds of discovery and invention that play makes possible. AR is more concerned with "what-if" than with rules.

Piaget said that too much assimilation was boring, and too much accommodation was overwhelming. To grow, we need a balance of both—the equilibrium we talked about earlier. The comfortable way we feel when we understand enough about something (assimilation) to play with it enables us to walk off the edge of our known worlds into something new (accommodation). We create something new and therefore create *more* of ourselves as well. We learn. We enlarge our repertoire. Each time we do this, Piaget found, we have the same reaction and good feelings that babies do. We may display it differently—we don't usually wiggle, gurgle, and chuckle—but we, too, feel good inside and find pleasure in practicing our newfound abilities, whether they are mental (discovering a new computer tool) or physical (discovering how to stop while skating). A *playground* is a place to recreate. When we play, we re-create. And we frolic.

So, why, you might wonder, are these qualities and characteristics important to action researchers? They are important to all of us, researchers or not. But they are especially important to action researchers. Take a minute to think about this. Go back to our definitions of curiosity, wonder, creativity, and play, and think about action research. Now what do you think?

Does it seem surprising to think of the words *play* and *research* in the same sentence?

Action researchers are . . . meddlers! They are searchers who inquire into their own experience. They meddle into what they did not question before. When they try something different, they upset their routines. To do that, they have to be inquisitive, interested in what is going on. To search means to look at something from different points of view. Action researchers are creative. They ask themselves, What is going on here? and What if I try this out? In a sense, action researchers have to be able to turn experiences inside out and to pose and entertain possibilities. And that takes a sense of wonder and curiosity, an openness to surprise, because you don't know what you will find. Yes, action researchers construct new ways of doing things and of framing and portraying these things to others. Often we get too busy to remember the value of keeping these things alive within us. The sparks that drive us get covered over, and our senses dulled. Action research is a way to rediscover and cultivate these qualities and to enhance our capacities for further questing. By paying attention to the conversations in our heads about our practice, to the feelings that take hold of us, and to the ideals we hold as possibilities, we will define questions that transform us into scholars and our classrooms into learning communities. As a scholar who looks ahead, think about how you will organize your work (Stepping Stones 8.1).

STEPPING STONES 8.1

Getting Organized in the Beginning of a Study

Getting organized at the beginning of a study in order to keep track of actions and data can save endless hours later on. Here are a few things to consider.

- Develop a filing system for everything that must be saved. Date all documents, reports, artifacts, interviews, and so on.
- Any student work that you intend to photocopy will need to be on good-quality paper and written with high contrast ink. Newsprint and colored paper make poor copies.
- Make one copy of everything and keep copies in a separate place (one set at home, one set at school).
- Do not write on or mark up an original document, especially one created by a student. Keep originals as original and use duplicate copies if needed.
- Think through things you may want to purchase at the local office suppply store: index cards, sticky labels, Post-its, paper clips or binder clips, page protectors, graph paper, permanent marker pens, highlighters, file folders, three-ring binders, hole puncher, large rubber bands, pocket folders, tape, calculator, a filing box, and computer supplies.
- Consider who can help you with your study. Teacher colleagues, spouses, friends, and roommates can help tally, count, and double check.
- Decide on a procedure you will use each time you collect data or perform some aspect of your study to keep track of what you did, how much you did, where you will keep it, who might help you.
- Create folders in your computer for files pertaining to your study, and back up your files.
- Sharing files among computers can cause problems. Send shared files by e-mail attachment rather than via shared disks or drives when possible.
- Take advantage of emerging online programs and social software such as blog/weblog, wiki, various audio and video editing technologies, and electronic portfolio systems. This will help organize, modify, and share information with the other teachers and participants more easily in the long run. Chapter 18 will provide more information on various technologies that can be used to create texts and multimedia content, to communicate, and to collaborate.

How Do Questions Evolve?

Many fruitful questions begin with a sense of curiosity. You want to know how something might work. Or you may wish to better understand your students: Perhaps you wonder what it is like to be a child with a hearing disability in your classroom. Perhaps you have attended a workshop on multiage grouping, and you wonder what it would be like to teach in such a setting. Perhaps you are dissatisfied with how long it takes to do routine tasks and wonder if there is a more efficient way. Or you want to study an aspect of your practice that you feel needs some attention; for example, testing and the time you devote to it (preparing for tests, administering tests, communicating with parents about tests, changing schedules to accommodate tests). And you also want to hold it up to a critical light: Is this time well spent? Importantly, what do the tests measure? Who designs them and for what purposes? Who do tests "advantage" and who do they "disadvantage"? You may or may not have an opinion at the beginning of your inquiry, but by following up on your curiosity, you will find yourself making more informed decisions based on this kind of critical reflection.

These types of questions emerge from the three domains of knowledge that Habermas (1972) described: technical interest in how things work, a practical need to understand, and a critical sense of the social, cultural, political, and economic realities that form the context of our teaching. They also illustrate the many ways in which curiosity works to fuel our explorations. It is

- A *wish to understand* ("I wonder why inclusion isn't working?").
- A *dissatisfaction* ("We don't *live* democratically in this classroom!").
- A *concern* ("This is an improverished reading program. I wonder what we could do to bring it to life for the students?").
- A *challenge* or *problem* ("How can I help Jen to learn?").
- An *issue* ("What are the consequences of the testing program at my school on our first graders?"). Issues have multiple and conflicting perspectives. They may be highly controversial, such as imposed testing, student privacy rights, bilingual education, school uniforms, and special education with "inclusion" and the challenges this offers to both parents and systems. *Issues* are the basis of questions that often get coverage in the media.

The stance we take toward our topic is important. If we maintain a sense of wonder and curiosity, as opposed to one of judgment, we may be able to view the topic from multiple perspectives. Viewing the topic (question) as a problem or a possibility, an issue or a concern, will influence the design, conduct, and consequences of our study. Maintaining curiosity throughout the research process is almost a guarantee of success.

Questions evolve over *time*. While many action researchers enter an AR class knowing exactly what they want to study and how, more often they enter with vague and general questions. They may have a hunch or an uneasy feeling about a topic. Although refining our thinking to define a question can be a lengthy process, often it is not. If you have a fuzzy question right now, that's fine. By the end of the chapter, with its exercises, you will likely shape your question into one that can be researched.

Lenses for Inquiry: Zooming In, Zooming Out

Questions can evolve as we work with them over time. We use a process of thinking about a question and shaping it as we ponder responses to the questions we posed earlier: What is my research interest? What is my question? What do I already know? What do others know? What do I expect to find? Our focus can become clearer as new aspects of the topic come to mind, as we sort out key elements: background, foreground, main events, and processes. Noticing one element and its relationship to other elements makes us more aware of our focus and the context within which it sits. The process is not unlike an inquisitive meddler poking around with a zoom lens inspecting this; zooming over there, up and down, and all around; visually taking things apart and putting them back together, just to see how they work.

Many travelers, especially photographers, pack camera equipment for their journeys so that they can capture a wide-angle view of a region as well as a close-up of a rare insect, flower, or flying monkey (microcosm). Just as photographers do, action researchers need multiple lenses to study different aspects of their topics. As we conduct our inquiries, we need the flexibility to zoom in and out, between and among different perspectives. This is a continuous process. We need a wide-angle lens (macrocosm) to view the phenomenon from larger contexts (the big picture). From snapshots at these different levels, we get much more detailed and comprehensive pictures of our topics, and we can use these to construct an album or portfolio for others to view and then discuss our work with us.

We may choose to focus on an individual student or group of students, a classroom, a school, a district, a state, or a province. Whatever we select as our focus, we will need to zoom in and out, alternating between perspectives: the child, the classroom, the schools, the child, the community. Figure 8.1 displays these lenses as concentric circles, with a pie-shaped cutout to show questions that cut across all lenses.

Focusing on one student.   Action research can be focused on one child or on a small group of children. Perhaps we wonder about *an individual student* (the innermost circle in Figure 8.1). Perhaps a student looks tired, disinterested, or unengaged in lessons. Perhaps, as in Shawn's case, a child needs special attention. What is the best way to meet Jen's needs?

Lesley, a kindergarten teacher, had a child in class who was delightful, confident, and amusing, but performed academically and socially like a much younger child. "Timmy fits better with a class of preschoolers than with a group of 5- and 6-year-olds," Lesley thought. Timmy's delightful personality frequently made him the center of attention. Yet, as others in the class began to develop more advanced literacy behaviors, Timmy was not yet ready for academic work suitable for his classmates.

Some investigation revealed a thick folder in a school office. Timmy had been born prematurely and spent his first months in a neonatal ward. His family had received many social services since that time. Lesley investigated characteristics of

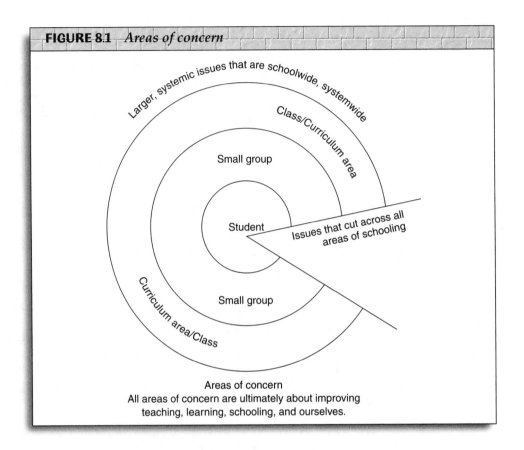

FIGURE 8.1 *Areas of concern*

Larger, systemic issues that are schoolwide, systemwide

Class/Curriculum area

Small group

Student

Issues that cut across all areas of schooling

Small group

Curriculum area/Class

Areas of concern
All areas of concern are ultimately about improving
teaching, learning, schooling, and ourselves.

premature babies and found that his behavior was, in fact, typical of such young-sters. What was perceived as "premature" could more accurately have been applied to the curriculum he was (unsuccessfully) being forced into! A push to make him function at a higher level than his development allowed was as nonsen-sical as expecting a flower to bloom without a stem. The teacher's action research enabled her to be an informed advocate for the child. She aimed to prevent deci-sion making that could be damaging to the child.

Another action researcher conducted an in-depth study of a man who could not read or write. The man was attending evening classes at an adult education facility where the researcher worked. The researcher's intent was to understand this individual and his issues about learning and literacy, and to find ways to help him. Studies like Lesley's and Shawn's often result in single-subject designs, which are discussed in Section V. When our focus is on teaching a single student, a single-subject design can be useful.

Studying a small group of students.   You may be concerned with a small group of students who become the focus of your action research (see Figure 8.1). You may have several students who do not thrive in spite of your best efforts, and the efforts of support services. We know many teachers who design studies around small groups of students who present the greatest challenges to them as professionals.

A kindergarten teacher studied the six youngest children in the class to delve more deeply into their perceptions and their needs. Realizing that the range in most kindergarten classes is diverse, the researcher knew that better understanding of the needs of the youngest children would also benefit future students.

At the other end of the developmental scale, one researcher felt that the program in which he taught was inadequate for the most advanced students. A nagging sense that these students could be more academically challenged led to finding new and better ways to meet their needs. Similarly, one kindergarten teacher designed a study around a handful of Chinese second-language students, much as Shawn did with Jen.

Studying a curriculum area.   At times, a curriculum issue is the focus of research. The issue can affect the entire *class* or classes that you teach (the middle circle in Figure 8.1). It could be the way spelling is taught, the reading program that is used, the lack of critical thinking, or the didactic teaching of science or social studies. Perhaps a lack of student enthusiasm or the ineffectiveness of a program has been observed.

Terry and Jon were veteran teachers concerned with a curriculum problem that was affecting the entire class. In some ways, the problem was a result of school policy with which they did not agree—the ability grouping of entire classes for teaching (tracking). Those practices ran contrary to their values (and much research). They wanted to implement more effective practices in the curriculum— and they were committed to students labeled *at risk*. They felt that students considered to be less proficient than others were systematically denied opportunities provided to more advanced students for critical thinking and creativity, which meant that "low" students would likely stay "low" through no fault of their own.

Jonathan, a middle school math teacher, initially thought that the use of math journals would be beneficial to students by raising their grades on pupil progress reports. Bonnie, a French teacher, thought foreign language teaching needed an overhaul when she noticed that none of the techniques and strategies she'd been learning about first-language literacy were applied to communication and literacy in a second language. She decided to try the same type of dialog journals (Fulwiler, 1987) with French I students that she saw English teachers using with success.

Margie, who taught in an urban school with mostly African American students, wondered if third graders would spell more conventionally if they increased their journal writing. Then there was Kelly who knew that vocational students disliked her English class, viewing English class as a distraction in their day filled with the vocational classes they so enjoyed. But, Kelly wondered, would students respond more enthusiastically to reading and other literacy-related activities if she used the daily newspaper instead of the existing, somewhat mundane materials? Her students seemed quite interested in current events.

Maureen, a teacher of 11-year-olds, taught students identified as gifted and talented. Feeling that her curriculum wasn't engaging, she began to think that she could bring new life into her class by applying Gardner's theory of multiple intelligences (H. Gardner, 1993). Her focus on curriculum would cut across all areas of study; it would serve to help her identify student strengths, to better know herself as a teacher, and to explore new ways of teaching to student strengths.

Patti knew her high school students were as bored as she was with how vocabulary was taught. Vocabulary teaching was an issue for the entire high school English department.

Studying a larger issue.   No matter what the focus of a study, there is a larger context or arena within which it takes place (the outer circle in Figure 8.1). Kyle, a student teacher in a middle school, was concerned when it became apparent that students enrolled in music appreciation weren't learning anything about the appreciation of music. These students spent most of their music time in what was essentially a study hall, because the priorities and resources for music education were devoted to students specializing in music performance through chorales, the school band, or orchestra. The "average" student, it seemed to Kyle, was short-changed with this method of allocation. This posed a challenge, a chance to create something and make a difference. Kyle wondered what could happen if, in fact, music appreciation were to become a reality during the study hall. This was a complex issue because it involved addressing a school district and community's priority for performance over appreciation and exploration. Middle school philosophy, on the other hand, advocates student exploration and appreciation of a wealth of curriculum and career options.

Jon and Terry's desire to change the curriculum for at-risk readers also had roots in a systemic issue. Their district, as a matter of policy, grouped classrooms by ability without questioning the practice, in spite of the plethora of published literature and research against the practice, often called *tracking* (Oakes, 1985; Slavin, 1988; Wheelock, 1994). This district practice had long been unquestioned, and would be difficult to change. Consequently, Jon and Terry focused their concerns on what they could control—the manner in which those so-called low-ability readers were taught. Both teachers harbored the hope that they could prove a point to their colleagues and their district—that children labeled *low ability* will respond to exciting literature and excellent teaching as their more successful peers do, and, in the end, will look less and less like low-ability students. Ultimately, the teachers might even begin to see all children as unique and worthy of the best conditions for learning.

In doing AR, many teachers find that their concerns challenge district, state, or national mandates, policies, or traditions that have an impact on education as a system of interrelated rules and practices. Kallie's study of how to help vocational students pass the state writing proficiency test led her to ask many questions: Why did the school assume that these students were incompetent? Why were teachers and administrators at the school not permitted to judge the suitability of this test? Furthermore, what was the value of a test that would reinforce students' feelings of failure and further encourage them to drop out of school?

Kallie learned to question the *system* and the mandates. Presenting the results of her study, Kallie threw her notes down in frustration, saying, "I don't care anymore about whether or not my students passed this test!" What Kallie learned while implementing a comprehensive writing program for these students was that they *needed* to write because they had important things to say, that writing was a valuable form of expression. Once she enabled them to write, which was difficult at first, a flood of heart-wrenching stories poured out onto paper. She got to know the students. Kallie's study, like many action research studies, turned out very differently from the original plan. The study led her to be more politically aware and active, and thus to influence local and regional educational policy.

Studying social issues in a classroom.   Social issues can cut across ages, disciplines, regions, and boundaries (the pie-shaped cutout in Figure 8.1). Some aspects of the implicit curriculum, such as unspoken cultural norms of behavior, are critically important to educational success. Learning is a socially constructed process, and schools present unique contexts with their own structures, features, and governing relationships. These types of issues are possible topics for action research.

Toni's story provides a good example. As a middle school health teacher, Toni was concerned about how disrespectfully students in health class in the urban, low-income neighborhood treated one another. Toni's question touched on not only the content of the teaching, but also the idea of bringing harmony to the group so that teaching and learning would be embedded in a more pleasant, open, accepting, and supportive community. Students seemed to rejoice in each other's misfortunes; they engaged in name-calling and put-downs. While some students seemed to control the class dynamics, others were nonparticipants. With all these dynamics at play, very little productive work was being done. Toni wondered if, in one semester, this situation could be moved toward greater respect and a greater sense of community support. Toni would not be able to feel satisfied with the curriculum while such negative classroom dynamics persisted. What could Toni do to improve the situation?

Tracy, a middle school social studies student teacher, began to understand that males dominated the class. Why was this so? Was it something about this age group? Was it related to how lessons were structured? Was female participation simply less overt? Tracy, like Toni, wondered if this situation could change so that student participation would become equitable between genders, and girls could be helped to feel comfortable and empowered to express their views and ideas. Tracy felt it was essential to have students profit equitably from class discussions and lessons.

Roberto's S.T.A.R. (Students and Teachers Advancing Relationships) Club is another prime example of studying a social issue. Despite a functioning inclusion model (students with special needs integrated into regular classrooms), students with and without multiple handicapping conditions in Roberto's school were not interacting with one another in meaningful ways. Roberto's commitment to the "special" students and his willingness to try to achieve the long-term goals of inclusion spurred the study that led to starting the S.T.A.R. Club.

CHAPTER SUMMARY

In summary, developing a curiosity into a question can begin with self-study: Why am I interested in this topic? Through self-study, we can awaken ourselves to our democratic commitments. By nurturing curiosity through creativity and play-fulness, we move beyond asking, What *should* be, to asking, What *if*? By zooming in and out, constantly focusing and refocusing, we are able to gain new perspectives on our topic.

There is an important cautionary note in our efforts to frame a research question. Although many researchers are able to pose a question and follow it through an entire study, others begin in one place and meander to a related question. We like to think that we are getting smarter in our wanderings. We call this process of getting more focused and sure-footed in our direction *progressive focusing*. It can be a natural part of the cycle of action research.

For example, a science teacher may begin by asking, How can I use my own enthusiasm to motivate my science students? But the teacher may decide after a while that even though a teacher's interest and enthusiasm for the subject matter are important, what is really of interest is helping students engage in subject matter in ways that link to their own lives. The new question becomes, How can I help students find relationships between their own personal interests and the subject matter?

In the next chapter, we will explore our questions further by considering problematic taken-for-granted assumptions underlying our questions. To do this, we will explore not only what we already know about our topic, but also what others have to offer.

CHAPTER 9

Exploring and Problematizing Our Practice

What's going on here? Are there better ways to engage these students? Teachers often begin with broad questions. We want to understand more of the complexities of learning and classroom life. As we explore our questions and unwrap the issues that surround them, we often find them to be even more complex than we knew, yet at the same time simpler. This process of unwrapping the multiple layers in which our topic and curiosity are embedded is called *problematizing* our practice. We focus on two sources of making our work problematic: inside sources (what we already know) and outside sources (what others know). We follow this with a brief look at the importance of keeping track of our expectations about how the project will go.

What Do I Already Know?

Taking into account what we already know about our topic is an important first step in defining our research interest. Often we doubt our own experiential and intuitive knowledge. These doubts are not surprising, because we are inundated with media from a variety of sources that discount what teachers know in favor of the promises of expert "wizards," who willingly provide easy, step-by-step remedies for all that ails our educational system. But as explorers of our own terrain and developing scholars of our own practice, we know that meaningful understanding and change demand a kind of wisdom that begins at home.

Perhaps your question is about a student. So you ask yourself: What do I already know about this child? Her family? How she learns?

What gets in the way of her learning? What do I already know about how groups of students become engaged in subject matter? Perhaps your concern is about a group of students. What are my students' attitudes toward learning, and what skills do they already possess? Some researchers call this knowledge *baseline data*, and it may be found in the observations we have noted in our journal or grade book, surveys we have administered, and student work and performances. This knowledge helps us to form hunches about a student's potential for success, about how students might respond to a particular curriculum.

But to *explore* implies the unexpected, that we don't always know what we might find. We follow up on a curiosity with the hope of discovering something we don't know. Further, to *problematize* is to explore with a *critical* stance. It requires that we become skeptical of familiar territory, that we "question the historical, social, economic, political, and cultural realities that shape our lives" (Leistyna, Woodrum, and Sherblom, 1996). It has been said that to problematize is to unwrap "professional routines" that "are, by definition, seldom, if ever challenged or consciously engaged" (Tripp, 1993). As we investigate, we can explore (and expose) our implicit assumptions and theories. By taking an interested and nonjudgmental approach to making the familiar unfamiliar, we can better weather the loss of the somnolence and comfort of our unexamined practices. So, not only do we want to draw on what we already know, we want to question that knowledge.

We can revisit several routines that are common practices in many schools. Here are some examples:

- Grouping students by "ability"
- Lining up students in rows
- 40-minute classes
- Starting school at the crack of dawn and ending school in the early or middle afternoon
- Determining promotion and retention
- Giving homework
- Standardized testing
- Teacher-led parent-teacher conferences
- Orientation programs that prepare students for the next level of schooling
- Organizing levels of schooling
- Fat pencil and wide lined paper in primary grades
- Foreign language teaching starting in adolescence

We have plenty of unexamined routines in teacher education, too. Why do students begin their program with observing and end (until recently) with full-time teaching? Who dares to question these practices—despite the almost-universal comments by students that they "really start to learn" during their full-time teaching experience? We can become so entrenched in the details of our teaching lives that we rarely even *think* to question them, let alone have the courage to challenge the way things are "always" done and to question cultural norms.

And what questions would we ask? Let's look more deeply at the example we mentioned earlier of Chuck, our daydreamer, and his teacher. Let's imagine that Chuck's teacher has asked a critical colleague to help her problematize her teaching.

Problematizing the Story of Chuck

Chuck's teacher: What an amazing occurrence! I have mixed emotions. Here Chuck is, seemingly oblivious to the class, while I am straining to explain a math concept in a way that the children can understand. I try to snap him out of his biological excursion, and instead he leads the class into understanding! How do you figure?

Critical colleague: Yes, strange. You seemed pretty frustrated all right. Why did you think he was daydreaming?

Chuck's teacher: Well, I didn't actually think he was daydreaming. I mean, he was so wrapped up in the squirrel and bird play going on outside the window that he didn't have time for daydreaming or for what was really important to me: math. And, yes, I was frustrated. I pulled out every trick in the book, and I couldn't seem to help the children make the connections they needed to. And then zap! Chuck did it!

Critical colleague: What do you think was going on?

Chuck's teacher: Now that I can look back on it, I realize that he already knew the math I was trying to teach. I also know that my method of teaching wasn't working—but I knew that before!

Critical colleague: Tell me more about your method of teaching. What did you assume about teaching and learning with the methods you were using?

Chuck's teacher: That's an interesting question. I was caught between two worlds with my teaching. I hadn't thought about it consciously until you asked, but I was trying to teach the way I think children learn, with manipulatives and having the children work in small groups. But I was also trying to have a whole-class discussion when I realized that most of the children weren't getting the concept as quickly as I thought they would. So I went back to the way I was taught, the lecture.

Critical colleague: Were you caught between "encouraging their exploration" and "direct teaching"? Did you think you had to do one *or* the other?

Chuck's teacher: Precisely. In a sense, I didn't trust the newer way of teaching, although that is really where my intuition tells me we ought to be moving. I slid back into the way I was taught, and it didn't work. I was frustrated with myself, although I didn't know it at the time. I had a whole lot of "shoulds" buzzing in my head: "They should be getting it faster! They won't be ready for the proficiency tests!" *"Do something!"* And in the *"do something"* voice, I was the fount of all knowledge; and if all eyes were not on me, well, how could they possibly be learning?

Critical colleague: And Chuck wasn't helping, was he?

Chuck's teacher: No. He was like a match to gasoline! And now I see that match was just what *I* needed! I was part of the problem; Chuck was part of the solution.

Thanks for helping me to process this. It really helps to reflect on this with you. I don't feel that you are judging me, and I can hear my own words as I reflect honestly on my teaching and on what the children were telling me. Thanks!

We will add a few footnotes to the story. What if we told you that Chuck is now a well-respected biologist? Does that make any difference in how you interpret the story? Does that one piece of information enable you to see the whole situation from a different frame of reference? Might the scientific, logical mathematical gifts of this young child have enabled him to quickly grasp the concept *the way the teacher was teaching it*, and teach his classmates in a way that most other people, including the teacher, could not? Might his interest in the bird and squirrel have been what was *really* important and in his best interests, despite the belief of his teacher, *at the time*, that it wasn't?

Chuck's teacher is not alone in her frustration with trying new ways of teaching and reverting to the way she had been taught. Although the case in point took place over 30 years ago, recent research in mathematics education bears out her belief that children learn mathematical concepts by working them through in concrete ways, by themselves and in small groups, not by working on abstract problems presented by the teacher (Rowan and Bourne, 1994). Why don't we more readily adopt the most current methods of teaching? A simple response is: It is harder than it looks! For example, once we "know" something it is a physical trace in our brains, and new learning takes considerable experience (or a powerful experience) to make a new connection that is stronger than the first; we automatically refer to the earlier learning (Zull, 2002), and often, it is "both" (small-group learning and mini-lectures) not "either-or."

In spite of a plethora of research studies that demonstrate the value of new ways to teach math, teachers continue to teach in ways reinforced by the dominant cultural norm—that students learn best when teachers talk to the whole group and students listen. Historically, that is the way it has been done. Students have been moved through the educational system like cars on an assembly line, each getting the same treatment and each being labeled as able or not. The lecture method has been considered to be the most efficient in terms of money and time (and politically it is wiser to do things the way those in power are accustomed to).

Remember when we talked about Piaget and how we need to assimilate and accommodate and come to new ways of seeing and being through our own constructions of reality? This is as true for Chuck's teacher as it is for Chuck. (It is also true for cultural change.) Seeing and believing that a new way of teaching is more effective isn't enough to make it so. Chuck's teacher is going against much of what she was taught, and it can take time and reflecting on critical incidents to help her make a transition to more inclusive and effective ways of understanding and teaching mathematics.

By examining this story through *cultural, psychosocial, political, economic,* and *historical* lenses, we can begin to identify the underlying assumptions that govern so many routines. These unexamined assumptions serve as collective blindfolds. With the help of our critical colleagues, the possibility for growth occurs. And as this happens, we may see our questions in new ways. For example, if Chuck's teacher were investigating her teaching, we can imagine her initially asking, How can I keep my students on task? With her new insights, however, her question might become, How can I examine the way I structure learning in my class so that I can better understand how my students learn and what I can do to facilitate their learning?

At the risk of belaboring the point, let's use the dialog between Chuck's teacher and her critical colleague as well as our cases (Shawn, Jon and Terry, and others) to construct some critical questions and examples that can help us practice problematizing. The questions will shift our focus to looking inward, looking methodically and contextually, and looking ahead.

A Scaffold for Problematizing

In developing a topic area or question for your action research study, you may want to work through these questions. The most challenging questions are ones we honestly ask ourselves about our practice.

What are my feelings? Chuck's teacher had a range of feelings about the episode: *hope* and *optimism* at new ways of teaching, *frustration* that it didn't seem to be working, *anger* at Chuck who wasn't helping, *fear* that the children would not be ready for the proficiency tests, and finally *surprise* and even *incredulity* at how Chuck saved the day! And she is still telling the story decades later! Ruby felt *frustration* about how students in her civics class treated one another, and Terry and Jon felt *anger* that their students were required to use inferior curriculum materials. Shawn was *excited* about having a new student, and Roberto was *disappointed* with student interactions. First feeling our feelings, and then pondering what they might be trying to tell us, is one of the most important indicators that we are ready to learn something new. Bringing intelligent thought to areas that attract strong feelings can open many areas for growth.

What are my motives, assumptions, and actions? Are they in alignment? For example, while Wendy's motive was to help her sixth-grade students to develop a love of reading, there was a discrepancy between this motive and what happened in the classroom and in the children's minds. One day Wendy told the class to "get ready for reading." Mickey, a sensitive child, said under his breath, "Yeah, but when do we get to read?" In the frenzy of working with the school's new reading series and its slick pretests, skill lessons, posttests, re-teaching skills lessons, retest, and workbook exercise, which one assumed would help children succeed in reading, there was precious little time for enjoying the stories! Mickey knew it and so did she! Because of this critical incident Wendy was moved to begin graduate school to learn more about reading. See Stepping Stones 9.1 to try out identifying assumptions.

What are my biases? We have biases in all directions. It may be easy for Jon and Terry to recognize that they have a bias about how children learn to read, but more difficult for them to recognize and admit is that they feel more comfortable around some children and less comfortable around others. It is difficult for most of us to realize and to act on the realization that race, social class, and gender are issues for us, too. Unearthing our biases is one of the most important aspects of our professional work.

How do I—and can I—visualize this? If Ruby were to close her eyes, relax, and summon an image of what a democratic civics classroom might look like, she

STEPPING STONES 9.1

Identifying Assumptions—

Practice	**Assumptions**
Writing spelling words five times each.	Repetition, or rote learning, will take place with practice. Students will memorize the spelling and remember it when they need to write the word at another time.
Grouping students by grade levels.	Students learn better when they are grouped with those closest in age. Teaching is more effective with learners who are similar. Learning is a hierarchical and sequential process.

What are assumptions underlying these practices?

Answering questions at the end of a chapter.

Looking up a new vocabulary word in a dictionary and using it in a sentence.

Writing a book report.

might visualize a vibrant discussion among students. She might diagram or draw a picture with arrows from students who initiate discussion to show the range of engagements and interactions. Next she might think about the class as it currently functions and visualize a conversation in which very few of the students are engaged. The quantity and quality of the conversation would be quite different in her two images. She could draw a picture with arrows from initiating students, but it would be mainly from the teacher and a few students. Another simple and powerful way to get an image of a situation is to let an image come in the form of a symbol. In Ruby's case the first image might be a growing pulsating organism; in the second, a plant with only vestiges of green, the rest withering or dead.

One of the benefits of visualization is that we can focus on different aspects of the topic. Our emotions, motives, biases, and aims are culturally shaped and housed, so that the social and cultural contexts within which we conceptualize our work need equal attention. The following questions help us to focus methodically and contextually.

What are the elements of the topic, and how do they work? Many, if not all, topics can benefit from visualization and working with symbols to represent and explore dimensions of the topic, and to uncover implicit knowledge. Along with the synthesizing that takes place with visualization, we can benefit from analyzing elements or parts of a topic. We cite two examples: Amy, a second-grade teacher, was interested in integrating math and poetry. She read an inspiring article that pointed out how the two areas are both symbolic processes, and that one could support the other in curriculum development and teaching. Intrigued at the notion, she designed her AR around it. Her question had multiple parts. She had to understand the math and poetry areas and begin to make connections between the two.

Judy, a middle school teacher, wanted to know why so many eighth graders failed the newly mandated writing proficiency tests. Pursuing this question has several obvious parts: the test, the students, and her roles and responsibilities as the teacher. Judy had to learn about the nature of the tests. What were students unable to do on these tests? What could she learn about the students and their needs? What were their weak spots? This would give her an opportunity to critique the test in the process. She would have to get to know more about students who failed. Could she develop lessons and strategies as an intervention for students who would be retaking the test in the near future?

How does my topic compare to something else? What might be learned from related experiences? For example, perhaps you have designed a curriculum project that flops. Remember the social studies curriculum project titled "Man: A Course of Study," in which one of the finest teams of subject-matter curriculum specialists put together an exemplary curriculum, and it flopped because they didn't involve teachers and parents in the process? Might there be any lessons from this project to apply to yours? Ruby had this problem too and took it seriously. As she thinks about how she can help foster a democratic classroom, she involves others, most importantly her students, in the process.

In what ways does time enter into the picture? Jon and Terry's fifth graders are labeled "low ability" because according to *time* they are not performing at grade-level norms. They are "behind" the typical and expected time line. The time it takes second-language students to learn and adjust to a new language is considered lost time. Successful bilingual programs exist in which "content" and language studies continue in a first language while students are gaining proficiency in the new language. With Shawn's student, this opportunity isn't available. Who *could* teach Jen social studies or science in her own language? Lesley, the kindergarten teacher concerned with the child born prematurely, foresaw problems because the child could not meet district-articulated and developmentally inappropriate goals. He would be "behind" his age-mates *timewise*. Time is an intriguing issue because we usually take it for granted and make unquestioned assumptions about its boundaries.

Time is treated as a commodity in our culture (Bloome and Katz, 1997). We pay people based on *time* worked. We divide school days and the school year into time segments. We note "typical" benchmarks and measure our children's growth by time. Time is a cultural construct. Indigenous peoples in recent memory who were nontechnological have no words in their native languages for clock-driven time. The cultural use of time (timed tests, assignment due dates, changing classes by a bell) is difficult for many students from nondominant cultures (Kasten, 1991). As we consider our research questions, *time* is an important variable to problematize.

In several chapters, we allude to constructivist and developmental theories and their implications for teaching and learning. How is time construed in these theories? Is a child premature (is this even possible?) or is the judgment premature? Are we lacking knowledge and understanding of both the child's and mother nature's time frame? Are Jon and Terry's students behind in their reading, or are our observations and the theories we use to understand growth and development inadequate to describe the students' realities?

What are the cultural and historical contexts? What is valued? If culture is composed of ways of thinking, valuing, and believing (Heath, 1983), what are the norms and practices within which you will conduct your study? One model in sociology uses the terms *high* and *low* culture to describe different cultural orientations (Hall, 1976). In a high-context culture, people are closely linked, more dependent and interdependent, work together, and are more long-term, family, and relationship oriented. A low-context culture is characterized by use of technology, individualism, and independence, which are more highly valued, and relationships in general are tied to specific events, opportunities, and circumstances.

The Amish culture, a group of people originally from Germany (many of whom are now living in the Midwestern United States) who live much as they did in small farming communities 100 years ago, is a good example of high-context culture; the postmodern upper-middle-class suburbanite is an example of low-context culture. Images help to bring this concept out: Picture a family at home together after a day working on the farm, spending a leisurely hour or so together enjoying roast beef, mashed potatoes, cole slaw, and rhubarb pie. Contrast this with a person or two spending 15 minutes at a drive-in for a Big Mac, fries, and soft-serve cone on the way to a soccer game after work.

High and low cultures can be that marked, but the distinctions also become muddier as cultures mix and change. The point is to begin to look at the different ways people live together, their shared values, and what this means for your work. History has a considerable impact on culture and thus on teaching and learning. What are people's beliefs about what is important? What are their ways of working, together and singly? How do some of these beliefs look in practice?

In Jon and Terry's school, for example, the staff is mature; they have been together for a long time, and no one has questioned the way children are grouped or how the curriculum is "developed" and "delivered." It is a relatively low-context culture in which independence is valued as long as people conform to and respect school norms and policies. Until recently, there were relatively few collaborative projects in which teachers, parents, students, and administrators worked together in creative ways. Jon and Terry will take this into account as they move their study along. Roberto may discover that the culture of segregating special students from other students has been in place for so long, and is so entrenched, that the effort to change may be met with resistance. Ruby's reading and personal life experiences as a student activist and mother of school-age children, as well as extensive reading in critical democracy, have prepared her to understand the culture of the school and to work with this knowledge in her project.

What forces are supportive of and resistant to change? Twenty years ago in the curriculum field a process called *forced field analysis* was popular. Forced field analysis is a way to assess and evaluate the possibilities for change in a cultural setting. Simply put, it entailed listing factors that were in support of change and factors that served as constraints to change. Let's see what Shawn might find.

Factors supporting change

I am committed to teaching each child.
I can get info off the Web about Korea.
I can observe carefully and try
    things out.
The principal said she would help.
I can work with the ESL teacher.
Jen is bright and enthusiastic.
The children want to make friends.
I know quite a bit about child
    development.

Factors constraining change

I know nothing about Korea!
I know almost nothing about Jen.
Jen doesn't speak *any* English.
No one I know speaks Korean!

For Ruby, trying to initiate a democratic classroom will go against tradition and the norms in her school. Some of her obstacles, then, are political. For students who benefit from the traditional system, the new system could provide a rude demotion, and fallout. The force most powerful in supporting change is her commitment to do so, which comes from her conviction that a democratic system works.

For Terry and Jon, there were several forces that made change unlikely: a group that set policies for the district curriculum, past experience of teachers who had been "innovative" finding themselves unemployed, and a lack of resources and curriculum materials appropriate for their proposal. One of their strongest assets was that there were two of them. They each had considerable experience and confidence, and they were willing to make this a major project—planned, documented, and evaluated—with shared results. They were willing to put in the time to research and prepare a professional proposal for change and to communicate with all necessary parties.

As we look inwardly, outwardly, and contextually, we keep coming back to our purpose. Where are we heading? The last two questions help us to frame our topic from the perspectives of long-term effects—ones that we may not be around to deal with. Decisions can be made with myopic vision, and if we are not mindful, short-term goals may jeopardize long-term goals and violate our vision for the future.

What are my long-term aims, and how do these fit with my short-term goals? Ruby
thinks that if her students live the democratic process today, they will come to "own" it and will be more likely to take an active interest in voting and the world around them later on. Jon and Terry want their "low-ability" readers to enjoy reading today, finish school, and continue to read as adults. Their reasoning is that if students fall in love with books, there's a better chance this will happen. They are not alone in this belief. Reputedly, some states plan future prison beds based on elementary test scores in reading.

It is easy to get caught up in everyday issues that overshadow democratic processes, and in "skill and drill" that kills the very processes that encourage democratic living and the motivation to learn in ways that only reading can support. Regular revisiting of long-term aims is an important practice to cultivate, not only among ourselves, but with parents, students, and the wider community.

Goodlad (1984) asked more than 27,000 people how learning and long-term goals were served in their districts. Results were remarkably consistent. Most people wanted high academic standards in schools that were humane and caring places. In general, parents and teachers have similar long-term goals: to have children grow into good citizens, communicators, problem solvers, critical consumers, and parents, and learn to live happy and fulfilling lives. Each community defines what is meant by *good*, but the categories are similar. Although it is important to jointly determine aims and goals as a framework for planning (if we want all students to graduate from school, we need to anticipate practices and policies that may in fact hinder students from graduating), as problematizers, we also want to question goals that simply maintain the status quo at the expense of students and families who are not privileged by the current system.

What are the consequences of change? At first glance, we might say that those people best served by maintaining the present circumstances will lose their benefits with that change, and that those most disadvantaged by present circumstances will benefit from changes that are in their best interests. However, this assumes that change must advantage and disadvantage some people. This may be so, or seem so, in the short term. However, by taking a longer-term perspective, it may be that *both* or, more accurately, *all* groups will be advantaged. Is the child who "shines above all others" in a competitive, stepped, "single-intelligence," hierarchical system really better off than he or she would be in a system in which all children are enabled to grow and shine, in which collaboration, multiple intelligences, and continuous progress (formative) are acknowledged, valued, and supported? Does not an inferior education for Jon and Terry's students affect the quality of education within the school, and thus the quality of education for all students?

Taking time to examine the consequences of change from both long- and short-term goal perspectives for all people involved is well worth the effort in terms of both individuals and communities. To see how one practice can be problematized and unpacked through responding to critical questions and scrutiny, go to Travelers' Notes: Problematizing the Honor Roll in Your School.

Although exploring and problematizing on our own are important, we are mindful of the need to work with colleagues to mutually expand our own knowledge and scholarship. How we can work with these colleagues is the subject of the next section.

What Do Others Know? Students and Colleagues as Resources

Think of the many resources available to us as we try to make informed decisions about our work: other teachers, counselors, social workers, psychologists, parents, business and community partners, media specialists, friends, researchers, and theorists quickly come to mind. Talking over a cup of coffee to a teacher who has helped second-language learners might be a first stop in Shawn's exploration. E-mail list servers, chat rooms, and Internet sites instantaneously open up our world to distant colleagues. Libraries give us access to the scholarship of researchers, thinkers, and teacher-researchers who may have pondered the same questions that puzzle us. They have developed their own ideas and theories that can inform our thinking. We would be remiss in our research if we did not consult available resources. Although we will focus on one resource—scholars who have written about a particular topic—we do so not to diminish the contributions of others, but to highlight the importance of scholarship in helping us expand our knowledge about our research interest.

Reviewing the Literature

Exploring the library and the Internet related to one's topic can be not only informative but downright invigorating as we discover more about the terrain we are traveling and the resources available to us. We can use relevant literature to help us shape our inquiry. In fact, a single article can change the way we think about a topic; it can act as a catalyst for our thinking and help us to define the study and our direction. An article or book can be a gold mine from which to draw much of our review. It may contain a list of references that, when reviewed carefully, can provide key sources for further investigation. *Using* the wheel, rather than reinventing it, may enable us to move further down the Yellow Brick Road.

One action researcher we know learned a related lesson the hard way. She was interested in *buddy reading* (children read back and forth to one another without teacher supervision). After several weeks of frustration with students' lack of interest, she went to the literature and found a wealth of research and materials that helped her to understand the process and how to proceed.

Many times, consulting the literature at the beginning of one's thinking about a topic is advisable, but sometimes it is advisable to conceptualize and begin the study, after which the literature may become useful. The traditional bias has been to do the former. With AR, however, it is at times advisable to do the latter. There are studies in which the literature is not essential, or even necessary, even though the study itself may contribute to it. It all depends on one's topic and purpose. By laying out some of the possible benefits and cautions in reviewing the literature, it will be easier to determine the best approach for our studies.

A review helps us to map out the terrain, locate resources, define and refine our topic and questions, and save time. The cautions include allowing the literature to shape our questions when we are in a better position to do so, getting sidetracked or distracted by other issues, and feeling the need to read beyond the point necessary to conceptualize one's study. One way around these potential problems is to read critically and to keep summarizing our thinking about our studies as we proceed through a limited body of literature. We have learned from action researchers who have searched libraries and Internet sources for scholarship that helped them to develop their questions. We include a few of their ideas for your consideration:

Read broadly and generally at first, then read in a more focused way. If you are interested in using cooperative learning, first you may want to read a book that describes all kinds of cooperative learning strategies. Then you may want to focus in on articles, chapters, or books that focus on the particular approach that makes sense for you and your students. To read broadly, browse through catalogues and stacks to discover some general and useful information: Is the topic considered to be controversial? Is there agreement about the topic among professionals? Has information on the topic changed greatly over recent years? What are key works and who are key scholars concerning the topic? What do experts consider to be unexamined central issues? You may stumble on research syntheses that provide many different perspectives on the topic and a list of references leading you to specific works that will narrow your focus. See Figure 9.1 for sources to consider when browsing. *When you are researching a novel topic that seems to have few resources, look for related topics and then synthesize them.* The first people who wanted to study children and computer use would have been unable to find information in professional journals on their topic. Instead, as they progressed in their inquiry,

---

FIGURE 9.1 *Scholarly sources for reviewing literature*

- **Journals from learned societies.** Publications sponsored by organizations central to a field of study are instrumental in setting national and/or regional standards for the field. Referred to as *juried, blind-reviewed,* or *refereed,* anything going into these journals has been evaluated by at least three readers to whom the authors are unknown. Thus the work has been judged on its merit and not on the fame or connections of the author. The purpose of refereed journals is the dissemination of knowledge. Writers and even editors are generally not compensated.

- **Online journals.** Many learned societies offer online journals that are refereed, like their paper counterparts. Web addresses are generally available in paper journals and from colleagues, media specialists, and society Web pages. Some journals have access fees. Some online journals are free; most require subscriptions either through your Internet browser or through your academic institution. Be cautious about information obtained from the Web when the source cannot be documented as scholarly or reputable. Anyone with minimal computer knowledge can post Web information. When in doubt, consult a reference librarian. Some online sources are not intended for scholarly use, but are more like electronic encyclopedias with concise information for use by the general public.

- **Professional books.** The market for books to inform teachers and others is rich and exciting. Certain publishers cater to the needs of educators, and nearly any topic that has been around for a few years has a book on the subject. Consult reputable publishers in your discipline. Your action research mentor can assist you in finding out which publishers are appropriate. With a professional book, the credentials of the authors are provided. Professional books, like journals, have been reviewed for quality throughout the publication process. Be cautious of books or other print materials that are self-published or published by the author-owned company, although they can be as reputable as known sources. Reference librarians have publishers' directories that include all legitimate publishers and information about their ownership. Similar to online journals, more and more professional books are accessible online as e-books purchased individually or through online databases that libraries or institutions can subscribe to.

- **Conferences.** While attending a local, regional, national, or international conference of educators, you may have the pleasure of hearing a speaker whose words or handouts you would like to use in your research. Publication manuals list rules for citing such sources. Differentiate between conferences sponsored by scholarly, learned societies where proposals were reviewed by a proposal committee and commercial, for-profit conferences or workshops that are primarily business enterprises (the quality nonetheless could be good), as the latter often lack checks and balances to ensure quality. Materials from the former are generally safe to use in a literature review.

they found that literature on how children learn and on computer processing could be useful to their research. They became synthesizers of these two bodies of literature and brought them together in new ways. In these instances, the researchers make their maps as they go. The entire map becomes visible only in hindsight!

Consult primary sources where possible. When the first generation of babies born addicted to "crack" cocaine arrived in kindergartens around the United States, no one was prepared for the difficulties these children would have in school. A library search would not have been useful. But local hospitals and agencies that serve families of preschoolers were aware of some of the issues, had research studies in progress, and had reports and resource people prepared to share information. Getting information firsthand from those conducting the research and publishing their findings is to consult *primary sources* and is preferable to using *secondary sources* (sources that build on, quote, and use other people's research). Having said this, we acknowledge that it is not possible to use only primary sources. Use as many primary sources as is possible and feasible, and check secondary sources to make sure that the information quoted is accurate.

Ask for help. Sometimes information is difficult to find. The terminology or the databases you are searching may not be suited to the question. A few well-placed questions to a librarian, media specialist, and colleagues can be helpful in these instances.

Read enough to get started, but not so much that you become too exhausted to conduct your study! Those pursuing advanced degrees may want to read until they see ideas repeat themselves. Those whose interests are more immediate may simply read until ideas are framed in a context that makes sense for their purposes. To read everything on cooperative learning would be senseless if you discover that your primary interest is how to form groups of students. Read with a critical eye. Each of the questions we reviewed for problematizing can be posed to sources in our literature reviews. What are the theories, assumptions, and frameworks of the authors and researchers? Are they plausible? Are they consistent with what you know? What is explained? What is left for interpretation? What are the credentials of the author(s)? Do they take themselves into account as part of their study? The public theories that we read in the literature can enhance the development of our emerging private theories.

Stepping Stones 9.2 and 9.3 help us to look ahead and think through ways to keep track of our tools, data, and other resources, and provide suggestions on using names in action research.

What Do I Expect to Find?

Action researchers are continually mindful of their own thoughts, feelings, values, assumptions, and biases. We realize that only through self-reflection will we develop into professional scholars of our teaching. Being mindful of our own expectations for

STEPPING STONES 9.2

Looking Ahead: Considerations for Managing Information

- *Consider permissions.* To conduct your study, you may need clearance from the institutions involved. In addition, you may need permission from families of your participants. This is especially important if you plan to use audio recording, video recordings, student work, or photographs in your work and in your report or presentations. Consult your action research mentor as well as school district personnel for local guidelines.

- *Consider exploring baseline data.* Often teachers give assignments at the beginning of the year (such as writing or interviews about content knowledge) or surveys to parents about prospective students. Others take reading samples on audiotape, or videotape early school-year behavior. Also, schools maintain cumulative files with data from previous school years. Some of this information may be useful in your study design and analysis for identifying focus participants, for comparing growth in a subject area, or for making numerical comparisons from available test scores. Local policies may affect how and when these files are accessed and used.

- *Shop for supplies.* As smooth journeys most often require careful and compact packing, research requires organizational skills and procedures. Consider how you will keep track of readings. (Notebooks? Index cards?) How will you keep track of data? (File folders? Binders? Envelopes?) How will you keep track of what you have done and what you still need to do? Where will you store these things? Will they be on computer files? Where will you store backups? Sometimes colored labels, files, or highlighters can help separate different kinds of data.

- *Protect your work.* As you collect data, date and name every item. Photocopy written materials. Maintain backup files on your computer and on diskettes. Be careful transporting files between home and school. Don't leave important parts of your research in unsecured places. Carefully documenting can prevent a last-minute scramble for citations and page numbers. If, at the last minute, you discover one part of a citation is needed, a reference librarian can generally help retrieve the missing information.

- *Know your library and your librarians.* Take time to get to know your library and its services, especially interlibrary loans, online sources, and the magic library staff—the *reference* department. They are knowledge-able about finding and obtaining information. *Ask for their help.* Most academic libraries have a *reference* desk. Talk with a librarian knowl-edgeable about your area of interest.

STEPPING STONES 9.3

Do I Use the Real Names of My Students and My School in My Action Research?

Many teachers question whether or not to use pseudonyms for their students and their school, or whether they should seek permission to use real names to honor the work and accomplishments of their school and their students. Here are some considerations when making this decision:

- Action researchers must collect permission from all students' parents and from their school administration whether they use real names or pseudonyms.
- The topic you are researching comes into play here when, for example, it may make sense to maintain anonymity of the school and students. For example, could something in your research embarrass the school or some of the staff? If this is the case, use pseudonyms.
- Having conversations with colleagues and administration at the site of the research is recommended to gather information on any policies in place as well as the general feeling and consent of the school staff. Here are two examples:
  - You are studying the effects of authentic audiences on student writing, and you are having students write wonderful and creative school-published books on the country they are studying to have on display in the city or regional library after the project. *It makes sense to use real names in this study*, even to have your local newspaper cover the story.
  - You are studying all the seventh grades in your school that have been ability tracked all year. You are exploring these students' perceptions of schooling, and the amount of time each track of students has opportunities for quality, hands-on, experiential learning. *It might make sense to use pseudonyms.*

where our questions may lead us is also a way to keep track of how our own lenses filter the way we look at our journey. Traditional researchers call this expectation a "hypothesis." For example, Ruby expected her social studies students *to want* to participate in a democratic process. She hypothesized that through active engagement students would find meaning in civics (and it would be remembered).

CHAPTER SUMMARY

Problematizing our questions and our practice is perhaps the most challenging part of our action research journey. By beginning with what we already know and adding the wisdom and critique of colleagues (teachers, students, researchers, theorists, and others), we may be able to move beyond the confines of the Yellow Brick Road, to a little more dangerous but richer territory and journey.

SECTION SUMMARY

In this section we met the teachers who will accompany us on our journey. We explored how we can turn our curiosities into researchable questions, and we learned how to problematize our practice—all important elements in AR. We conclude this section by recalling the questions that the teachers in our case studies developed over the course of their action research projects. What can you learn from them?

1. How can I best teach a child who speaks a language different from that of the rest of the class?
   - How will Jen fare when immersed in a new language?
   - How will Jen learn English?
   - How will Jen's lack of English affect her learning and social relationships?
   - How will I learn about Jen's culture? How will that learning inform my teaching?
2. How do children who have had difficulty with reading respond to a rich literature-based approach with the use of trade books, literature response journals, and the opportunity for meaningful discussions of literature, when they have grown accustomed to reliance on basal readers?
3. How can I create a democratic classroom environment in my civics class?
4. "I just don't get it! I know these kids [students placed in regular education classes] have been with our students [students placed in special education classes] in inclusive classes in the past, but the regular education students act as if they have never seen a child with disabilities. Why isn't inclusion working? Is it because it is not cool to hang around kids perceived to be different"?
   In each case, the questions relate to personal values and commitments:
   - A desire to help a child who speaks another language feel included and an eagerness to learn about the child's culture.
   - A belief that learning to read requires a variety of rich and interesting resources and meaningful discussions with peers and adults.
   - The idea that it is important to model a democratic classroom if we expect students to become active citizens.
   - A belief that all students, regardless of how they are labeled by a school, need to be and feel included.

Their beliefs form the commitments that, combined with curiosity, fuel their desire to know. Questions that lead to illuminating studies are fueled by curiosity and commitment to a set of values. Such questions focus on interpreting and critiquing one's own practice and center on matters of consequence to the researcher. Although the results of such studies may be useful to others, their purpose is not to generalize.

The beginnings of journeys are usually rich with potential, but they can also seem rough and dangerous for lack of knowing exactly where our interests may take us, how our journey will unfold, and what the journey may teach us about ourselves. To move closer to the Emerald City, let's take time to make use of what we have explored and further frame our research questions in "Exploring the Forest."

Exploring the Forest

From Curiosity to Research Topic: Asking Critical Questions

In the chapters of Section IV, we offered many suggestions to begin to define and shape a study topic and questions. These explorations and exercises are designed to assist you in being the educational conductor of your own professional work. They will help you to develop professional judgment. As you proceed, you may choose to change your idea anywhere along the way, as you acquire new information and make it part of your developing reportoire. Give yourself a few minutes for each exercise. Just write, don't think. You can always return and expand on your ideas if you decide that would be beneficial. Do a free-write for the first three items that follow.

1. What are three things you are curious about related to professional practice?
2. What are three concerns you have about being a caring and committed teacher?
3. What three problems (or dissatisfactions) do you have, or foresee, with your teaching and professional work?

Now, look at the nine things you have listed.

4. What larger issues come to mind? Are any of these related to others on the list? Can you find an issue related to each curiosity, concern, and problem? What different perspectives or viewpoints are inherent in each? What (if anything) is controversial or contestable in each? Take one issue that holds promise as a research topic, and do a free-write about it. Focus your thoughts, ideas, experiences, and questions on this possible topic.
5. Take the issue you wrote about in item 4, and turn it into a statement of the problem (curiosity) you (tentatively) will investigate. Pose a question or two

or three that go to the heart of what you think the problem is. Limit yourself to one page.

Do you notice anything about what you have just done? What connections did you make as a result of writing? What thoughts and feelings did you have as you did this, and about the process itself? You now have a tentative topic and questions for a study. You have also generated ideas that you can take through the same process and develop into an area for investigation, perhaps an action research project. The next section will take you further into thinking critically (problematizing) about teaching, learning, and curriculum development.

6. Make a list of several teaching or instructional practices in your field of study. For example, you might list the practice of students expanding their vocabularies by looking up words from a list in the dictionary and then using the words in a sentence. Some other common practices might be writing spelling words for practice; answering questions in science or social studies at the end of the chapter; conjugating verbs in a foreign language; memorizing multiplication tables in math; diagramming sentences in English grammar; or asking students to identify the elements of art in well-known paintings. Ask yourself, and a few colleagues, questions about the practice and the assumptions that seem to underlie it. This is a good activity to do in a small group. Although we cannot be sure of what someone else assumes unless we ask them, we can think through what seems to follow logically from the activity. Here are some questions to frame assumptions.
    a. What might be assumed about how learning takes place in this activity? What might be assumed about how children learn? Adolescents? Adults? What might be assumed about students' roles and responsibilities in this learning? What might be the assumptions about the teacher's roles and responsibilities in this teaching and learning?
    b. What is assumed related to the student's overall education? Might we assume that this will make the student a "better" or "more educated" person? What is the warrant for this assumption?

7. Identifying assumptions is one way of problematizing practice and this process can take us back to our roots (as we explored in Section III) and to the critical question of "Whose eyes can see what?" Return to your autobiographical writing, or, write a brief autobiography. Read this autobiography and ask yourself, **How would your autobiography be different if you changed your**
    • gender
    • birth order
    • economic circumstances
    • abilities
    • family values
    • race or ethnicity?

8. Select several issues from a prominent journal in your field or discipline. In small groups, select several articles and read only the literature reviews. The

literature review will be easy to locate—it will summarize many studies. Have each group member read the same two or three literature reviews. Then, as a group, decide how to describe the literature review and the role it plays in the article. How do the literature reviews vary? What do they have in common? How might the article be different without this section? Share your findings with the group or class as a whole. These literature reviews may serve as useful examples later, if you need to write one. Keep in mind that the references you make in your own study may be used sparingly—just enough to get you started on your journey.

9. Write a draft of an introduction to your project. You many find that you can use this again later as an introduction to your report. Include the following in your introduction:
   - What is my research interest?
   - Why am I interested? (What are my values, beliefs, and assumptions?)
   - What is my question?
   - What do I already know?
   - What do others know? (From the literature, from other professionals, from family, from the community, and from technological sources.)
   - What do I expect to find?
   - Who will benefit from this study and in what ways will they benefit?

Limit this draft to a page or two. Be concise and stick to the topic. It is appropriate to write in the first person ("I"). Trade drafts with critical colleagues or classmates, asking them to react to your idea and your writing. Ask them to tell you, in their own words, what they believe you said.

10. Select an issue or controversy in your school or in the news (school uniforms, year-round schooling, multiage classes, national teacher testing, national standards, etc.). Using the chart based on the three orientations of Habermas in Chapter 4, frame an argument either for or against this issue or practice: one from the *technical* orientation, one from the *practical* orientation, one from the critical or *emancipatory* orientation. For example, the issue of out-of-school suspension has many aspects that can be debated. From a technical point of view, how effective and efficient is out-of-school suspension in punishing students? Do students return to school with a better attitude toward learning? Are they less of a threat to other students? From a practical point of view, we may want to know if out-of-school suspension allows us to better understand these students. From a critical perspective, we may want to know which students are suspended. Is any ethnic or socioeconomic group overrepresented? Here are some issues to try out with this exercise. Try these or generate your own:
    - As a teacher, you notice that your "nonmajority" students continually score lower than the group as a whole on the standardized test used by your district. You are considering this as a research question.
    - Your state or region is talking seriously about retaining all eighth graders who do not pass a local mandated proficiency test, preventing them from

proceeding to the next grade level. You and your colleagues are concerned about this policy.

- You have been teaching vocabulary in your high school the same way for years—separate from the context of literature. You are bored with it, and the students are bored with it. The parents highly value the fact that vocabulary is taught this way, as they believe it will help their adolescents score higher on college entrance examinations.

11. Using the list of questions for problematizing in this chapter, examine the issue or practice you just explored in item 9 or revisit the vignette about Chuck, the child who wasn't paying attention to his teacher during a math lesson. Or take the research topic and question that you are considering for your own action research project. Ask a critical colleague or a group of colleagues to think with you to clarify your research interest. Let them know that while you value their advice, this is not an advice-giving session. Rather, you want them to ask you questions that will help you clarify the situation or problem or interest. Begin by writing a few sentences that describe your research interest or problem. Read them out loud to your colleagues. Next the questions begin. Close the session by asking a colleague to reflect on what she or he heard and saw and felt about you and the way the process went. Many researchers find this kind of "think with me" reflection to be one of the most beneficial parts of beginning an action research study. Finally, reflect on what you have learned through this process. Were you able to see things from perspectives that were not apparent before? Do you have new insights into the research interest or into yourself? How are you involved in the situation? How might you play a part in the problem?

V

Designing and Planning an Action Research Study

This adventure [with monstrous beasts] made the travelers more anxious than ever to get out of the forest; and they walked so fast that Dorothy became tired. . . . To their great joy, the trees became thinner the further they advanced . . . suddenly they came upon a broad river . . . on the other side of the water they could see the road of yellow brick running through a beautiful country.

"How shall we cross the river?" asked Dorothy.

"That is easily done," replied the Scarecrow. "The Tin Woodman must build us a raft so we can float to the other side."

. . . When they reached the shore . . . they knew the stream had carried them a long way past the road of yellow brick. . . .

"What shall we do now?" asked the Woodman.

"We must get back to the road in some way," said Dorothy.

"The best plan will be to walk along the river bank until we come to the road again," remarked the Lion.

The Wonderful Wizard of Oz
L. Frank Baum (1900)

In this section, we will explore how professionals address their questions by carefully planning a road map. We will explore the kinds of data that professionals produce and evaluate to make adjustments in even the best-laid plans. By the end of this section, you will have designed a thoughtful study to address your own questions. Helpful hints in boxes called *Stepping Stones*, examples taken from action research studies called Case Studies, and exercises in "Exploring the Forest" at the end of the section are provided to guide the design of your study. Now let's take a look at the plans that our teachers have developed to address the questions posed in Section IV.

CASE STUDIES

Shawn

Helping Jen Learn English as a Second Language

Shawn knew having a child who spoke Korean in an English-speaking classroom would be a challenging experience. Shawn's respect for Jen as a learner from a culture different from her own provided the impetus for the study. After deciding to make this into an action research study, Shawn had to decide how to proceed. Because Jen was the focus of the study, a single-subject case study approach certainly made sense. Shawn immediately began keeping a researcher log in which she noted observations about Jen. In the beginning, Shawn wasn't sure what to write in the logbook, but was confident that as time went on, interesting and informative anecdotes would need to be recorded about Jen's development.

Reading, language, and socialization were of primary concern, as these would influence nearly all other learning for Jen. The literature on ESL offered many suggestions for ways to enrich the language learning of ESL students as well as all students in a classroom. Shawn's plan for Jen included working with a self-selected buddy, hands-on activities, modified written work, drawing and labeling of pictures, a picture journal, and independent computer work. An integral part of the study was for Shawn to learn about Korean culture.

With each new strategy, Shawn decided to save Jen's journals and analyze her progress. Shawn planned to conduct interviews with the ESL teacher in the school both to become more informed about strategies to use with Jen and to collect the other teacher's insights on her progress. Shawn systematically saved all Jen's written classroom work for later analysis to look for progress in literacy and language development. Finally, Shawn decided to give three periodic quizzes of commonly used words for second graders to assess Jen's progress in knowledge of common but vital vocabulary. These four data sources would provide multiple ways of looking at her progress.

As in many action research projects, Shawn was uncertain exactly how the study should proceed. One thing was certain—a number of things would have to be tried out. Shawn would observe Jen's responses, note changes in a researcher log, keep tabs on progress as evidenced in the student's journal, and adjust teaching as things were learned along the way. One of the members of Shawn's university research class agreed to be a critical colleague.

Shawn knew that the report would be presented in the university action research class for which this study was being conducted, so permission was obtained from the university Human Subjects Review Board prior to actual data collection. In addition, Shawn obtained written permission from Jen's parents, who were eager to participate in any way they could. The principal of Shawn's school had suggested that a brief presentation at a faculty meeting would be beneficial to staff.

The Literature Circles Study

Jon

Terry

Jon and Terry decided to conduct their study with a class of 20 fifth graders tracked as the lowest-ability fifth-grade readers in the school. All these students were labeled *at risk* by their school. Within this class, literature circles were selected for special focus. The goal was to help students become enthused, engaged, and excited about reading in hopes that they would become lifelong readers. Specifically, the goal was to help students become self-confident in reading and language and develop critical thinking skills.

The teachers decided to implement literature circles (Daniels, 1994; Kasten, 1995) in which groups of five students would meet daily for approximately a 5-week unit to read award-winning juvenile novels, keep written responses to their reading, and conduct student-led discussions. The literature circles would replace the basal reading program put in place by the district, which consisted of anthologies of short stories, questions about each story, and workbook exercises of skills that were decontextualized from the stories.

The "Reader Self-Perception Scale" (Henk and Melnick, 1995) was to be administered to the class at the beginning and end of the semester as pre- and posttest measures of student attitudes toward themselves as readers. Student journals would be collected, and one group's journals would be analyzed for evidence of higher-level critical thinking. Jon and Terry designed a form for students to self-assess their participation, their contribution to the group, and their understanding of the literature. Selected student discussions would be audiotaped for evidence of critical thinking and level of engagement with the story. The teachers also planned to take anecdotal notes about students and group process skills. A close look at student responses on the attitude scale, the content of the student journals, and their own researcher logs would hopefully reveal some patterns that would help them make some good decisions about how best to use literature circles to develop student interest in reading and student critical thinking.

Because of their review of the literature, Jon and Terry were aware of some kinds of expected written and oral responses and planned to look for those plus other kinds of responses that might emerge from all these data sources. In the back of their minds, they were thinking of how to demonstrate student progress at the end of the one-semester study to other teachers. They suspected that they would find that "at-risk" readers can respond to literature in engaging ways. It was not necessary to obtain written parental permission for this study because blanket permission for action research studies was obtained through the principal's office at the beginning of the school year. However, Jon and Terry did write a letter to parents informing them about the plans, hoping that they would encourage their children to talk about their selected books at home.

The S.T.A.R. Club Study

Roberto

Roberto's study focused on creating situations in which "typical" middle school students would be more accepting of the sixteen students in two multiple handicapped (MH) classes. The sixteen students had been diagnosed with Down's syndrome, cerebral palsy, language disorders, vision impairments, and autism.

Roberto considered several alternative actions before deciding on a *peer club* as an extracurricular activity. The sole purpose of the club would be to increase the time for social interaction between "typical" students and students with multiple handicaps. This option was appealing for two reasons. First, it addressed the social needs of both groups of students. Second, it supported the middle school philosophy of providing choices for all students to participate in the life of the school. The group would be called the *S.T.A.R. (Students and Teachers Advancing Relationships) Club*. Interested students could sign up with a friend and be paired with a peer with special needs.

During first semester, Roberto would organize the club: find interested peers and teachers, pair them up, and think of club activities. During the second semester, the club would sponsor one activity per month. Roberto thought activities like a pizza party would be fun for everyone involved and would be a natural way to increase social interaction and acceptance.

To triangulate the data, Roberto decided to use a personal journal to keep track of observations and personal reflections, a before-and-after survey of student attitudes toward peers with disabilities, and a focus group interview of S.T.A.R. Club members to probe more deeply into their attitudes. Roberto would consult with an advisory group of teachers for feedback, and he would test emerging hypotheses for disconfirming data. He would analyze data in relation to the literature on inclusion and his personal experiences of working with students with special needs. He would inform administrators, teachers, and parents about the results of the study. Because Roberto was interested in seeing if the S.T.A.R. Club would make a difference in social interaction and acceptance, he used a before-and-after study design that also looked at feelings and activities *during* the year.

The Democratic Classroom Study

Ruby

Ruby gave some serious thought to ways she could address her question. She wanted to help her ninth-grade civics students develop knowledge, skills, and characteristics that she felt were necessary for active, involved citizenship in a democracy. Her goal was to develop a sense of community among the students in three of her college preparatory civics classes, something she saw lacking during her practicum observations. Drawing on readings about community development in classrooms, she decided to start out by focusing on building a collaborative ethos. She brainstormed ways to enhance collaboration between teachers and students and between students and their peers. Her ideas ranged from student choice, to group work, to discussion of controversial issues, to a classroom compact.

Ruby realized that she would need to collect evidence to determine the consequences of her efforts. She considered this evidence to be *formative evaluation* of progress toward the development of a sense of community in her classroom. She also knew that she would have to verify that the results of her study would hold up to the judgment of others—her mentor, her university advisors, and her fellow student teachers when she made a presentation to them at the end of the term. So as she decided on data collection strategies, she kept these things in mind. In an effort to save time, rather than interview all her students individually, she decided to survey students about their sense of community, both at the beginning of her student teaching and toward the end. Rather than develop a survey of her own, she was able to obtain one from a journal article recommended by her research advisor. This, too, saved some time. She would also collect student work and student journals. The journal would be a source of information about student attitudes about collaborative work. Her own journal would be a source of private reflection on how the study was progressing and what she was learning. Here she could record her hunches and thoughts about issues that were emerging. She decided the best time for her to write would be in the evening after she put her children to bed. Observations by herself, her mentor, and her university action research adviser would provide information about student group work and participation. She knew that she would need their continued support as critical colleagues in order to carry through her plans.

With all these perspectives, she felt that any conclusions drawn would be fair and reasonable. Before drawing conclusions, however, she planned to examine her data closely, looking specifically for things that contradicted her own hunches. She planned to interpret her findings in light of experience (her own and that of other teachers) as well as the reading she planned to do. The next steps would come as the study evolved. Before administering the first survey, she told her students about the study and gained written parent permission and support.

Let's briefly reflect on the journey of the teachers in our cases as they explore their options and develop their plans of action. The English as a Second Language Study and the Literature Circles Study are conducted by veteran teachers aware of the detours and obstacles that may redirect their journey. For this reason, they plan tentatively. The S.T.A.R. Club Study and the Democratic Classroom Study are conducted by novice teachers whose limited teaching experience is both wonderful and problematic. Strong commitments and ideals motivate their work, but like their more veteran counterparts, they must work within existing classroom and school structures that moderate their plans. All these detours and obstacles (classroom and peer culture, school or district, mentor and student "agendas") inform the professional judgments made by our teachers.

Each of these studies is based on a strong commitment to understanding the self as teacher, the setting, and students, and to action that is consistent with a vision for teaching and learning. In this section, we explore specific tools of inquiry that will provide "data" for the professional journal. In the following section, we will see not only how the stories unfold, but how these teachers develop professional judgment that relies on both careful analysis of data *and* intuition (and ingenuity) that leaps beyond the immediate and concrete evidence.

CHAPTER 10

From Research Questions to Planning a Study

If you have developed a question in the previous section that you would like to carry out as an action research project, this chapter can be used to help you quickly design a study. Or you may want to develop a "trial" question and use this chapter to design a study for practice. The idea that we introduce here—design—is developed further in the next chapters as we design and carry out our own studies.

What Is Design?

Design is a plan and a process. Design is a personalized road map for teaching and learning. Design is part of our everyday lives. Selecting the clothes we wear to create a certain image or feeling, choosing and arranging furniture to create a special kind of living space, and customizing a car for safety, comfort, or utility are all examples of design.

Action research involves designing our teaching and our relationships with students. Just as Dorothy and her friends deal creatively with obstacles, action researchers face seemingly unsurmountable obstacles (such as standardized tests for students, checklists for teacher evaluation, and bureaucracy). Internal obstacles are just as difficult to overcome. Unexamined personal and professional assumptions about the way things *ought* to be can easily become our own roadblocks. It takes creative energy and thought to design an educational journey.

Why create a plan? Planning a study in advance may be the glue that holds the research together when things do not go smoothly. Plans are a starting point. Planning necessitates stepping back and thinking about where we want to go, knowing full well that we will make changes in response to what we learn along the way. Many teachers plan for action research before school begins—before students arrive and the thousand details of the school year demand their attention.

For student teachers unfamiliar with the classrooms in which they will teach, planning ahead might seem difficult. To ease into their studies, our students spend time in their classrooms prior to student teaching, making observations, reading research, and talking with their teachers. If this is not possible, the first weeks of student teaching can be spent formulating questions. Small learning communities of student teachers can be formed based on their common interests. The written plan usually comes *after* time is spent in teaching and in reflection on our aspirations. As a general rule, start by designing a short, easily manageable study.

Designing a Quick Practice Study

Think of something you did recently in your teaching that didn't work. Perhaps it worked previously, or it has come up for the first time and you had to figure out how to make it work. Now jot down some notes about it in your journal. You may wish to follow this up in "Exploring the Forest" at the end of this section.

The following example illustrates how one teacher thought about her teaching. Kathy, an experienced kindergarten teacher, started to question the value of "letter of the week," a practice for reading that she had carried out consistently as "a firm believer" for many years.

> As I continued to use the letter of the week, I noticed my enthusiasm for teaching the alphabet began to lessen. I was no longer excited or enthused about activities. I noticed the children felt the same way. There seemed to be an overall attitude of "I will do this because I have to, not because I want to do it." I also noticed that the children who functioned at a lower level were not learning sounds and the letters in isolation. As I began to seriously take a look at what I was doing, I asked myself, Does teaching the letter of the week really suit the children's needs? . . .
> The thing that bothered me the most, though, is that I have always been a strong advocate for a developmentally appropriate curriculum and thought that I was really teaching one! But as I looked at my classroom practice, I really began to question whether I was actually providing a developmentally appropriate curriculum for my children. I began to search for other ways. . . .

Kathy identified an emerging question based on what was happening in her classroom.

What did *you* do as a result of *your* situation? Jot it down in your journal. Now see what Kathy did.

> I began to read, and I attended a conference and came away with new ideas and enthusiasm . . . a better understanding of phonemic awareness. With the help of Dr. Timmons and numerous resources, I implemented [a more comprehensive]

phonemic awareness [program] in my classroom. This simple change in my teaching has given me a whole new enthusiasm for teaching. I am really pleased with what is happening in my classroom and have documentation through an action research project to prove that it works!

(Kathy, journal excerpt)

Louise, a teacher unknown to Kathy, struggled with a similar problem. Let's look into her journal reflections:

In looking back at my journey, I discovered that teaching in isolation does not work for every child. I began my study by focusing on phonemic awareness and letter sounds. I thought that by teaching these concepts children would be able to see and/or hear a word and have the ability to segment the word by letters. I believed that the children would then be able to read and write the sounds they heard and/or saw. I assumed that because the children would be taught the skills, the enthusiasm, the enjoyment, and the understanding of literature would come with it automatically. I was wrong. I was able to teach the letter sounds and phonemics awareness, but there was something missing. The children were not enjoying the literacy experience as much as I had anticipated.

(Louise, journal excerpt)

By thinking about something that didn't work and what you might try differently, and then actually trying out ways to make it work, you are engaging in an initial cycle of action research. To remind you of this cycle, we have included Figure 10.1.

Now, let's design a study. Quickly answer the following design questions:

1. Describe a hitch in your practice—something you would like to improve or try out for the first time. Select something that might take a week or so to try out some different actions.
2. What can you try out?

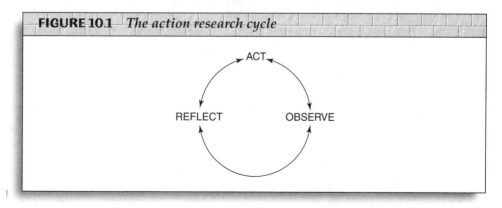

FIGURE 10.1   *The action research cycle*

3. How will you document the process?
4. How will you report and discuss it with others?
5. How will it make life better?

In thinking about your hitch in practice or your aspiration, you were reflecting. By trying out some alternative actions, you were acting. By documenting the process, you were observing the consequences of your actions. By reporting and discussing it with others, you were engaging in collaborative reflection. By thinking about how these actions would make life better and planning for your next steps, you were again reflecting on the consequences of your actions and moving toward more action. You can develop these ideas in "Exploring the Forest."

In research terms, you have just designed a brief proposal for a study, complete with research questions (How can I improve?) and methodology (What can I try out? How will I document the process? How will I report it to others?). You have also given some serious consideration to your own value commitments when you reflected on how it would make life better. This is called a *proposal* because of the tentative nature of design—it needs to be responsive to events and ideas as they unfold.

To be action research, the design (proposal) needs to reflect the characteristics of action research. It is based on (1) ethical commitment to improvement, (2) a cycle of reflective practice, (3) collaborative work, and (4) making our work public for others to examine and critique. Figure 10.2 shows the research language that is used to describe the cycle of action research in the beginning stages of design. As the design process proceeds, we will add ideas to the research cycle that can be used in planning to assess our teaching.

In the next chapters, we will expand on this brief proposal, adding some questions. Even though you may not be ready to tackle all the questions, you will at least be aware of them.

The questions you addressed in the practice study form the framework of your design. They are the elements of design in an action research study. In the next chapters, we fill out that framework with additional questions and practical suggestions. See Figure 10.3.

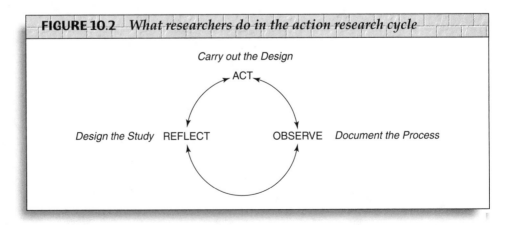

FIGURE 10.2   What researchers do in the action research cycle

Carry out the Design

ACT

Design the Study   REFLECT   OBSERVE   Document the Process

FIGURE 10.3 *Framework for AR project design*

1. What is my research interest? (Chapters 8 and 9)

2. What will I try out in order to improve my practice? (Chapter 11) (McNiff et al., 1996)

3. How will I document the process? (Chapter 11) What are the ethical considerations? Are permissions needed? (Chapter 12)

4. How will I verify that my judgments are trustworthy and credible? (Chapter 12)

5. How will I interpret the data? (Chapter 13)

6. How will I portray what I have learned and make it public? (Chapters 15, 16, 17, 18)

7. How will these actions make life better? What will I do next? (Chapter 14) Who will my critical colleagues be? And the cycle continues. . . . (Chapter 12)

CHAPTER SUMMARY

In Chapter 10, we modeled how to think about hitches, or dissatisfactions, or frustrations in teaching. Through writing about these personally meaningful issues about teaching, we saw how two teachers helped to frame researchable questions from their concerns and reflections.

CHAPTER 11

Elements of Design: Planning and Documenting the Action

In this chapter we think through the actions that might be taken to address research questions. We carefully monitor our actions and document the consequences. Documenting the consequences can be useful in evaluating and assessing to inform change. We try something out and assess the outcomes, both the ones that we predict and the unexpected ones.

What Will I Do to Improve My Practice?
The Action Plan

What is the "action" in action research? Is it activities? Strategies? Or is it something more? Action for Hannah Arendt (1958), involves people engaging with others to effect change. She believes that when people exercise agency in their actions, they experience freedom as they learn who they are. A "good" action accommodates individual voices.

Consistent with Arendt, John Elliott (2003) places action research in the "context of teachers' attempts to effect changes in the conditions governing life in classroom and schools for themselves and their students" (p. 25). Rather than basing actions on the goals and objectives of others, Elliott believes that an action should be driven by the participation of equals (students, teachers, parents) who aspire to realizing their freedom and dignity.

What kind of actions can we carry out in our classrooms *with* our students? How will we ensure that individual voices are heard so that the actions we plan help us to realize our aspirations? Answering the questions *why, who, what, how, when,* and *where* guides our thinking as we design a study. See *Case Study: Ruby's Action Plan* for an example of an action plan. Later in the chapter, we address how the action will be documented. Documentation is an important element of design because the consequences of action are never totally predictable. Accounts are needed so that participants can negotiate and renegotiate meaning and actions.

Ruby's action plan.   Let's take a look at Ruby's action plan as she followed through from the "why" of her study to the "how" she would manage it.

1. Why.   The why of a study reveals our aspirations, our values, our desire to create a just and empowering classroom community. Each time we hitch our practices to our dreams, we create energy. When we hitch our dreams to the dreams of our students, we create energy in our classrooms. When we hitch our mutual dreams to a collective wish for a better life, we create schools with the potential to enhance the quality of life for many students and their teachers.

CASE STUDY

Ruby's Action Plan

Ruby

1. Why:	These activities were chosen for their potential to build a democratic community in my class and model democratic principles that are the foundation of the civics curriculum.
2. Who:	Ninth graders in three college-preparatory civics classes.
3. What:	Community-building activities focusing on collaboration between teachers and students and between students and their peers.
4. When:	A variety of activities tried out and analyzed throughout the 12 weeks of student teaching. Activities will last from a few days to a few weeks.
5. Where:	A large comprehensive high school in a middle- to upper-middle-class, predominantly white suburban community. There is dissension among students, put-downs, lack of respect.
6. How:	Group work (learning pairs, jigsaw, and chapter talks), student choice in selecting groups and topics, and preparation for playing a variety of group roles. Work with mentor in observing and making decisions.

2. Who.   The participants (*who*) of the study engage in action. The teacher-researcher is a participant as are students. Some teachers want to study an aspect of *all* their classes and *all* their students. Progressively they begin to focus their attention on a few classes or a few students. The Literature Circles Study is an example of this focus—what we affectionately call the "big data–little data" design. In this design, data are collected for all students, but analyzed for only some.

Or after collecting data for the whole group at the beginning of a study, we narrow our focus to a smaller group. We may be drawn to study students who resist our efforts, or who excel in spite of our hunches that they will not do well. As our questions become more focused, so, too, might our samples. In some studies (e.g., Jen), a case study design of an individual is most appropriate right from the beginning. If we are tutoring students, we may, for example, want to conduct an action research study with them.

In summary, we can start with a wide-angle lens and progressively focus, or start with a zoom lens and shift outward to a broader perspective. No matter the size of the sample, our new knowledge becomes a part of our teaching for all our students.

We can describe participants as individuals or as members of a group. For individuals, we can describe what we know about them, how they respond in class, what we know of their knowledge, how they interact with other children, family context, and so on. We can provide a rich description of our students and classrooms based on our observations and insights.

For example, Ruby wrote in her proposal: "My cooperating teacher and I noted that the students in the civics classes rarely participated in class discussion. . . . a few students tended to dominate, opinions were rarely supported by evidence, and there was little interest in civics as a course of study."

We can also include available demographic information that describes students as members of a larger group, information such as ethnic background, socio-economic status, gender, and academic achievement. This is sometimes referred to as *objective* or *face sheet data*. If appropriate, we can include test scores, inventories, or other information gathered from a counselor, social worker, special education teacher, tutor, and so on, as part of a larger evaluation process.

We use the term *participants* rather than *subjects*, the term typically used in many types of research. Participants can take roles in planning, directing, analyzing, and interpreting, whereas the term subject implies a more passive role. Students, parents, community members, other teachers, and administrators can be fully involved members of your research team.

3. What and how.   Before deciding on *what* to do and *how* to do it, consider a variety of alternative actions. Brainstorm strategies from the literature, colleagues, and experience as effective starting points. Keep in mind the purpose of the study; the criteria by which to judge outcomes; the time, effort, and resources that will be required; and the strategies likely to help us to accomplish the task.

Shawn wanted ESL strategies and practices that would benefit all students' language development and additional strategies that could be applied to helping

CASE STUDY

Ruby

Excerpts from Ruby's Schedule

Date to start	What will happen?	For how long? How often?	Who will be involved?
February 10	Pretest: Classroom community survey	15 minutes	All 86 students in three civics classes
February 11	Bill of Rights	Every day for 2 weeks	All 86 students
	Project—students choose topic, group members, due date	10 weeks	
February 12	Weekly student reflection journals	Students write twice a week and turn in on Fridays	All 86 students
March 25	Classroom compact activity	3 days	All 86 students
April 5	Posttest: Classroom community survey	15 minutes	All 86 students

Jen in language, reading, and socialization. A larger vocabulary was one criterion for success, so a periodic vocabulary quiz was a way to accomplish this. Shawn also monitored Jen's daily journal for evidence of Jen's developing use of written English.

4. When.   *When* refers to a time period and schedule of activities. When will the study start? How often will a particular strategy be used (frequency)? For how long each time (duration)? For how long will data be collected? Which participants will be involved at what time? When will the study conclude? How will you know? By developing a schedule that breaks the study down into a sequence of steps, we make what may seem to be overwhelming, more manageable. The key is to remain flexible. *Case Study: Excerpts from Ruby's Schedule* is a schedule for Ruby's Democratic Classroom Study.

5. Where.   The *where* of a study is the physical, social, and cultural context. We might describe a school building as old but comfortable, in a neighborhood of small, tidy homes. Or we might describe a school building as a massive three-story brick building with a leaky roof, a maze of darkened hallways, and chipped metal bars over the windows in a neighborhood forgotten by municipal services.

Some of us have little knowledge about the overall student population we serve or the family and community context in which students live. To know our students involves knowing about their communities. While our own classroom, team, or school provides an immediate context, our district, state, province, and country also shape our lives and the lives of our students. School districts provide demographic data (ethnic composition, social class) and ways in which students are categorized for services (gifted, limited English proficiency) and percentages of students in those categories. The location of the school (urban, rural, suburban, small town) can be a useful descriptor. Realtor Web sites also provide demographic information.

How Will I Document the Process?

The reflective teaching process necessitates ongoing documentation. A scholar *learns from experience.* We will talk about many ways to document experience in this chapter and ways to "house" those data in an organized fashion so that we can draw evidence from them in order to interpret and make public our new understandings.

Use your journal to reflect and store data. Although we each must develop our own ways of organizing and making sense of our data, you may want to section off the journal so that you can easily maneuver between data sources: a general section for daily recording and another section for autobiographical writing, such as we did in Chapter 6, and then sections for interviews, observations, and documents. If your journal is electronic, create separate files for each section, as it will be easier to locate, add to, modify, and analyze data.

In documenting the process of AR, noting the consequences is important. The term *consequences* is a useful one because it alerts us to the importance of paying attention to what happens to student learning, to ourselves, and to our situation when we try out something new or modify an existing practice.

Because we are inquiring into our teaching (actions) *and* the self (motives, assumptions) that teaches, data are often not separate from self as is the case in other forms of research. In traditional research, collecting data is a means of accumulating information (that becomes evidence). Explicitly or implicitly we may be trying to prove a point; for example, that one method of teaching is better than another. But in AR, our data are often *in* our teaching. Data are used to problematize the many assumptions we make about teaching and to redefine our relationships with one another (we shall soon see how a student's poem helps Ruby and her students reconsider their relationships with one another).

The term *consequences* is not to be confused with the way it is used in other types of research. As you might recall, in experimental studies researchers seek cause-effect relationships. If the teacher does X, then Y happens. Classroom life is much more complex than a one-way relationship between our actions and what happens to our students. We know, for example, that our assumptions "color" what is happening. (Recall the teacher on the Native American reservation who thought her students were not interested in books?) For this reason, action researchers build multiple sources of data into their studies and consider multiple points of view as they interpret the data. Not only must we be cautious in thinking that we *cause* specific things to happen, but also we must pay close attention to *how* we and others are constructing the situation.

The term *evidence* is an apt description of the information a teacher gathers related to the consequences of actions taken. Just as an explorer looks for evidence of cultural life in footprints, pottery, clothing, furniture, and written artifacts from ancient civilizations, good teachers look for evidence of the social, intellectual, and ethical consequences of actions in student learning, personal and professional growth, and equality of relationships. So a corollary question to *How will I document the process?* is *What evidence will I collect to show the consequences of these actions?*

Brought to critical colleagues and students, data provide an opportunity for discussion. In verifying "truth as we see it," we come to learn the values and beliefs we share. The rest of this chapter is about how groups come to verify particular data as evidence of growth, learning, and equality of relationships.

Every day we are bombarded with lots of *information*. Some of it is useful; for example, the telephone number of a friend. Much is not. For information to be useful, it has to fit our purposes. That a student scores in the 25th percentile on a test of reading comprehension is information. What makes it data is our interest in this student's score as a baseline. As a researcher, you gather information and when (and if) you invest it with interest, it becomes *data*. Data may also become further differentiated into *evidence* if you use it to make a point in your study. Simplified, it might look something like this:

Information ➙ Data ➙ Evidence ➙ Interpretation and portrayal

We continue to filter information related to our purposes. Finally, we interpret what it means in the context of our projects, and we portray it to share with others. The latter processes, interpretation and portrayal, are very important to the success of our efforts. We will talk about these in Chapter 13 and Section VII. What this process and all the terms have in common is that they depend on professional judgment. Harry Wolcott (1994), a well-respected ethnographer, places more emphasis on what you *do* with these data and evidence (that is, how you interpret and portray data) than on what you gather in your fieldwork.

What we *do* (analyze, interpret, portray) with what we have depends, at least in part, on our professional judgment, and this takes us back to those domains of development we talked about earlier: cognitive, moral-ethical, and psychological. We grow toward cognitive complexity, moral-ethical commitments, and psychological maturity and health as we exercise our professional judgment. These qualities are inextricably linked to ongoing assessment of our students and ourselves. To conduct ongoing assessment or, more broadly termed, formative evaluation, we use different *methods of data collection, verification,* and *interpretation* (the latter two will be developed in greater depth in Chapter 13).

In what ways might you observe, interview, and study documents prepared by others? You probably already use many of these and have not considered them research techniques, but that is what they are. In Figure 11.1 we have adapted from Wolcott (1992) three major forms of data collection and sampling techniques. Notice that there is some overlap in that one technique may seem to fit into several different forms of data collection.

Each tool may be loosely or tightly structured, depending on where we are in the study and the purpose of our studies. Interviews can be standardized or casual and open-ended. Observations can be as open and expansive as the horizon, or as close and highly focused as observing the sounds of particles of sand slipping through the hourglass.

The scholar's tools are often complementary and used together to study life in classrooms. For example, we may interview our students based on our observations of their work and/or analysis of their papers (artifacts). And then, as a result of our interviewing, we observe differently. We might also teach differently, and students' work may change as a result.

Next we will present each of the major forms of data collection used by action researchers. We have included a variety of examples and practical tips of the work of action researchers as a starting point for thinking about data collection strategies you may want to develop.

FIGURE 11.1 *The tools of professional scholarship: Data collection*

Observing	Interviewing	Examining Documents and Other Data Sources
Experiencing Through Our Senses	*Inquiring into the Experiences and Thoughts of Others*	*Examining Documents and Artifacts*
Note taking and field notes	Informal interview	Personal-experience methods
Shadow study	Formal interview	Student work
Anecdotal record	Questionnaire	Photographs and video and audio
Log, diary/video diary, journal	Attitude scale	Recording
Checklist	Checklist	Technology
Rating scale	Rating scale	Physical traces
	Critical incident interview	
	Sociogram	
	Projective technique	
	Creative visualization	
	Focus group interview	

Three categories are from Wolcott, 1992.

Observing

Observation is foundational in research. Whether we decide to observe at a distance (intervening as little as possible into what is observed) or to become a full-fledged *participant-observer* (engaging to different degrees with the observed person or activity), or anything in between, knowing what to look for, how to apprehend it, and how to describe it for later reflection is a key element of the evolving repertoire of scholars.

A key element of being an observant scholar is intuition. Although we may think that research is a strictly procedural process, intuition is as important to observation as the techniques we will share with you in this section. In fact, many of us, including Albert Einstein, think that intuition and its friend, imagination, are more important than knowledge. Thankfully we can use all three in our research.

Intuition is based in part on experience and points us toward certain kinds of information, which can lead to knowledge. At the same time, knowledge can make certain kinds of intuition possible. (In "Exploring the Forest" at the conclusion of this section, we will help you make use of your intuition.) How we describe what we see is as important as what we see, for when we describe a phenomenon, we open the possibility of seeing it differently. The richer the description, the fuller the observation will be—and the richer the eyes that behold!

While it may be easy to look into our classrooms, it is much harder—and much more fun and profitable—to *see* into them. Looking is an act; seeing is an accomplishment (Eisner, 1985). John Moffit has written a poem that makes this point very well.

To Look at Any Thing

To look at any thing,
If you would know that thing,
You must look at it long;
to look at this green and say
'I have seen spring in these
Woods,' will not do—you must
Be the thing you see:
You must be the dark snakes of
Stems and ferny plumes of leaves,
You must enter in
To the small silences between
the leaves,
You must take your time
and touch the very peace
They issue from.

Source: Dunning et al. (1966, p. 21).

We develop the ability to see by looking with intent, by practicing conscious looking and seeing. This is part of what it means to be a scholar—to develop our abilities and capacities to see. We have also used the terms *educational connoisseurs* and *critics*. This is what Kathy did when she started to see what was going on in her classroom. She started to develop her ability to see as she focused more carefully on her children's responses to the letter of the week. And she did it by paying attention to her feelings. They told her something wasn't right, and she did something as a result. The results were a product of her courage to take *informed* action.

Our aim in observing is to develop understanding and empathy. We can do this, in part, by writing what is often called *thick description*. It is the difference between describing the reeds in the pond as tall green grass and as "dark snakes of stems and ferny plumes of leaves" where you "enter into the small silences between the leaves."

Because we are so immersed in classroom life, we "know" a great deal about what is going on. But for us to be action researchers, we must step back from our intense involvement and become more *self-conscious* of our roles as participant-observers. This may require us to give up some of the beliefs that limit our vision.

In the early stages of research, our observations tend to be broadly focused. Who is here? What is going on? What are the emotions that are being expressed (our own included)? When are things occurring? How long do they last? How is space being used? In other words, we make general observations about who, what, when, where, and how, taking into account participants, activities, goals, emotions, time, and space (Spradley, 1980).

As we describe our observations and record hunches, these may in turn shape the focus of new observations. Like photographers, we might survey the broad landscape and then zoom in on specific views and zoom out again to broader views. In this way we can see events, artifacts, and people in context. This process of zooming in and out enables us to better ground our observations and interpretations.

A story will illustrate our point. Franki, a third/fourth-grade multiage teacher, schedules the first hour of each day as exploratory learning time in which students choose from a diversity of activities. One pair of boys, Franki observed with worry, did the same thing each day. One of the pair constructed a building from Lego-type building toys, and the other constructed a vehicle from the same materials. At the end of the exploratory hour, the boys staged a huge crash, destroying both structures. Franki's initial judgment was that the pair was acting out violent and aggressive behavior. She held back and observed for weeks, debating whether to intervene. Finally, she decided to query the boys as to their project. They explained carefully and articulately how after each crash, they studied the weak points in their respective structures. Each day, they tried to engineer a modification to their respective structures that would better withstand impact. Franki's first assumptions didn't come close to understanding the sophistication and complexity of what was going on. By observing and reflecting on repeated observations, Franki illustrates the kind of professional judgment used by "complex thinkers," "socially responsible feelers," and "emotionally mature adults."

At other times we might miss a great deal if we wait too long to make judgments. By making tentative hypotheses early on, we can then produce and examine data to confirm or disconfirm those hunches.

Another consideration in using observational methods is whether to focus on an individual, a group, or both. Most often we use a combination, perhaps starting with a group and then zooming in to an individual or vice versa.

Note taking and field notes.   Recording notes about observations (as well as interviews, artifacts, and documents) is the most common method used by the action researcher to describe what is occurring. Field notes are direct observations of what is being said and done as well as impressions or hunches of the observer. They are called *field* notes because they are taken in the field—the classroom or school setting. In the shadow study described next, the notes taken in the space provided in the chart would be called field notes.

Writing down our observations and reflecting on them helps us to become aware of the point of view from which we observe. *We are never neutral in our observations.* We observe with a limited eye, both informed and constrained by our cultural lenses. We may observe with a sympathetic eye because we have ourselves been in such a situation. We may observe with a critical eye for the injustices we see in the way students are treated. We may observe with an eye toward seeing how efficiently things can be done, or an eye toward understanding the perspective of the other. Being fully present and open to experiences around us allows us to see and understand more of the complexity of our classrooms.

Recording that complexity through rich detail will help us as we try to analyze and synthesize what we have observed. In Chapter 15 we will further explore the possibilities of writing down our observations. You may want to turn to those beginning pages of Chapter 15 on *writing up, writing down,* and *writing about* before you read further in this chapter. They may inspire you in your note-taking adventures!

There are a variety of types of field notes:

- Running record—recording regularly occurring events such as attendance.
- Time intervals—recording what is happening at regular intervals, such as quickly "sweeping" the classroom every 5 minutes to see what kinds of conversations students are having during computer time.
- Specified events—recording every time a specified event occurs, such as students asking questions of their peers during discussion (as opposed to asking the teacher).
- Critical incident—recording moments that seem to be pivotal points in a study, such as the moment a teacher realizes that it is only the male students who are objecting to reading a particular novel, not the entire class.
- Anecdotal record—recording incidents that show growth over time (more on this later).

A variety of time-saving approaches are possible. Recording the date, time, and focus of observations helps to locate data and verify findings. When recording multiple events or using multiple columns, one for each category is useful. At other times, keeping a wide right-hand margin for impressions and hunches is preferable. Either way encourages the researcher to begin analyzing data early on, which may lead to focusing the question. Ongoing analysis may also lead to a change in research strategy. For example, by reading over field notes, a researcher might decide to write in the margins that note taking during interviews detracts from the ability to listen to what students are saying, hence the decision to get permission to tape-record. (While this may seem an easy solution, keep in mind that for every 7 minutes of tape recording, it takes about 1 hour to transcribe it!) While we typically associate note taking with a pen or pencil and paper, technology can be helpful, too. Laptop computers and even handheld "palm" computers may speed up note taking and increase accuracy. Suggestions for note taking are presented in Stepping Stones 11.1: Note Taking.

Several observational techniques are useful to action researchers. These techniques allow us to focus on individuals, groups, classrooms, and larger contexts. We will begin with techniques for gaining appreciation and empathy for the experiences of our students.

Shadow study.   A shadow study of an individual student can be good practice at focusing our observations, and it can help us derive insights from firsthand experience of what it is like to be a student. When we immerse ourselves in the life of another, we can develop an understanding of how that person makes sense of school, knowledge that is of critical importance for understanding how we can negotiate our own roles as teachers (Bullough and Gitlin, 1995).

There are many ways to conduct a shadow study. Here are a few strategies that researchers have found helpful.

1. Select a student whose experience of school is considerably different from your own experience. Gain written permission from the parent and verbal permission from the student to spend an entire day shadowing the student.
2. Record information about the student that is readily observable or available, for example, grade level, gender, ethnicity. At 5- to 7-minute intervals, record the specific behaviors your student is engaged in. In separate columns record information about the environment of the classroom, study hall, hallway, and so on, and any impressions, hunches about what is going on, ideas, and personal feelings.
3. At some point during the day, conduct an informal interview with the student to check out emerging hypotheses or to gain further insight into the student's perception of school. For example, you might ask: Is there an adult at this school in whom you can confide? What is your favorite class? Your least favorite? What do you like most/least about this school?

Case Study: Excerpts from Shadow Study of Joe was conducted by Rick in the weeks just prior to student teaching. Rick, whose own high school experiences were in the college-bound accelerated mathematics program, spent the day with a more relaxed, vocational student named Joe. The example illustrates several ideas: the importance of separating our opinions (to the extent that we are able) from observable facts; the way in which hunches propel our observations to test out

STEPPING STONES 11.1

Note Taking

Keeping field notes can be time-consuming. There are a few shortcuts that inventive teachers have designed to make the task more efficient and less disruptive to teaching. Power (1996) suggests the following:

1. Set goals for each note-taking session.
2. Establish a routine—if outside of the classroom, find a favorite place, a favorite pen, favorite music, a set time with a "Do Not Disturb" sign.
3. Experiment with different times (during or after the fact) and different places.
4. Experiment with different tools—index cards or address labels for anecdotal records that later can be arranged in a way that makes sense; project planner paper with two columns, one for student records of the day's events and one for teacher comments; a computer; a transcribing machine; loose-leaf paper; carbon paper, saving the time of going to a copy machine; a large notebook to store tools.
5. Develop personal shorthand codes, such as T for teacher or S for student. This will help to speed up writing.
6. If you are a fast typist, you may want to consider the following technical devices:
   - Carry a laptop with you and type your notes directly using a Word processing program. Or if you can connect your computer online, you can also use an online program such as blog or wiki. Although known as a search engine, Google offers lots of convenient tools online such as Word and Spreadsheet (http://docs.google.com/).
   - Take a PDA (personal digital assistant) with you. It is common for a PDA to be a cell phone at the same time. You can make phone calls, use Microsoft Office tools, e-mail, text message, record voice, take pictures and short videos, and play music with this device. In addition, attaching a folding keyboard to the PDA allows you to type using a regular keyboard. With a USB connection, you can connect a PDA to a computer and transfer files and data between the two.
   - Take a digital recorder with you to record your thoughts. Sometimes you may just want to think aloud to sort things out. You can later play back and write them down. In fact, you can also use a voice recognition software such as Dragon Naturally Speaking (http://www.nuance.com/naturallyspeaking/) to convert your voice automatically into a text format.
7. Make sure you have enough batteries or battery power for any electronic device you use so that you will not lose power in the middle of note taking. Using a technical device may appear to be inconvenient at the beginning, but it will save time typing and organizing notes in the long run.

Excerpts from Shadow Study of Joe

Student Pseudonym: Joe   **Grade**: 11   **Age**: 16   **Gender**: Male
Racial/Ethnic Group: Caucasian **Regular/Special Education/Ability Group**: Vocational
Date: Nov. 19   **Starting Time**: 7:50 A.M.   **Ending Time**: 2:45 P.M.
Observer: Rick

Time	Specific Student Behavior at 5- to 7-Minute Intervals	Environment (what is happening in class, halls; teacher, activities, room arrangement, sounds . . .)	Researcher Impressions, Hunches, Ideas
7:50 A.M.	Fidgeting, looking up and around	First period social studies. Older, white male teacher. Quiz on Spanish-American war. Twenty-six students seated in rows.	Student forgot to meet me in hall. I went into class without him. Body language is telling me that he is uncertain about answers.
7:55 A.M.	Raised hand and told teacher that he would only be in class for 10 minutes the following day because of his involvement in the play.	Teacher writes in grade book; turns out lights and starts movie on Spanish-American War.	
8:00 A.M.	Holds his head while watching movie.	Teacher grades papers; handful of students looking drowsy; movie sounds coming from next door.	"The Indians would never rise again. . . ." This violent cartoon version of conflict with native people was too simplistic.
8:05 A.M.	Watching, holds up head; looks at nails.	Teacher grades papers; interjects, "Remember this information"; students are fidgety.	"With leaders like Roosevelt, we had to find new worlds to conquer" is such an imperialistic attitude— this movie bugs me.
8:10 A.M.	Watching, holds up head, looks at nails; yawns.	Eight students have heads on desks.	Students have no opportunity for engagement in learning during movie, which seems so stereotypical and removed from their experiences.

Later that day

10:28 A.M.	Operating cash register in school restaurant. Taking orders, ringing them up, bantering with students and teachers.	Fourth period, culinary arts. Teacher is absent so restaurant is closed except for carry-out. Phone continues to ring with orders.	Hectic atmosphere, but Joe seems to enjoy it. This would be exciting for me if I did this. No such experience for me as a college-preparatory high school student.

Excerpts from Shadow Study of Joe

Time	Specific Student Behavior at 5- to 7-Minute Intervals	Environment (what is happening in class, halls; teacher, activities, room arrangement, sounds . . .)	Researcher Impressions, Hunches, Ideas
10:35 A.M.	"Out of $5? Is that $4.25 or $3.75?"	Cash register clicking out bills. Students standing in line, some poking each other.	I just sit and watch, hungry, but should I order lunch? I decide to just be an observer, though my stomach is growling.
10:40 A.M.	"Did you come to bother me? I don't have time for this! . . . I don't care what he said. She loves me cause I was born on Walt Disney's birthday." Gets a little flushed when teacher discusses change for order. Takes a minute to figure it out.	Hectic. Ten students waiting for orders.	Seems to have settled into the pattern. Getting past the hectic time. Gets more talkative. He takes things in stride and seems to juggle work and play.
Later that day			
1:57 P.M.	"It's the gingerbread man," Joe announces himself to the class.	Eighth period, geometry. Teacher walks around to check homework. Students settle down.	In between classes Joe said he dislikes most classes except English and culinary arts. He doesn't mention anything about geometry—probably because he knows that I am a practicum student for the geometry teacher. Even though he seems open, there is that subtle student reservation around me as a teacher—I don't like this!
2:00 P.M.	Yawns and looks at nails and writes something down.	Says, "We'll go over homework for the next 20 minutes."	Most of day seems to value intellectual work over physical work. Are these classist notions of work? I must remember to do some more reading in this area.

those hunches; and the way in which we can use observations to zoom in and out from individual to group, to larger context.

Notice how in the columns for behavior and environment Rick describes the actions of Joe and the classroom environment without interjecting personal opinions or feelings. In the column labeled "Impressions, hunches, ideas," we learn a great deal about what Rick is thinking and feeling. This column includes hunches, personal feelings, and ways to change the methods used to conduct the shadow study.

Rick's use of the final column illustrates the development of his emerging theory about student engagement. We often have our own ideas about what student engagement means, and we observe students to see if they are raising their hands, responding to questions, doing their assignments, and participating in activities. But Rick begins to pay attention to the quality of the *opportunities* to engage in meaningful learning and hypothesizes that we do not always provide these opportunities for students. Rick's concern that schools reinforce classist stereotypes (for college-bound "upper-class" students, schools emphasize the importance of the intellect whereas for vocational students the physical is emphasized) is one that will require investigation beyond this brief study. This hunch, however, is rooted in careful observations and problematizes the concept of engagement.

Rick's decision to forgo lunch and remain an observer was a methodological decision. Reflecting on and noting changes (changes in planned activities), we are making important decisions about methodology. Keeping a record of these changes can help us to make better informed decisions.

Finally, we may want to record experiences from our personal lives that may shape how we observe and how we act. Moods, prior experiences, and mental and physical health all influence our teaching and our observations. Rick's negative attitude toward what he perceives to be a shallow, imperialistic portrayal of Native Americans in the movie is important to keep separate from Joe's attitudes. Joe may or may not share those feelings.

Often the student being shadowed will request to look at the notes. Share them! If you want to record personal commentary, not appropriate for a student to see, record it in a separate place. (This piece of advice applies to any type of data collection activity. Many teachers keep separate journals at home for private reflections that help them make sense of their school life.)

Occasionally prospective teachers are uncomfortable with the idea of shadowing a student. Their concerns center on invading privacy. This issue should be taken seriously. Feelings of discomfort are natural; they tend to diminish as the day goes on. Students who agree to participate in shadow studies typically welcome the interest of another person. One resource that has been helpful to those hesitant to undertake such a study is Fine and Sandstrom's (1988) *Knowing Children: Participant Observation with Minors*.

Anecdotal record.   Anecdotal records are factual descriptions capturing incidents that a teacher observes. They are useful in recording changes over time, particularly when they include a separate interpretation of the incident. Anecdotal records are like a verbal camera that records what is being observed.

Joanne recorded anecdotal entries as part of a study of students' use of journals in a graduate course. One incident involved Terry, a student in her middle forties who was returning to school for the first time in 20 years. See *Case Study: Anecdotal Record and Reflection from Joanne's Master's Degree Class.* By filing anecdotal records on index cards, adhesive labels, or in the computer, the action researcher can easily organize and reorganize them for later data analysis.

Log, diary, journal.   As we discussed in "Exploring the Forest" in Section I, there are many different types of personal written documents and, depending on the discipline, there are slightly different definitions of terms. Some people use *diary* and *journal* interchangeably, while others use *journal* and *researcher log* as equivalent. On our journey together we use journals as the evolving and reflective professional

CASE STUDY

Anecdotal Record and Reflection from Joanne's Master's Degree Class

Class: Curriculum and Organization in the Middle Grades

Date: July 17   **Student:**   Terry

Place: College of Education   **Observer:**   Joanne

As students filed out of class after picking up their journals, I asked Terry if I could speak with her. She looked terrified. "Have I said something wrong in my journal?" she asked.

"I am just concerned about several comments you made in your journal that my expectations of you are too high, particularly in your journal writing," I replied. I assured her that her work was exemplary. "Are you feeling overwhelmed by all the requirements in a 5-week summer session? Do your ideas differ from mine about the purpose of a journal? [I had asked them to reflect on readings and class activities, and her writing was more of a summary.] Or do you truly feel that my expectations of you are too high?"

Tears welled in her eyes as she haltingly said, "I just lack confidence. It has been so long that I have been in school, and your enthusiasm for what we are learning is somewhat intimidating. I am not sure I can be as excited as you are for what you want us to do. I also think that a journal is a place to say whatever we want to say, and I resent having to do the kind of reflection you want us to do."

Reflection

Terry's work was always creative and thorough. But when it came to the journal, she did not reflect on readings and class activities as I had asked. I asked students to use their journals as a place to reflect on *academic* matters because I myself did not like to write personal reflections to be read by an instructor whom I hardly knew. When asked to do so, I revealed very little about how I really felt. By structuring the journal in this way, I sought to minimize the invasion of privacy that I assumed everyone would feel. I still need to explore with students how journals can be used in academic settings. I think that we overuse them, and sometimes it can turn to abuse.

document that holds our perceptions, plans, descriptions, explorations, and exercises, as well as our trepidations and interpretations. They contain diary and log-type writing and become richer as we continue to develop. As our research evolves, we will use the journal in more specific and complex ways. We will return to our descriptive data to interpret and make sense of them from different perspectives. Logs and diaries, case records, field and dialogue journals, and many other kinds of documents can be used as data sources to record and study observations.

1. *Log.* Have you ever watched Star Trek? The Captain's Log, like other ships' logs, can contain considerable detail and be important in establishing events and circumstances. Simply put, a log is a running record of transactions. Incidents such as phone conversations with parents and daily attendance, while simpler than a ship's log, can provide useful information for the researcher and are here referred to as researcher logs. *Case Study: Ruby's Researcher Log of Classroom Activities* shows how Ruby's log was used to keep track of the various activities designed to create a more democratic classroom. Each activity was carefully developed to respond to situations that arose in the classroom. Another type of researcher log can be found in *Case Study: Roberto's Researcher Log* in which Roberto uses detail in a functional, concise, and highly focused way.

2. *Diary or video/audio diary.* A diary is a personal, unedited account of feelings and thoughts. For example, you might keep a diary of personal conversations related to your research to return to later. Videotaping might be preferable for those who enjoy verbally and visually recording personal reflections. Videotaping oneself at regular, convenient intervals such as in the evening after dinner, Saturday mornings, or during lunchtime may provide clues, for example, to understanding one's development as a teacher.

As a personal document, the journal is a potent tool to collect, analyze, and interpret data. A journal can take many forms. Perhaps you can add to this list.

CASE STUDY

Ruby's Researcher Log of Classroom Activities

Date	Community-Building Activities
2/11	Jigsaw discussions—to emphasize importance of participation.
2/17	Presentations on Bill of Rights—to emphasize the importance of rights.
3/5	Class compact—to encourage students to examine values and build agreement.
4/15	Show movie "Rigoletto," film about prejudice based on physical appearance.
5/4	Personal values project—students demonstrate a deeply held personal value.

Ruby

CASE STUDY   Roberto's Researcher Log

Roberto

Log for Week of November 17

Observer: Roberto

Note: Students with multiple handicaps are referred to as students A, B, C, D.

Wood fabrication (inclusion class): Student A came into the classroom, and typical students did not talk to him or pay attention to him. A typical student said "hi" to student B as he walked into the classroom. Student C initiated a conversation with a nonhandicapped peer by asking, "Do you like the car I made?" The typical student answered, "Yes."

Cafeteria: Typical students move from a table where their peers with disabilities are eating lunch.

Hallway: A typical student waved and said, "Hi, how's it going?" to student D. (They had gone to elementary school together.)

Home economics (inclusion class): One of the typical students did not even talk to her own cousin, a "special" student integrated in home economics.

3. *Dialogue journal.* A dialogue journal is used to converse with someone else about thoughts, feelings, and incidents. It may be used by both teachers and students to describe, interpret, reflect, and evaluate. In a dialogue journal, teachers respond to the writer's questions, concerns, and thinking on topics chosen by both students and teachers. These interactive journals allow writers (students, colleagues) the opportunity for a one-on-one tutorial and provide teachers with curriculum ideas to extend and enrich development. The journals also give students and teachers the chance to evaluate their curriculum experiences. A traveling journal is an ongoing conversation among a student teacher, mentor teacher, and university mentor that travels among these three people.

4. *Researcher journal.* A researcher journal is a place to record issues that arise related to research, such as research methods; hypotheses; evolving research questions; reminders to ourselves to follow up on things, such as books to read, people to consult, and additional data to collect related to hypotheses; and analytic memos (ongoing analyses and interpretation). Shawn's Researcher Journal was a comprehensive recording of the development of Jen's literacy. A few entries shown in *Case Study: Shawn's Researcher Journal of Jen's Literacy Development* illustrate the dramatic leaps in learning that occurred in a very short time.

   Shawn's journal entries note daily observations as well as periodic benchmarks. The growth in Jen's vocabulary from February 24 to March 14 is

CASE STUDY

Shawn's Researcher Journal of Jen's Literacy Development

Shawn

1/27 (first entry)

I have been working with Jen on a one-to-one, daily basis. We are keeping a journal and labeling pictures that she has drawn. I am having her form "sentences" about the picture. She seems to be good at writing and labeling the things that she knows. She has a hard time sounding out the names of unfamiliar things. She is not aware of the text that she is creating.

2/24

Today I quizzed Jen on basic sight words commonly used by second graders. Out of 108 words, she recognized 47 words. She was able to correctly use 30 of the 47 words in a sentence or phrase. I could see that she was understanding the meaning of the words.

3/14

I quizzed Jen on basic sight word flash cards. Out of 100 words, she was able to correctly read 79 words and use 68 of them in phrases or show me what the word meant.

one source of evidence that her language development and literacy are both proceeding rapidly.

Roberto's researcher journal contained systematic observations of the social interactions of students with multiple handicaps and their "typical" peers—in the hallways, cafeteria, and classrooms. Several journal entries show the development of Roberto's hunch that there was little interaction between the students in his class and other students. He used this hunch to focus observations.

Noting the pattern of alienation that occurred repeatedly during the week, Roberto concluded: "Somehow the relationships that inclusion was supposed to be fostering were just not happening" (November 24, Roberto's journal).

Roberto used the data to problematize a belief held by district advocates of inclusion—that it would naturally foster the social acceptance of students labeled *special education students*. Based on these focused observations and years of experience, Roberto decided to start the S.T.A.R. Club.

5. *Multiple text journals.* A multiple text journal (such as the one used in the shadow study) is a type of journal that allows the researcher to record different kinds of observations and reflections. Forming columns is one way to organize the data.

In addition to the information we have provided, there are several useful sources on logs, journals, and diaries. They include Holly's (1989) *Writing to Grow: Keeping a Personal-Professional Journal*, Connelly and Clandinin's (1988) *Teachers as Curriculum Planners: Narratives of Experience*, and Grumet's (1990) *Retrospective: Autobiography and the Analysis of Educational Experience*.

Checklist.   The checklist is a structured observation instrument. It is "a list of points to notice in direct observation [and] used to focus the observer's attention to the presence, absence, or frequency of occurrence of each point of the prepared list as indicated by check marks" (Hopkins and Antes, 1985, p. 467). Checklists may include data that remain the same, such as ethnicity/race, gender, and time, and data that describe attributes that may change, such as *withdrawn* or *extroverted*. A checklist might simply list the relevant points and ask, "Yes or no?" Points on the checklist need to be related to the goal of the study, and as many action researchers have found, using a checklist developed by someone else may be confusing if the points are not directly related to the study. For that reason, many action researchers, such as Jon and Terry in their Literature Circles Study, prefer to create their own checklists. They created a checklist indicating student preparation for literature circles and participated in group activities to look for when their students met in literature circles. See *Case Study: Checklist of Literature Circle Indicators Showing Participation and Preparation*.

Rating scale.   Another structured observation instrument is a rating scale used by an action researcher or student to evaluate a particular behavior or activity along a continuum. McKernan (1996) suggests that they are particularly useful in observing social and personal development in areas such as cooperativeness,

CASE STUDY   **Checklist of Literature Circle Indicators Showing Participation and Preparation**

Student_____   Date_____   Y = yes, N = no

Jon

Terry

Brought materials to class	_____
Participated in discussion	_____
Worked cooperatively	_____
Completed assignment	_____
Took notes	_____
Made predictions	_____
Used context to understand	_____

industriousness, tolerance for difference, enthusiasm, and group skills, among others. We present four types:

1. *Category rating scale.* The rater selects the category that best describes what is being rated.

    How often does the student participate in discussion?

    Never ___   Seldom ___   Occasionally ___   Frequently ___   Always ___

2. *Numeric rating scale.* Rating on a numbered scale from 1 to 5 (or any number up to 10) lends itself to later statistical analysis.

    Student explains problem situation

    (1) Very clearly . . . ; (5) Very unclearly

3. *Graphic rating scale.* The rater places a check mark along a lined continuum. The advantage is that the rater is not restricted to a particular category or number. It is widely used.

    During literature circle discussions, the student participates:

Always	Frequently	Occasionally	Seldom	Never
1	2	3	4	5

4. *Pictorial rating scale.* This can be used by teachers to rate observations and provide feedback on student work. Students are often asked to express their attitudes about something by using a humorous cartoon-type rating scale. For example, the smiley faces in *Case Study: Pictorial Rating Scale* have been used with young children.

In constructing a rating scale, we suggest that it rate substantive as opposed to trivial activities; that the scale use no less than three and no more than seven points; that more than one rater be used; that it avoids putting personal biases into the wording of the question, avoids double negatives, and keeps the items short, rating one item at a time. It is also important, as with other types of structured observation instruments, to test it first with a small sample to work out the kinks.

CASE STUDY   **Pictorial Rating Scale**

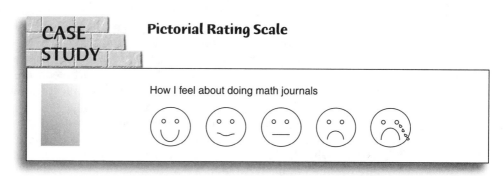

How I feel about doing math journals

We have found several useful resources for constructing observation instruments. They include Borich's (1999) *Observation Skills for Effective Teaching*, Hubbard and Power's (1999) *Living the Questions: A Guide for Teacher Researchers*, and McKernan's (1996) *Curriculum Action Research*.

Careful observation and thoughtful description are especially important in the beginning stages of research because they help us to develop a context, focus our research interests, and gain appreciation for others' perceptions. Because of its valuable role in evaluation, many teachers are now building observation time into their schedules. Based on observations and the questions and hypotheses that emerge from them, action researchers can follow up observations with interviews to create a richer picture of what is happening.

Interviewing

In trying to understand the perspectives of students, teachers can conduct interviews, both formal and informal, as a regular part of teaching. The interview may be as informal as Shawn asking Jen to label pictures of things commonly found in the classroom, Jon and Terry asking a literature circle to tell them how the group went that day and what the most valuable part of being in a literature circle was, talking with a student during an editing meeting, or asking a mathematics student how she or he solved a particular problem. In each of these cases, the teacher is trying to *understand* what the student is thinking or doing and how that person views the world.

On the other hand, an interview can be as formal as Ruby's Democratic Classroom Survey, adapted from a survey she found in a journal and administered at the beginning and end of her student teaching. Or, it can be as formal as evaluation instruments that we ask our students to complete at the end of a course. Formal interview instruments are typically designed to enable the researcher to explain a pattern of student responses. Interview questions and answers can be written, drawn, or verbal, or a mixture of these. Questions can be open-ended, eliciting responses without shaping them, or closed, thus limiting the responses to the choices provided. And even though we provide examples of teacher-led interviews, the interviews can be conducted by students, parents, administrators, and other outside observers.

Informal interview.   The aim of the informal interview (or as some might say, a *purposeful conversation*) is to understand the perspective of the student (or parent, etc.). The interviewer poses a question related to the research interest, then uses the responses as a lead for the next question. As in the following example, extraordinary revelations are made in what might start out as a very ordinary moment. Jimmy, a child born with fetal alcohol syndrome, was a constant challenge in Danny's first-grade classroom. Jimmy had spent the last year watching his mother drink herself to death. His erratic behavior in school paralleled the erratic support he received at home from his father, who also had a problem with alcohol. Frustrated with the father's unresponsiveness to a variety of initiatives, Danny finally got the father to come in for a conference. *Case Study: Danny's Informal*

Interview with Jimmy's Father is a summary of the conference (informal interview) as recorded in Danny's journal.

The lines of communication opened because Danny cared enough about Jimmy to engage his father in an authentic conversation characterized by give and take, openness, and empathy. Danny gained the father's trust. For most of us, the rules of formal interviewing simply don't apply: Techniques such as maintaining objectivity, withholding opinions, and consistently asking the same prepared questions are inadequate for our desire to establish the trust we need in our everyday relationships. When we speak authentically, from the heart, these techniques become less important if not irrelevant or counterproductive. As one feminist researcher pointed out, there is "no intimacy without reciprocity" (Oakley, 1981). Reciprocity is at the heart of action research. The action researcher learns from her or his students and parents as well as the other way around. Reciprocity is a moral and ethical cornerstone of action researchers, not merely a methodological concern.

Formal interview. Sometimes referred to as structured interviews, formal interviews have set, standard questions that are asked of all interviewees and are often recorded using a predesigned coding scheme. All interviewees receive the same questions in the same order. In the case of verbal interviewing, the interviewer does not give his or her opinion, does not interpret or modify the question, but is attentive and shows interest in responses that help the student to feel comfortable. The formal interview techniques we will discuss are questionnaires, attitudes scales, critical incidents, sociograms, and projective techniques that can be administered orally or in writing. This is followed by a discussion of creative visualization and focus group interviews.

CASE STUDY   **Danny's Informal Interview with Jimmy's Father**

At this first conference, I wanted to know how Jimmy's father thought he could help his son succeed in school. But I didn't ask him specifically about how he helped his son with homework, or whether he checked his son's backpack after school each day. Nor did I ask him why the forms were never signed and returned. Rather, I spoke from my heart to his heart. I asked him if he knew how much Jimmy desperately needed a father—someone to play an active role in his education. Then the floodgates opened. He expressed doubts about being able to do this as a single person, and I assured him that he could be a good father and that I would support his efforts. He shared his grief, his fears, and his tears. Then *he* asked what he could do, and we talked about different ideas. It was at this conference that the lines of communication opened.

April 4, Danny's Journal

Questionnaire. When it is not possible to interview everyone, the action researcher may want to use *questionnaires* (or attitude surveys or group interviews, discussed in the next sections). Questionnaires are written questions requiring responses about facts, attitudes, or values. Ruby adapted a questionnaire from Schaps et al. (1996) to measure classroom community, and we have excerpted it in *Case Study: Excerpts from the Classroom Community Questionnaire.*

In constructing the questionnaire, Ruby asked the same question in several ways, some worded positively and others negatively. She tried to make her questions neutral so that students could not guess how she felt about the class. These are *closed* questions because they force a response from a list of possibilities. Because responses are numerical, it will be easy for Ruby to average the scores of each student and look for trends across students.

What Ruby learned from her survey (which she gave at the beginning of student teaching and near the end) was that the fifth-period civics students rated their sense of community the lowest of all her classes. In fact, she found that as she poured her efforts into *creating* a sense of community, the amount of disrespect among students actually increased in *all* classes, even the ones that had a fairly high sense of community at the beginning! Notice how Ruby uses multiple sources to examine classroom community: what students say (on surveys and in interviews), what her mentor says (in the classroom profile and follow-up conference), and what Ruby suspects (and records in her journal).

CASE STUDY   Excerpts from the Classroom Community Questionnaire

Ruby

For this set of questions, use this scale:

1—Disagree a lot

2—Disagree a little

3—Don't agree or disagree

4—Agree a little

5—Agree a lot

_____ Students in my class are willing to go out of their way to help someone.

_____ My classmates care about my work just as much as their own.

_____ Class is like a family.

_____ The students in my class don't really care about one another.

_____ A lot of students in my class like to put others down.

_____ Students in my class work together to solve problems.

An open-ended questionnaire, on the other hand, allows students to respond in their own words. For example:

What communities do you belong to? What makes each a community?
In what ways is our classroom like a community?
In what ways is it not like a community?

Although open-ended questions are more time-consuming to analyze, they also can yield more specific and meaningful data. Many times it is most useful to use a combination of forced-choice and open-ended questions in a questionnaire.

Online survey tools.   With an online survey tool, you can create various types of questions, such as multiple choice, rating scales, drop-down menus, essay questions, and matrix of choices. Some programs are free of charge for publicly funded, non-profit educational institutions. Following are some popular online survey software:

- SurveyMonkey: http://www.surveymonkey.com/
- Hot Potatoes: http://hotpot.uvic.ca/(free)
- Flashlight: http://flashlightonline.wsu.edu/
- Vovici: http://vovici.com/

Attitude scale.   Attitude scales are designed to measure the strength of an attitude or opinion to get at underlying beliefs. By numbering each item on the scale, for example, from 1 (strongly agree) to 4 (strongly disagree) with a 0 for uncertain, the range of attitudes within a group can be studied. In Roberto's study, the question was how "typical" students felt about special education students; he asked them to circle words that best describe their attitude on a Likert-type scale.

I would be interested in spending more time being a friend to a student with special needs.

Strongly agree   Agree   Disagree   Strongly disagree   Uncertain

It is not necessary to scale or measure attitudes to explain how students feel. On another section of the survey, Roberto had this question:

Circle the words that describe your feelings about this statement:

Students labeled as students with special needs make me feel

| Sad | OK | Pity | Happy | Nothing |
| Upset | Fine | Friendly | Like helping them | Other _____ |

Checklists and rating scales, discussed in the section "Observing," may also be appropriate as a means of collecting interview data.

Critical-incident interview.   *Critical incidents* are turning points, revealing moments that, when uncovered, provide insights for interviewer and interviewee. For example, in a study of primary-grade student attitudes toward learning in a multiage classroom, researchers asked each child to recall a critical incident:

> Think of a time in school when you really learned a lot and enjoyed what you were doing. Tell me about it—What did you do? Whom did you work with? How did it go? What did you do first, second, . . . What did you learn? What did you like about it?

Because multiple researchers conducted the interviews in several classrooms, each interviewer asked the same questions. Rather than perform numerical analysis, the researchers will later look for concepts that emerge as consistent patterns in student responses and incidents that illustrate the patterns.

A major problem in formal interviews is that students will often give socially desirable responses to please the interviewer. Sam's middle school science students, for example, were reluctant to reveal negative attitudes toward "environmentalists" because their teacher was a "nature lover." Sam had to figure out another way to get at their attitudes before constructing a unit on the environment. Students may not want to reveal their opinions, or are too shy or embarrassed to reveal their thinking. Other, more indirect and nonthreatening, ways of interviewing students, such as sociograms, projective techniques, and focus groups (as well as observations, documents, and artifacts) may be helpful.

Sociogram.   A sociogram is a technique for studying peer networks and relationships to determine a student's position within the social structure of a classroom. It is a way to identify those students who are revered by peers or who stand out in some way. It may also help identify people who are isolated and in need of extra social support. It has been used by teachers to help in understanding discipline problems and student preference for curriculum and groupings. Hubbard and Power (1993) have developed a useful protocol for this type of interview:

> You meet with each child and say, "I want you to give me first, second, and third choices in response to this question." Then you give the sociogram question. You might ask, "If you could work with anyone in the class, whom would you work with?" or "If you could play with anyone in the class, whom would you play with?" (p. 39)

Case Study: Sociogram of Sixth-Grade Girls' Preferences for Field Trip Partners is an example of a sociogram that describes sixth-grade girls' first and second choices of partners for a field trip.

The sociogram suggests that Cheryl, Jan, and Kathy are a tight group, popular, and other students desire to get to know them. Sally and Elizabeth appear to be friends, although they would like to be associated with the three most popular girls. Melinda does not choose one of the popular girls. Betsy is chosen by no one and is usually seen working and playing alone.

Projective technique.   A projective technique is an open-ended type of self-report interview in which the interviewee "projects" her or his feelings, attitudes,

CASE STUDY

Sociogram of Sixth-Grade Girls' Preferences for Field Trip Partners

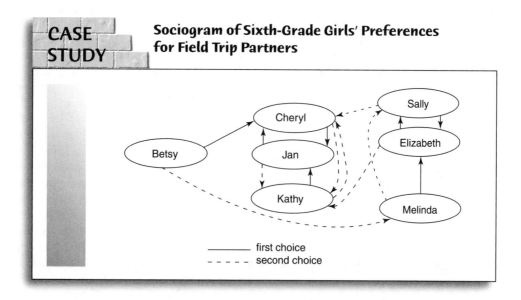

———— first choice
– – – – second choice

beliefs, and values by answering open-ended questions. It is like an ink blot test. One method is to present a hypothetical situation. If, for example, we wanted to know how student teachers really felt about doing action research, we might say:

> There are some faculty members and former students who have concerns about action research being a requirement of student teaching. If you were responsible for the student teaching seminar, how would you handle the action research component?

The distance established by using the hypothetical situation may enable some students to be more honest than if they were asked the question directly.

The incomplete sentence is another way to help interviewees project themselves. Sentences may be presented verbally or in writing. For example,

The best thing about math journals is . . .
The worst thing about math journals is . . .
I am happiest as a teacher when . . .
The thing that I am most worried about as I begin student teaching is . . .

Incomplete sentences are a useful diagnostic as well as evaluative tool.

Creative visualization. Asking people to use their imaginations in creative ways can yield rich data. One technique is guided reflection, sometimes called *creative visualization*, in which you ask the person or group to close their eyes and to visualize how something might be or was. You ask them to take themselves there—to that time and place—and to engage their senses. Then they can tell you what they see, or they can draw or write about it. In some of our classes we do all three. Students, for example, are asked to take themselves back to childhood and to recall an incident in school. Perhaps it is the first day of school. Who is there?

How do you feel? What do you see? Do you see yourself? What are you doing? What do you smell? What do you want to do? After students have drawn their visualizations (skill in drawing is beside the point—in fact, sometimes we have them draw with their nondominant hands so that they forget about "I can't draw"), they turn them over and do free-writes describing the experience in words. Finally, we discuss these in class and include them in our journals.

Focus group interview.   As we mentioned earlier, students can be reluctant to open up and speak honestly during individual interviews. Their reluctance is with good reason as people have too often been exploited or punished for being honest. This puts a considerable burden on the researcher to come from an ethical base that honors the respondents, regardless of their responses. Students may not want to participate, they may want to please the teacher with the "correct" answer, or they may simply be too shy to talk privately with someone in authority, no matter how much we may try to establish trust and to diminish status differences. Sam, the middle school teacher and environmentalist, had to figure out another way to get at their attitudes before constructing a unit on the environmental education that would address their prior conceptions and stretch their thinking. The focus group turned out to be just the right technique.

A *focus group interview* is a group discussion addressing a particular topic or issue. Before breaking into groups, Sam led a brainstorming session in which students generated topics, questions, and issues related to the environment. One of them was, What do we think of environmentalists? The class was then divided into groups of five students. They moved to round tables, all of which had tape recorders except one. Students who did not want to have their discussion recorded selected the table without a recorder. A student at each table was elected to facilitate, and the discussion began, focusing on the topics they had brainstormed. Sam walked around the room, but didn't stay at any table for more than a minute. After listening to the tapes and transcribing them, Sam found the terms *nerd* and *tree hugger* as well as descriptions such as "They don't bathe very often" when students referred to environmentalists.

No wonder they didn't want to reveal their attitudes in the whole-class discussion to their "tree-hugging" science teacher! Sam knew that any unit on the environment would have to address these negative attitudes.

Suggestions for using focus groups are developed in Stepping Stones 11.2: Focus Groups.

The advantages of a group interview over the individual interview are that it encourages elaboration, it aids in recall, and it is stimulating to have multiple respondents interact. When the teacher plays only a minor role, focus groups also provide leadership opportunities for students. On the other hand, one person may dominate the group discussion, or the group culture may dominate individual speech with "group think" as the result. When students are prepared for facilitation roles, the potential hazards are lessened.

We hope that our discussion and examples demonstrate the potential of the interview to democratize the research process (Carspecken, 1996). The interview

STEPPING STONES 11.2

Focus Groups

The following suggestions for conducting a focus group are adapted from Tripp (1996):

- Form groups of three to six.
- Students elect a facilitator or a teacher facilitates, keeping in mind that questions are to be directed to the group, not individuals.
- The topics for discussion can be the teacher's, the students', or a combination.
- Time limits encourage coverage of the topics.

It is a good idea to obtain permission for audio or video recording the focus group sessions using a digital recorder or a camcorder. This helps you, as the interviewer, to pay attention to what each individual has to say at the moment instead of focusing on note taking. Often, you will hear or observe details from the recordings that you did not notice while at the scene with the focus group participants. Some participants may feel uncomfortable knowing that they are being recorded at the beginning; yet, they will soon forget the recordings after the focus group session has started. This method also applies to other kinds of interviews.

does more than build on the rich descriptions created through observation. By inviting students (and parents) to have more of a voice in the classroom and a chance to challenge our understandings and actions, we are establishing conditions that encourage reciprocity out of which genuine understanding can grow.

Suggestions for conducting interviews are included in Stepping Stones 11.3: Interviewing. We have found a section called "Student Feedback" in Tripp's (1996) *The SCOPE Program* and Spradley's (1979) classic, *The Ethnographic Interview*, to be helpful for various approaches to interviewing.

Examining Documents and Artifacts

Artifacts and documents provide descriptive records that can enable the researcher to derive insights different from those provided by observations and interviews. Through observations we see with our own eyes. Through interviews we inquire into other peoples' perspectives. Just as clothing, jewelry, furniture, and stoneware of ancient civilizations tell us a great deal about the beliefs and practices of long-ago cultures, examination of records, texts, and products of work provides *physical traces* of the culture of students, classrooms, and schools.

STEPPING STONES 11.3

Interviewing

It takes time and practice to become a skilled interviewer. Here are some tips:

- Select the interview approach that best suits your study. Interviews can be informal and routine; they can be very open ended if you are open to student opinions and have the time to listen; or they can be targeted for what you are seeking.
- Be aware that the way you phrase questions can signal the interviewee that you want more information (such as "What else can you tell me about . . .). Others signal that you do not want to continue (such as "Anything else you want to add?") Be aware of your purposes and choose your phrasing accordingly.
- Understand the difference between different kinds of questions:
  - *Open-ended* questions—These leave things vague and responses can be varied. Examples: How do you feel about social studies? What do you think about using journals in math? Is there a difference in participation between boys and girls in our class discussions?
  - *Targeted* questions—These get at what your concerns are. Examples: Compare the way we learned social studies today with the way we usually do it. Do you think you learned something new by using a math journal? Do you think girls are reluctant to share ideas in front of boys?
  - *Why* questions—Questions that probe more deeply into participant thinking. Examples: Why do you think social studies was better the new way we did it? Why do you think girls are shy talking in front of boys? Why do you think you learn more when you write in your math journal?
  - *Should* questions—Questions that get at values of participants. Examples: Should social studies be changed for all students? Should all math teachers use journaling? Should girls and boys participate equally in discussions?
  - *Affect* questions—These questions get at how participants feel. Examples: How did you feel after our change in social studies teaching? How did it feel writing regularly in math journals? How did you as a girl/boy feel in your class discussions?
  - *Leading* questions—These questions steer participants in a highly targeted direction. Common in journalism, they are less useful in research, as they signal what the interviewer wants to hear. Examples: What was better about social studies after we changed our teaching? How are math journals better than other things we do in math? Don't you think girls should be encouraged to participate more?

STEPPING STONES 11.3 *Continued*

- *Recall* questions—These questions get at remembering something important. Examples: Can you think of the first time you began liking social studies classes more? Can you tell me a concept you understood better because you had written about it in your math journal? Can you think of the first day you took a risk to speak up in class when it was otherwise difficult?
- *Comparative* questions—Questions that are open ended but specifically target a comparison or contrast. Examples: How would you compare the way we used to teach social studies to what we do now? How would you compare math journaling to learning without journals? How would you compare the participation of the boys and girls in your classroom now with participation at the beginning of the term.
- *Experience* questions—These questions get at behavior or experience with something. Examples: Have any other teachers used historical novels as part of social studies? Have you ever kept a journal to help you learn content in any other classes? Have you ever had classes that separated boys and girls for some discussions?
- *Demographic* questions—These questions collect demographic data around the inquiry. Examples: Is this your first year taking social studies? What are your previous grades in math like? Do you attend any all-girl clubs, such as scouting or "Rainbow" girls?

Expanded from McKernan, 1996, pp. 130–131.

Examining documents and artifacts is an unobtrusive way of collecting data that is becoming more common for classroom researchers. Portfolios, for example, provide physical evidence of what students (and we ourselves) know, believe, and have accomplished. Teaching portfolios might include video clips, student records, awards, statements of our philosophy, lesson plans, and articles we have written. When rubrics based on either internal or external criteria are used to examine the pieces in a portfolio, for example, rubrics based on the standards developed for scientific literacy or classroom environment, we call the design an *evaluation study.*

As he was doing his dissertation, Sam wanted to become more aware of the beliefs and potential biases he brought to his qualitative study. So he examined documents he had created throughout his doctoral program: comprehensive examination, pilot studies, and papers for courses. Each formed a part of his story of scholarship. They provided a database from which he could derive insights into his beliefs about middle school science.

Personal experience methods.   In Chapters 6 and 7 we outlined many techniques to explore the beliefs, values, and identities that form our own personal-professional road map. Among them are self-talk, examining personal artifacts, interviewing family and friends, recalling significant others, generating metaphors, recalling critical incidents, and creating a time line of incidents and people.

Each of these techniques can also be used to gather data from students about their own personal experiences. Student experiences, as John Dewey and many since him have told us, are central to learning. School learning occurs when students are able to link their own experiences and purposes to academic content. Personal experience methods play an important role in helping students to make these connections. Thus, gathering data about student experiences can be helpful to students and teachers as we work together to construct our own learning. Jo's story provides an illustration of how a teacher's assignment can draw on students' personal experiences. These student experiences can, in turn, help students make connections to subject matter.

An initial questionnaire in Jo's middle school Spanish class indicated the presence of many cultural stereotypes by students. The study's purpose became to help students gain a deeper appreciation and acceptance of cultural practices in Spanish-speaking communities. Through a series of individual and group activities, students were asked to make connections between their own experiences and the experiences of Marta, a female Mexican protagonist in the movie "Sweet 15." In their final essay, in which students were to compare their own struggles to the struggles of Marta, Jo noted a shift in their thinking. Examples from student essays (see *Case Study: Excerpts from Student Essays About Marta*) illustrate this development.

The ethical dimensions of using personal experience methods requires serious consideration of who we are in our student's stories (Clandinin and Connelly, 1998). When we enter into a research relationship with participants and ask them

CASE STUDY   **Excerpts from Student Essays About Marta**

Marta showed her responsibility by helping her father become a U.S. citizen. Marta and I also must show some independence and trust. We have to show that we are able to do things by ourselves to gain our parents' trust.

Marta's parents didn't believe that she was an adult yet. My parents feel the same way about me. They don't understand how much having adults accept you as one of them means to us.

I think I am very lucky to live the life that I lead. Marta's life as a teenager is not as easy as most people's, including mine. . . . she was a Mexican in an Anglo-dominated society.

to share their stories with us, we shape their stories as well as our own. We must also pay attention to what happens after the research. Helping students deal emotionally with revelations they uncover in personal stories becomes part of the ethical responsibilities of action researchers who use these methods. Reminding students that stories told in class must remain there, maintaining anonymity, and using pseudonyms are ways to protect the privacy of participants. On the other hand, privacy and anonymity become less important if we seek full participation of students and colleagues.

Student work.   Student essays, poetry, problem solving, musical compositions, journals, and the many types of performances that students use to demonstrate their understanding and appreciations are ways to document student learning. A good source of ways to document student work is Barrell's (1995) *Teaching for Thoughtfulness: Classroom Strategies to Enhance Intellectual Development*. Working with students to document their growth in portfolios also helps us as teachers to understand how we might address issues in our own teaching.

Shawn saved Jen's computer-generated work to keep track of her literacy development and to illustrate and make visible Jen's remarkable progress over a 4-month period. Jen's progress was traced by examining illustrated stories she developed with a computer program. See *Case Study: What Jen and Her Family Did Over Spring Vacation*, and *Case Study: Jen's Writing Sample*.

By examining Jen's entries for overall number of words, words spelled conventionally, increased vocabulary, and change in sentence structure, Shawn noted significant changes in Jen's writing.

Photographs and video and audio recordings.   Photographs and audio and video recordings may get at evidence of spiritual, aesthetic, and religious sensibilities and experiences that go beyond what is available through written work. Photographs and video recordings, found or researcher-produced, are underused data that can create powerful images. They also allow the researcher to relook at what happened. Whether the photographs were taken in the past (such as in the case of the student teacher who documented her transformation through photographs of herself as an overweight kid hiding behind others to a newly "blonded" cheerleader and prom queen) or are taken by the researcher for the purpose of telling a story, photographs and video can become powerful evidence. Since they can elicit emotions and record objects, people, or events, we must be careful to provide the context in which they are taken. We need to keep in mind that what we select to frame in a photograph or video represents our own understanding of the subject.

One researcher ran a video recorder in a center area in one part of her classroom. Her primary-aged children soon ignored the presence of the camcorder on a tripod. What the tapes revealed about interstudent conversations and language among these ethnically diverse students identified as severely "language-impaired" was fascinating and revealing. Analyzed segments demonstrated the role of language in the social construction of knowledge. One picture can tell 1,000

CASE STUDY

What Jen and Her Family Did Over Spring Vacation—April 15

Shawn

> Skiing is ts veery coid. It is snowing. Ji Woo and Eun Woo we are skiing

stories. It can be interpreted differently by each observer! Remember those multiple selves we explored in Chapter 6?

A vocal music student teacher made and shared audio recordings of her young adolescent male students to help them through the period when their voices were changing. (After listening to the recordings, our class had a far greater appreciation for vocal music teachers who want to be inclusive rather than exclusive in selecting students for their programs.) An elementary teacher, eager to attempt student-led group discussions of books but curious about whether discussion would be productive, placed audio recorders on each student table. She listened to them in her car on the way home and later categorized their responses.

Technology.   Technology provides new and rich sources of data and its analysis to help us understand our students. One teacher was working with her students on a project and using the Internet as a resource. She wanted to see what sites the students used and how long they stayed there when browsing the Web for information. She used the history file from the browser. This file indicated the first and last time they visited a particular site and how many times they visited it. She then went to each site and bookmarked it. At the end of the students' project the teacher determined whether their search for information progressed to the use of more complex materials, if they stayed longer at the sites, and if they incorporated the material in their reports.

Another teacher took advantage of the school system's networked computer system. He and colleagues from across the country set up a virtual project for students in their social studies classes. The teachers noted how students' communication differed when they used chat and e-mail correspondence as opposed to

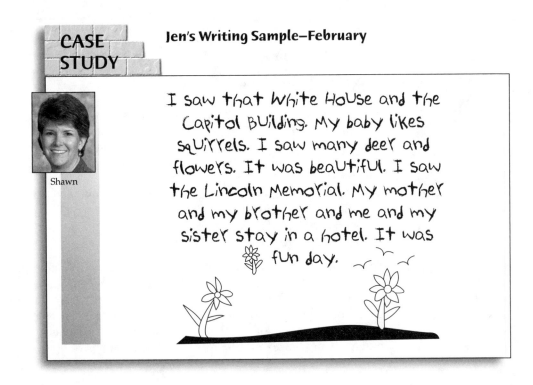

CASE STUDY

Jen's Writing Sample—February

Shawn

I saw that White House and the Capitol Building. My baby likes squirrels. I saw many deer and flowers. It was beautiful. I saw the Lincoln Memorial. My mother and my brother and me and my sister stay in a hotel. It was 🌸 fun day.

regular classroom conversation. They began to collect e-mail and chat logs, comparing them to the quality of the discussion within the classroom. Digital cameras, palm pilots, chatrooms, MOOs (multiple-user, object-oriented environment), Listservs, e-mail, and so on, offer opportunities to record events, conversations, information and other forms of data in ways that were not possible a few years ago.

Technology also makes data analysis easier and more systematic. While there are software packages available to aid in data analysis, for example, ethnograph, a beginning researcher might simply want to use a search function such as "find" to locate key words.

Technology offers a whole new world of opportunities for student learning. Just as with other methods, researchers need to be mindful of the ways in which they protect student privacy and anonymity.

Physical traces. Evidence of learning and development may be found in some unexpected places. A sixth-grade social studies teacher learned through a survey that her students hated social studies. She asked the school media specialist to provide her with a printout of circulation records just before and during the time she introduced historical fiction to increase student enthusiasm and involvement with social studies. By examining student choices, she could document whether there was an increase in the number of historical novels or social

STEPPING STONES 11.4

What Documents and Artifacts to Save

- *Samples of work produced over time*—journals, math problems, laboratory experiments, artwork, writing samples, audio or video recordings.
- *Correspondence*—notes, memos, journal, diary, field notes.
- *Records*—attendance, grades, certificates, minutes of meetings, library records.
- *Curriculum materials*—lesson plans, textbooks, CD ROMs, Internet sites.
- *Accounts*—newspaper clippings, journal articles, video clips about classroom, or larger work context.
- *Accretion and erosion* of any of the above.

Identifying work by labeling and dating needs to be a routine part of our work. If students forget to date their work, a student can be assigned the task of stamping the date as work is turned in. Labeling work by describing the assignment and identifying the author by name, which can later be removed to protect privacy, or by some other method such as numbers or letters can be done either directly on the work itself or by attaching an adhesive note.

studies-related books checked out by her students. An art teacher counted fingerprints on glass cases after a field trip to an art museum to determine which kinds of art and sculpture were most appealing to students. And a technology teacher monitored interest in his homework Web page by recording the number of hits made every evening. Webb et al. (1966) call the buildup of physical traces *accretion*.

Erosion, on the other hand, is the wearing away of physical traces. A quick look at the wear and tear of student textbooks indicates the extent to which they are being used. Popular paperbacks often have no remaining covers at all! Another researcher studied teaching styles by the types of supplies teachers used up over a school year. Gathering artifacts and documents with accretion and erosion in mind may lead to some very creative research designs!

Suggestions about what documents and artifacts to save and how to organize them are presented in Stepping Stones 11.4: What Documents and Artifacts to Save, and Stepping Stones 11.5: Managing Data.

We have made a chart of the numerous possible situations the action researcher might find herself or himself in and ways to collect data in those situations. Can you find your emerging study in this chart? See Figure 11.2.

Finally, while most of this chapter is devoted to data that the action researcher creates in context, we must not overlook the wealth of "data" that are available outside of our classrooms. Other people, theories, empirical studies, electronic

FIGURE 11.2   *What do I want to know? How do I get at my question?*

If . . .	Then . . .
I want to know how students perceive something or feel about something	I probably need feedback from interviews, surveys, or questionnaires.
I want to know how their attitudes or perceptions about something *change*	I probably need to collect feedback at least twice, whether it's a survey, interview, questionnaire (pretest, posttest).
I want to know something about parents, their ideas, perceptions, input about their children, etc.	I probably need to survey or interview them, in person, by letter, by phone, etc.
I want to see if what I'm doing impacts quality or quantity of student work in some way	I probably need to collect examples of related student work at intervals (once a week, once a month, etc.) or study selected students' work over time in some depth.
I want to know how my students make use of something existing or introduced (such as a library center, particular books, study aid)	I probably need an observation instrument that is a checklist, log, anecdotes, audiotape, etc.
I want to know how students use consumable items or collections	I may need to track the use of the items or depletion of the supplies related to the topic.
I want to know how students use something new I'm teaching them	I may need to track their use of the thing or strategy in a desired context.
I want to see if one intervention works	I need to decide what signals "working" and track the progress in observation, or artifacts, or student comments or feedback.
I want to compare more than one intervention	I need to document each intervention through student work and/or student opinions and/or observation.
I am studying one learner in great depth for whatever reason	I probably need a comprehensive and regular researcher log in addition to interviews with the student and about the student with others, and I need to collect artifacts the student has done related to my topic.
I want to know if what I'm doing influences something students do outside my classroom	I'll need to collect data outside my classroom from parents, librarians, other teachers, or wherever I want the influence to be.
(Self-assessment) I want to assess *my* effectiveness at something I'm doing with my students	I might examine artifacts to see if I'm getting what I want; I might directly ask students; I might ask them to write about their understanding; I might interview them about it; I might listen to related comments, nonverbal comments.

STEPPING STONES 11.5

Managing Data

Systematically and coherently managing the large amount of data that accumulates in an AR study is of critical importance in data collection, storage, and retrieval. Because data management is so closely connected to data analysis, the subject of the next chapter, we will mention here only those things that will help the action researcher before the data collection even starts.

1. If we know what the categories are that form the rubric for a study, then simply filing data in those categories is the most logical way to organize data. A portfolio with standardized categories for evaluating teachers and students is one such example. As additional categories emerge from preliminary and ongoing data analysis, the portfolio can be expanded to include them. Organizing by types of data, such as interviews, artifacts, documents, field notes, journal, will make it easier to add to and retrieve the data.

2. Numbering pages; developing a table of contents; summarizing contents; labeling documents and artifacts with relevant information such as date, time, length, place, type of data (e.g., interview), preserving original student work; and filing them on a regular basis are strategies that will prevent the task from getting out of hand. Notebooks, index cards, colored file folders, storage boxes or file drawers, and computer software that were described in Chapter 6 are the typical tools of data management.

resources, and philosophical inquiries are valuable resources that we have highlighted in earlier chapters. Moving between these sources enables us to gain multiple perspectives and deeper insights.

CHAPTER SUMMARY

Trying out a variety of actions and documenting those actions strengthens our awareness of the consequences of what we often take for granted in our teaching. Most of us are constantly trying out new ways to better reach out to students. We are now learning the tools that can help us make *informed* decisions. In the next chapter, we will look briefly at some of the other elements of design that strengthen our decision-making powers.

CHAPTER 12

Elements of Design: Verification, Interpretation, and Portrayal

In addition to planning and documenting the action, other important elements of design need to be taken into consideration prior to launching a full-blown study or at least in the early stages of a study. Verification, interpretation, portrayal, action planning for next steps, and ethical considerations are dealt with briefly in this chapter and developed more fully in chapters to come.

How Will I Verify That My Judgments Are Trustworthy, Credible, and Respectful?

As we design our studies, we want to build in assurances for ourselves and for others that our professional judgments are trustworthy, credible, respectful, and reflective of our values. See also Chapter 13.

A simple way to enhance the verification process is to plan ways to triangulate the data by using observations, interviews, and other data sources discussed in Chapter 11. What do I observe? What do students say? What do I see in student work? Multiple sources of data collected systematically provide opportunities for credible interpretation of this data.

How Will I Interpret the Data?

While interpretation (making sense of the data) is the focus of Section VI, planning how we will interpret the data is part of designing a study. Because analysis and interpretation are an ongoing part of the action research process (e.g., we check on student progress throughout a unit of study, not just at the end), we want to consider how we will make sense of the data. When will I read over my journal entries? How often and when will I collect and assess student work? What will I look for in the data? What indicators will I use to determine the quality of work? Are there any theories that I can use to guide my interpretation and understanding of student learning and my own growth as a professional? (We often write about those theories in the "What is my research interest?" section of the proposal.) Researchers are often fearful of what they will do once they have collected all their data. By anticipating *how* we will make sense of these data, analysis and interpretation become more manageable.

How Will I Portray What I Have Learned and Make It Public?

Even as we begin designing our studies, we need to be aware of the possible ways to portray and make public what we have learned. Will we use critical incidents? Photographs? Will we create aesthetic representations through music, art, sculpture, dance, drama, or poetry? Video or audio tape recordings? Student work?

Who are potential audiences? In other words, with whom will my research be shared? Parents? Colleagues at school, university or professional conferences, or elsewhere, such as on a Listserv? Students? School board members? How will our collaborators participate in sharing what we have learned? Will it be formal or informal? As we collect data, we want to keep in mind these audiences and the kind of evidence they will most appreciate and value. In Section VII we will explore the many options open to action researchers, some traditional to research and others in emerging forms.

How Will These Actions Make Life Better? What Will I Do Next?

Action research requires that we examine critically the consequences of our work.

When we speak of making life better, we have in mind the professional commitments that we discussed in the first three chapters of this book: collaboration, community based on justice and equity, participation of those with whom we work, authentic communication as a way of building strong relationships, and so on. Commitment to these qualities as well as to our own professional growth is the cornerstone of what we mean by *better*. For example, if we believe in collaborative and participatory education, then an element of design we will want to consider is how we might involve our students and parents.

What Ethical Considerations Need to Be Made?

When we speak of making life better, we are considering not only the consequences of our actions, but the research process as well. Earlier in the book we said that to teach well is to inquire well. Yet action research involves a wider audience than does traditional teaching. As a result, ethical dilemmas may arise. These dilemmas revolve around procedural issues (e.g., how, when, and from whom to gain permission); legal and institutional issues (e.g., compliance with Human Subjects Review Board regulations, turning over documents such as journals to legal authorities in cases of child abuse and neglect, etc.); relational issues (e.g., building trust, using data to build up the community as opposed to using data only to further one's career); and role confusion (e.g., according to Zeni [1999], multiple responsibilities of action researchers to research, to students, and to parents).

Zeni (1998) argues that the dilemmas that arise are related to underlying issues:

1. *Representation*—how students and the school are represented to others. Is it accurate? How do others feel about the way they are represented? How open is the communication between researcher and participants, so that differences of opinion can be taken into account?
2. *Ownership*—who owns what data and who has a say in how it can be used? The student, the teacher, the school, legal authorities?
3. *Responsibilities*—our primary responsibility as action researchers is to our students. How is potential abuse, of those over whom we have power and whose trust we have gained, minimized?

These considerations relate to the values that undergird action research. We can think these through with others affected by our study. Consult Figure 12.1 for ethical guidelines to be used as new situations arise.

CHAPTER SUMMARY

Keeping in mind the elements of design presented in this chapter and the dilemmas that planning and documenting action may pose can help increase the power of your design and get you off to a good start. While modifications are usually made along the way, planning for the journey may prevent or alleviate detours and delays.

SECTION SUMMARY

A design is tentative and provides a road map that can change and evolve as we gather data and reflect on what we are learning. Where we end up can bear little resemblance to where we thought we would. Often design begins after much data collection has already occurred, data that provide evidence that we need to address a particular aspect of our teaching. Toni, for example, had been studying

---

FIGURE 12.1 *Ethical guidelines for teacher action researchers*

Obtain permissions: If research is a natural part of teaching, why is permission needed? We have emphasized the importance of making research public in order to contribute to a knowledge base for teaching. Whenever we make our practice public, research participants may be at risk of public scrutiny. Let your students and their parents know what you are doing. Obtain written permission to conduct the study from parents and oral or written permission from students. If the study is conducted through a university, appropriate Human Subjects Review Board permission is often required. The school or district may also have guidelines for research. Reciprocity between a school district and a university is preferable so that the researcher does not have to file separate applications. If students can be identified (through the use of video, audio, or photographs), special permissions are needed indicating this fact. If private records are needed, gain school permission to use them. When possible, obtain permission to use quotes and student work, negotiating with participants how they are represented to others.

The process of obtaining informed consent involves written permission from parents and oral permission from children. In each case the researcher provides the following:

1. Topic.

2. Purpose.

3. Brief description of study and how participants will be involved.

4. Description of potential risks and benefits (risks are usually minimal, but if there are any that the researcher is aware of, they need to be stated).

5. Procedures for anonymity/confidentiality (except in the event that participants opt to waive this requirement because of the cooperative nature of the study).

6. Students' option to stop participation (except if it is regular course work) without fear of reprisal.

7. Phone number of researcher (and research advisor or university researcher officer) and invitation to contact one of them with questions.

8. Space for agreement. For example,

   I agree to (take part/let my child take part) in this project. I know what (I/she/he) will have to do and that (I/she/he) can stop at any time.

   _____   _____
   Signature   Date

FIGURE 12.1 *Continued*

Involve participants: Encourage the full participation of those who will be affected by the study, and give them credit for their work. Encourage participants to help with design, data collection, and interpretation. Be willing to extend or clarify accounts for the purpose of enhancing fairness, relevancy, and accuracy. Share your progress with those involved, and seek their ideas. Seek out the points of view of those involved, especially if those points of view differ from yours. Then include their points of view in your report, along with yours, so that the readers or audience members can form their own judgments.

Ensure confidentiality: Building a classroom environment based on respect is the first ingredient of ensuring confidentiality. Students and other participants need to trust that what they say in private will remain private, particularly in their journals and diaries, and that their thoughts and feelings will not be used against them. However, students need also to be aware that in the event they reveal information leading the researcher to believe that the student is suffering from some sort of abuse or neglect or is engaged in illegal activities, it is the responsibility of the researcher to report this information to the proper authorities.

Ensure anonymity: Generally, anonymity is preserved through use of pseudonyms or the exclusion of student names from any documents or examples used in a report. Blurring images and distorting audio clips are other ways to ensure anonymity. It is difficult in most classroom situations to hide the identity of students when making reports to parents, colleagues, administrators, or school board members. Zeni (1998) suggests alternatives to pseudonyms: composite rather than individual portraits and interchanging physical description, grade level, gender, etc. There are times when we do not want to keep identities anonymous, particularly when our students are coparticipants in our study and the report will be presented to larger audiences. For example, in a study of how students respond to writing for authentic audiences, student work will be displayed in a public library. Since the work is of high quality and students are proud, using student names is appropriate.

Inform participants of the right to withdraw: Students need to know that they may withdraw from the study at any time without fear of negative consequences. In most cases, if the study includes teaching activities and curriculum that are part of the regular teaching process, withdrawing is not an issue. For example, if all students were participating in small group work related to a topic in social studies, they would not withdraw from the study. They might, however, choose not to participate in a survey about how they felt about the group work or their partners.

Build relationships of trust: Open communication, trust, and reciprocity are the cornerstones of action research. Whether we like to admit it or not, as teachers we are in positions of power, and we may intimidate students into complying with our research agenda and interpretations by virtue of our status. We need to consider how we will continue to justify the trust that students and parents have in us.

Be self-reflective: Include self-reflection as an integral part of the study. How does this research fit with your values? Consider ways in which you as a researcher influence or do not influence what happens in your classroom, so that you will interpret and portray the evidence you have gathered with honesty, respect, fairness, and accuracy.

These guidelines reflect several sources: our own experience as teacher action researchers, application for approval to use human subjects in research (Kent State University), Zeni's (1998) article titled "A Guide to Ethical Issues and Action Research," and Hopkins's (2002) book titled *A Teacher's Guide to Classroom Research.*

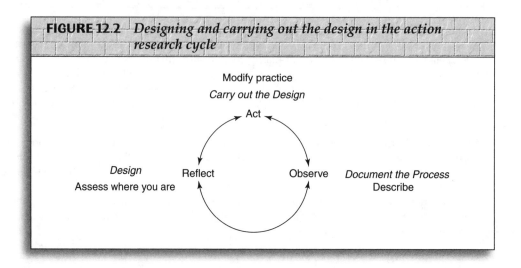

FIGURE 12.2 *Designing and carrying out the design in the action research cycle*

math journals for a year before realizing that two students with special needs were having the same difficulty with solving equations, thus motivating Toni to launch a case study of these two students.

Thus, we return to the cycle of action research. To the basic cycle of *reflect, act,* and *observe,* we have added the research layer of design, carrying out the design, and documenting the process. This blending of teaching and research becomes the mark of the scholar as we continuously assess where we are, modify practice based on informed decisions, and describe what we are learning. See Figure 12.2.

In Figure 12.3 we summarize how the elements of design fit together as a basis for developing a proposal for an action research study whose goal is to develop professional judgment and improve classroom practice. A proposal is simply a way of getting our thoughts organized and of saying (to ourselves, our colleagues, our students, and others), "This is what I plan to do to address my questions and concerns."

There are several resources on research design that provide a good overview of methods and issues: Marshall and Rossman's (1999) *Designing Qualitative Research*; Creswell's (2003) *Research Design: Qualitative, Quantitative, and Mixed Methods Approaches*; Stake's (1995) *The Art of Case Study Research*; Maxwell's (2005) *Qualitative Research Design: An Interactive Approach*; and Schram's (2006) *Conceptualizing and Proposing Qualitative Research*. For design related specifically to action research, see selected chapters and cases from Carson and Sumatra's (1997) *Action Research as Living Practice*; Kemmis and McTaggert's (1988) *The Action Research Planner*; Atweh et al. (1998) *Action Research in Practice: Partnerships for Social Justice in Education*; Stringer's (2004) *Action Research in Education*; and Herr and Anderson (2005) *The Action Research Dissertation: A Guide for Faculty and Students.*

FIGURE 12.3 *Designing an action research study*

Questions	Methodology: How to address the question					Consequences
What is my* research interest?	*What will I* try out in order to improve my practice?*	*How will I document the process?*	*How will I verify that judgments are trustworthy, credible, and respectful?*	*How will I interpret the data? (decide whether this section is needed in the proposal)*	*How will I portray what I have learned and make it public?*	*How will these actions make life better? And what will I do next? Who are my critical colleagues?*
What is my question? Sub questions? (How can I . . . ?) Why am I interested? (values, beliefs) What do I already know? (through my experience) What do others know? (literature and colleagues) What do I expect to find? (my hunches)	Who are the participants? What will I try out? When will the actions take place? How often? (time line) Where will the actions take place? How will the action unfold? Why try these actions and not others?	Data are collected to give evidence that shows the consequences of actions. Data are gathered through • Observing • Interviewing • Examining artifacts and documents What permissions are needed and how will they be obtained?	Verification is process of making judgments by • Making your standpoint clear • Using multiple perspectives (triangulation) • Applying indicators • Providing raw data • Writing descriptively • Being systematic • Being reflective	Interpretation is an interactive process of giving meaning to data by • Analyzing: What are the parts? • Synthesizing: How are the parts related? • Theorizing and making assertions: What do I make of all this (with reference to personal and public theory)?	The form of portrayal takes into account the audience and purpose of the study. Forms include: • Presentation • Written report • Video/audio recording • Art work • Drama • Video diary • Photo essay • Photograph • Multimedia presentation • Poem • Mural	The "so what"? How will changes in myself, my students, and my situation foster a more democratic learning community? What will I do next? Who are the critical colleagues who will challenge my thinking and also support me?

(Continued)

FIGURE 12.3 *Continued*

Questions	Methodology: How to address the question				Consequences
Criterion	**Criterion**	**Criterion**	**Criterion**	Potential audiences:	**Criterion**
Significant to self and others.	*Doable process that addresses the question in a way that brings action in line with values.*	*Provides for rich description, multiple perspectives, and a plan to obtain permissions.*	*Use of multiple techniques to ensure sound and ethical judgments.*	• Teachers	*Clear link between proposed actions and values.*
				• Parents	
				• School board	*Critical colleagues have the potential to challenge and support.*
				• Community	
			Criterion	• Students	
			A general plan to guide analysis, synthesis, and theorizing is presented.	• University	
				• City council	
			Criterion		**Criterion**
			Method of portrayal matches the audience and purpose.		

*If a study is conducted by an individual, use "I" and "my"; if conducted by multiple researchers, use "we" and "our."

In Section IV we focused on questions and how to develop them. In Section V we have focused on the actions we can try out and the data we can collect to document the consequences of those actions. In Section VI we will offer suggestions for analyzing, verifying, and interpreting the data we have collected. In Section VII we will look at ways to portray for others what we have learned, so that they can learn from our actions and critique the claims we make. The *substance* of each of these chapters, however, goes beyond methods and techniques and is concerned with how to make our classrooms and schools more democratic and just places. That will make analysis and interpretation much more engaging and productive. But first, let's explore the forest with our new-found tools for design and fieldwork.

Exploring the Forest

Designing an Action Research Study and Doing Fieldwork

In Section V, we devoted our attention to designing a study. In these exercises you will conduct fieldwork in your classroom or school by observing, interviewing, and examining artifacts and documents—in other words, collecting data for your study. By completing these exercises, you will be designing your study.

Design

1. If you have not yet designed a *practice* study, now is a good time to do so. By answering the design questions provided in Figure 10.3 on page 127 and then carrying out your plan for about a week or so, you will get a good feel for the action research process.

   Share your plan with a critical colleague, someone you feel has insights about teaching that would be helpful to you. In a week or so, check back with the colleague with a progress report. If you need help in documenting the process of your action, invite the colleague to collect and examine the data.
2. Now that you have designed a practice study, select a question you would like to pursue in your action research project. It might be the one you selected in Section IV or the one in the practice study. Or it may be something that occurred to you while you were reading Section V. Write out your question. Have you already collected some information about the topic? If not, you might interview knowledgeable people, search the Internet, and read articles, chapters, or books on your topic, paying attention to different ways you can address the question.
3. Now comes the fun. Think of possible actions to address your question. Based on the information you have gathered and your own personal

experiences, brainstorm possible actions. Think of at least five. In brainstorming, allow ideas to flow freely without editing them. Free-writing is a good technique for this. Have a critical colleague and/or your students brainstorm with you.

After you have a list of ideas, categorize them. Are some related to the same idea? Perhaps an even better idea will come to you by this clustering. From all these ideas, which ones seem to fit your beliefs about teaching and learning and life in your classroom? Which ones seem most like you? Which ones could you commit to working on for awhile? Which ones seem most achievable in your classroom? Which ones seem right at this time (or do they require something else to be done first)? Which ones hold the greatest potential for the amount of effort you plan to expend? Which ones best match resources? Which ones fit with the ethical commitments of action research, a commitment to the improvement of yourself, your practice, and the larger community through the principles of equal relations, shared leadership, authentic communication, inclusive involvement, and active participation? Are there any other criteria that come to mind?

Now, using the criteria that makes most sense from the previous exercise, select an idea you would like to start with, saving others that meet your criteria for another cycle. Write down *why* you selected this approach and what you will do.

4. Answer the questions concerning who, what, when, where, why, and how about your proposed action. Be as specific or general as you would like, knowing that you will develop each more fully in your final draft. Look back into Section V for details about the kinds of information you can gather to answer each question. Use Figure 12.4 as a guide for your action plan.

5. Develop a schedule for your action. This is much like an action plan. It will make the plan much more real and doable when a list of activities, times, and participants is laid out. You might want to use the chart in Figure 12.5 as a guide. Share your schedule with a critical colleague. Ask what he or she thinks about it.

6. Before you try out your plan, think about how you will collect data to show the consequences of your actions. What do you think is going on? And how do you know? By using multiple sources of data, you will be in a better position to respond to both questions. You might want to use the format presented in Figure 12.6 to help you triangulate.

7. What will you look for in the data (as evidence that your values or goals are being realized)?

8. What do you expect to find? Stating your hypotheses (hunches) based on experience, intuition, and other resources is important because as you test your hypotheses you may adjust or formulate new ones.

9. Complete the data collection plan (an example is provided in Figure 12.7) as a starting point for your design.

FIGURE 12.4   *Action plan*

Why? (dreams and aspirations)	
Who? (the participants)	
What will you try out? How will you do it? (the action plan)	
When? (the schedule)	
Where? (the context)	

FIGURE 12.5   *Schedule for action research proposal*

Date to start	What will happen?	For how long? How often?	Who will be involved?

FIGURE 12.6   *Strategies for triangulation of data*

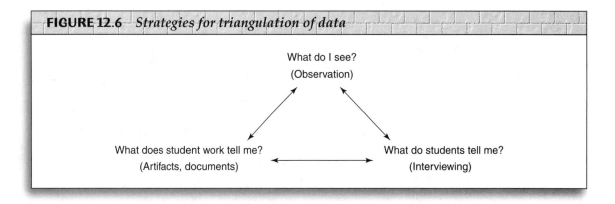

10. With whom will you collaborate? Who will your critical colleague(s) be? In what ways will full participation of your students (and others) be encouraged?

FIGURE 12.7 *Data collection plan*

| Topic: Problem Solving | Research Question: How can I improve student problem solving in science class? |

What are you trying to accomplish?

Improve student problem solving through direct teaching of the scientific method.

Your plan:

What will you try out?

1. Present a series of four problems throughout the semester and guide students through the scientific method.
2. Provide additional opportunities for students to solve problems.

What data will you collect to provide evidence of the consequences of your actions? How will you gain multiple perspectives?

1. Student written responses to four problems using a scoring rubric to keep track of how they are doing.
2. Mentor observations of student problem solving during laboratory time recorded in a log.
3. Informal interview with students as they are presented with problems during laboratory time.

What will you look for in the data?

1. Clear statement of problem.
2. Increasing number of alternative solutions.
3. Selection of alternative solution with greatest likelihood of success.
4. Willingness to try out solutions.

What do you expect to find?

I expect that students will become better problem solvers when I am more direct in my teaching of problem solving and use the rubric to assess their problem-solving abilities. I then will modify my teaching based on what I learn.

---

11. What permissions are needed, and how will you get them? An example of a letter asking for informed consent for parents is provided in Figure 12.8. Figure 12.9 is a letter for informed consent for students, and Figure 12.10 is an example of protocol for verbal assent.

12. In the following chapters, we will explore other important design questions: How will I verify that my judgments are trustworthy and credible? How will I interpret the data? How will I portray what I have learned and make it public? How will these actions make life better? And what will I do next?

FIGURE 12.8 *Family consent letter*

Dear Family Member:

Under the direction of my KSU professor, I/we will be conducting a study in my/our classroom(s). This process, called *action research*, helps teachers inquire into methods or strategies for teaching our students more effectively. The sorts of things we do are in keeping with regular and expected educational experiences that take place in classrooms except that we will be asking more questions, saving and analyzing data, and more systematically examining an area of teaching and learning in depth. This study also fulfills a requirement for my/our Master's Degree in Education.

As in all research, this study has been approved by the KSU Human Subjects Review Board for appropriateness in working with students. I am requesting your permission for your son or daughter to participate. Participation by part or all members of my class will not in any way interfere with regular educational experiences. The potential benefits are considerable as I explore ways to improve student learning and my own teaching. Your son or daughter has the right, at any time, to change his or her mind and choose not to participate. No real names are ever used in reporting about the results. Everything is done anonymously.

The title of my/our inquiry is:

If you would like more information about this study, please call my research mentor, (Professor name), at (phone number), or (Research Director) at the (office) (phone number). If you are willing to have your student participate, please fill out, sign, and return this form. Thank you in advance for your support of my continued professional development.

Yours truly,

Teacher

+++

Student name _____

I, (parent name) _____, **give / do not give** (underline one) permission for my son/daughter to participate in the classroom action research study.

Signature_____ **Date**_____

FIGURE 12.9 *Consent letter from Roberto Diaz*

(on school letterhead)

Social Interaction Study

Dear Student:

I would like to conduct a study of the social interactions of typical students and students with multiple handicaps at our middle school. I want to do this study because I would like to increase the positive social interactions between students.

I would like to invite you to become a member of the S.T.A.R. club (Students and Teachers Advancing Relationships). This is a social club in which students with multiple handicaps and typical students will be involved in voluntary social activities during lunch time and, on a few occasions, after school.

At no time will regular educational activities be interrupted. All information collected through interviews and surveys will be kept confidential and will not be used to influence your grades. You will not be identified in any way in any report that is written about this study. It will not be held against you if you choose to decline participating in any interview or survey.

Participant Consent: Social Interaction Study

I [student name] agree to allow my teacher to collect data on this project. I know what I have to do and that I can stop at any time.

_____   _____
Signature of participant   Date

Parent/Guardian Consent: Social Interaction Study

I [parent/guardian name] agree to allow my child to participate in this project. I know what he or she will have to do and that he or she can stop at any time.

_____   _____
Signature of participant   Date

FIGURE 12.10 *Verbal assent protocol*

If participants are between the ages of 5 and 12, written permission is needed from parents but not from students. Instead, provide participants the opportunity to give verbal assent. The following is an example of a verbal assent protocol to which details from your study could be added. The teacher reads the protocol to the students.

Project Title:

1. Hi, [child's name]

2. My name is _____, and I am trying to learn more about [description of project in appropriate language].

3. I would like you to [description of what you would like the child to do; include data collection procedures].

4. Do you want to do this? [the "this" refers to any activities that are beyond what you would normally do in the classroom, such as data collection procedures].

5. Do you have any questions before we start?

6. If you decide you do not want to [be interviewed, be a member of the club, or other activities that are beyond what participants would normally do in your classroom], just tell me.

You may or may not want to fully address these questions until you have read Sections VI and VII, but by thinking about them now, you will anticipate what these chapters (and your study) hold in store for you.

Practicing Data Collection

13. Try out your action and practice your observation skills. In your journal, label a section "Field Notes." Develop a format for your field notes that makes sense to you. Remember to leave wide margins on either the left- or right-hand side of notebook paper for your hunches, methodological decisions, and personal notes. At the top of the note paper, write your name, the setting of the observation, the date, and the focus of the observation (if you have one). For example, in your first observation of your students during an activity, you might want to look at *who* is doing what. Describe. *Where* is the activity taking place? Drawing a picture might help with later recall. *When* do things occur? Is there some regularity? Now write for 10 minutes.

    Read over your notes and insert information that enhances or extends the description. Add hunches, impressions, methodological decisions, and ideas that come to mind.

14. Select someone, a group, or your whole class to interview. What will you try to learn in the interview? How does the interview relate to your research question? How will you design the interview? Will you use a survey,

questionnaire, informal interview, or formal interview? Does a focus group interview make sense? Develop your interview questions or survey in such a way that it will be easy to analyze. For example, a Likert-scale from (1) *highly agree* to (5) *highly disagree* is easy to score, but it does not have the richness of an open-ended interview. During an informal interview, take notes, and get direct quotes where possible. As soon after the interview as possible, go back to your notes and fill in details.

15. Examine artifacts or documents produced by your students. Make sure that names are written clearly on the work and that the work is dated. Ask the students if you may keep the original; or if they are keeping it in a portfolio, ask that the portfolio be kept where you can retrieve the works you want to examine. Begin by examining them. What do they tell you about the student? About what they are learning? About the assignment? What else could you note in your journal?

Getting Organized

16. Begin to develop a data management plan that will work for you and the space that you have, be it a drawer, a shelf, a file cabinet, a box, or a binder. Make sure that everything you save is labeled, named, and dated. How will you organize the interview and observational notes and artifacts? Ask your colleagues for suggestions about how they organize their offices, their homes, and their student work. Share your plan with your critical colleague.

Writing a Proposal

17. Use the chart "Designing an Action Research Study" (see Figure 12.3). Examine the criteria for each section of the proposal. Write a proposal for an AR study, labeling each section. For example, the first section is "What is my research interest?" Write a few paragraphs, using the questions and criteria from the chart as a guide. Your proposal can be written in an informal, first-person narrative style. The length is up to you, but it is not usually more that five to eight double-spaced pages. Include a reference list for works that you have cited in your literature review. You may want to review Roberto's proposal in the Travelers' Notes B to see how one person designed a study.

VI

Analyzing and Interpreting Data

> *T*he four travelers walked up to the great gate of the Emerald City and rang the bell . . . [They] passed a sleepless night [waiting for Oz to see them] each thinking of the gift Oz had promised to bestow.
>
> *The Wonderful Wizard of Oz*
> L. Frank Baum (1900)

You have already sensed what is ahead. We offer many ways of exploring data and some of the "Aha's" will probably come from putting together small puzzle pieces in our minds.

Piero Ferrucci (1982), an Italian educator, said it well: "The moment we see the range of possibilities opening in front of us, we are filled with a sense of wonder and enthusiasm. But we should also beware lest this enthusiasm lead us astray; certain distortions and consequent dangers are . . . widespread" (p. 24). He goes on to say, "Perhaps the most fundamental distortion is the belief that the technique itself is the main transforming agent, rather than the way in which it is used" (p. 24).

So, you see, we need it all: intelligence, courage, and heart, as we move through the gate. Ferrucci (1982) is suggesting that an all-important factor in our journey is the *attitude* with which we use our research tools: "We can use them with attention and patience as tools to transform . . . Or we can use them mechanically . . . and just waste our time. We can make use of them what we want; in themselves they hold no guarantees" (p. 24).

185

We have been so diligent in laying out our path and carefully monitoring our actions. We are ready to open that door—to learn through critical reflection what insights we may derive from the data. Our case studies will take us through the gates of Oz, where we hope to find some answers to our questions. As we know, Oz holds surprises for us.

In Section V, we showed how action researchers monitor and keep track of their actions and how information becomes data through the filter of our questions. In Section VI we will *transform* data into evidence, using our creative and analytic powers. Then, examining the evidence from many perspectives (with heart, mind, and courage), we will interpret and make sense of that evidence. Finally, these interpretations will guide our actions in ways that further the development of just and caring classroom communities. Transformation is the key.

CASE STUDIES

Helping Jen Learn English as a Second Language

Shawn

Shawn's classroom already had an integrated focus, using only a few texts and mostly authentic assessments. With a balance of small and large group lessons, Shawn would have to decide for each lesson and activity the extent to which Jen could participate, or how to include her in the activity.

Jen's progress would be monitored through several means. First, Shawn was keeping a daily and fairly detailed researcher log. At times, Shawn would do some preliminary data analysis by writing what might be called an "analytic memo." Through these memos, Shawn gained a different perspective on things that would not be perceptible on a daily basis. A log of entries detailed the flow of the lesson and how Jen fared during a particular kind of activity.

Second, Shawn kept and dated all Jen's writings, from the earliest ones that were mostly drawings, to her first attempts at written English, to her fully developed sentences and stories. Shawn also designed a quiz of common English words that would be important for a second grader to know. Three times during the study Shawn administered the exact same test, which asked Jen to read and define common words. In addition, Shawn interviewed the ESL teacher during the study.

Shawn logged Jen's quiz scores as evidence of her increasing use of common English words and examined her journal in detail to look for changes, which, as it turned out, were large and easy to describe. Jen's last journal entry during the data collection period was a written entry about a trip Jen had taken with her family. It consisted of 45 English words, and seven syntactically and semantically appropriate sentences. Only one sentence contained a syntactical miscue with incorrect verb tense.

The Literature Circles Study

Jon

Jon and Terry carried out their plan for a literature-based program for all students in Terry's fifth-grade class. They decided to study six students in depth. All students had completed a "Reader Self-Perception Scale," known as the RSPS, at the beginning and end of the study. Jon and Terry also analyzed the written responses of students, collected as part of the strategy, and an instrument that included a checklist that tracked activity of all group members in terms of their role and participation in the groups. Each student also completed a written self-assessment of his or her role and feelings about participating in the book groups. In spite of the short duration of this study, many students began to see themselves as better readers. They also wrote more substantive entries in literature response journals as a result of their reading.

Terry

The S.T.A.R. Club Study

Roberto

Sensing that "typical" students had negative attitudes toward students with disabilities and feeling curious about their survey responses, Roberto immediately analyzed the data collected at the beginning of the study. He categorized the kinds of feelings students expressed about their peers with disabilities and arranged them on a continuum. Their attitudes ranged from "sad" and "pity" to "fine" and "like to help them." Next, he tallied the number of responses in each category. He found that the responses were more positive than negative—43 responses indicated that students were "fine/OK," "comfortable," or "happy" or would "like to help," while 31 responses indicated discomfort, sadness, or pity. But what he thought really interesting was that while all 30 students had classroom experiences with special needs students, only 13 chose to have lunch with a student with special needs and only 13 indicated interest in spending more time being a friend to a student with special needs. The remaining 17 indicated that they did not want to develop such relationships.

Roberto reread observations recorded in his log. What stood out was the absence of meaningful interactions between typical students and students with disabilities. He conducted a focus group interview with typical students who also indicated relatively positive feelings about students with disabilities but had relatively few social experiences with them. Putting this all together made him even more committed to taking some action. He wondered whether increasing social interaction outside the classroom would encourage the desire for friendships. Would typical students choose to have lunch with their peers with disabilities? He journaled regularly during the S.T.A.R. Club activities, noting that typical students began to show interest in their peers with disabilities. He repeated the final survey and found some heartening results.

The Democratic Classroom Study

Ruby did not wait until the end of student teaching to carefully examine her data. She planned each of her actions based on the unfolding story that her data opened to her. Right from the start of her study she recorded observations of her students'

Ruby

participation. Conferences with her mentor supported her hunch that only a few students participated in discussion. Then, in order to understand the student perspective on citizenship and what it entailed, she administered a Citizenship Survey. When she found that students thought that participation and knowledge of government were unimportant to citizenship, she planned activities to encourage collaborative and participatory work.

Another way she tracked student perceptions of community was through the Classroom Community Survey, which students took near the beginning and near the end of her student teaching. Analyzing the results of the "before" survey confirmed her hypothesis that fifth period had a lower sense of community than her other classes. Her teaching would have to address this problem. She continued to monitor her activities and carefully reflect on them throughout student teaching, verifying her own interpretations by consulting with her mentor and her students. She kept in mind her goal of encouraging strong student–teacher collaboration and student–student collaboration as a means of creating a classroom community that would ultimately result in students showing more care and respect for one another.

In spite of her efforts, things seemed to be getting worse—lack of respect among students, particularly those in fifth period, seemed to be increasing rather than decreasing. One student's poetry reading taught the students (and Ruby) a lesson they would not soon forget.

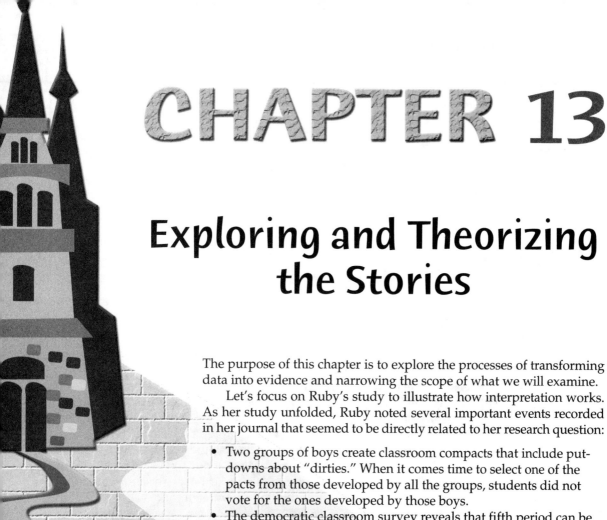

CHAPTER 13

Exploring and Theorizing the Stories

The purpose of this chapter is to explore the processes of transforming data into evidence and narrowing the scope of what we will examine.

Let's focus on Ruby's study to illustrate how interpretation works. As her study unfolded, Ruby noted several important events recorded in her journal that seemed to be directly related to her research question:

- Two groups of boys create classroom compacts that include put-downs about "dirties." When it comes time to select one of the pacts from those developed by all the groups, students did not vote for the ones developed by those boys.
- The democratic classroom survey reveals that fifth period can be characterized as less collaborative and more disrespectful than the other periods.
- One of the "dirties" reads a powerful poem to class about an outcast who learns to be invisible. The class reacts with complete silence, and then breaks into applause: "Give her an 'A'"!

These data drew Ruby's attention and begged for reflection. Taken together, they became the *issue* that drove her to make sense of what was happening: As Ruby struggled to create a democratic environment for learning, some of her students were becoming tyrannical! To make sense of the irony of this situation, Ruby relied on her intuition *and* her power of analytical and logical thinking. While logic would tell her that she was doing everything "right" according to what she read about classroom community, her intuition and the data told her that something was different.

Sometimes, we rely on intuition rather than logic and analysis to make immediate sense of a situation. Roberto, for example, saw two cousins sitting next to each other in home economics class. One was a

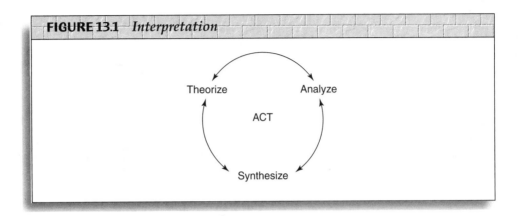

FIGURE 13.1 *Interpretation*

student with disabilities. The "typical" student did not acknowledge his cousin's existence in spite of repeated attempts to make conversation. Roberto *knew* that something was wrong. Further observation and analysis might uncover clues about the relationship between these two cousins.

Interpretation is a process used to explain, to give meaning, to make sense of the many disparate events and ideas that we encounter as teachers. Often we take data apart (analyze) and put them back together in new ways (synthesize), and this helps us to make assertions (theorize) that propel us to action, all the while seeking verification. We proceed systematically, using our logical and analytical powers to make inferences and draw conclusions about actions to take. At other times, an appropriate response is obvious without further analysis and interpretation. Our experiences, insights, and intuition provide all that is needed in these instances. If we learn to think critically *and* to relax, creating spaces for the unexpected, these spaces might quietly fill with understanding. Taken together, logic, intuition, and artistry can come together in transformative ways.

The transformative process of interpretation (and action) is an interactive one. (See Figure 13.1.) We analyze and *intuit* to inform our actions. Analysis helps us to synthesize—to get a better picture of the whole. We synthesize and go back to the parts to check out our hunches, and we create a whole upon which we can base our assertions, which leads to action, and so on.

In the remainder of the chapter, we will provide ideas and additional resources for analysis, interpretation, and verification of judgments based on the data collected. There are many paths to take in this process. We will cover some commonly used ones.

Ongoing Interpretation

Interpretation (making sense of the data) is not a separate part of action research that comes at the end of a cycle: we are constantly trying to understand our students, their work, their world, *and* ourselves. Interpretation is an ongoing process that begins as soon as we decide to study our own practice. Thus it includes everything from making sense of baseline (initial) data to making sense of selected pieces of data even as we write up the report. The meaning we attach to the data depends on how we look at it—on our circumstances, on our motives and hopes, and on our expectations.

Here are suggestions for interpreting data *while* your study is in progress.

1. *Continually narrow the focus.* Think of a funnel—wide at the top and narrower as your study progresses. This process will also narrow the scope of the data you collect. For many of us, the action research process entails focusing and narrowing until at the end of the study we begin to get a sense of what is important to study—and the cycle begins again. This may mean focusing on fewer students, or selecting only three of the ten questions on a survey for analysis.

   At the beginning of the study you had broad questions that may change and develop as you learn more about your students. At first Ruby was interested in learning how to create a democratic classroom. While this remained her general question, she began to look more carefully at how she could increase tolerance and respect among students. Her data led her to new questions and issues. Recall that this process is called *progressive focusing.*

2. *Use what you learn from your data to plan further data collection and action.* Ask yourself, What have I learned here? How will I document what is happening next? Perhaps Ruby could focus her next observations on students who are the most intolerant. Roberto might spend more time observing those two cousins to learn more about the nature of their relationship. Jon and Terry might focus on their most successful group to learn what makes this group successful and use that new knowledge to help groups that are less effective.

3. *Record your thoughts and feelings.* Write personal comments about methods, hunches, ideas related to your field notes, and interview notes on sticky pads that can be attached to student work, and so on. As patterns emerge, note them. Label them as O.C. (observer comments). For example, Ruby wrote in her personal journal:

   > **O.C.:** I am beginning to think that I should have done the Classroom Compact at the beginning of our class rather than wait until the middle. It might have provided the kind of common commitment to one another and to learning that seems to be missing.

4. *Write analytic memos.* After several days or weeks of data collection, read through your data and write a memo to yourself about what you see emerging: *patterns of behavior, words, key ideas, events.* Record *methodological dilemmas*—what to try next and *hunches* about what is happening. Perhaps we need to read something or talk to critical colleagues or to a student's guidance counselor. The analytic memo can remind us to look for something in our next observation, or to develop a particular idea or theme in our next journal entry. Shawn, for example, began to note changes in Jen that were

separate from the research questions about her development as a speaker of English. Since Shawn was studying Korean culture, she realized Jen's behaviors were considered disrespectful in her home culture. Perhaps Jen was "testing" the limits and rules in her new surroundings. Shawn had to react to Jen's behavior as well.

Analytic memos are personal field notes to ourselves, helping us to notice things that we did not notice before. Written periodically during data collection, analytic memos can help us look carefully at our data. They can also be incorporated into the final report. See the example of an analytic memo written by Ruby for her Democratic Classroom Study in the case study on page 193.

5. *Make creative comparisons.* So often we become bogged down in the concrete particulars of our data that we cannot see the possibilities they hold for us. By asking ourselves, *What is this similar to?* or *Is this idea familiar?* we may gain powerful insights. Mary Lou was stumped about how to think about a teacher in one of her studies. He seemed to have everything going for him, the right educational background, the right words to use in describing his classroom and students, . . . but something was not right. She thought to herself, *What does he remind me of?* And it came to her in an instant—a "tarnished spoon." By letting her mind range freely, Mary Lou came to have a clearer understanding of this teacher. After this flash she wrote about why the image fit so well. She included details and evidence that enabled her to create other visual images. With considerable talent, the teacher was, at the time, not able to shine, and only later realized how difficult a time his tarnished period had been.

6. *Visualize ideas.* Create pictures that show relationships or organize ideas. Visual devices can be used anywhere during the action research process. Circles and arrows, lists, charts, graphs, diagrams, or even sketches of people or classroom space are ways to both break data down into parts and put them back together.

7. *Check out your insights with participants.* What do they think about how you are interpreting the event or conversation? Are you on target?

To give you a concrete example of how Ruby's analysis proceeds while she is teaching and collecting data, we have included a table that shows what she planned to do week by week. (See the case study on page 195.)

8. *Check out your insights with critical colleagues.* What does someone who is not close to your study think about your interpretation? See suggestions for ongoing data analysis in Stepping Stones 13.1: Ongoing Data Analysis.

Ruby constantly compared one set of data with another to make decisions about what to do next. When she found that things were not going as she had expected, she looked in different directions, especially in her own private reflections of experience. She examined her own assumptions about participation and the political process and began to reflect on her students' understandings of community.

The Democratic Classroom Study
Analytic memo written by Ruby

Ruby

Week 12

Analytic Memo

I was anxious to look at the results of the "after" Classroom Community Survey. I wanted to compare student responses to the "before" survey. I arranged the data in a chart so that I could look carefully at the questions that related to teacher–student collaboration (questions 1, 2, 3) and student–student collaboration (questions 4, 5). Here is my chart:

A comparison of means on the before and after Classroom Community Survey

Class periods	Question 1		Question 2		Question 3		Question 4		Question 5	
	Before	After	Before	After	Before	After	Before	After	Before	After
4th	3.2	3.5	2.7	3.7	3.6	4.0	1.9	2.5	3.8	3.5
5th	3.1	3.5	2.2	3.1	3.3	3.7	3.0	3.4	2.7	2.1
8th	3.0	3.6	2.5	3.5	3.3	3.7	3.0	3.4	3.0	2.7

What I noticed is that in all three classes in the 6 weeks between the first and second surveys, students sensed an increase in teacher–student collaboration as evidenced by responses to questions 1 (Students make decisions about what is going on), 2 (Teacher involves students in decision making), and 3 (Students in my class work together on solving problems). On the other hand, I noticed that there was an increase in disrespect in all classes and particularly in fifth period, as evidenced by a decrease in the mean scores of students on questions related to student–student collaboration: questions 4 (A lot of students in my class like to put others down) and 5 (Students in my class treat each other with respect) where the higher the average, the less the respect. Something isn't working! I wonder what is going on? I suspected all along that my fifth-period class was not showing respect toward one another. When we did the classroom compact, the boys in those two groups made so many put-downs about the "dirties" that many of the students in class were visibly upset. Thank goodness the rest of the class had better sense and voted on a classroom compact that was more respectful of others. I am going to have to address respect and tolerance for others more seriously between now and the end of student teaching. I think I'll have them watch "Rigolleto," so that they can explore the theme of tolerance. I may also give them time to work on a final project in which they can express their own ideas about democracy.

This is so discouraging. I wonder if I am cut out for teaching!

STEPPING STONES 13.1

Ongoing Data Analysis

1. Narrow the focus of your study as needed.
2. Use what you learn from your data to plan further data collection and action.
3. Record your thoughts and feelings.
4. Write analytic memos.
5. Make creative comparisons with data.
6. Visualize.
7. Check out your insights with participants and critical colleagues.

Qualitative Data Analysis Software

When you handle rich text-based information, where deep levels of analysis on both small and large volumes are required, you may want to consider using a qualitative data analysis program. Such a program removes many of the manual tasks associated with analysis, including classifying, sorting, and arranging information, which will allow you to have more time to explore trends, build and test theories, and ultimately arrive at answers to questions. The following are some popular qualitative data analysis programs; check for new links and URLs, as these change often.

- Atlasti: http://www.atlasti.com/
- Ethnograph: http://www.qualisresearch.com/
- HyperResearch: http://www.researchware.com/
- MAXQDA: http://www.maxqda.com/
- NVivo: http://www.qsrinternational.com/

Among the above, NVivo is probably the most used in higher education. When choosing a qualitative data analysis software, you may want to consider which of the following factors, features, and functions are important for you and your research: cost, paradigm, mapping/graphic, management of data or documents, coding, and analysis.

Online Tools for Statistics

Check for new links and URLs, as these change often.

- Rice Virtual Lab in Statistics: http://onlinestatbook.com/rvls.html
- StatCenter Sampler: http://www.psych.utah.edu/learn/statsampler.html (Free Open Source Tools for teaching and learning science, methods, and statistics online)
- Virtual Laboratories in Probability and Statistics: http://www.math.uah.edu/stat/

Ongoing interpretation, exemplified by Ruby's thinking, relies on our ability to use three important research tools—comparing, asking questions, and speculating.

1. *Comparing.* We compare one piece of data to another. For example, "So many of the students in this morning class are saying the same thing as my afternoon class. Both classes are saying they just don't get the point I am trying to make!"

2. *Asking questions.* When comparing, we ask questions of the data, look for key ideas, categories, issues and patterns of behavior, thinking, and ideas. For example, "Why can't the students in my comparison group answer the simple question, *Who is your favorite author?* Kids in the other class did."

3. *Speculating or theorizing.* We make educated guesses about what might be happening, basing those guesses on hunches, critical self-reflection, and

CASE STUDY

The Democratic Classroom Study
Excerpts from the time line Ruby used in analyzing data

Ruby

Week	Activity	Data Collection Strategy	Analysis
1	Collect baseline data about student perceptions of "citizenship."	Citizenship survey. Bi-weekly researcher journal.	Compute means. Discussion with mentor. Look for patterns in journal.
2	Read literature on collaboration. Conduct community-building exercises.	Informal interview with research advisor. Classroom Community Survey. Researcher journal. Student journal.	Discussion with action research group. Compute means. Read journals.
3–4	Bill of Rights project.	Student projects. Student journal. Researcher journal.	Use rubric to evaluate projects. Read journals. Write analytical memo.
12–13	Assess student collaboration. Classroom Compact.	Classroom Community Survey. Student compacts. Researcher journal. Student journal. What can we do to create a community?	Compute means and compare with "before" survey. Look for patterns in journals. Write analytical memo. Discuss patterns with mentor.
14–15	Personal values project.	Student projects and presentations. Researcher journal. Student journal.	Use rubric to evaluate a project. Analytical memo.

dialogue with others. We think critically about what we have in front of us and what we still need to know. We conjecture. For example, Wendy asked students in different settings, "What was an assignment the teacher gave from which you learned the most? The least?" Wendy noted that with the exception of students from a small island in an English-speaking country, most students responded that they learned when they had choices. The students from the island were all unable or unwilling to answer the question. Wendy then had to speculate about why. Was the phrasing of the question unclear? Did these students think that they were being asked to critique their teacher and their school? And if so, were they unable for some reason to do this? Another word for this process of conjecturing is *hypothesizing*. Hypotheses are formed from careful analysis *and* from making creative leaps. We talk more about that later.

We will now go into greater detail about the process of *interpretation—analysis, synthesis,* and *theorizing,* which allows us to make *assertions*—that helps us to make decisions that are not only logical and intuitive and artistic, but ethical in their commitments to creating a just and caring environment for learning. While we present it as a linear process, it is, in fact, cyclical, interactive, and spontaneous, as we will shortly see.

Analysis

Analysis usually necessitates taking things apart. We use analysis to "get it right" (Wolcott, 1994). To get it right, we carefully look at data, identify the parts, and develop them. We look for the holes, the patterns, the secrets, the mysteries, for what is in between the stones, the hidden assumptions, the disguises that we find when we follow the path that wanders off almost silently into the forest where the Yellow Brick Road disappears. To work in a systematic way with existing data and data that have not yet been interpreted, working with them in such a way that they yield insights that are dependable, accurate, reliable, *and* irrationally right is no small accomplishment.

For example, Meridith, a student teacher interested in how her "reluctant" readers would respond to young adult literature, was disturbed by responses to *The House on Mango Street* by Sandra Cisneros (1991), a story narrated by a young Latino girl, alienated from U.S. culture. Comments such as "Yeah, and they really are that way—those Spics" confirmed her suspicion of racism.

Students sneered and called her a feminist when she asked them to consider the portrayal and treatment of Hispanic women. Comments such as "I hate this book!" and "This is stupid!" made her question her original hunch about the potential of young adult literature to turn on these young people to reading. Their comments left her concerned that their racism and sexism would interfere with their experience with young adult literature. Had she ended her inquiry at this point, it is easy to see the conclusions she would have drawn about her students and the potential of young adult literature.

But she noted the silence of the female students. When she asked students to write their reactions to the novel, the female students resonated with the perspective of the female protagonist. Perhaps their silence was the result of enculturation into a world of male "voices."

Tools for analysis can help us to get at the data in systematic, intuitive, and creative ways. They are presented here in numerical order; analysis is less orderly and discrete.

1. *Get ready.* Assemble the data informally and conduct an inventory: What data do you have? (Researcher log, diary, student journal, student work, interviews, questionnaires, analytical memo.) Is it complete? Are there missing responses on some surveys? If it is too late to have students fill in missing data, adjust your calculation to take this into account. Is everything labeled and dated? Is there order to the piles, folders, index cards, and so on? For example, are all the interviews together, either on successive word processing files or in a folder or binder with pages numbered? Likewise, is student work organized in a way that makes sense to you?

   If you are working with numbers, such as calculating averages to compare student scores on different surveys, tests, or rubrics, now is the time for initial processing. Although much of what you want to do can be done manually or with a calculator, you may want to explore the option of using a spreadsheet, which is often part of a software package that comes with your computer. Either way, you will be "entering your data" into a matrix or table and calculating means, percentages, or in some cases correlations, making the data ready for close examination. We have included examples or graphs and simple calculations of means, median, and mode in Traveler's Notes C: Organizing and Visually Displaying Data.

   Remind yourself of what you are going to look for in the data: What is the research question? What issues concern you? What hunches do you have about what you might find? Keep your eyes and mind open to seeing things that you do *not* expect to find. Find a comfortable, quiet place and uninterrupted time when you can spread out the data in front of you. Take a deep breath and . . .

2. *Read and reread.* Immerse yourself in your data. What is going on here? Who? When? Where? How much? Why? What is *not* going on here? What jumps out at you by its presence? Or by its absence? In wide margins of your notes or on adhesive note paper, write your impressions, your questions, your speculations. Read for evidence related to your question and your issues.

   Roberto reads his own journal entries and researcher log, looking for evidence of improved student attitudes toward children with disabilities, examining observations of student's body language and communication, and reflecting on what others have observed as well. What strikes him, even shocks him, is the absence of interaction. Ruby looks for evidence of community in exchanges between students and between students and herself, in survey responses, in comments made by her mentor. She identifies a lack of peer respect. In searching for ways to include Jen in the classroom, Shawn looks for evidence of language development and notices huge leaps. Jon and Terry, wanting to create a holistic literacy-learning environment, look through student journals and survey results for evidence of reading development related to literature circles; they begin to notice a move toward critical thinking and more positive attitudes toward reading.

When reading over surveys, questionnaires, or interviews, we often find that some questions are more relevant and illuminating than others. Since we cast a wide net at the beginning of a study, we may want to later select only those questions for analysis that now seem important.

Here is an example of what one action researcher did. On a survey about reading habits and preferences, one pair of researchers asked students whether they visit their neighborhood library. After they read the set of responses, it was clear that many students were unfamiliar with their public library. On further thought, the researchers realized that the neighborhood where the respondents lived was very far from a library and that most families in this neighborhood had limited access to cars. This question, then, did not reflect anything that the child as a developing reader could control. The researchers decided against using it in their analysis.

On the other hand, you may find that responses to one or two questions offer important clues—analyzing those questions, while keeping the others in the back of your mind, may lead to some important insights. One researcher developed a student attitude instrument with 10 questions and discovered that one question was so informative that its response would predict the results of the rest of the questions. A one-question instrument would have been just as valuable. Try out questions on a small sample of students before giving them to the entire class.

Finally, make time to walk away from the data, sleep on them, to talk them over with others. And then . . .

3. *Look for the parts.* Skimming the data, look for words, phrases, behaviors, ways of thinking, events that seem to repeat themselves. Look for parts related to your issues and questions. Look for things that jump out to you as well as the subtleties. Look for patterns, or lack of them.

   a. Grouping these ideas together is a process of *categorizing*. Categories can be ideas, issues, themes, dilemmas. Make a list of categories. Open a file in your computer for each category and write about each. Include quotes, descriptions, critical incidents, and your thoughts. As your study continues, look for data to add to each file. (Files can be in your computer, on index cards, in your journal, wherever it makes sense to you.) Be open to the possibility that the categories (like your questions) may change. While it is preferable to develop your categories so that they accurately reflect what is happening in your situation, action researchers sometimes use categories developed by other researchers or theorists. Here are some examples of both kinds of categories from our case studies. See *Case Study: Categories Developed by Roberto, Shawn, Jon, and Terry* which follows.

CASE STUDY

Categories Developed by Roberto, Shawn, Jon, and Terry

Roberto

Shawn

Jon

Terry

Roberto's categories, developed from the focus group interviews, describing student attitudes toward children with disabilities (the S.T.A.R. Club Study).

- Comfortable

- Empathic

- Uneasy

Shawn's categories describing Jen's progress (helping Jen learn English as a second language):

- Vocabulary

- Word recognition

- Written expression

- Social adjustment

Jon and Terry selected these categories from Daniels (1994) to describe reader progress (the Literature Circles Study):

D/C	Drawing conclusions
P	Predicting
S	Summarizing
E	Enthusiasm
Q	Questioning
C	Connecting
I	Illustrating

In some studies the categories are more like issues or dilemmas or tensions. In a study that Joanne conducted with her graduate students, she felt student resistance to course content was a major issue. She decided to look for the points of resistance to understand the dynamics of power that were in play in her classroom. The forms of resistance she noted are listed in *Case Study: Forms of Resistance to Power.*

In another study, this time a study of the first year of a newly formed professional development middle school, Joanne and her teacher-researcher colleagues noted several dilemmas in their study of multiple perceptions of the new school. See *Case Study: Dilemmas Faced by Teachers, Students, Parents, and Other School Professionals in a Newly Formed Professional Development Middle School.*

CASE STUDY

Forms of Resistance to Power

- Emotional resistance to power—doctoral students reacted strongly (both favorably and unfavorably) when they were asked to critique their own fields of inquiry.

- Conceptual resistance to power—doctoral students found it difficult to make assertions about power relations in their own fields.

- Political resistance to power—doctoral students openly critiqued the power vested in the position of professors who claimed to have the authority of knowledge in their respective fields.

- Moral resistance to power—doctoral students questioned the moral authority of Foucault's challenge to the existence of absolutes or moral truths.

- Ethical resistance to power—doctoral students felt that studying Foucault's notions of power made them question the ethics of things that they had previously found acceptable.

CASE STUDY

Dilemmas Faced by Teachers, Students, Parents, and Other School Professionals in a Newly Formed Professional Development Middle School

- The dilemma of discipline: We want students to be self-directed, and we want to impose discipline.

- The dilemma of involvement: We want involvement, but we are frustrated by it.

- The dilemma of the orderly school: The ideal school is both orderly and caring.

This is how the process of categorizing worked for one action researcher. Jennifer made audiotapes of oral discussion at each table in her elementary classroom where literature groups were meeting. She listened to the tapes every night on her commute home. After playing each tape several times, she began to invent labels to express what was taking place in those discussions. With her list of labels, she relistened to the tapes and coded each for the type of response and the frequency of each type of response.

Certain discussions were harder to code than others, so she asked a critical colleague to listen to them. This collaborative process helped. Jennifer ended up with 12 categories of oral responses from simple ones such as

STEPPING STONES 13.2

"Prompts" for Categorizing Data

- *Setting* includes school demographics, location, per-pupil expenditure, classroom arrangement, and classroom environment.
- *Definitions* include how students and teachers define key concepts such as *discipline, engagement,* or *good student* and what political, religious, or socioeconomic orientation shapes their perspective.
- *Rules and norms*—the ways in which things are routinely done, such as reviewing math homework at the beginning of each class—are often expressions of underlying rules, values, and beliefs.
- *Roles and relationships*—roles such as mother, caretaker, and police officer and relationships such as mother–child, nurse–patient, police officer–criminal, leader–follower, and boss–worker—often emerge as important ways to understand how people do or do not see themselves.
- *Processes*—time periods, steps, chronology, turning points, benchmarks, transitions—are ways to organize data to show changes and growth.

Source: Adapted from Bogdan and Biklen. *Qualitative Research for Education,* 2/e. Published by Allyn and Bacon, Boston, MA. Copyright © 1992 by Pearson Education. Adapted by permission of the publisher.

predicting what would happen next in the story or *clarifying* story details to more sophisticated ones such as *judging character's actions* and even *judging author's choices and writing.*

The categories that emerge often come from the theoretical perspectives of the researcher. A constructivist-oriented researcher will most likely develop a different set of categories than a behaviorist-oriented researcher. Joanne's categories, for example, related to resistance, emerged in a context of a class that was studying power and its effect on teachers and teaching.

We find that for beginning researchers, it is often helpful to have a set of *possible* ways to categorize data. The following "prompts" are adapted from Bogdan and Biklen (1992). See Stepping Stones 13.2.

To make it easy to locate these categories in the data, researchers devise different ways of organizing and coding their data:

- Color-code each category (highlight positive responses with green, and so on).
- Develop a code for each category through numbers, symbols, abbreviations, letters, and so on. For example, P indicates the reading strategy of *predicting;* the computer symbol :-) indicates a positive attitude toward children with disabilities.
- Sort data into piles, into file folders, into boxes, into word processing files.

- Using the search function in a word processor, retrieve words that relate to the concept that is emerging. Use the word count feature available when you do a spell check. There are many data analysis software packages on the market, some fairly sophisticated and probably not necessary for the typical teacher-researcher.

CASE STUDY

The Literature Circles Study
Analysis of Sam's Student Response Journal Entries Following Discussion

Jon

Terry

D/C = Drawing conclusions   P = Predicting   S = Summarizing
Q = Questioning   C = Connecting   I = Illustrating   E = Enthusiasm

Date	Words	D/C	P	S	Q	C	I	E
8/31	27		I	I		I		I
9/18	50		II	I		I		
9/23	13	I						
9/24	56	I				II		I
9/25	41		II			I		
9/26	17	I		I				
9/28	30			I	I			I
10/1	49				IIIII			
10/2	61		II	II				
10/3	28		II					
10/28	52		I	I		I		
10/29	67	II		II				I
10/30	61	I	I	II				
11/4	38	I	I			I		
11/5	32		I	I		I		
11/6	49		II	II				
11/7	43			II		I		
11/11	56			I		II		
11/12	78	I		II		II		I
11/13	84			I	II	III		
11/14	64	I			III	I		I
11/15	32	I			I			I
Total		10	15	20	12	17	0	7

b. The next task is to see whether the *categories selected fit the data.* Does the label need to be changed to more adequately and powerfully reflect what we are finding in our data? Are categories overlapping, so that a list of 10 categories might be reduced to 5?

c. *Develop these categories* by defining them. Definitions provide specificity. For example, Shawn sees Jen's *social adjustment* as *participation,* which included *speaking* in discussions, *sharing* her work with other children, and *volunteering* to take a nonspeaking part in a play. She also notes that sometimes she participates in a *quiet* and *shy* way and sometimes in a more *assertive* way. These italicized words are descriptors of what it means to "adjust socially."

Developing and understanding the categories is a major challenge of analysis. And researchers often find useful ways of organizing their work to facilitate the development process. Jon and Terry did exactly that. After combing through student responses for categories, they developed a table and tallied the number of times they saw evidence of predicting, summarizing, and so on, in student journal entries. See *Case Study: The Literature Circles Study.*The tally sheets on Sam, one of the focus students, revealed that as time went on, he moved past the simpler skill of summarizing to skills such as connecting and questioning, skills associated with critical thinking. But using a table to tally the recurrence of a particular skill or concept is only one way to organize and use categories. See Traveler's Notes C: Organizing and Visually Displaying Data for a variety of visual displays.

Synthesis

Synthesis is the process of combining parts to make a whole. Once we have taken things apart in our analysis, we need to put them back together and ask ourselves, How do the parts relate to one another?

Synthesis is a creative process. In fact, one expert on creativity, Silvano Arieti (1976), calls creativity the *magic synthesis.* While it might sound as if you simply take your data apart and make sense of the parts (analysis), and then make sense of the whole by reassembling the parts and putting them back together (synthesis), that isn't what really happens. We have separated the two processes because we feel it will be easier to understand them this way.

Analysis and synthesis take place simultaneously, usually without our notice. While in the research process, analysis and synthesis are as natural as inhaling and exhaling, and are taking place much of the time. In this process, we are *finding patterns* (analysis), and then *making sense* of those patterns (synthesis).

1. *Find patterns.* Learning is change as a result of experience. Finding patterns in experience facilitates learning. Noticing patterns in experience, from the simplest to the most complex, enables us to draw our data together in new ways. As researchers, we keep our questions and issues in mind and look for the ways in which the parts relate to one another. Does one part always occur

when another part occurs? Does one part happen more often than others? Do parts happen simultaneously? What are the conditions under which this or that happens? What is the role of power? What happens when the data are "disaggregated" by gender, race, ethnicity, ability, social class, achievement level, time, or age? As action researchers, we look for changes in thinking, behavior, feelings—for developments in ourselves and our students—that could be consequences of our actions.

To determine whether changes were occurring in student collaboration, Ruby arrayed the "before" and "after" survey data in a table. In her analytic memo shown earlier, you can see how she displayed these data. Were students becoming collaborative? Did one class work more collaboratively than another? If so, in what ways? When examining her journal, she looked for clues to her frustration: What is my contribution to the disrespect my students show toward one another?

Roberto noted that instances of uneasiness decreased over the course of the year. Neutral and negative attitudes were replaced by more positive, helpful attitudes in which typical students expressed interest in becoming more engaged with their peers with disabilities. He asked, When did this occur? And he noted that after S.T.A.R. Club activities had been going on for some time, typical students asked him for information about students with disabilities. They began to sit together at lunchtime.

Shawn noted that Jen gradually changed from being a shy, reserved, and physically passive student to one who volunteered to participate in class. Shawn's analysis of data found that this change happened in a context of peer support. Jon and Terry noted that over time, students in the literature circles summarized ideas less and moved to more substantive responses including raising questions, judging characters, evaluating the author's style, and relating events and actions to their own lives. These teachers knew from their literature review that these changes are associated with increased critical thinking.

We may want to look at the conditions and contexts surrounding these thoughts, behaviors, and feelings—these patterns. We can do this by asking questions of our data. What are possible causes? What are possible consequences?

We most often think of patterns in terms of frequency. How many times do students participate, or look bored, or sign books out of the library, or complete their homework, or score an A on a test? But this is only one type of pattern. In Figure 13.2 we illustrate the rich list of possible patterns that can be found in data and examples of each. We have adapted this list from David Tripp's SCOPE Program (1996).

Because frequency of occurrence is an often-used and important pattern, we have included information about how to calculate the mean, median, and mode in Traveler's Notes C: Organizing and Visually Displaying Data along with an example of how to construct a means table. Each pattern that we notice becomes the basis for making sense of the data. However, many

FIGURE 13.2 Patterns in data

Patterns	Questions	Examples
Frequencies	How often does this occur? How often does "this" occur in comparison to "that"? Does it occur constantly and evenly? Does it occur periodically and in waves?	How often do children visit book corner during free-choice playtime? How may French vocabulary words taught in class appear in the journal writing of French I students? How often do girls and boys seek help during science lab?
Timing	What things occur simultaneously? Do the similar things occur during similar periods, or at similar times of the lesson, day, week, year? What things occur in a sequence?	Who arrives first in class each day and who leaves last? During what time during the lesson do my students seem most engaged?
Spaces	How are things connected in space? Close or distant? Above or below? Beside or opposite? Crossing or parallel? Inside or outside? On or off? Over or under?	Where do the boys sit in class? The girls? The academically successful students? The academically unsuccessful students? Who stays inside for lunch? How does room arrangement enhance or frustrate learning?
Interactions	What is this acting on? What is this reacting to? Who is interacting with whom?	To what are students responding when I ask them to write a journal entry about what we have learned today? Do they respond to what they think I want to hear, or to what they are reading? Or to something else?
Causes	What are the possible causes of this? What does this cause?	Why do some students do better on tests when they study in groups and others do not? What are some of the possible causes of student misbehavior in my classroom?
Effects	Is the effect of this to increase or decrease that? To balance or unbalance that? To change or maintain that?	What are the effects of student participation in school decision making on their sense of autonomy? What are the effects of interdisciplinary teaming on students' sense of belonging?
Conditions	Is this a necessary condition for that to happen as it does? Under what circumstances does this occur?	What kinds of control do adolescents need over their environment to feel that their work is meaningful? What are the effects on children, if any, when the teacher engages in sustained silent reading with them? When black, white, and Latino middle school students participate in a multicultural awareness workshop, what are the effects on the ways they socialize in and out of school?
Speeds	Does this happen as fast as that?	Do children who are taught holistically develop at the same speed on reading tests as those taught with phonics only? Does one method of word processing instruction produce faster typists than others?

Tripp, D. (1996). *The SCOPE Program*. Perth, Western Australia: Murdoch University Centre for Curriculum & Professional Development. p. 20.

relationships are unimportant, and we need not follow up on them. Key questions to ask about any pattern are, *So what?* and *What does this mean?*

2. *Look for confirming and disconfirming data.* While we have made the point that it is important to continually look for evidence in the data that confirms our hunches about patterns we see emerging, we must also look for disconfirming evidence—evidence that does not fit into our emerging understanding of what is going on. Disconfirming data can be *very important* to understanding what is going on. Joy, a shy, attentive, gentle, and generally slow in movement and response second grader was out of character on Thursdays. Mary Lou, who was one of the teachers, recorded in her notes that instead of watching out for the younger children in the class as she would normally do, Joy would become bossy and agitated.

When exploring this further, Mary Lou discovered that on Wednesday evenings, the entire family went to a long church service—Joy would not get to bed until after 11:00 P.M. When Mary Lou shared with Joy's parents what was happening on Thursdays, the parents made arrangements to get Joy home earlier from the church service. We may find important secrets in those instances that just don't seem to fit into the dominant pattern. In this case, a pattern in Joy's classroom behavior was disrupted, and through data collection and analysis, another pattern was noted—Thursdays.

Theorizing and Making Assertions

So what? What do I make of all this? What does it mean in light of my original question and my new question? What does it mean in the context of my study? How do I explain the patterns? What do others make of all this? What assertions can I make based on what I have learned? These questions we can ask when we are theorizing about our teaching.

Assertions can be statements that direct action. When Ruby says, "My own experiences in politics and my understanding of the Bill of Rights should have warned me that a democracy that relies too heavily on rights cannot create a safe community." She is making an assertion. It is not new knowledge, but knowledge that is tacit and given new meaning in the context of her teaching. The potential for her teaching is clear—emphasize both rights and responsibilities.

Assertions can also be claims to new knowledge. Roberto's concluding remarks exemplify this: "My original impressions about the 'typical' students and their interest in students in special classes were erroneous. These middle school students had mostly positive attitudes about those with disabilities. The problem was that they no longer had the same opportunities to socialize as they did in the elementary classroom." In each case, assertions are made with forcefulness and understanding.

Our assertions are often based less on recently acquired facts than on our own personal frameworks for seeing the world. Ruby is immersed in political science and critical theory. Roberto's thinking is shaped by experience as an elementary school teacher where inclusion worked by virtue of the extended time students spent together in self-contained classrooms. Shawn, Jon, and Terry are enrolled in a master's degree program that describes itself as constructivist. Students are encouraged to be change agents, creating classrooms that are more holistic and constructivist in orientation. Rethinking our personal frameworks can be accomplished with the help of our friends.

The point of interpretation is to generate many possible hypotheses. The richer the range of possibilities, the more complete the interpretation can be. Here are some examples of ways to generate multiple hypotheses to stretch your thinking.

Assume the *role* of an interested party. How might a frustrated parent view the patterns? A struggling student? An accountability-minded principal? A budget-minded community member? A contentious colleague? A novice? An expert? We are trying to stretch our thinking, to move away from our taken-for-granted view of ourselves, our students, and our situation by taking the perspective of someone else. The point is to "take the attitude of the other" (Mead, 1934) and develop empathy for that person's position. Our assertions need to be made in interaction with others. Interpretation is thus a "catalyst for mutuality and reciprocity" (Brennan and Noffke, 1997, p. 25).

There are times when our theorizing and assertions are blocked. We have too much data. We are too close to the situation. We have too much conflicting information. At times like this, it might be best to stand back, relax, and allow the spaces between these facts to open up to our creative powers. Metaphorical thinking is a valuable tool. How are these students' lives like a tapestry? How is my classroom like music? What kind of music?

Theorizing also draws ideas from the larger body of literature and the public theories that have been developed by researchers and thinkers relevant to your field of inquiry. In this way we join an ongoing community of scholars, which, over time, adds new ideas and modifies existing theories.

And finally, assertions are made in a context. We are not generalizing to all students, or all teachers, or all classrooms. Rather, we are making statements that seem to apply in our own situations. Roberto's assertion that inclusion is not working is made in the context of a middle school in which students move from class to class, as opposed to an elementary school in which students become more connected to one another in the self-contained classroom.

The process of analysis, synthesis, and making assertions is illustrated by the work of Mary Schwartz, a fifth- and sixth-grade teacher who decided to invite parents and members of the community to present their ideas at a math workshop. She showed students the connection between classroom math and the real world by presenting their ideas. Part of the data collection was a letter students were asked to write, telling Mary how they felt about the math workshop. To analyze the data, she first read over all the letters, noting the ideas that continually appeared: *relevance, enjoy, motivation, organized, confidence,* and the role of the *teacher.* She then reread the student letters and wrote codes in the margins (R for relevance, E for enjoy, M for motivation, O for organized, C for confidence, and T for teacher). See *Case Study: Coding Data.*

Coding Data

> Dear Mrs. Schwartz,
>
> Thank you for creating the Math workshop. I thought it was pretty cool. I learned a lot about math from Mrs. Lungu, Mr. Patrick, Mr Zizzo, and
> (R) Mr. Peaslee. I didn't Know that a lot of jobs use math. I liked the math
> (E) workshop because it was exciting and I learned something at the same time. I learned chemistry, (I didn't Know it involved science) sports statistics, how Mr. Peaslee uses math to help people that have an injury, and how math is used in our culture. This was a great idea because it also shows how important math is in the world. I think this
> (M) helped me to love math more than before!!! I learned so many new and cools things from these parents. I hope we can do this next year.
> (T) Thanks Mrs. Schwartz and parents for making math fun.
>
>   From your student,
>   Nadine Masagara

Categories of Student Responses to the Math Workshop

Relevance	Enjoy/fun	Motivation	Confidence	Important role of teacher
"How Mr. Peaslee used math to help people with a sports injury."	"It has been the most fun thing in school."	"I want to get a good job using math."	"I now know I can get it [math]."	"When teacher is motivated and excited, it spills over to students."
"I realize I need math no matter what I do."	"I liked the math workshop because it was exciting and I learned something at the same time."	"I think this helped me to love math more than before!!!"	"I feel stronger in practicing my math."	"You make it fun."
"I do math around the house."		"I will put more effort into math."	"I know how to learn."	"You show us the relevance of math."
"I used to not care, but now I see the impact on people's lives."		"I want to be a really good student."		

Next, she opened files in her word processor for each of the categories and added the words or phrases from each student letter that fit into that category. See *Case Study: Categories of Student Responses to the Math Workshop.*

Based on this analysis, she created a concept map that synthesized the emerging connections between the categories: When students see the relevance of math in everyday life, their confidence seems to grow. See *Case Study: Synthesizing and Showing Relationships.*

With this assertion about the relationship between the categories, she wrote assertions about each individual category and developed each assertion with student quotes to illustrate her points. She incorporated the resulting paragraphs into the section of her report called "What have I learned?" For an example, see *Case Study: Developing the Category of Relevance for the Written Report.*

CASE STUDY

Synthesizing and Showing Relationships

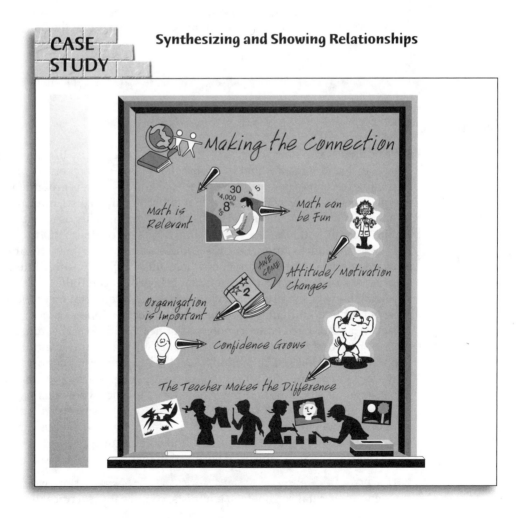

CASE STUDY

Developing the Category of Relevance for the Written Report

Relevance

I had hoped that the Real World Math Workshops would help the students see the relevance of their classroom math. The student letters evaluating the workshops revealed that the students had indeed made the connection. Their comments included phrases like "I realize I need math, no matter what I want to do" and "I used to not care, but now I see the impact on people's lives." They also said, "I know how grownups use it," particularly "how Mr. Peaslee used math to help people with a sports injury." "It is something more than what we do in school." "I do math around the house!" One fifth grader said that now when her family goes to dinner and to the movies, she calculates how much it will cost for the family. These sample comments show that students now recognize the importance of math in their daily lives.

Verification

Verification is knowing when you "got it right." We ensure that the judgments we make will lead to action that is "right." For action researchers, *right* has a special meaning. As you may recall, we said that action research is grounded in an ethical commitment to improving society (that is, become more just), improving ourselves (that we may become more conscious of our responsibility as members of a democratic society), and ultimately improving our lives together (building community).

When Roberto interprets the indifference of regular education students toward special education students as a result of lack of positive interaction rather than a lack of caring, his interpretation is based on carefully collected data and a growing body of literature on inclusion. Ruby's interpretation of the growing disrespect among students (in spite of her direct actions to create harmony and respect) is placed in a larger context of political life. She recalls from her own studies that "a democracy that relies too heavily on rights cannot create a safe community." Her self-reflections lead her to understand how she herself is involved in creating conditions that undermine her teaching goals. Blame, prejudice, anger at students, and a desire to be a "savior" were feelings she sought to temper with empathy, equanimity, understanding, and acceptance of her own limitations as a person and teacher. Ruby's interpretations are thus made within her multiple commitments to justice, self, and community.

There are several aspects of verification that we might consider:

1. *Our judgments are made from a particular standpoint.* We are women, men, environmentalists, liberals, feminists, conservatives, critical thinkers.

Understanding and clarifying our positions and values is important information to share with others. Carspecken in his book *Critical Ethnography in Educational Research* (1996) argues that *all* research is political because "all researchers seek some form of self-empowerment through their work, just as all people in everyday settings seek recognition and dignity" (p. 170). He goes on to say that all research claims are made in complex social and cultural situations in which power relations are naturally present. Critical researchers argue that the more we reduce power differences so that participants have an equal "say" with researchers, the closer we come to making valid statements. The action orientation of critical researchers is not, however, without pain. By opening up the research process in a way that gives equal say to all participants, we open ourselves to being "wounded" (McLaren, 1992). Ruby can certainly attest to that, as can any teacher-researcher who really listens to students. We can be hurt by student responses. But by being open to our students through our commitment to equity, we (and our students) may grow personally and professionally.

2. *Critical researchers also argue that validity and truthfulness lie within consensus among participants.* Stringer (1996) reminds us that "we are not looking for the 'best' or most 'correct' explanation, but one that makes sense or can be accommodated by all of the stakeholders" (p. 93). From this perspective, how groups come to verify particular data as evidence is more important than overcoming the "threats" to validity, such as adequate sample size, randomization, history, and maturation. For teacher action researchers, then, claims of "truth" are developed and tested within a group. Using this line of thinking, securing broad consent may allow us to generalize.

3. *To find the truth, we need to seek out the voices of our participants, and ensure that even the most quiet or most contrary will be heard.*

4. *Self-reflection and self-awareness are an integral part of making claims to knowledge.* As we try to transform our classrooms, we also need to become aware of ways in which we need to transform ourselves.

5. *Reciprocity in relationships characterized by mutual trust, caring, and awareness will help us to shape judgments respectful of others involved in and represented in our research.*

6. *Commitment to justice, respect, and the dignity of our participants and a desire to improve the lives of our students will influence our interpretations and claims to knowledge.*

Lincoln (1997) says that making quality judgments is about "how we can trust each other and the things we write, and how we can translate our inquiries into meaningful, purposeful individual and collective social action" (p. 66). The image of a triangle is offered by interpretive researchers as a means to get closer to a "truth" or a consensus. We build triangulation into our studies by using multiple sources of data, multiple methods, even multiple theories to develop diverse perspectives. If and when these perspectives converge (and sometimes the points of view that are brought to a study are vastly different), we are encouraged to believe that the *findings* of a study are credible and trustworthy. But can we be sure that three different perspectives will find a fixed point on the horizon in the same way that sailors use the stars to triangulate their location?

Truth is elusive. What is right in one context may be wrong in another. We have found that Richardson's (1998) image of the crystal to be a more robust way to approach the world. Rather than a three-sided, fixed triangle, a crystal is multi-dimensional and changeable. It reflects the external world, but it also refracts within itself, "creating different colors, patterns, arrays" as it casts off light in different directions. "What we see depends on our angle of repose" (p. 358). The image of the crystal breaks down the notion of validity as the search for a single or ultimate truth. It reflects the possibility that there is no single truth and that the data we study (such as writing, oral communication, body language, photographs, drawings, music) have multiple meanings and validity. Rather than finding the complete truth, we find that truth is partial and culturally constructed. And although we feel that our knowledge is growing because of the complexity we begin to see, we are left with doubts about what we know.

There are several methods that action researchers use to verify the claims they make. The methods we suggest aim for trustworthiness, credibility, and respectfulness. Here are some suggestions for maintaining veracity in the inferences we make from our data:

1. *Make your standpoint clear,* to the extent that you are able. Let others know your values and positions on relevant topics.
2. *Use multiple perspectives* of various people, theories, and methods. They offer a rich array of possible ways to transform and crystallize data into evidence related to our questions. There are several ways to gain these multiple perspectives:
   - Triangulation and crystallization of people, methods, theories is a way to cross-check data sources and open up, for argumentation, the veracity of possible interpretations. To triangulate with people, we might select students, a colleague, and a mentor to observe our classrooms and provide feedback. To triangulate with methods, we might use observations, interviews, and documents produced by others. To triangulate with theories, approach the analyzed data from the perspective of a developmentalist, a behaviorist, a constructivist, or a critical theorist. While triangulation suggests three sources of data, two or more than three might be appropriate. The concept of crystallization suggests that using multiple sources is not a search for truth, but rather a search for clarity on the perspective we each bring to data and its analysis.
   - Revisiting data—individually or with a group—can open up possibilities of uncovering meanings that did not appear the first time around. Sometimes we are too close to our situations to stand back from data; we can't see the forest for the trees. But revisiting data, a week, a month, even a year later, may help us see things in a new light. Focus group interviews or informal group discussions with colleagues or other

interested stakeholders may open up the data to the "mind-constructions" (Brennan and Noffke, 1997, p. 39) of others.

- Member checking means taking data or interpretations back to the people most affected by it to ascertain their perspectives on what you have found. It is a valuable way to gain understanding, clarity—and veracity. Member checking can point out potentially valuable omissions or errors. It can also send the researcher back into the forest to rethink the data, or the research question that prompted the study. Member checking serves to democratize the research process by equalizing power relations between researcher and participants; it values the perspectives of others. Member checking can be accomplished through an interview or a discussion or by simply writing up what you have learned and giving it to participants to read. This can take courage. What happens if a student disagrees with an action researcher's interpretation of the data? Such disagreement can lead to a productive discussion and to mutuality. By including both interpretations, the reader or audience members can make sense of both perspectives.

3. *Applying indicators* to the data can add legitimacy to the interpretation. Indicators are criteria that can be used to judge the quality, or worth, or adequacy, or completeness, of data and interpretations. Involve community (students, parents, professional groups) in developing indicators that will be applied. For example, Trish wanted to document students' problem-solving skills over time, so she developed a list of indicators of what a good problem-solver actually does. The list included exploration of the problem situation before writing a problem statement and willingness to generate alternative strategies for addressing the problem. Based on these indicators, she then developed a rubric to study a series of four problems that students were given over the course of the semester. In addition to researcher-developed indicators, action researchers may choose to use externally derived indicators. Standards and rubrics developed by testing companies, professional teaching associations such as the National Council of Teachers of English, and state or provincial Departments of Education provide indicators for accountability. Teachers often use external indicators as one *source* for their own personally developed list.

4. *Provide raw data* so that readers can make their own interpretations.

5. *Write descriptively* so that the reader can imagine what you saw or heard or felt or smelled. When readers resonate with what you have said because they can imagine a similar experience, your situation becomes plausible.

6. *Be systematic.* By carrying out research in a systematic way and making our research processes transparent, we make our interpretations and explanations more credible. It means checking out our emerging hypotheses in a systematic way by discovering categories and patterns of behavior, and looking for confirming and disconfirming evidence of our hunches. But being systematic is not as linear as it may appear. It is an evolving process that relies on judgment all along the way. You may be more systematic in the telling of what you did than is obvious to you during the process. Following a hunch may lead you away from your original plan but have a coherence when you

reflect back on the process. Describing how you carried out your study helps the reader make judgments about your inferences.

7. *Be self-reflective.* Is your interpretation based on knowledge of your role in the situation? Is it based on mutual trust and caring?

The action researchers from our cases have used a variety of methods to ensure the veracity of their interpretations. One example will serve to illustrate the power of these approaches. Had Ruby relied only on her understanding of students' disrespectful behavior, she would have failed to see her contributions to the problem. Without revisiting those data, she might have continued to lay complete blame for student misbehavior on students. Without consulting critical colleagues and friends, she might have overemphasized her perceived failure.

Oral Inquiries: Making Interpretations and Assertions in Community

Although much of what we have described in this chapter shows *individuals* engaging in systematic yet open-ended reflection, these same interpretive processes of analysis, synthesis, and theorizing in order to make informed decisions may best be accomplished through collaborative inquiry with colleagues. Oral inquiries (or the descriptive review process), as described and used by teachers such as Patricia Carini (1986) at the Prospect School in Vermont and Rhoda Drucker Kanevsky (1993) at the Philadelphia Teachers Learning Cooperative and others illustrates a way of knowing about teaching and learning in community that enriches our understanding of students.

What follows is a process for learning more about a specific student by meeting with other teachers. You may have a question about a student who is having a problem. For example, "How can I help this fifth grader become more visible in my classroom?" Or "How can I support this student's learning in my classroom?" In some cases, a teacher may simply want to explore the talent or potential of a particular student. For example, "What are this student's capabilities in my classroom and the classroom of other teachers?" In any case, a teacher may want to consider presenting this particular student to colleagues so that together they might learn more about this child, and teaching in general, through a collaborative reflective process. This could be compared to what teams of colleagues do regularly in special education when they are attempting to better understand a student and plan the most effective learning program possible.

In preparing for this collegial review process, a teacher may want to consider a student in five areas: physical presence and gesture; disposition; relationships with others; activities and interests; and more formal learning. Using these five headings, the initiating teacher writes down everything possible based on observations, student work (including art and written work), anecdotes, comments from other teachers, anything that will portray the student as a whole person, "trying in her own way to create meaning in the world" (Drucker Kanevsky, 1993).

The descriptive review session has six steps:

Step 1: Convening the session. The chairperson convenes the session of teachers by presenting the name and age of the student, family information that is directly known, and the focusing question. The group may be teachers on a team, teachers at a particular grade level, specialists, or a study group interested in learning more about teaching and learning. Ideally, these are teachers who know the student or who have observed the student for the purposes of this review.

Step 2: Describing the student. In an uninterrupted time period, the teacher decribes the student in five areas: physical presence and gesture, disposition, relationships with children and adults, activities and interests, formal learning. The other teachers listen carefully to the presentation. The teacher describes not only the student, but also what the teacher has done.

Step 3: Restating the themes. The chairperson briefly restates the portrayal and summarizes the major themes that run through the picture that has been presented.

Step 4: Other descriptions. Other teachers who have had contact with the student or who have made observations of the student for this review may offer descriptions. The chairperson gives a description of the student's previous school history and any relevant information about family that is directly known and not hearsay. If a family member is a co-presenter with the teacher, this person may want to add additional information.

Step 5: Questions about the student. The chairperson opens the session for questions and comments of the participating teachers. The questions reflect their own assumptions and expectations for teaching and learning. The teachers are careful to separate questions from recommendations. The teacher presenting the student may want to add additional information.

Step 6: Recommendations. The chairperson summarizes new information; restates the focusing question; solicits recommendations based on assertions generated through analysis, synthesis, and theorizing; groups the recommendations; initiates plans for a follow up; and asks for a critique of the process.

The descriptive review is a way of knowing. It may offer new interpretations to the teacher who initiates the discussion. Resulting recommendations are then based on a broadened view of the student and the situation. By starting with a particular student, teachers can then move to students in general and to larger educational issues.

CHAPTER SUMMARY

In this chapter, we explored the process of transforming data into evidence about the consequences of our actions. We discussed evidence and found that it can be based on method, intuition, artistry, and ethical commitments. Transforming data involves taking things apart (analysis), putting the parts back together in new and creative ways (synthesis), making assertions (theorizing), and assuring ourselves and others that what we have learned is credible and trustworthy (verification). Interpretation relies on our ethical commitments—our personal frameworks, experience, and insights. It is both method and artistry.

We attempt to glean the essence of our data and to provide a context for that essence. We focus our evolving questions and issues to narrow the scope of what we will examine.

Note: You may want to read Section VII on report writing, and then come back to Chapter 13. The ways of writing up a report and portraying what you are learning in multiple formats may yield insights for both how data are collected and how they are analyzed. For example, if we know that our audience is a school board, we may want to consider presenting a videotape of student study participants. Putting together the videotape is a process of analysis and synthesis. Since action research is cyclical and rarely a linear process, you may find yourself going back and forth in this book many times throughout your study.

CHAPTER 14

Taking Action—What Will I Do Next? How Will Life Be Better?

In completing one cycle of action, observation, and reflection, the action researcher takes the knowledge and understanding he or she developed and moves to a new cycle. These new understandings can lead to actions that are in line with the aspirations that served as the impetus for inquiry.

The goal of action research is NOT to produce findings that are generalizable to other teachers, students, schools, and families. Generalizations may be used to control others. When, for example, someone in authority says, "based on research, this is the best way to teach your students," the person in authority is using generalizations to control teachers and students.

Chapter 13 contained strategies for reflection about action. We called this theorizing and posed it as a means to improve the quality of our decisions and actions. But this is not the kind of theorizing that results in generalizations. This theorizing reflects our aspirations, values, beliefs, knowledge, and intuition. We develop theories in action and use them to inform actions and to understand, articulate, and alter our practice and relationships. Thus, teacher action researchers use theories to support student authority and their own authority as learners.

Without action, there is no action research. An easy way to think about this is to list all the things that we have learned about ourselves, our students, and our situations, and to think about what we will do as a consequence of what we have learned. We think about how these next steps will make life better.

Ruby's reflections about next steps will help us to see how she turned what she learned into actions to direct her teaching and her thoughts about herself as a teacher. Ruby's follow-up action plan contains ideas about next steps; we often realize that we need to reevaluate our position, and our values. (See *Case Study: Ruby's Follow-up Action Plan.*) Her savior spirit, one that she had prized throughout her life, did not serve her well as a teacher. It got in the way of helping her students take responsibility for their own actions.

Ruby plans to use her knowledge about creating a democratic classroom in her social studies classroom. She wants the challenge of working with early adolescents. Roberto is already planning his next S.T.A.R. Club program. Shawn is making plans to become certified as an English as a Second Language (ESL) teacher. Since their study, Jon and Terry conducted Literature Circles workshops for other teachers.

Each teacher has in some way transformed understanding of her or his practice. They do this by theorizing about their practice in light of their ethical

CASE STUDY

The Democratic Classroom Study
Ruby's follow-up action plan

Ruby

What have I learned?	What will I do as a consequence of what I have learned?	How will this make life better?
A democracy that relies too heavily on rights cannot create a safe community.	I will create a classroom compact earlier on, at the beginning of class. Then, when students act in disrespectful ways, I will bring them back to the compact and remind them of agreements they had made.	We will establish a common ground of the responsibilities that democracy entails.
I have always wanted to be a type of "savior," wanting to stop the war in Vietnam, wanting to reverse the ills of society in the civil rights movement, and now trying to create a type of classroom that champions the rights of students.	I need to temper my savior spirit. I will keep reminding myself (with a little help from my friends) that I can easily burn out as a teacher if I take everything too seriously. I think that my journal will be my lifelong companion.	I will be more realistic about what I am able to do while maintaining the ideals that shape my commitment to teaching. I hope that I can remain in teaching for the rest of my career.

commitments. Frequently, insights and interpretations lead into another cycle of action research.

Transformation

We also want to acknowledge the multiple and overlapping barriers to action and change that daily present themselves to classroom teachers trying to improve their practice. Hargreaves et al. (1996) summarize a large body of literature on the difficulty of educational change in their book *Schooling for Change: Reinventing Education for Early Adolescents.*

Change is a technical process of managerial efficiency that requires special planning, design, and structural alignment. If not all elements of the system, from the district level to the classroom level, support the change, teachers are likely to feel frustration at their individual efforts.

Change is a cultural process that requires building effective collaborative and consultative relationships in an environment that encourages individuality. It is a process that requires understanding and involvement. Critical colleagues who challenge our thinking and actions and at the same time support efforts to change are invaluable companions for our journey.

Finally, change is a political and paradoxical process. Not only do people fear change because it presents something new and uncertain, but also educational change is often contested. Formal education is a gatekeeper to opportunity and a powerful distributor of life changes. In a socially divided and culturally diverse society, what education is and how it is defined favors some groups and interests over others. So attempts to change education in fundamental ways are ultimately political acts. They are attempts to redistribute power and opportunity within the wider culture. This kind of change is not a matter of more, better, or faster, it is a matter of *transformation*—as John Elliott would say "doing things differently." As you contemplate change you may want to respond to A Few Questions for Personal Reflection (Stepping Stones 14.1).

STEPPING STONES 14.1

A Few Questions for Personal Reflection

Now that my study is drawing to a close:

- What might I change in my teaching?
- What have I learned about my personal ethical commitments?
- Who else needs to learn about what I discovered?
- How could I help others learn what I know?
- Is there action I am willing to take as a result of my study?

The Tension Between Democracy and Control in Educational Change

In taking action and planning for next steps as we discuss here, the tension between democracy and control is often evident. The scenarios we are about to describe involve classroom teachers and teacher educators.

The democratic impulse is evident in many action research arenas:

- Helping teachers participate in change—evident in the school-based curriculum development projects in the United Kingdom in the 1960s and the "process" approach to teaching writing in the United States today.
- Equalizing relationships in the classroom—evident in the many efforts to give students a voice in classroom decisions.
- An explicitly emancipatory project—evident in the studies of ways to end discrimination toward Aboriginal students in Australia and efforts toward ethnic and gender equity in classrooms.

While we may act in democratic ways, we also may be complicit in acts of control by:

- Mandating that teachers do action research to improve teaching.
- Helping teachers adapt to change, instead of (or simultaneously with) encouraging their empowerment to shape change.
- Working toward changing teachers' attitudes toward research. ("If you hate most kinds of research, I promise you will really like AR.")
- Developing hypotheses about the ways teachers develop, that is, studying teacher development as an action research project instead of (or simultaneously with) supporting collegial development.
- Working toward changing students' attitudes toward school, instead of (or simultaneously with) working to change the conditions of schooling that make it undemocratic.

The point is that we need to take care not to impose our theories on others and undermine the purposes of action research. To bring about fundamental change, those responsible for student learning need to transform classrooms, policies, and structures that inhibit the agency of students and teachers.

CHAPTER SUMMARY

While we have just touched on the surface of the issues that emerge when we contemplate changing our practice to be more in line with the democratic impulses we have outlined in earlier chapters, we encourage you to think about your own situation and the paradoxes and conflicts that may arise with the changes you propose. Involve others in thinking through issues. This can be the first step in securing support to accomplish even small goals. Questions to guide thinking about "next steps" are included in Stepping Stones 14.1: A Few Questions for Personal Reflection.

SECTION SUMMARY

The process of interpretation is presented in Figure 14.1. It shows our conception of the cyclical process of the search for meaning in which we transform data into evidence. To make sense of experience, we analyze (take things apart), synthesize (put parts together), and theorize (make assertions). This is a natural part of reflective teaching used by professional teachers to make informed judgments and decisions about how to act.

In this section, we presented the tools of interpretation used by action researchers. We summarize them in Figure 14.2.

You may want to turn to Traveler's Notes C for strategies that have been developed to help teachers analyze student writing and mathematical understanding. We focus on these two areas because of the attention they are receiving on local and national levels.

In Section VI, we saw the need to use all our powers—our heads, our hearts, and our courage—to transform our practice.

In Section VII we'll see about portraying and sharing what we have learned in a public forum. But first, let's develop tools for interpretation in "Exploring the Forest."

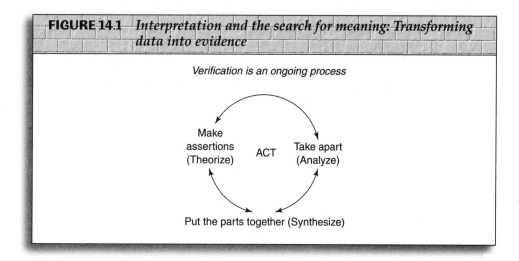

FIGURE 14.1 *Interpretation and the search for meaning: Transforming data into evidence*

Verification is an ongoing process

Make assertions (Theorize)

ACT

Take apart (Analyze)

Put the parts together (Synthesize)

FIGURE 14.2	*Tools of interpretation*

Tools of Interpretation	
Analysis: What are the parts?	Get ready. Read and reread. Look for the parts— the categories (issues, concepts, dilemmas, themes). Check the categories to see if they fit the data. Develop the categories.
Synthesis: How do the parts relate to one another?	Find patterns. Look for confirming and disconfirming data.
Theorizing: What assertions can I make to guide my actions?	What does this mean to me? To you? In this context? Is it related to a "public" theory? How are my ethical commitments furthered or modified?
Verification: How do I know I am right, that the interpretations and judgments I make are trustworthy, credible, respectful, and reflective of my aspirations?	Make your standpoint clear. Use multiple perspectives. Involve community in developing indicators to be applied. Provide raw data. Write descriptively. Be systematic. Be self-reflective.
Using Our Interpretations as a Basis for Action	
Action: What will I do with this knowledge? And how will it make life better?	How can I use what I have learned to improve myself, my situation, my students, and my teaching to reflect my aspirations and commitments to equalizing relationships?

Exploring the Forest

Developing Tools of Interpretation

If you are conducting your study as you read these chapters, these exercises will help you analyze and interpret your data. If you are conducting a mini-action research study, you can use those data for these exercises. Or you can simply read the exercises and return to them later when you have an action research study underway. Create a section of your journal labeled *Analysis and Interpretation*.

1. Tracing our evolving questions is a key aspect of reflecting on our development as teachers. These questions become important tools of data analysis and interpretation because they guide us as we look into our data to see what secrets we can derive from them. Create a section in your journal for a log of questions that arise as your study unfolds.

2. Read through the data you have collected thus far, and write an analytic memo (a note to yourself about what you see emerging as categories and patterns of behavior, words, key ideas, and events) to place in your journal. The analytic memo is a way to record and solve methodological dilemmas about what to do next. Record hunches that point in new directions for actions and data collection. They serve as reminders about what to look at more closely. Write freely. When the data are still fresh in your mind, you will be surprised at the insights you may uncover. These memos may form part of your written report.

3. In Section VI we discussed several processes that are part of interpretation:
   - Analysis: What are the parts?
   - Synthesis: How are the parts related?
   - Theorizing: What assertions can we make?

Now we are going to practice using those tools in the briefcase exercise. Briefcases often carry a diverse array of items that may be revealing. The purpose of the activity is for a group of researchers to analyze the contents of the briefcase as if it were a set of data. The directions that follow are for leaders to use in instructing participants of the briefcase exercise.

• *Ask questions and describe.* Prepare a briefcase, real or contrived, for every five- to six-member group. You may want to ask members of your group to share their briefcases.

• Using tables or the floor, instruct members of each group to empty the contents of a briefcase. Members of the group can take turns describing items—in rich detail. Looking at the contents as a whole, what question would they like the contents (data) to answer? Some possible questions include, How is this briefcase used? What can the contents of this briefcase suggest to us about its owner? What might be some of the issues in the owner's life? Group members can ask questions about each item and what it represents to the owner. Who is in this photograph? Why are you carrying it in your briefcase? How long has it been there? What does it mean to you?

• *Look for categories.* Keeping in mind the question that is being addressed, begin sorting the contents into categories. How many categories will you need? Each category will need a label ("office supplies"), a definition ("anything that is used in a part of work in an office setting"), and items that can serve as examples of that category (paper clips, index cards). To help organize the data into categories, you may want to use chart paper, a chalkboard, or word-processing table to create a chart such as the one in Figure 14.3.

 Next, check to see if the data fit the categories. If not, you may want to modify the labels for the categories until each of the pieces of data seem to fit into one. If there is an outlier that does not seem to fit anywhere, you might want to consider what that particular piece of data is all about.

• *Look for patterns.* Do certain words, items, behaviors, ideas repeat themselves? Are there categories? How does one category compare with another? In other words, what are the relationships, if any, between the categories? It is often helpful to create a visual display to identify relationships. Graphs, charts, and concept maps are useful devices. For example, if you want to see the frequency of items in each category, a bar graph might be useful—it would show which category had the most items and which the least. This information might be helpful in later interpretation. But frequency is only one pattern. You may want to refer to the list of patterns presented in Figure 13.2. For other types of patterns (or relationships), such as cause-effect, a flowchart or concept map might be better than a bar graph. See Traveler's Notes C for samples of visual display. This is where playfulness comes in! After you look at your visual display, do you have any hunches about what is going on or about

FIGURE 14.3 *Organizing data into categories*

Issue/Category/Theme	Issue/Category/Theme	Issue/Category/Theme
Evidence	Evidence	Evidence
Include quotes from interviews, observations recorded in field notes, excerpts from documents.	1. 2. 3.	1. 2. 3.
For example, from the Briefcase exercise:		
Category 1: Work-related items		
Evidence:		
Scissors		
Manuscript		
Textbook		
Calendar		
Office supplies		

what these categories reveal related to the research question? What issues seem to be emerging?

- *Revise the categories and patterns.* Now it is time to go back into the data to see if these preliminary categories and patterns still apply. What if one item doesn't seem to fit anywhere? What do you do with it? You may either adapt the category so that it will include that item, or you may want to create all new categories. Or you may keep the items that don't quite fit (the outliers) separate and look at them again when you interpret the data.
- *Synthesize.* After taking things apart during analysis, we need to put things back together—this time in a way that we perhaps have not thought of before. Visualizing data is a powerful tool to see data in a new way. Charts, graphs, concept maps, flowcharts, drawings—these are the tools of synthesis! We take our categories and arrange them in ways that will help give meaning to them.
- *Make assertions.* Finally! The point of analysis and synthesis is interpretation—making sense of what we have. *What does all this mean?* If the work-related category is much larger than the others, can we interpret that to mean that for the briefcase owner work may be more important than leisure? Or, that the "stuff" of work simply requires more concrete objects, or . . .? *What dilemmas or issues emerge?* Do the categories reveal a person who may be struggling to achieve some sort of balance in her or his life, balance between work and play and family? *What are the perspectives of others?* What if another group doing the same exercise comes up with entirely different categories and interpretations? Great! That is why multiple perspectives are important. If several groups conduct the analysis with the same items and come up with different interpretations, it might be worthwhile to discuss those differences and go back to the data with new questions. Action researchers connect emerging theories to experience and imagine conditions where life could be lived differently. *What assertions can you make?* What statements can you make about what you have learned? For example, "The contents of this briefcase reveal a person who struggles between balancing multiple personal interests with work commitments." Remember that these are only possible interpretations that require further study. The fact that a briefcase is full may lead some to believe that the owner is very busy. What are other explanations? Might the briefcase just be in need of a good cleaning out? The presence of things such as a crossword puzzle book, a pocket video game, and a novel may lead one to assume this person works to balance his or her personal and professional lives. But there may be another explanation. This briefcase may serve as an airline carry-on and serve as a storage place for idle-time activities. Make a list of new questions that the data bring up for you. Why does this person travel? Does she or he have children, or might those crayons be used for something else?

Discuss how one might find answers to such questions. What types of data would be needed and how can those data be obtained (interviewing, observing, etc.)?

Discuss insights about the research process gained through this activity. What further questions do you have about data analysis and how this process can be applied to your data?

4. Now it is time to analyze and interpret your data. Try using the process we have outlined in item 3. Invite a critical colleague to join you in the process as you are doing it, or after you have completed it. Does the critical colleague interpret the data in the same way you do? Does the critical colleague introduce new interpretations? Is the possible interpretation richer for your two perspectives?

5. There are many frameworks for interpretation, but we suggest that examining your data from the lens of adult and professional development may be a fruitful approach. This lens provides a framework for exploring and learning from data. See Figure 14.4.

For example, is what I am learning about the situation in my classroom informed by my ethical responsibilities to create a more humane and participative environment? Am I able to view my students in more complex ways, using my tools of inquiry, rather than looking for easy solutions to difficult problems? When confronted with obstacles, am I able to use the courage of my convictions to make the changes that I believe are necessary? Am I able to accept the limitations of my study without feeling inadequate?

Reflect on these kinds of questions as part of your data interpretation and include them in your journal. They will be a valuable part of the "What I have learned" section of your paper.

FIGURE 14.4 *Examining the consequences*		
What have I learned?	**What will I do as a consequence of what I have learned?**	**How will this make life better?**

FIGURE 14.5 *Frameworks for interpretation*

Three Domains of Adult and Professional Development

	Cognitive and Conceptual Complexity	Moral, Ethical, and Social Responsibility	Psychological and Emotional Maturity
What am I learning about myself?			
What am I learning about my situation?			
What am I learning about my students?			

6. Create an action plan based on what you have learned through your study. Reflect on what you will do next with respect to yourself, your students, and your situation. Reflect on how this will make life better. Examine your values. Are there any shifts or changes? Use the chart presented in Figure 14.5 if you think it will be helpful.

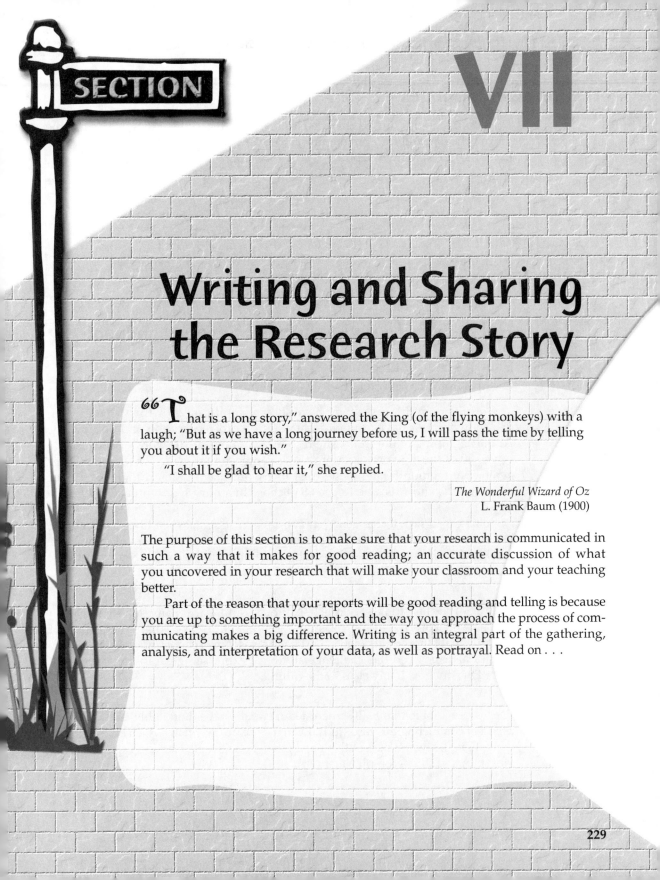

VII

Writing and Sharing the Research Story

"That is a long story," answered the King (of the flying monkeys) with a laugh; "But as we have a long journey before us, I will pass the time by telling you about it if you wish."

"I shall be glad to hear it," she replied.

The Wonderful Wizard of Oz
L. Frank Baum (1900)

The purpose of this section is to make sure that your research is communicated in such a way that it makes for good reading; an accurate discussion of what you uncovered in your research that will make your classroom and your teaching better.

Part of the reason that your reports will be good reading and telling is because you are up to something important and the way you approach the process of communicating makes a big difference. Writing is an integral part of the gathering, analysis, and interpretation of your data, as well as portrayal. Read on . . .

The Journey Continues

Let's check in with our classroom teachers. Each has come a long way since the journey began, and they are reaping the rewards of their study. What follows are excerpts of their written reports.

CASE STUDIES

Shawn

Helping Jen Learn English as a Second Language

Shawn's Student from Korea

Excerpts from Shawn's report

The results from this case study have shown significant growth in all areas. Jen has shown a vast development in her sight word recognition and vocabulary. At the beginning of the study, she recognized 47 out of 100 words. She was able to use 30 of the 47 words in a phrase or sentence that made sense. I tested her again about a month later using the same word list, and Jen recognized 79 out of 100 words and was able to use 68 of those in a phrase or sentence that made sense.

I have also seen a change in Jen's social adjustment. When I began observing her in January, she was somewhat reserved. She often did not share during our weekly "show and tell" sessions. She did not volunteer to answer questions. Slowly, I saw a great change.

* * * * * * *

I enjoyed this study very much. Not only did I learn many new strategies to teach all the children in my classroom, but also I discovered another aspect of teaching that I thoroughly enjoy. . . . I have also let my school principal know how much I have enjoyed this challenge and have expressed great interest in having more ESL students in my class in the future.

* * * * * * *

I chose a topic that really interested me and I have thoroughly enjoyed every aspect of completing this case study. Even the literature review, which I thought was going to be the worst part of this paper, was an enjoyable learning experience. . . . I feel proud of this accomplishment.

The Literature Circles Study

Excerpts from Jon and Terry's study

Jon

During this time, Mrs. S (Terry) had been reading the response journals, looking for signs of progress toward more critical thinking. Specifically, she was looking for drawing conclusions, questioning, predicting, and illustrating using pictures or graphic organizers. To keep track of the growth and give concrete evidence to students' growth, she developed a tally sheet. In initial responses, students focused more on summarizing and predicting. As they became more comfortable and practiced with literature circles, the responses became more expansive with an increase in questioning, connecting, and drawing conclusions.

* * * * * * *

Terry

The results of the study were encouraging. We were able to abandon the basal and use authentic literature successfully with students at risk. A definite move toward more critical thinking was observed. We expect this progress to continue as we expose these students to more authentic texts.

* * * * * * *

We have noticed a marked increase in motivation and enthusiasm as well as an increase in self-esteem for these children. With this in mind, we have met our goal in providing all students with open membership into the "literacy club."

* * * * * * *

As other teachers in the building have heard us discussing our study, many have shown an interest in what we've been doing. One teacher went so far as to "borrow" a misplaced evaluation sheet left on the copy machine. Several teachers have stopped by the classroom to watch the literature circles in action. We plan to present our findings and share strategies to implement literature circles at a future staff meeting.

The S.T.A.R. Club Study

Excerpts from Roberto's report

Roberto

My original impressions about the "typical" students and their interest in students in special classes were erroneous. These middle school students had mostly positive attitudes about those with disabilities. The main problem was that they no longer had the same opportunities or time to socialize with one another as they did in the elementary classroom. Their schedule did not allow them to stay in one classroom and get comfortable in one environment. Each time they switched to another class, they were with new students. What I perceived as a lack of interest was largely a lack of opportunity.

* * * * * * *

I found the research process interesting, thought-provoking, and sometimes staggering. As a special education teacher, I was usually accustomed to planning and implementing activities for 16 students. This research project compelled me to organize approximately 70 students for various social events. The commitment to the research, the activities, and the club members could be exhausting, but I felt it renewed my devotion to teaching.

The Democratic Classroom Study

Excerpts from Ruby's report

Ruby

Everywhere people bemoan the state of U.S. society and the destruction of democracy. Pundits argue that civility has declined, aggression has increased, and U.S. citizens grow more cynical about the political process. Fewer and fewer people register to vote; not all those who register, vote. Fewer and fewer people write letters to the editor, wear campaign buttons, try to convince others about an issue or a candidate, or donate money to a campaign. Those who are concerned about these developments say that people are too willing to give up control over the decisions that affect their lives, thereby giving too much power to too few and leaving the citizenry vulnerable to manipulation.

* * * * * * *

Now that we have revisited our teacher colleagues and their work, let's look at how *we* can write and share ours. In this section we will talk more about the processes and products of writing. We start out by discussing the process of *writing as a research process* and revisit a question we posed earlier: *Whose eyes can see what?* We will extend our discussions on *writing down, writing up,* and *writing about* our work to share it with colleagues and others. We will discuss some of the many options for point of view, voice, and form in report writing, and we will provide general and specific information about preparing research reports. Part of the mystery surrounding research can be dispelled by understanding the importance and meaning of language, style, and the points of view in reporting research. Finally, we will discuss ways to share what we have found, both to strengthen our findings and to spread the work and contribute to an evolving library of professional knowledge. In "Exploring the Forest," we will try out some different kinds of writing for our studies.

CHAPTER 15

Writing as a Research Process

Writing is a powerful process for learning; for describing, synthesizing, analyzing, interpreting, and communicating experience; for coming to terms with what we know, how we know it, and why it is important—if it is—to know. This last part, the value of what we know, depends on our points of view. And that brings us to our eyes (and hearts and courage)—and what they *can* see and *want* to see, for these are usually related. The question is: *Whose eyes can see (and tell) what?*

Those exploring writing in the late 1970s and early 1980s talked about writing as thinking, as cognition. Their theses outlined how writing is, in itself, a most complex and engaging process that is multifaceted and contains many subprocesses, such as planning, analysis, synthesis, and sequencing, to name a few, making writing a heuristic process (Emig, 1977, 1982; Flower, 1981; Flower and Hayes, 1980; Perl, 1980, 1981).

Writing is not only a cognitive process, but also a political process. We observe and write from a point of view, actually from many points of view. Since we are normally unaware of these processes, we don't perceive the options we have for conceptualizing and portraying research.

As we explore options in this chapter, we can begin to perceive the possibilities—and responsibilities—that come with conscious knowledge. For example, as we try to live our values in our teaching, we have the responsibility to make those values known. *What* we select to focus on and *how* we record it will determine to a large extent the data we have to analyze and interpret. It also matters what we decide *not* to focus on or record, and what does not enter into our consciousness. Writing is not an automatic or inconsequential act.

Follow this process one more step into consciousness, and we find that "Representation . . . is always self-presentation. . . . The Other presented in the text is always a version of the researcher's self" (Denzin and Lincoln, 1998, p. 319). This means, at the most basic level, that our studies tell as much about us as they do about others. Because there are almost an infinite number of ways to represent experience (Brady, 1991), and each of these ways carries its own interpretive lens, the reader, as well as the author, needs to think critically about what is recorded, analyzed, and interpreted.

Each of the paradigms and theories that we discussed in Section II has its own orientation. A person from a constructivist orientation, for example, will ask different questions, collect different kinds of data, interpret them in different ways, and portray the data differently than a person with a behaviorist or feminist orientation. Even if by some unlikely twist of fate these three groups had the same data and research questions, they could still write very different reports, calling attention to different aspects and elements of the study.

Let's make this even more complicated. Depending on our purposes, we write from different perspectives and we choose how to portray what we have learned. We may want to choose a very concise, scientific type of report, or we may want to write a more conversational, narrative account. We may choose to discuss informally what we have learned with a teacher research group (in person or through the Internet) or present our study at a conference. It may also be a source of relief to realize that whatever format we choose, we are providing an account of a phenomenon at one point in time rather than a definitive study of a topic.

You needn't be concerned about "getting it right for always." The writer Henry Miller once said that "writing is a voyage of discovery." The personal and professional discovery that AR makes possible happens throughout the research process—from capturing and writing down data, to writing up our results, to writing about our work in ways that lead to further discovery with others. We will explore specific options for writing, but first let's revisit and extend our discussion of the process of writing.

Writing Down, Writing Up, and Writing About

Recall from Section V that *observation* is key to all good research and, as we can surmise from what we just discussed, observation is always from a point of view. We develop our observation skills as we observe and as we put what we observe into words. This is how we develop as connoisseurs and critics (Eisner, 1985).

So, what does that have to do with writing *down* and *up* and *about* you might be wondering? Plenty. Connoisseurs appreciate the significance of the topics they choose to study. Careful observation makes it possible to document and record *(writing down)* what you see so that you can return to it later, analyze and play with it, and put it into a form that makes sense of the pieces and that shows relationships of one aspect of the data (or data sets) to others. That is what we call *writing up* the results of a study. Once you have written up your report, you have a base from which to *write about* the study for presentation to others in the form of publication or presentation. When writing about your study, your options in terms of audience, form, and style are more than accoutrements: They carry the meaning of the story. As critics make their keen observations public, so, too, do action researchers. The richer the database from writing down, the stronger the foundation for analysis and interpretation, and for writing up and about the research later on. This means documenting and snooping, probing around corners, asking challenging questions about what you see to get different angles and perspectives to record.

Oftentimes the more work you put in early on collecting the information, the better. The more comprehensive and organized the proposal, the easier it will be to conduct the study. This isn't always the case though.

Sometimes people start with less "well-developed" or "comprehensive" proposals and do marvelous studies in less time than other people, who prepare very thorough proposals and find themselves so stuck to their plans that they miss the main event or clues that will take them to it. They do not see what is in front of them if it doesn't fit "the plan." Sometimes researchers follow their instincts without much fanfare, and it works. Some of our greatest discoveries happen in that way. They *aren't* laborious. They *flow*.

That is not to discourage carefully prepared proposals; good ideas come in many ways. Some come in flashes, others in uneven tempo, and we need to be open to our intuition and visits from parts of ourselves that may know more than the rational parts. For example, an author of a delightful, award-winning children's book wrote it in less than a day! The ideas had been growing inside her since childhood when she lived the story the first time. What happened was a magic synthesis. And that can happen to each of us. Had she labored at it, she may have lost the pulse and we might have been deprived of this treasure. Writing in its many forms—from free-writing possible ideas for research to writing about research for publication—is a powerful tool. Since we have been writing in different forms all through our journey, perhaps it is time to stand back and put a simple framework around writing and a few of the many forms it takes in carrying out research. See Figure 15.1. Although the forms may be seen as progressive, one leading to the next, and indeed this can be the case, it is also true that these forms take place throughout the research. Free-writing, for example, can be useful no matter what stage or part of the action research cycle one is in. Ideas for *writing about* can occur to one at any time, and can be noted in one's journal for future use.

The kind of writing we are talking about here is professional writing. It helps a professional to be just that. We have done quite a bit of free-writing, and we have written our proposals. So let's extend a few ideas that we sprouted in the last two chapters related to the last three terms. *Writing down* is the process of recording observations. As we discussed in Section V, there are many ways to take notes and make records. Sometimes we record the landscape and take a broad sweep; at other times we focus more narrowly, carefully (and for the Wizard's adventurous postmodern mind, **creatively**), with a connoisseur's eye for detail. Recall the

> **FIGURE 15.1   *Writing related to research***
>
> **Free-writing:** writing without taking time to think about it, to edit (either internally or externally), or to labor over our writing; giving the creative parts of our minds free reign. There is usually no audience for free-writing other than the author.
>
> **Proposal writing:** focused and disciplined writing often informed by ideas from free-writing with the purpose of proposing a study.
>
> **Writing down:** developing the art of observation and data collection; capturing rich, detailed information. The audience may be oneself, a student, professor, colleague, funding agency, or others.
>
> **Writing up:** analyzing and synthesizing the results of our observations and data in writing; refers to rendering our considered observations and interpretations in written form (portraits, case studies, research reports). This is usually available for outside audiences; it is part of making research public.
>
> **Writing about:** taking our reports and creating products from these to share; usually moving beyond the report in rendering it in other forms (presentations, articles). This kind of writing is usually prepared for presentation with an outside audience in mind.

"dark snakes of stems and ferny plumes of leaves" from John Moffit's poem "To Look at Any Thing" in Chapter 11. This is an example of the rich detail we are aiming for in recording our observations. We are acutely aware and fully present. What do we see with our ears? (Silence in Moffit's poem.) What do we see with our eyes? Detail. What do we see with our noses? Dampness and green. This is the opportunity to be the young child who literally sinks into what she sees. The clearer our vision, the richer the database for description and later interpretation. Some researchers capture the essence of what they see in lines and phrases to use as they write up their observations.

Mary Oliver, a Pulitzer Prize-winning poet, provides a good example of each of these points: *careful focusing* by *being fully present* with *all senses open for engagement*, with a *childlike sinking into experiences*, and *capturing, in sentences and phrases*, material from which to write up in a story or poem. In *Blue Pastures* (1995) Oliver gives us a glimpse into her work and provides a good illustration of these points. She carries a notebook with her and captures phrases and ideas as they occur. Following are four examples from *Blue Pastures:*

- Little myrtle warblers kissing the air
- You there, like a red fist under my ribs—be reasonable.
- Just at the edge of the sea, a dolphin's skull. Recent, but perfectly clean. And entirely beautiful. I held it in my hands, I was so excited I was breathless. What will I do?
- Something totally unexpected, like a barking cat.

Can you see and feel, smell, and hear these? Do these words and their images transport you there? From a research perspective, Mary Oliver is collecting data, *rich* data. Once she has written down these rich data, she will make sense of them as she *writes them up* in another form.

Perhaps you are thinking, "But I can't do this! She is a prize-winning poet!" Ah, but you can. We all can. We can accept the invitation into a connoisseur's world to cultivate the powers of our senses. Does the child in your room *walk, bound, saunter, shuffle,* or *vault* to the drinking fountain?

Because we have long written up our research according to canons seeded centuries ago, "value-free" and modeled on science, we have few examples in education to draw upon. From the seventeenth century on, for example, the world of writing was divided into two streams: *literary* (fiction, narrative) and *scientific* (nonfiction, expository).

"Fiction was unfortunately considered to be 'false' because it invented reality, unlike science, which was considered 'true' because it simply 'reported' 'objective' reality in a single, unambiguous voice" (Richardson, 1998, p. 350). Today, since fiction is defined as human experience in narrative form, we would not call fiction false. In our own time, what has been called *realism* with its "objective, precise, unambiguous, noncontextual, nonmetaphoric" scientific voice was so strong that for a time even poets and novelists tried to adhere to realism's guidelines. "By the late nineteenth century, 'realism' dominated both science and fiction" (Clough, 1992, in Richardson, 1998, p. 350), and its effects can still be felt. In postmodern times, neither scientific nor literary writing is in a higher position. Today, no one can "know all" with realism's precision, but each can "know something" (Richardson, 1998, p. 350).

If this sounds complicated, relax. Not knowing everything is not a bad thing. People *never knew it all*, but they *didn't know that they didn't know it all*. With postmodern thinking, we are free to know what we know and to question that knowledge as well as what we don't know. We can provide evidence for our claims, but we don't have to pretend that we have discovered truth or that we know more than we do. This is very freeing.

Recall that writing up is drawing on what you have written down, and interpreting and developing it further. Mary Oliver makes poems out of her notes. As you draw on your data, trying to make sense of it, making connections, noting patterns and findings, and synthesizing elements of the study, you begin to write up your cogitations, too.

Writing up detailed description, all by itself, can easily seem to be "enough" analysis—after all, we are taking something that *wasn't* obvious to us before and making it visible in new ways. But for AR, rarely is this enough. Since issues usually undergird our research (fairness, etc.), the careful presentation of data, as creative and suggestive as it might be, is not usually sufficient. We must probe and develop our results so that we, and our readers, can contemplate the "So what?" of our research. What does this finding mean related to the underlying issues that frame my research? What do these results mean to my classroom?

"When I began observing her [Jen] in January, she was reserved. She often did not . . . " Here, Shawn writes up her analysis of the data she collected. Often in writing up results, the researcher makes a statement about the data and provides examples as evidence to support the statement. Such evidence might include "plays with other children, takes part in recess activities, and works in collaboration with her science group."

In writing up the results of their Literature Circles study, Terry and Jon wrote, "In initial responses, the students focused more on summarizing and predicting. As they became more comfortable and practiced with Literature Circles, responses became more extensive with an increase in questioning, connecting, and drawing conclusions." Examples, such as, "Myron, Abbey, and Gerald's group spent four times the amount of time questioning the text, and five times the amount of time discussing their conclusions and what these meant to them, than they did three weeks ago," lend credibility and clarity to the findings. The use of time in this case need not necessarily show growth, but as an indicator, it can point in that direction, especially when combined with further evidence, such as "Whereas during the first few weeks of the study Myron dominated the discussion, providing 'answers' to questions he had before the other children were able to grasp the ideas and pose their own questions. By the end of the study many more children contributed to the discussion; Myron made certain that each child had the opportunity to contribute."

What the teachers found, simply put, was growing and consistent evidence of higher-level thinking skills; the children moved from literal questions (Who is the main character? What did she like to do?) to higher levels of thinking (posing questions, making judgments, thinking critically). Their next step could well be to relate these findings back to the larger context or issue: "So what do these results and related examples suggest for enabling children to think critically and creatively? What can *we* do differently in the classroom to encourage further growth in critical and creative thinking?"

Another way would be to write up examples first, and *then* make a general statement. Then readers could conjure up their *own* ideas. That is the way it often happens both for readers *and* writers. As researchers write up the examples, they begin to discover the importance and relationship of one example to another. In a real sense as researchers, we *write into understanding*.

Writing about your study after you have presented a preliminary report can be fun—regardless of your paradigm. Think about *writing about* as if you are an artist who has just completed a pencil drawing of a landscape. You have the landscape, now you can make something else out of it: Paint it, zero in on one part of the painting and blow it up large, combine a few parts of the painting to make another painting. Perhaps you can use multimedia to emphasize different aspects of the painting. Writing about your study, once you have prepared a report, leaves you open to many of these options, some of which will be influenced by those to whom you want to present your work. Writing up includes literally *writing*, as in a form for publication or other forms of distribution, and *presenting* or telling about your study from alternative perspectives. Later in this section we will talk about audience.

As you start thinking about how you will approach writing up your report, you may find the suggestions in Stepping Stones 15.1 helpful.

STEPPING STONES 15.1

Practical Considerations in Preparing for Writing Up Your Report

- What word-processing software best suits your report writing? Will you likely want to construct tables or graphs, or incorporate PowerPoint or streaming video? Who knows software and can serve as a consultant? Who do you know who might have written reports of a similar nature?
- What major folders will you need to develop?
- What subfolders, or files, will you have in each folder? (These may evolve as you continue to develop your project.) Setting up a framework, or architecture, for your report can simplify the process and enable your intellectual and creative juices to go into analyzing, synthesizing, and portraying data as you draw on these easy-to-find files and information.
- How will you protect your files from loss (due to computer malfunctions, stealth of the wicked witch, loss of your computer, house fire, flood, or other unintended happenings)? We know one student who sends her files to a friend for second-copy safe-keeping; others use thumb disks and multiple computers for storage.

Do you feel excited to start your report? You can select what way your energy will go: "Can't wait to get started!" Or "Good grief, what if . . . ?" The energy is the same: What you use it for makes all the difference. How, for example, might you write about your study in ways that enable you to see it differently? What forms might you create to share your work with others? What different stories might you tell? This leads us into the whole idea of narrative, or story. We have been using narrative (and writing it) all along our journey.

CHAPTER SUMMARY

In this chapter we discussed writing as a vital part of the research process. The quality of our observations as we record them reflects a point of view and provides the material for analysis and interpretation. We termed this gathering-of-data process *writing down*. After we have the data, we *write up* our findings, providing analysis and interpretation. The third general type of action research writing is *writing about* our study to communicate with others. This is often overlooked and yet is an important way to share our research and through the process to further develop the ideas embodied in the report. In Chapter 16 we discuss narrative writing and some ways that we can tell our research stories.

CHAPTER 16

Narrative Writing

It is hard to conceive of a report without narrative, so it is important for us all, regardless of the type of report we will prepare, to give narrative writing some thought. With the rise in the use of qualitative methods to study educational issues, there has been a concomitant increase in the use of qualitative, or *narrative*, reports, which often are longer than more traditional reports. They are different in nature. Just what is narrative, and what is a narrative report? Why would we want to write a narrative report?

Narrative Defined: A General Term, a Process, and a Product

According to Donald Polkinghorne (1988), a student of narrative, "The most inclusive meaning of 'narrative' refers to any spoken or written presentation" (p. 13). In common usage, we often think of narrative as the parts of a document that are words and sentences in contrast to the parts that are numbers, tables, and figures. The same can be said for an oral presentation of narrative research. Narratives, whether written or spoken, are the explanatory commentary of a report. In qualitative research, which much of action research is, narrative reports take the reader to the data in personal and highly descriptive ways. Narrative, as Polkinghorne uses the term, stands for both the process and the results. We use the term *narrative* in both ways here, as the process of narration and as the product, a narrative. Here, we are talking about a narrative report.

" '[S]tory' is equivalent to 'narrative' " (p. 13), according to Polkinghorne. Although there are a few qualifications to keep in mind when referring to our research writing as a story, we find that "story" has more benefits than liabilities. Stepping Stones 16.1 contains a few of each that you can consider and add to.

Entertain the idea that if people are more likely to read a narrative story, that alone is reason enough to try using narrative when writing.

Storytelling is perhaps the *oldest* method of teaching. Long before there was even the term *research,* let alone "methods" of it, there was story, a way to pass along culture from one generation to the next. Long before our brains were as highly educated as they are today, we responded to life and made sense of experience through stories. Story, then, speaks to us on multiple levels, including the primitive level, and conveys meaning in ways that more rational (seemingly more pointed and straightforward) approaches are unable to convey. Story speaks to us in a tempo and form that allows us to entertain information that we would not otherwise consider. Direct presentations can be threatening and perceived as irrelevant, so much of what they might have to impart never reaches consciousness.

It is rather like Ken Macrorie's (1980) suggestion to "show, don't tell" in writing and teaching. Stories show. While there are those who think "No pain, no gain!" and scoff at the idea of research engaging the audience in creative and playful ways, we can learn much through story—and often happily so.

STEPPING STONES 16.1

Benefits and Liabilities of Using Story

Some action researchers report their research in a creative story format.

Benefits of using story

- Easy to understand
- We think in stories rather than linear ways
- Aids understanding on multiple levels
- Reader less resistant to considering results
- More inviting to read
- Connects with reader on a human level
- Uses story conventions in creative ways
- Reader brings imagination and intuition to the text

Liabilities of using story

- Data may not easily "fit" into story line
- Easy to dismiss its importance because most people associate "research" with traditional reports
- If reader is looking for traditional research report categories, main points may be missed
- Story calls on participation and nonlinear processing of reader
- Findings may not be as clear and unequivocal as in a traditionally structured research report

We have all sorts of ways to protect ourselves from new ways of thinking. And for those steeped in traditional forms of research, narrative methods can be disconcerting, or more likely, dismissed. There are conventions for narrative writing just as there are for more expository and scientific writing—the data are no less important, and the engagement of the researcher with the data is no less rigorous. As Denzin and Lincoln (1998) point out, researcher's narrative stories are "couched and framed within specific story telling traditions" (p. 4).

Think of narration as the way you describe and make sense of your experience. Narrative is the story you weave to make sense of your life and world; it is the glue that holds experience together in a coherent way. As we narrate, we link, synthesize, integrate, connect, and make meaning of our experiences.

Because action research is rarely as neat, tidy, and sequential as suggested by report formulas familiar to many of us (purpose, rationale, research question, hypotheses, literature review, methodology, results, conclusions, discussion, references, and appendices), we may choose to use different ways to write up what we have learned.

Jean Clandinin and Michael Connelly (1998) make a useful distinction between the stories we live and tell and those told by narrative researchers: ". . . people by nature live storied lives and tell stories of those lives, whereas narrative researchers describe such lives, collect and tell stories of them, and write narratives of experience" (p. 155). The perspectives of narrative researchers can take many forms depending on the writer's purposes.

Writer Perspectives

The narrative report can be written from many different perspectives. We have drawn from the work of Robert Stake (1995), John Van Maanen (1988), Thomas Mallon (1984), and Eliot Eisner (1985) to compile a list of possible perspectives from which the author can write.

- The *chronicler, biographer,* or *historian* narrates the story, giving the reader an event-by-event accounting of the historical case as it develops, focusing on key components (Mallon, Stake).
- The *researcher* or *experiential authority* tells the story of developing the research, what it looks like from this person's point of view, methodologically and substantively (results and meaning of results) (Stake, Van Maanen).
- The *describer* or *connoisseur* offers rich, thick description of major components of the research (Stake, Eisner).
- The *documenter* or *journalist* or *traveler* puts you there as the story unwinds, privy to details that stand for typical behaviors, patterns, places (Van Maanen, Mallon).
- The *culture member* tells the story from the perspective of the member of the cultural group that is being studied, using her or his own accounts, quotations, language, cliches (Van Maanen).

- The *confessor* engages in truth telling beyond what is needed or wanted, including more about the field worker than about the study; what is key to the reader and to the author is muddled (Van Maanen, Mallon).
- The *impressionist* offers personalized interpretations of selected elements of the research and does so in a dramatic form (Van Maanen).
- The *ecologist* tells the story from many vantage points and dimensions (Mallon).
- The *pilgrim* comes from a point of view and values that are obvious to the reader; the story is told explicitly from this point of view (Mallon).
- The *apologists* "wish to explain, to justify, to plead the case before history . . . at least to get their versions on the record" (Mallon).
- The *creators* create the story as they go; interpretations and images are rich and thought-provoking. The creators sometimes explain the detail and its meaning, sometimes not. The story can be a collage, either with a clear beginning and ending, or not.
- The *prisoners* escape into writing; they come alive through writing and are far braver in this form of communication than in direct conversation, which is a surprise to people who think they know them well (Mallon)!

You might be thinking that these don't look like reports you've seen in schools. And you might wonder aren't we supposed to be neutral and *objective?*

To start with, you probably have read reports that represent different perspectives. Sometimes educators are eager to present experiential authority and we have more than a few chroniclers who want to share their stories. With this list in mind, you may find other research accounts in which a particular perspective is embedded. Now, let us throw you a sticky wicket. How can one be an insider (one who writes the point of view of a person inside the culture studied) and yet look at the data as an outsider (able to gain distance and look at the phenomenon under investigation with a stranger's fresh new perspective)? It *is* possible.

Being an insider or an outsider in relation to the data and participants is a discussion still being carried out among modern and postmodern researchers. The insider/outsider perspective is a paradox of sorts, seeming to be a contradiction with some truth in it. Once, it was believed that if a researcher got too involved or too close to the data, the study was contaminated. As you may recall from Section II, others, from a more qualitative orientation, argue that there is no such thing as objectivity. They are joined, oddly enough, by physicists who confirm that the eyes of the observer influence what is seen. This is termed the *observer effect.* We construct meaning from who we are, our experiences, our gender, our world views. Recording data, its analysis, synthesis, and interpretation, enables one to return to it, to bracket it, and to critique it from alternative perspectives. One can record as an insider, and along with others step outside the data to critique it as an outsider. This is by no means inevitable, but for many researchers, it is possible. Another issue involved with the current insider/outsider debate concerns the researcher's rights, responsibilities, and capabilities to write other people's stories with or without their corroboration or comment. Whose story is it? For what purpose is it written? So, the first issue is, can a researcher write from insider and outsider perspectives, and the second issue is, *should* and *can* the researcher write from alternative perspectives?

Whereas once reports were viewed as simply writing up objective results of the study, we now realize that there are many issues to consider and that our insider's eyes shape all forms of writing—down, up, and about as we make connections, analyze, synthesize, and come to new understandings. The underlying element in all these perspectives is the telling of the story, which, according to Jean Clandinin and Michael Connelly (1998), is "the closest we can come to experience" (p. 155). Our experiences are "the stories we live" and in the telling of them, we "reaffirm them, modify them, and create new ones . . ." (1998, p. 155). We will soon present some different kinds of report formats, but before we do that, let's entertain a few of the ways that we can create new ones and thus enlarge our understanding in the process. We present a few newer forms of writing, what Laurel Richardson (1998) calls "evocative forms of telling," which necessitate relating to the data differently and thus coming to know data from alternative perspectives and angles. We plant these here as seeds, as new ways of thinking, not to provide comprehensive descriptions or ways to proceed. Richardson charts a path into new forms of telling, and we can travel with her for a few minutes.

Some evocative forms of telling include:

- *Narrative of the self.* "This is a highly personalized, revealing text in which the author tells stories about his or her own lived experience." They use the writing techniques of fiction rather than those of traditional ethnography, and they are therefore not concerned with accuracy, but with the "literary criteria of coherence, verisimilitude, and interest" (Richardson, 1998, p. 356). The narrative of the self might easily be the culture member's story.
- *Ethnographic fictional representations.* These are products of the imagination where the author is "seeking a format in which to tell a 'good story.' " The story can be about the author but is more generally about the people or culture studied. Techniques such as "flashback, flash forward, alternative points of view, deep characterizations, tone shifts, synecdoche, dialogue, interior monologue, and, sometimes, even the omniscient narrator" are used (Richardson, 1998, p. 356). The chronicler could well adopt ethnographic fictional representations and its techniques to enliven the research story.
- *Poetic representations.* Poetic writing is often closer to how people actually talk than is the typical style of most academic writing. Writing up an interview in a poetic form can come closer to the reality of what was said than a verbatim transcript or a summary of it might convey. "Settling words together in new configurations lets us hear, see and feel the world in new dimensions. Poetry is thus a *practical* and *powerful* method for analyzing social worlds" (Richardson, 1998, p. 357). The connoisseur might find poetic representations the most meaningful way to portray and convey research.
- *Ethnographic drama.* "Drama is a way of shaping experience without losing the experience." Drama can incorporate many different forms of representation and technique—poetry, visual and oral arts, literature—and

thus make multiple ways of appreciating the "text" possible. Importantly, drama can be used to "give voice to what is unspoken, but present" (Richardson, 1998, p. 357). The impressionist might select ethnographic drama to tell the tale.

- *Mixed genres.* Mixed genres give perhaps the most creative license to present one's work. The author can draw upon "literary, artistic and scientific genres, often breaking the boundaries of each of those as well" (Richardson, 1998, p. 357). Looking at a study from these multiple points of view enables a wealth of possibilities for portrayal and understanding. Creators and prisoners would find a wealth within mixed genres to tell their respective research stories.

You may want to experiment with some of these newer kinds of portrayal, as they will give you more options for your writing. You may also want to explore digital storytelling (Lambert, 2006) and other forms of media and multimodal composition (Selfe, 2007) that can be used in writing and sharing your research story. There are two other forms of writing used in narrative reports that can be used in most of, if not all, the possibilities we just explored, from chroniclers and pilgrims to ethnographic drama. These are *portraits* and *vignettes.*

Portraits, Portraiture, and Vignettes

A *portrait* presents a likeness of a person, place, time, event, or circumstance. "The portraitist takes liberties and artistic licence to create the sense or essence of the [portrayed]" (Holly, 1989, p. 105). Robert Coles, a well-respected child psychiatrist, used portraiture to call attention to the inside stories of children's lives (a Pulitzer Prize-winning series titled *Children of Crisis,* 1967, is a good example) and of men and women over the years. Coles is a qualitative researcher who argues persuasively for the use of stories. In fact, his book *The Call of Stories* (1989) makes the case for stories by presenting examples of telling stories in teaching, therapy, and research. The research from which his stories come is based on an immersion into the setting in which he observes, interviews, collects artifacts, and documents what he sees and hears and experiences. Each of Coles's books offers the student of portraiture and qualitative methods a feast, not only from the stories themselves, but also from his discussions of his research. Of portraiture, he says:

> The essential thrust is toward a reasonably accessible and suggestive "reading" of a given person's life. The writers become mediators; through them another life reaches toward the reader, and if the work has been successful, stays with the reader as a guest, a "spirit," whose mind and heart and soul have been registered upon the consciousness of distant strangers. (Coles and Coles, 1980, p. 4)

Portraiture is now considered to be a "genre of inquiry and representation that seeks to join science and art. . . . [It] is a method of qualitative research that blurs the boundaries of aesthetics and empiricism in an effort to capture the complexity, dynamics, and subtlety of human experience . . ." (Lawrence-Lightfoot and Davis, 1997, p. xv).

Vignettes.   *Vignettes* and portraits are representations of life on paper or in an electronic form. Vignettes are "small literary sketches of life that often fade gradually into larger pictures; they are segments that begin a story, and they are the smaller stories within a story; small centers of interest within a landscape or a painting or a life" (Holly, 1989, p. 105). Vignettes can stand by themselves. They provide mental images and pictures of past and current actions. Life histories are often constructed using biographical or autobiographical vignettes, which, when integrated, can form patterns and themes and provide materials for the construction of portraits.

A critical incident vignette captures a turning point in the story. The point may turn on a sudden insight—the moment Ruby realized that students need to be given responsibilities along with freedom. Or, from a more critical perspective, that she herself may have fed into the problem by taking shortcuts on her way to building a classroom community. In Ruby's case, she made these incidents critical during her process of reflecting on what she had learned through her study. Weaving incidents together may help us see our own development as critical researchers and help readers understand how knowledge is and can be constructed.

Here is a vignette that is part of a larger portrait constructed by Robert Coles in *The Political Life of Children* (1986). The first paragraph is a small part of the portrait of Kate, who lives in Dublin, Ireland. This paragraph leads into the vignette that follows in the second paragraph.

> She was, at twelve, tall for her age, with lanky legs and utterly straight brown hair, with a touch of red. The hair came down almost to her shoulders. When she got anxious or angry, she put her hands through her hair repeatedly, or lowered her head abruptly, so that her hair suddenly all came forward, covering much of her face. She wore a crucifix on a chain around her neck, and often played with it, sometimes stopping to look down intently at it. She was "deeply religious," the sisters told me: "Kate might become one of us when she's older, for all we know. She may have a vocation. She may!"

With this information, we have a context for the vignette in which Kate speaks for herself:

> As for Kate's idea, at twelve, of her vocation, it went like this: "If I could choose what I'd be, I'd be a surgeon! I'd be in a hospital someplace in Belfast, and I could help take care of our men, who get hurt. If I went with them, to fight the Brits, I could sew anyone up, who got hurt. If I saw a Brit, and he needed to be sewed up, I'd just walk away. I'd never give any of them help! They look down on us, and they never listen to what we say.

> If I could *really* have my choice, I'd be a soldier! I'd be in the Irish Army and we'd cross the border and fight the Brits and beat them. Then we could tell the Orangies: Stay here, and we'll be nice to you—nicer than you've been to us—or go back to your Scotland, if it means all that much to you! They've taken me in for being a 'public tease' to their soldiers, but if I was a soldier, I'd not get upset when some kid, a girl like me, starts saying what I said. I'd stop and listen to her! I'd ask my friends to listen."

Notice the pacing and shape of the text. Where do we go next? The pacing and intensity of the vignette are broken as there is a shift in both. The text is pulled back as Kate "pulls back." Very simply, Coles invites us, too, to contemplate what has just been said in the vignette.

> She stops there. She has begun to notice my incredulity—and maybe her own. She pulls back somewhat, acknowledges that it would be an exceptional soldier who would be that honest and open—even to a child. Anyway, she admits, she isn't exactly a child: "The Brits say we're all grown up—that's what they say when they arrest us! They told me I'd go to jail the next time. . . ." (Coles, 1986, p. 119)

When writing vignettes and portraits, authors often include direct quotations from the people they portray. Coles makes extensive use of the language of the persons portrayed. At the other end of the scale, some authors use such quotations sparingly. In general, the trick is to be judicious in using quotations. Coles probably uses a small portion of his data in his books; but since he has more data than most to draw from, he is better able to use them. If a quotation is important to the story and the person says it best—use it. Scholars such as Robert Coles and Sarah Lawrence-Lightfoot (*The Good High School*, 1983, provides excellent portraits of very different "good" high schools) can weave magic with the language of the portrayed. In their writing, a book can be read as if it were the story told by the portrayed. In our experience this is not easy to do—but it is a highly effective way to report scholarship, when done well.

You might be thinking: Here we go again—more prize-winning authors. Excuse me, but we are *not* experienced researchers. Who are *we* to tell a story our own way, create our own vignettes and portraits, and all that? We're not experts. We might get it wrong.

Think about it. Is this not your journey? Are you not the one who experienced it? Who else has focused so carefully, systematically, and self-critically on this little corner of your professional practice? And besides, you are not alone. You have each other and these good witches and critical colleagues to assist you, to provide you with alternative perspectives. Telling *your* story is not a matter of being *right* or *wrong*. It is a matter of being *authentic and telling it with integrity*. Was Kate right or wrong, or is it more fruitful to ask if she was telling her truth? As a researcher, you tell *the story as you see it.* Based on the questions you asked, and the methods you used to collect and make sense of your data, this is how you interpret it. You take care to let the reader—or listener—know what you did and how you did it and then they can enter into the conversation and draw their own conclusions. This is one way that the profession grows, by entering into each other's professional worlds and providing multiple perspectives.

CHAPTER SUMMARY

In this chapter, we defined narrative as "any spoken or written presentation." We use the term *narrative* as equivalent to *story*. We discussed several perspectives from which a narrative can be written, including that of the historian, the creator, and the ecologist. There are new forms of writing termed by Richardson (1998) *evocative forms of telling* that include ethnographic fiction and drama, poetic representation, and mixed genres. We concluded with examples of portraits and vignettes that can be used in many of these different types of writing. How we tell the story influences what people can derive from our scholarship, what they can see, hear, and comprehend. Now, in Chapter 17, we look at the commonalities that cut across the many different ways to write up what we have learned through our journeys.

CHAPTER 17

Report Formats

This chapter explores report formats, sections, and organizational ideas.

There are a variety of ways to organize a report. In this chapter, we present three for your perusal: a "traditional" report (Figure 17.1), a more issues-oriented narrative report (Figure 17.2), and a report based on the proposal format we presented in Section V (Figure 17.3). We include a column for estimated number of pages for each section, but only you will know what fits for your study.

The traditional report is typical of standard research reports. To make it more suitable for action research, we have added a section called "changes" to show how the study may have been modified from the initial proposal and a section called "reflection." You might want to weave the changes throughout the methodology and the reflections throughout the report. Modify Figure 17.1 to suit your study.

The second format we present, Figure 17.2, is an adaptation of a way to organize a case study report presented by Robert Stake in *The Art of Case Study Research* (1995). One of the reasons we recommend this type of format, and the way Stake organizes his framework, is that it enables the action researcher to develop the *issues* indicated in the study. Especially in action research, with its overt agenda, the "questions, the contexts, the history, the case itself need more than to be described, they need to be developed" (p. 123).

The third type of report format, presented in Figure 17.3, is the one we have detailed in previous chapters. See Traveler's Notes E and F for examples: Ruby's report of the democratic classroom and E-folios: Motivating Our Students to Speak More.

Use these possible frameworks as catalysts to think about what may be a suitable format for your study. You may want to take a few minutes now to jot down some ideas on how you might organize your report. The section that follows is designed to help you to further refine your thinking about your report.

FIGURE 17.1 *Outline for a traditional report*

Abstract	Composed at the conclusion of the study, this is a concise summary of researcher questions, purposes, methods, and findings/outcome(s).	50–100 words
Introduction	This section tells why and how the study came about, including personal motivation, rationale, need for study. It usually concludes with a statement about what researchers hope to learn.	1–$1\frac{1}{2}$ pages
Review of literature	This section summarizes what other researchers and theorists have learned about the topic of your study. Tell readers how review is organized. Present what you've learned in chunks, depending on how things fit together, complete with a summative statement, paragraph, or bridge to design section.	3–5 pages
Design and methodology	Indicates who (participants), what (what you tried), when (how often, how long), where (setting), why (why you chose this approach and not some other approach).	3–5 pages
Changes	Few AR studies proceed exactly as planned. Save a section to record changes from your original plans.	Whatever needed
Results	These include findings, results of analyses (tallies, frequencies), tables, graphs, graphics, and your theorizing about these. Divide into subsections if needed.	4–8 pages
Reflections	What would you do differently next time? Do you have new questions? What was your journey like? How do you feel about what you have done? What have you learned about the topic? What have you learned about action research? What have you learned about yourself, your situation, and your students?	1–3 pages
References	Include all the sources referred to in your paper.	1–3 pages
Appendices	Include copies of survey (sample only), interviews, artifacts, permission letters, excerpted research log, and whatever else is pertinent.	Varies by study

FIGURE 17.2 Outline for an issues-oriented narrative report

Abstract, story, vignette, or anecdote	Start with a brief summary that incorporates the main ideas of the study, or use a short descriptive or suggestive scene to introduce the study: poetry, dialogue, brief story, or vignette, within the study.	50–150 words
Researcher's perspective, issues, purpose, method	Invite reader to delve into the perspective of the researcher, why the interest in this study, the issues, purposes, and methods used.	3–6 pages
Defining the study and its context	Give an extensive description of the context, database, and related research.	3–6 pages
Development of the issues	Drawing on other research and data, more fully develop the issues mentioned earlier, which will lead into the data analysis and interpretation in the next section.	3–6 pages
Presentation of data: descriptive detail, vignettes, quotations, triangulation of data	According to Stake (1995), this is "the place for experiential data" including what the researcher does to confirm and disconfirm her or his observations (p. 123); it can provide a portrait that presents data but refrains as much as possible from interpretation.	2–4 pages
Assertions	Stake (1988) suggests providing information that "allows the readers to reconsider their knowledge of the case," and presenting a summary of what is understood about the case, and how these understandings may have changed during the study (p. 123). These assertions are based on the researcher's interpretation.	2–4 pages
Closing vignette	A vignette or story serves to point a direction, or leaves the reader with an issue or sense of the main idea (if there is one), or opens out into another question. It can be a thought-provoking end to the report.	A paragraph
Appendices	Include selective data and other materials useful to interpreting the study, its context, and issues.	Variable

Category ideas adapted from Robert Stake (1995), *The Art of Case Study Research*. Thousand Oaks, California: Sage Publications.

Abstract	Composed at the conclusion of the study, it is a concise summary of study including major learning related to the research question.	50–100 words
What is my research interest?	What are the issues, concerns, problems, curiosities? What is my question? (How can I. . . ?) Why am I interested? (values, beliefs) What do I already know (through my experience)? What do others know? (literature, colleagues) What are my hunches? What do I expect to find?	2–3 pages *Criterion:* *Question is significant to self and to others. Addressing it has potential to bring practice in line with values.
What did I try out in order to improve my practice? What problems arose and how did I respond?	Who are the participants? What did I try out? When did the activities take place? (time line) Where did the study take place? How did the action unfold? Why did I try these particular things and not others? What changes occurred in my plans as a result of what I was learning?	3–6 pages *Criterion:* Actions related to values; addresses research question or evolving question.
How did I document the process (as I monitored my actions)?	How did I record observations? What did I observe? How did I conduct interviews? What kind of interview format did I use? Whom did I interview? What documents and artifacts did I save? What literature did I read, or what people did I consult with? How did I get permission from students, parents, and school to collect and share data?	1–2 pages *Criterion:* Rich description of observations, critical reflections on actions, multiple perspectives.
How did I interpret the data?	How did I analyze data? How did I synthesize the parts into a whole? How did I formulate my theories? Did I use public theories to help me? Did I make assertions? Include charts, tables, pictures, and other processed data, but refrain, as much as possible, from interpretation.	1 page *Criterion:* The process used for making interpretations that allow for reasoned thinking, intuition, and creativity is clearly explained. However, no interpretations are made.
How have I verified that my judgments are trustworthy and credible?	Researcher's perspective is clearly stated. Multiple perspectives are drawn upon. Indicators (internal/external) are applied. Raw data are provided (transcripts, student work, survey results). Hunches are confirmed and/or disconfirmed. Researcher reflects on self and on action.	1 page *Criterion:* The basis for making judgments is grounded in insights gained from several verification processes.

FIGURE 17.3 *Continued*		
What have I learned and what is the basis of making those interpretations? (Results and analysis)	Include assertions related to research question and the evidence for those assertions.	3–6 pages *Criterion:* Multiple sources of evidence are used to support assertions that make sense in relation to research question.
How have these actions made life better? What will I do next?	What are the consequences of these actions for • Myself and my values? • My students? • My situation? And how are the consequences in line with my values (or not)? What are the implications for my practice? What have I learned about the action research process and becoming a scholar of my own teaching? What further questions do I have? What will I do next?	2–3 pages *Criterion:* Do actions relate to values of equality and democracy in my classroom? Is critical self-reflection evident?
References	List all sources used in paper.	1–3 pages
Appendices	Copies of surveys (sample only), interview questions, interview transcripts, artifacts, permission letters, excerpted researcher log, etc., should be included.	Varies by study.

* If multiple researchers are contributing to the study and report, an additional criteria for evaluating the report should be included: Is each researcher's voice heard in the narrative and is there evidence of collaborative reflection? See Chapter 9 for suggestions related to how to reflect collaboratively.

Questions to Think About Before Writing the Report

There are several things to consider in preparing most reports. Depending on the kind of report you decide to prepare, different questions will carry different weight. Think about the following questions in light of the kind of report you will prepare. There are two sections of questions and information: *questions to consider before writing the report* that might apply to any study and *questions related to sections of the report* and presentation.

1. *What is the purpose of my study and my report?* The purpose of a study and report (whether written or oral) is the foundation for all that follows; it is the touchstone that keeps the study and report focused. Ask yourself: Am I

keeping the purpose of my study in mind as I write? What literature relates to my purpose? Is my purpose evident in the design and analysis of data, in how I interpret the data? Has the purpose of my study changed as my study evolved? If so, how and when do I inform the reader?

Is the purpose of your report to fulfill a course requirement? To sell something to others? To inform? To fuel discussion? To enable others to benefit from what you have learned? To effect change in school policy or curriculum?

2. *Who is the intended audience?* The audience is closely tied to the purpose. Is the report written for a colleague, professor, your staff, the local board of education, a committee, parents, students, a professional community of teachers, or teacher researchers? Knowing the audience you can decide on the amount of detail to include, the format (e.g., concise report or dramatic presentation), tone of voice, and level of formality. Picture a variety of audiences. How might your writing differ or be the same for each group? Strive to be *clear* and *succinct*.

3. *What voice, point of view, and writing style are most appropriate to my purpose and audience?* Voice, point of view, and style are what makes our written and spoken journeys unique. If our journey is governed and told by the heart, by strongly held values, then the tale of our hearts will weave itself into the pages of our text. This tale may be that of the pilgrim. If it is governed by the mind, the researcher or experiential authority may tell the tale, and the intellect will be dominant. If the story is of inordinate courage, then tests of bravery may frame the narrative. The journalist may take you there, using ethnographic drama. Can you imagine the unique styles that our Oz companions can develop?

As to audience, a report to the board of education may well be argued in a crisp, expository style of the experiential authority or researcher with ample evidence from the research literature and one's own scholarship, whereas a report to teacher colleagues may usefully include the connoisseur's extended vignettes and examples of the students' work. Then again, your board of education may be more attentive to an illustrated story! Length, too, varies with the purpose and audience: short and concise for audience members who have little time to enjoy the vignettes you have crafted, longer for audience members who want to more fully appreciate the distinctions and nuances you have uncovered.

Whatever your perspective, *own your voice;* make it obvious to the reader. Where are you, the researcher, in this study? What are the values and commitments that prompted your study? What are your beliefs about teaching, learning, the purpose of schooling? Present your point of view so that audience members can interpret, question, challenge, and come to their own points of view. This is what developing professional judgment is all about— critiquing and forming one's own grounded opinions.

A technical aspect of owning one's voice concerns whether to write in the first person. Many of us were forbidden to use first-person point of view in report writing. Today, however, many professionals work to make their writing invitational. They work to make their point of view known, their claims, methodology, and findings clear. First person can help them do this.

Journal editors often encourage first-person styles. Oral presentation can also be more engaging in the first person.

In this next section, you will find thoughts on writing various parts of the manuscript. While there are many ways to write up a report, there are also conventions to follow. Thus, for solo authors, I is appropriate. For multiple authors, we is appropriate. See Travelers' Note D and E for examples of the use of I and we.

4. *What guidelines or rules govern style and the technical parts of writing?* Different fields use different "style" manuals, such as the *Publication Manual of the American Psychological Association* (American Psychological Association, 1994), that of the Modern Language Association, or the *Chicago Manual of Style* (University of Chicago Press, 1993), or the American Psychological Association (APA) style for referencing and citations. If you are taking a course or writing an article for publication, consult with the instructor or journal's editorial guidelines for directions about which manual to use. Consult a *current* manual for style and mechanical questions. These manuals will provide information about the parts of the manuscript (abstract, introduction, and so on), grammar, editorial style related to punctuation, spelling, use of quotations, citing references in the text, tables, figures, reference lists, appendices, etc. Therefore, we will not provide details on these technical aspects of writing, but we will address one frequently asked question. What about verb tense?

    The APA manual suggests that the literature review and results are best written in past tense. However, using present tense to discuss the project, findings, or reflections on the work will invite the reader to join you in your deliberations about the work (American Psychological Association, 2001).

5. *How do I get started?* There is no universal best way to get started in report writing or in presentation preparation. Some of us can hardly wait to put pen to paper or fingertips to keyboard. We have a beginning vignette in mind, and it sets the tone. Others of us would rather wash dishes, clean the garage, visit the dentist, or do income taxes than confront a blank page or computer screen. Our minds jump over the vast landscape of possibilities, and a hopeless, overwhelmed feeling descends upon us. If you are one of the former jump-right-into-it people, go to it! If you are one of the latter, never fear, for there are ways to conquer the malaise. Here are a few ideas.

    • Sift through all that you have saved. Look for patterns, critical incidents, descriptions, details, or moments that capture the essence of what you feel is important to convey. Now, just sit down and start writing.

    • Make a detailed outline, or a graphic organizer (like a flowchart or a web). Now, start anywhere on it, and proceed to other parts as they seem most relevant. Start writing a section that attracts your energy, a key finding or insight, or a powerful vignette or issue.

    • Robert Stake (1995) argues that topical outlines may give too much license to the writer to continue writing beyond what is necessary: "When each line in the outline has been handsomely developed, the 4 pages originally intended have become 8 or 12" (p. 124). Instead of using a topical outline, Stake uses a tentative table of contents and allocates the number of pages per section he will write, making him "ruthlessly winnow and sift" (p. 124). Try it.

6. *How can I introduce the report?* No matter what form of writing or oral presentation we choose, whether it is storytelling, poetry, drama, or expository writing, we want to portray our research interest. Think briefly through these questions:

- What are the issues, concerns, problems, and curiosities?
- What is my question? How can I . . . ?
- Why am I interested?
- What do I already know (through my own experience)?
- What do others know (other scholars, colleagues, parents, students)?
- What do I expect to find (hunches, hypotheses)?
- What do I hope to learn?

The exercises in Section V were designed to help you to develop the proposal that incorporated responses to many of these questions. Refer to your proposal when writing up your report, and make changes when needed. You may have used progressive focusing to identify your original questions. Did your questions change during the course of the study? In what ways did they change? Did you develop additional questions?

Use the introduction to bring your reader into the study and your purposes. Vickie Tapp, a sixth-grade teacher, does this by starting with a narrative that invites us to understand her desire to study the process of using math journals to help students construct mathematical meanings. This is how she began her report:

> In 1964, a blond, pixielike, third-grade girl skips home from school and runs upstairs to her room. She unloads her bookbag, opens the top drawer to her dresser, and quickly stuffs the math book under the clothes in the top drawer. She changes into her play clothes and goes downstairs. Her unwitting mother supervises her homework and sends her out to play. The next day, it is math time and the teacher announces, "We are going to play a game today. It is called 'Around the World' and we will use flash cards." All the children cheer. Well, almost all. This one little girl is frozen in terror. "I won't know the answer, I don't get math . . . I'll be so embarrassed." Too soon, it is her turn. Oh oh . . . too late! Lost again.
>
> Later in the same math period, the teacher gives out a computation worksheet. This little girl stares at the problems. Numbers dance in front of her eyes. She makes hashmarks on the side of the paper, then hides her hands under the desk and counts up on her fingers. Hot tears slowly trickle down her face, and she finds she is the only one not finished. The teacher takes her paper. Oh well, they were probably all wrong anyway. A few weeks later it is report card time. Our little girl is on pins and needles. Finally, she receives her brown envelope. She slowly opens the flap and peers inside. An *A* in reading, *A* in spelling, *A* in language. So far, so good. An *A* in social studies. Oh no, an *F* in math. How could that be? An *A* in all other subjects and an

F in math. What is she going to do? How will she tell Mom and Dad? School is no fun. Her attitude begins to change. Soon her mother has trouble getting her to go to school. She loses herself in reading, getting book after book from the library. Soon, she decides she is good at everything except math, so it is no use trying.

That little girl was me. An intelligent, capable child who for some reason got turned off to math. As a teacher, I have seen many students who are going through similar experiences with math. Some have a very negative attitude. Others have difficulty understanding the mathematical language. I have often wondered if there was some less traditional way of teaching math that might enable these students to use their language and communication skills to help change negative attitudes and bring them to a better understanding of mathematical concepts.

Vickie then discusses her growing understanding of the cognitive nature of the writing process, writing across the curriculum, and her desire to see if the use of writing in math will reduce math anxiety and foster better mathematical understanding among her students.

Jon and Terry begin their paper with a creative overview, inviting the reader to look into classrooms:

Down the hall another day is starting in Mrs. W's first-grade classroom. Seatwork is being assigned so that reading groups may begin. Students will spend 90 minutes on worksheets and workbooks as they cycle through ability-based reading groups using basal readers. This cycle is repeated in many first-, second-, third-, and fourth-grade classrooms up and down the hall, but in some rooms, this cycle is changing. Peek into Ms. S's fifth-grade classroom. No longer do we see the three distinct groups, but the whole class is receiving instruction that revolves on authentic literature and response. After a quick briefing on the day's discussion, students break away into their literature circles. By school policy, all fifth-grade students are homogeneously ability-grouped into four classrooms for reading. Ms. S has the readers who are struggling. Because of this, many of these children have been limited to the "basics." The focus of their instruction up to now has been skill-based basal instruction with few opportunities for what many refer to as enrichment literature activities. Since many of these children have not been members of the "literacy club" (Smith, 1988) in previous years of reading instruction, they have little enthusiasm or motivation to join a club that has excluded them from membership.

Our goal is to open membership in the literacy club to all these children. How can we motivate these children at-risk to take ownership of their reading and want to be members of the club? By using literature circles with authentic text and student-led discussion, we hope to ignite their desire to read. What strategies will best suit their needs—response journals, discussion, prompts, graphic organizers, role play, or cooperative projects? What management techniques have proven successful in other classrooms, and what adaptations of these techniques will be needed for success of literature circles in our classroom? We hope to see these children move from teacher-led activities to student-directed learning.

Jon and Terry cite Smith's idea about student exclusion from the literacy club as a way to confirm their own feelings and commitments.

7. *When, with whom, and how should I share during the writing process? Why* do you want to share? Do you seek a sounding board, serious feedback, confirmation? Do you want a witness to your explorations? Your responses to these questions form the basis for who to share with and how to do so. Do you have a critical colleague whose opinions or expertise you trust and value? How much and in what ways do you want her or his participation? What you seek from others, and who you seek it from, will vary with the time and task. In a period of incubation, where ideas are getting warm and coalescing, you may want a friendly witness, not another opinion. At another time, you may want challenging dialogue.

Report writing and planning presentations present great opportunities to invite collegial discussion. Professional writers rely on others. We can, too. Colleagues and family members can provide reactions and suggestions dealing with content, mechanics, and proofreading, and with audience response to your presentation ideas. Ask someone to read aloud what you have written. Read aloud to yourself and hear the syntax, the rhythm. Freeman (1997) advocates this for writers of all ages. The argument is that since we have often read fiction out loud in our schooling, we have developed an ear for the story, its cadence and rhythm. In writing this text, for example, the characters—

Scarecrow: Do they mean *us*?

Dorothy: I think so.

Authors: Sorry, that does put you into a box, doesn't it? Our point is not to be demeaning by lumping you all together. In fact it is the opposite, because you each have a unique voice, personality, and point of view. We could *hear* your voice when you wanted to speak as we typed our manuscript.

Using our *ears* helps us to edit our text. How does it sound? Do others respond with an understanding we think we intended? Are the main ideas fairly clear? Is there critical information missing?

After you find a critic to provide you with feedback, tell the person specifically what you would like her or him to do. "I want to see if I did what I started out to do. Do my purpose and findings relate to each other in a coherent way? What do you think?" "Please read through my recommendations and see if they follow from my data." "Please read through the interview with Jen and see what conclusions you come up with." "Am I giving a fair treatment to all the students in my report? What is missing?" "Is this argument persuasive?"

Questions Related to Sections of the Report

Although your report may not have traditional sections as we have organized six of them here, we hope that thinking through them will call attention to what might usefully be included regardless of which format you select.

1. Literature review. *What will you include, and where will you include it in the report?* There are two main ways in which literature related to your study can be particularly useful to the reader. The first way is the grounding that a theoretical perspective can provide in the way of context and lenses from which to understand your study. Literature usually informs your way of thinking about the topic at hand, and how you will study it. This could be called your theoretical basis or foundation. Normally we function from our own theories of how life and teaching and learning work, and as we discussed early in the book, these can be referred to as private theories, which, when we look into them, are usually informed by public theories (i.e., constructivist and structuralist theories, behaviorism, theories of language, or psychosocial or cognitive development). Are there theoretical bases for your study? If so, share them with your readers and let them know how those bases will be used for interpretation.

The second way in which literature is useful to both you and your readers is in positioning your study in a larger context. Where does your study fit within a larger arena? Often there are one or more studies that are quite relevant to your study, and citing important aspects of these can be instructive. Action researchers read and cite literature that supports and challenges their thinking, and provides ideas to try out. As critical readers, we read with a skeptical eye. By reviewing this literature we synthesize multiple dimensions of our topic and deepen our understanding of the contexts of our own research.

Many action researchers refer to relevant literature throughout their reports: in the introduction, design, or interpretation sections. Their references to literature are informal and interspersed throughout the text whenever the literature speaks to a point the researcher is trying to make. Other action researchers organize the literature review systematically in a separate section of the report and label it "Literature Review." The degree of formality and organization depends on your purposes. For example, a thesis or dissertation will most likely require a literature review section.

The literature review presents what you have learned about your topic. You may want to begin with an introductory sentence or paragraph describing how the literature review is organized. Try presenting the literature one aspect of the research area at a time. You might end the review with a summary of key points and a sentence connecting to what follows.

Stepping Stones 17.1 presents an organizer for a literature review. The topic was students' perceptions of school learning tasks. A group of action researchers was interested in making assignments more appealing to students. To gather baseline data, they planned to interview students about assignments from which they learned the most and the least, and one thing they might recommend to improve schooling. They also wanted to examine what others said about this topic. They found several big ideas through their reading.

STEPPING STONES 17.1

Graphic Organizer for Literature Review

Rationale for study citations (present first)
- Eisner, 1991
- Erickson and Shultz, 1992
- Kotter, 1996

Present next:

Studies done on middle school students
- Taylor and Roselli, 1993
- Wasserman, 1995

Then:

Student attitudes about school and curriculum
- Fouts and Myers, 1992
- Maroufi, 1989
- Shug et al., 1984

Finish with:

Student perceptions of teachers
- McCabe, 1995
- McDowell and McDowell, 1986

Several sources (Alvermann et al., 1996; Eisner, 1991; Erickson and Shultz, 1992; Kotter, 1996) provided a rationale for conducting the study. These ideas included the belief that students are key informants about education. Some suggest that students are the consumers of education and for that reason should be consulted. Others, among them action researchers, suggest that student experiences *should* be at the center of attention of all research that affects students.

Another pair of studies involved middle school students, and so clustering these two studies was logical (Taylor and Roselli, 1993; Wasserman, 1995). Other studies revealed attitudes of students toward schooling and curriculum in general (Fouts and Myers, 1992; Maroufi, 1989; Shug et al., 1984). The final idea that emerged was based on two different studies in which students were interviewed about their expectations of "good teachers" (McCabe, 1995; McDowell and McDowell, 1986). The researchers organized their outline as follows:

- Rationale for interviewing students.
- What middle school students like about school.
- Student attitudes about schooling.
- Student opinions about what makes good teachers.

Stepping Stones 17.2 presents suggestions for organizing the literature review and for citing references within the report.

STEPPING STONES 17.2

Organizing a Literature Review

1. Look for commonalities in the findings of research studies, and make a statement that summarizes the commonality. Then cite the authors who have jointly made this point, for example, "Many authors talk of the pitfalls of ability grouping and its negative effects on student performance over long periods of time (James and Roberts, 1990; Johnson, 1991; Jones, 1990; Smith, 1989)." Another way to write this is to incorporate the citations within the sentence that summarizes their idea, for example, "Smith (1989), Jones (1990), James and Roberts (1990), and Johnson (1991) all state that ability grouping is generally detrimental to long-term student achievement and motivation."

2. When you are paraphrasing, page numbers are not needed. When you are using direct quotes, provide page numbers.

3. Index cards and chart paper are two supplies you may want to use when trying to find the main ideas for a literature review. By noting bibliographic information and main ideas on index cards as you read, you can simply refer to these cards to look for commonalities when you are organizing the literature review. Then use the chart paper to list the main ideas and the authors you will want to cite in support of the ideas. You may also want to create a graphic organizer (a concept map or outline) to organize the key ideas you will develop in the report.

Software Tools for Publishing and Managing Bibliographies

Instead of spending hours typing bibliographies or using index cards to organize references, you can take advantage of software tools such as Endnote or RefWorks. Such software allows users to search, retrieve, and store citations from bibliographic databases such as ABI Inform, the Web of Science, Anthropological Literature, the MLA bibliography, or the catalogs of individual libraries. It can generate bibliographies, reading lists, and footnotes in a wide variety of styles, and because it links directly to word-processing programs such as Microsoft Word and Word Perfect, the software enables users to add and format citations to papers as they write.

- Endnote: http://www.endnote.com/
- RefWorks: https://www.refworks.com (a Web-based tool for managing references and creating bibliographies)

2. The design and methodology.   *What will you include about* **how** *the study was conducted?* You will recognize the following questions from the chapters on designing your study.

- What did I try out in order to improve my practice? What problems arose and how did I respond? (Who are the participants? What did I try out? When did the actions occur? Where? How? Why did I try this and not that?)
- How did I document the process? (observations, interviews, materials prepared by others)
- How did I interpret the data? (analysis, synthesis, theories, and assertions)
- How have I verified that my judgments are trustworthy and credible? (Is my standpoint clear? Multiple perspectives? Indicators? Raw data? Rich description? Systematic? Self-reflective?)

In this part of the report, provide information to the reader about *how* the study was conducted—*not* what was learned. For example, we include how our theories and assertions are made, *not* what our theories and assertions are. Refer to Sections V and VI, and Chapter 15, where we discussed writing down and writing up, for details of the sections as needed.

When instruments are used as part of the data collection, explain each briefly in the design section. If the test, checklist, or observation instrument has been borrowed from another researcher, mention and cite the source of the instrument. If the instrument was teacher-created but similar to one found in someone else's study, cite it as one's own based on the work of so-and-so. If you create the instrument for this study, note your last name and the year on the bottom of the instrument. This makes it officially copyrighted as your own; or use the copyright symbol, year, and person's surname (*Chicago Manual of Style,* 1993).

Note changes in the study. We often change planned activities. For example, Ruby modified her activities considerably as she realized that students were becoming less tolerant and respectful of one another. Note extenuating circumstances that influenced the research. Perhaps you had difficulty interviewing students when a flu epidemic hit the school, or when students were preparing for a test. These obstacles are real and part of the story. *Whatever happens is part of the research story.* And the things that happen that are unanticipated are just as important to what we learn as those things that we carefully plan.

3. Reporting what we have learned, and our bases for interpretation (results and analysis).   *What have you learned and how will you share it with others?* In this part of the report, tell what you learned related to your research question. Robert Stake (1995), whom we mentioned earlier, is a well-respected scholar whose pioneering of qualitative methods of research have opened up new possibilities in data collection, analysis, and portrayal. He might describe your primary task at this point (and into the next section) as one of coming to understand the case(s), to tease out relationships between issues and participants, to probe issues, and to search for patterns (or lack of them), consistencies, and inconsistencies within certain conditions. Report writing "must winnow and sift for the forest's sake" (p. 121). You continue to make sense of your results *as* you report them.

One way to formulate our learning is to make assertions. These statements are claims to knowledge. Ruby asserts: "It is not good enough to just encourage participants. I had to push for respect." What is the basis of this claim? Ruby goes on to argue that some students were so wounded by the classroom compact and teaching that she as a teacher had to intervene. She also provides a larger context for this assertion: "My own experiences in the political arena and my understanding of the Bill of Rights should have warned me that a democracy that relies too heavily on rights cannot create a safe community." Thus, Ruby relies both on her experience as a teacher and a political activist, and on the larger framework of the Bill of Rights to make her claim. In Ruby's report, she portrays the teasing and taunts aimed toward one another in such a way that we who have experienced similar situations can identify with Ruby's situation and will resonate with her assertion.

We want to *show* (rather than tell) the reader what happened (the consequences of your actions), and then speculate about why these consequences occurred (assertions). This is the process of theorizing described in Section VI. You might also want to make reference to the public theories that inform your own thinking or to critique those well-established theories if they run counter to your own emerging understandings, grounded in evidence that *you* have amassed.

We want to provide evidence in the form of data to support any claims that we make. But we may also want to move beyond the evidence in making assertions. There are many things we *know* to be "true" that lay beyond the statistics or interview quotes or grades or written documents produced by our students, or any patterns that we carefully and systematically note in our data analysis. Our intuition, as a kind of peripheral vision, can unlock mysteries that all the coded data in the world cannot reveal to us!

To help us to consider our evidence and the quality of the claims to knowledge that we make, we will want to consider these questions:

- Whose story are we telling? (How much is insider/outsider information, and how is it presented, as insider or outsider?)
- On what basis do I make my claims and assertions? (What is the context within which I claim and assert?)

There are questions related to the technical aspects of supporting our assertions and claims to knowledge:

- What data should be included in the report?
- What form should those data take?

Include charts, tables, and other graphics only when they can clarify or otherwise enhance the reader's understanding of the text. Sometimes, in trying to make meaning with the data, we construct tables or charts only to discover they aren't informative or compelling, or, even if useful to the researcher, are not necessary to the report. For example, if the research includes a survey with responses that can be quantified, a table showing the mean score on the responses to each of the questions will allow the reader to see how you interpreted the data. It also allows the reader to interpret the data for herself or himself. In this section, we may also refer the reader to transcripts of interviews, journal entries, documents, and artifacts. We let the reader know that they are available in the appendix and invite the reader to examine them.

What if the researcher interviewed 23 students? Should all 23 interviews be included in the appendices? Although it depends on the study, the answer is generally no. Include the interview questions and blank survey instrument, and sample responses that are typical of responses or that illustrate the point you are trying to make. If the data can be quantified, tables showing means, standard deviations, correlations, and other more advanced statistical analyses can be included. Within the text of the report, provide a brief description of these items and refer the reader to the appendix in which they are included.

Finally, a graphic organizer can help the reader (as well as the author) to see how the study flowed, the context for decisions that were made, and subsequent learning that took place. Refer to Traveler's Notes C to see examples of flowcharts and "snake" charts that summarize the overall studies of several action researchers.

4. Reflections and consequences.   *How will you reflect on the consequences of your actions?* Since this is the topic of our concluding chapter, we only briefly discuss it here. Reflecting on what we have learned, intentionally and unintentionally, is an important part of the report. Reflecting on the consequences of our actions (the *so what?*) has implications for future action. Since the ultimate aim of action research is to improve our professional practice, time engaged in planning how we can use our findings to improve our practice, student learning, and to foster equality and community, is time well spent.

5. The references.   *How will you acknowledge the authors and researchers referred to in your study?* Include all the references cited in the report in a separate section. Follow the guidelines provided in the style manual you have chosen for your study. For information on citing Internet sources, see Stepping Stones 17.3 on page 267.

6. The appendices.   *How and what will you include that enables the reader to see for herself or himself the artifacts of your study?* The appendices offer more detailed information to readers than can be written easily into the prose. Examples of instruments, student work, handouts during the project, rubrics, or other evaluation tools are all included for reader reference. Each appendix is labeled with a letter, e.g., Appendix A, Appendix B, and so on. There are no rules as to what goes first or second or last in the appendices except as it makes sense with the study. If a pretest was used, for example, it makes sense to have that appear earlier than the posttest (if there is one). After that, the order of the appendices generally correlates with the order in which they are mentioned in the report.

STEPPING STONES 17.3

Citing Internet Sources

There are now a wide array of journals online that are never printed in paper editions, as well as paper journals that are also published on the Web, either free or through a subscription the library purchases. Cite the journal, not the URL from which you accessed it.

- Cite the author, editor, complier, or translator of the article. **Last name, First initial**.
- Date of publication in parentheses—year, month, day, for example (1997, December 25). If the publication date is not known, use the abbreviation n.d. in parentheses, followed by a period, to indicate *no date*, that is (n.d.).
- Document title—the title of the article you are citing. In reference lists, capitalize only the first word, the first word after a colon or dash, and proper nouns.
- Publication information—For example, journal title, volume, number. Journal and newsletter titles are italicized. The journal volume number is italicized (and the comma after it), but the issue number is not.
- Statement of length—The pagination of the article as numbered in the printed journal, for example, 117–123. Note: It my take some deciphering to know the page numbers as they appear in the printed journal. The following examples from citations as they appear in journal databases may help you interpret the page numbering:

Example: No author given in the article

"Policies and procedures." (2001, December 7). *HR Reporter 18* (12).
Retrieved April 28, 2002, from Academic Universe Database.

Example: News source

Petit, C. (2002, January 4). "Tuning in to Einstein: Two giant instruments are set to listen for vibrations in the very fabric of space and time." *U.S. News & World Report*, 56–57.
Retrieved June 12, 2002, from SIRS Researcher.

Example: Books without a printed version; that is, the book is only an electronic one

Lee, H. (1998). *User*. Hsien-Chi Lee.
Retrieved May 14, 2002, from
http://www.duke.edu/~hlll/novel/novel.html

Each appendix needs a succinct but descriptive title (*American Psychological Association*, 2001).

Whatever format you select, use the guidelines from the style sheet you have selected to help you write the headings for each section.

CHAPTER SUMMARY

In this chapter, we looked into three formats for writing a report: traditional, issues-oriented, and one that builds on the design presented in Sections V and VI. We discussed general questions about report writing (purpose of report, audience, voice, guidelines, how to get started, introductions, when to share and with whom) and specific questions about report writing (review of the literature, presentation of what was learned, reflections, and consequences, as well as references and appendices). In Chapter 18 we go one step further and discuss ways to share our research in both paper and presentation forms.

CHAPTER 18

Building Learning Communities: Sharing Our Research

This book is about teachers as colleagues engaging in inquiry and professional conversation, creating knowledge bases for further action and learning. To develop our expertise as teachers, we need opportunities to engage with others who share our educational aspirations, for it is within these communities that ideas and knowledge about teaching can develop.

Knowledge about teaching is created when teachers open their practices and ideas to critique. See what worked for me? How does this work for you? Why? Why not? What are the differences in the way we did this? What are the consequences of this for serving the needs of my learners? Of your learners? Of all learners? As Hiebert, Gallimore, and Stilger (2002) point out in their article on creating a knowledge base for the teaching profession, "Over time, the observations and replications of teachers in the schools would become a common pathway through which promising ideas were tested and refined before they found their way into the nation's classrooms" (p. 12).

Thus, AR is a professional tool for teachers to *transform* themselves and the professional community of teaching. The "test" of the knowledge that is being generated is its ability to *transform* schools into democratic communities of learning.

If this sounds idealistic, it will remain so unless structures are put into place to help create the kind of community that enables the sharing and critique of knowledge to occur. Action research communities can provide this structure. They are developing within schools, districts, cities, states, regions, and even nationally and internationally.

In this chapter, we explore the structures for action research communities, ways of enlarging the growing conversations to larger communities, and resources for the traveler who wishes to move beyond the classroom walls.

Structures for Action Research Communities

Communities of teachers as learners take on many different names: learning communities, communities of practice, professional development centers, inquiry groups, study teams . . . and action research communities. The coin of the realm in learning communities is conversation, evolving networks of conversation that create a structure for continuing conversation. At the simplest level, conversations take place in communities where all who participate contribute and learn. They are safe spaces for innovation and challenge, where members are valued as colleagues, and authority shifts depending on needs. Learning communities have many purposes: to develop expertise; to solve problems; to share knowledge; to provide a social forum for the development of knowledge; to produce useful documents, tools, and procedures; and to mobilize forces for action. They are small or large, long lived or short term, homogeneous or heterogeneous, spontaneous or intentional, unrecognized or institutionalized, sharing the same location or different locations (Wenger, McDermott, and Snyder, 2002). They develop in many existing formal structures: interdisciplinary teams, local school councils, advisory councils, parent–teacher associations, departments, school districts, or university study teams, to name a few.

According to Wenger, McDermott, and Snyder (2002), these communities share three elements: (1) a common ground that creates a sense of identity and purpose built around what has value to its members; (2) a sense of community among its members that is based on mutual respect and trust; and (3) the practical set of tools that members use and master to form the knowledge base of the community. These are the conditions needed for teachers to make their ideas and actions public, to invite conversations of critique within and beyond the community. An example will demonstrate how a community develops and takes action in a difficult situation.

As a junior high school in Colorado tried to transform itself from a typical departmentalized, subject-centered school to a school based on middle school philosophy, teachers and parents posed several areas needing attention. Should interdisciplinary teams be heterogeneous (mixed ability) or homogeneous (students identified as "gifted" on one team)? Should cheerleading be limited to the most talented or should it be open to all who are interested? How best can the teams address the education of students with special needs? How can the school schedule be created to reflect the needs of all students rather than a select group who demand special consideration? What is the school philosophy that would guide decision making?

Short-term study teams of parents, teachers, administrators, and students were constructed. Each study team was comprised of members who had different opinions about how things should be. Members of each team read articles and books, did online searches, joined chat rooms with other middle school teachers and parents, visited other schools, talked to consultants, hired guest speakers, and engaged in dialogue with one another. Rather than building consensus, the goal was to learn about many possibilities and to construct a plan of action that reflected a diversity of perspectives, something creative and new. Each team presented its plan of action and rationale to the entire school community. Each plan was piloted, studied, and modified before it was institutionalized.

The common ground for each study team was a vision of middle grades schools driven by three goals: academic excellence, social equity, and developmental responsiveness (National Forum to Accelerate Middle Grades Reform). Even though discussions got quite heated, the ground rule of mutual respect for the perspectives of others guided the relationships among group members. Resources used to build a common knowledge included those listed previously (readings, online searches, school visits, etc.).

After months of study, the sports committee, as an example, decided that cheerleading would be open to anyone interested in participating and willing to practice to improve skills. Financial resources for cheerleading camp and uniforms would be provided by the community to anyone who needed it. The committee explained their decision to the entire school community in terms of the newly developed school philosophy and its basis in developmental appropriateness and social equity. The culture of adoration that developed when selection was determined by socially desirable appearance, athletic ability, and popularity did not fit in with the middle school philosophy. It had detrimental effects on the cheerleaders who were developmentally not ready to handle all of the attention they received. Nor was it fair to all of those who were never going to meet rigid (but well meaning) selection criteria. The sports committee invited critique. The response was amazing! People who had been fighting for months agreed to pilot the plan for one year. The carefully structured inquiry and dialogue within this action research community enabled the transformation of a school practice that by many was considered sacred.

New forms of action research communities are possible through the use of technology and offer opportunities for professional development with critical colleagues from different schools—not only within the same school district but also across a state, the country, or even internationally. In Ohio, for example, eTech Ohio, an agency within the Ohio Department of Education and funded by the Ohio legislature, offers opportunities for teachers across the state to take part in an online action research course in which they share what they are learning through their participation in a state-funded grant to integrate the innovative use of technology into their teaching. Critical colleagues within a school working on the same project may work face-to-face or in chat rooms as they figure out how to use technology to create student-centered classrooms. The same colleague groups share ideas, frustration, aspirations, and learnings with other groups across the state through a discussion board, at a state technology conference, and through an eTech Web site where their studies are posted (see http://www.etech.ohio.gov/programs/action/research/).

Participants from the 20 schools across the state agreed that without the help of their critical colleagues, they could not have accomplished what they did to change their teaching. The richness of discussion board postings related to technology and accountability, standards-based teaching, and professional relationships with parents and communities gives evidence of the challenges teachers face and the support they need when trying out something new.

Ways of Sharing with the Larger Community

There are many ways to share knowledge and invite critique. In this section, a variety of forms of representation will be explored, including journal articles, professional presentations, audio-visual presentations, performances, and communication through technology.

Papers for Publication

Have you thought about writing about your study for publication? Imagine an account that colleagues or others may find of interest. Consider the options for publication: a newsletter, a newspaper, a magazine, a book, or a journal. Each may be viable. We will address the journal possibility here. Once you identify a potential journal, a quick analysis of its contents can provide useful information. This analysis may include the following:

- *What can you learn from the table of contents?* Discern the types of articles and topics consistent with the journal's mission. Are there articles in your area of interest? How long are the published articles?
- *What can you learn from recent articles?* Can you envision your paper among these?
- *What can you learn from the directions for authors?* In the front matter, or on the back or inside covers, you will find information about submitting manuscripts: addresses where manuscripts are to be sent, number of copies required, style manual to consult, the mission and audience for the journal, and the kind of submissions the journal hopes to secure. Is there any indication of how long it takes for a response? Will the journal send reviewer critiques? Where can you write or call for further information?
- *Have you considered contacting the editor(s)?* Most editors encourage conversation about potential journal contributions. Is your paper appropriate for the journal? What is the likelihood of the journal's giving your paper fair consideration? Consider calling or sending electronic mail to someone on the editorial staff.

Consider collaborating on your first submission with an interested colleague—perhaps one with some experience, even if the colleague was not your coresearcher. Can you decide in advance how to share responsibilities for writing, manuscript preparation, and submission of the manuscript? Will your contributions be equal or unequal? Do you each have talents suited to different tasks? Typically, the person who drafts the copy becomes first author, while other author(s) contribute to rewriting, writing designated sections, preparing figures and graphics, editing, proofreading, and doing other parts of manuscript preparation.

Frequently, manuscripts are not accepted the first time, at least not without a request for revisions. Most experienced writers get requests to revise and resubmit. Reviewer comments and suggestions provide valuable opportunities for learning. Not all suggestions (even if more than one reviewer makes the same suggestion) are useful, or what's best for your paper. Do the suggestions seem reasonable and constructive? If so, give them serious consideration. Do the suggestions seem to miss the point? The reviewer may have misinterpreted or simply disagreed with your stance or premise, in which case you may choose to "stick to your guns" and not make changes. (Madeleine L'Engle, noted author of juvenile, young adult, and adult novels, enjoys sharing how *A Wrinkle in Time,* her Newbery Award novel, was rejected by 22 publishers before publication, most saying it simply "would not sell.") It pays to have confidence, courage, and persistence!

Many journals publish teacher action research. These are some of the better known journals:

Harvard Educational Review
Language Arts
The English Journal
Teaching and Change
National Writing Project Quarterly
Educational Action Research
Teacher Research: A Journal of Classroom Inquiry
Teaching Education
Teacher Education Quarterly
Action in Teacher Education
Teachers and Teaching: Theory and Practice

These are online journals that are very open to publishing the work of classroom teachers:

Action Research International
Action Research Electronic Reader
Networks
The Ontario Action Researcher

Many school districts now provide Web space on the district Web page for teacher action research studies. See, for example, Highland Park High School and

Madison Metropolitan School District. If your school district does not offer this opportunity, it might not take too much encouragement to do so.

Professional Presentations

Although teachers present ideas and facilitate dialogue with students on a daily basis, many become fearful and anxious at the mere thought of presenting their professional work beyond the classroom walls. But professional presentations can be an exhilarating experience, particularly when the purpose is to engage an audience in ideas that may result in meaningful action.

Tips for a typical oral presentation are outlined in Stepping Stones 18.1. The main thing to consider is how to actively engage participants in the presentation, first by inviting the audience to come along on the journey, and second by posing and encouraging questions around the issues involved in the action research study.

STEPPING STONES 18.1

Questions and Tips to Think Through for Traditional Presentations

- *Who is your audience?* Know the expertise of your audience, the numbers involved, their interest in your topic. A presentation to teacher peers may differ from one for parents or school board members. The size of your audience can influence the kind of presentation and activity you can accomplish.
- *What is the physical context of your presentation?* The size and shape of the room, the acoustics, the ability to use equipment easily and readily, the need for a microphone, whether people are seated facing you or at round tables, whether you'll be able to move from a podium, whether the equipment you use will be managed during the presentation by you or by someone else—all these can influence your planning. Ask questions about the arrangement beforehand to minimize unwelcome surprises.
- *How can you organize for success?* Will it be helpful to order your presentation on transparencies, note cards, or visuals? If so, number the transparencies or note cards for ease of presentation, and make sure that all fonts are large enough for audience viewing. During slide presentations lights are often dimmed. Be sure you can see what *you* need to in low-light conditions. If you are using handouts, arrange for an adequate number. Have a sign-up sheet of names and addresses if the audience is larger than expected. Get information out to others as soon as possible after the presentation.

- *How will you reach out to your audience?* How will you introduce yourself? Making eye contact and beginning with an anecdote, personal related story, humor, or a poem can help to establish rapport.
- *What about pacing?* Speak clearly and at a moderate pace. Many presenters speak too rapidly, slowly, or softly to be understood by everyone.
- *Will you use advanced organizers?* You may want to inform your audience, orally or with a graphic, of what your presentation will cover. This helps create a context for listening.
- *How will you use graphics to best effect?* If you display a table, graph, flowchart, photograph, and so on, narrate it for audience members. They will need time to grasp what by now seems readily apparent to you. Explain symbols or abbreviations.
- *Will you share the text visually?* Teachers often wish to share examples of student work. A PowerPoint presentation, transparencies, or handouts can be used. Large type and reading out loud can be useful.
- *Will you use video clips?* Is the video clip set in the right place and ready to go? Is the volume sufficient for the room size? Can all audience members see the monitor? Where are the room lights and who will dim and raise them? How will you prepare your audience? Are video clips brief and to the point?
- *How will you keep track of time and pacing?* It's easy to forget what you have said and what needs to be done. You may want to have an outline handy in large font for referral; or you may return to an overhead that gave your advance organizer, and remind people what is left at the same time. *Stick to your time constraints,* especially if yours is one of several presentations. Remember the last long-winded speech you endured? A clock or a friend or both can tell you that you have 5 or 10 minutes left.
- *How will you conclude your remarks?* The tone you leave your audience with often comes from your finale. Save a key piece of evidence, an issue, an inspiring piece of student work, a story, an anecdote, or a related poem for your closing.
- *Will you build in time for audience questions?* Find out ahead of time if there is time allotted for audience questions. This can be one of the most valuable parts of the session. Respond to all questions honestly and respectfully (even if you covered the point in your talk several times), and redirect appropriate questions back to others in the audience. The nature of AR is dynamic, and discussing unanswered questions can be informative for all involved.
- *Do you want to offer a few summary statements?* These can include what you have learned at the session from others both in preparing and in presenting your work. Thank the audience.
- *How can you enjoy and learn from the experience?* Presenting your work can be exhilarating. If you are engaged, chances are that your audience will be, too.

Many national and international educational organizations hold conferences and include action research presentations by teachers. A sample of these national associations include the following:

Collaborative Action Research Network (CARN)
International Conference on Teacher Research
American Educational Research Association (AERA)
AERA's Special Interest Groups (SIG): Teacher Research, Self Study, and Action
    Research
National Council of Teachers of English
National Middle School Association
National Association for the Education of Young Children

Many states have affiliates with the national organizations that also support the presentation of action research projects; for example, the Ohio Council of the Teachers of English and the Ohio Middle School Association.

Poster Sessions

Many professional conferences include poster sessions. They typically take place in a large room with movable bulletin boards, easels, or wall spaces that are segmented and designated for researcher displays. Those who attend these sessions walk around the room and discuss the ideas presented in the posters with the researchers.

A poster can be thought of as a composition with a background, middle ground, and foreground. What does an observer need to know about the context (background) to understand the issues behind the work? What does an observer need to know about the methodology and data (middle ground) that led to the decisions, actions, or results (foreground). What is the "so what" that frames the meaning in this research landscape?

The poster format required at some professional conferences contains traditional research elements: title of study, purpose of study, participants and setting, methodology, and key learnings and recommendations for action (complete with appropriate graphics). But other teacher-friendly venues might welcome more creative and engaging posters. Where is the energy in a study and how can it be portrayed? What symbols, images, or metaphors capture the essence of the study? How might participants be invited into conversation that goes beyond the study? A collage, photos, student work, rich excerpts from a researcher journal, or student quotes might capture the main idea in ways that invite an observer's own interpretation.

Technology and Multimedia Presentations

Technology enables the creation of action research communities that go beyond the school, district, or university. Action research studies can be posted to Web sites, e-mail, chatrooms, Listservs, and MOOs (multiple-user, object-oriented environments).

Blogs, wikis, cybercafés, simulations, and gaming offer the creative educator and student almost limitless possibilities to explore and practice. See Stepping Stones 18.2 for popular sites.

Listservs are a powerful means of communicating research results with a larger community. Members may join a list and send a message to the rest of the members. Members can choose to respond. If, for example, a science teacher is concerned about the quality of lab experiences in his physics class (they seem a little too contrived and unrealistic to his students), he might want to share the results of his action research project on hands-on lab experiences in physics with other physics teachers across the country through a physics teachers' Listserv. These teachers may want to try out the new approach and add what they have learned about this process on the same Listserv. Over time, these teachers will be creating their own knowledge base about lab experiences in physics.

Many professional organizations maintain Listservs for members. ARLIST-L is a multidisciplinary electronic mailing list. It is a free, moderated forum for the discussion of the theory and practice of action research. Participants can share what they have learned through an AR study or discuss methodological issues in conducting a study. This Listserv is considered low volume and includes members from schools and universities.

A MOO is one form of communication possible on the Web. According to Jan Rune Holmevick, a MOO is "synchronous online multiuser space . . . different from an asynchronous online discussion because it takes place in real time . . . unlike a chat because, in addition to real-time dialogue, a MOO is immersive: users move around a virtual space and can build rooms and create objects" (Holmevick and Haynes, 2000). Imagine having a coffee with other English-speaking teachers in Iraq, Germany, India, and Turkey. You are all teaching social studies in the days after 9/11 and want to explore ways to help students feel a sense of global community. For an hour and a half, you share student poetry, stories, photos, video clips, and music that may inspire your students. You decide to create something together for your students.

STEPPING STONES 18.2

Some Popular Simulation and Game-Based Technologies for Education

- SimCity (http://simcity.ea.com/): computer-based simulation puts user in charge of a growing city
- Civilization IV (http://www.2kgames.com/civ4/home.htm): a historic, turn-based strategy game where users guide their civilizations through the course of world history
- Second Life (http://www.secondlife.com/): a 3D virtual world entirely built and owned by its Residents

As we enter an era of "new literacies" with a wider understanding of what makes a person literate beyond print and oral representations, developments in technology have enabled new multimedia (nonprint) forms of making our work public. These can include multimodal compositions—combinations of visual art, video and film, graphics, motion, sound, and text. While the more static forms such as photography, photo essays, and simple PowerPoint presentations can evoke strong emotions and thoughts, the more dynamic forms that integrate video, graphics, audio, text, and photos provide details and evidence that require greater participation from the viewer. All of these forms capture a moment in time that can be replayed to form common understanding but also allow for layered interpretation and reimagining ways of understanding and acting.

Joanne Dowdy, a researcher at Kent State University, studied the narratives of students who did not complete high school in the traditional way and were working on their GED (Graduate Education Diploma). She created videos of interviews with the GED students to tell a story that she feels is more powerful and direct than a standard research report. The shifting of eyes, the tone of voice, body movement, the color of skin make participants become present—over and over again in ways that are unmediated by the researcher. Her interviews consisted of three questions: How did you come to get your GED certificate? What is it like to be a GED graduate? What does it mean to you? As a researcher committed to participation and empowerment, Joanne does not claim to "own" the data or the videos and invited participants to tell their own stories. One GED graduate, determined to share her story with others, played her video at a church gathering. "This is MY story" she said, in such a convincing way that a member of the congregation became determined to do the GED herself. A written account may or may not have had this effect. Since most of us are so video literate, we understand the language of film, thus diminishing the aura and often the fear associated with research.

Performances: Portraying What We Are Learning Through the Arts

Performance is an alternative way of interpreting and presenting the results of research. "A performance authorizes itself, not through the citation of scholarly texts, but through its ability to evoke and invoke shared emotional experience and understanding between performer and audience" (Denzin, 2003, p. 192). Through drama, role play, video, visual art, dance, and poetry, experience can be heightened symbolically, concretely, and dramatically in convincing ways. Performance is a particular way of knowing. It consists of "partial, plural, incomplete and contingent understandings—not analytical distance or detachment" (Denzin, 2003, p. 193).

Preparing the performance may need some thought: Who is the audience and what is the purpose of the presentation? Whose experiences need to be included? What themes emerge from the data analysis that represent the key experiences of the research participants?

Performances are no less work than writing a report. As a matter of fact, they may require more work because in addition to data analysis, scripts may have to be written, permissions may be required for performances, material might need to be secured for creating artistic renderings, and so on.

Several examples will serve to illustrate the power of performance to open spaces for new understanding and action:

A mural painted on the wall of a community center in a wealthy resort community in Florida depicts the lives of migrant students who attend the middle school. It was created by eighth graders and their team of teachers as part of a service learning project exploring the difficulties of moving into and out of school during the various growing seasons. At scheduled times, the mural formed the backdrop of journal readings. Students recounted their first day of school—a very different experience for the white and Latino students. The purpose of the project was to engage this very diverse community in a new awareness of the different cultural experiences of students so that actions could be taken to enhance everyone's education.

In another example of performance excerpts of life history, interviews of adults who could not read were audiotaped and broadcast on a local radio station to gain community support for an adult literacy program in the local high school. The researchers were teachers pursuing graduate work in adult literacy at the university. Their action research project began out of a desire to understand how it is that some adults in this small college town did not read and the impact of this on the literacy learning of their own students.

Online Resources for Action Researchers

A wide array of online resources (local and international) are available for those interested in becoming members of a larger action research community. We include a list of these Web sites in Figure 18.1. These sites include theoretical and

---

FIGURE 18.1 *Online Action Research Resources*

CARE Centre for Applied Research in Education (University of East Anglia, England)

CARN Collaborative Action Research Network (Manchester Metropolitan University, England)

Action Research Resources

Jack Whitehead's Action Research Page

CARPP Center for Action Research in Professional Practice (University of Bath School of Management)

Jean McNiff's Action Research Page

ARL Highland Park High School Action Research Lab

Madison Metropolitan School District Classroom Action Research

Johns Hopkins University Center for Technology Education—Action Research

methodological writing on action research; names of Web sites of key action researchers in the United States and abroad; action research reports written by teachers and university faculty; information about conferences; lists of related Web sites; lists of publications; and access to Listservs and discussion lists. You may want to explore these for what they have to offer. Specific addresses are not included because they may change over time.

Studies posted on these Web sites give evidence of professional growth, transformation, and knowledge development of teachers, principals, doctoral students, university faculty, and superintendents as they work to improve their practice. See Stepping Stones 18.3.

STEPPING STONES 18.3

Online Tools and Resources for Content Creation, Communication, and Collaboration

Synchronous Communication and Collaboration Technologies

- *Chat and instant messaging* allows participants to carry on a text-based conversation in real time. Popular programs include Yahoo Messenger, MSN, AOL, and Skype.
- *Web conferencing programs* help you share programs, windows, or the entire screen with participants. Popular application sharing tools include Elluminate (http://www.elluminate.com), Adobe Connect (http://www.adobe.com/products/connect/), and WebEx (http://www .webex.com/).
- *Audio conferencing* allows participants to talk with one another, such as Skype (http://www.skype.com).
- *Video conferencing tools* allow participants see and hear one another. Polycom (http://www.polycom.com/) is a good example.
- *Voting tools* provide a way for participants in an online activity to express their opinions about various issues. Some popular ones include Pollpro (http://www.pollpro.com/), Pollmonkey (http://www.pollmonkey.com/), and the Survey System (http://www.surveysystem.com/).

Asynchronous Communication and Collaboration Technologies

- *E-mail* enables the exchange of messages with other e-mail clients using the Internet.
- *RSS feed reader* is a free online service for searching, subscribing, creating, and sharing news feeds, blogs, and rich Web content. Examples

are Bloglines (http://www.bloglines.com) and Google Reader (http://www.google.com/reader/).

- *Online discussion boards* allow participants to post messages to a known location where other participants can read and respond to them. Yahoo Groups (http://groups.yahoo.com/) is a good example.
- *Course/learning/content management systems* use Internet-based software to allow participants, especially a course instructor or facilitator, to manage materials distribution, assignments, communication, and collaboration. Examples are Moodle (http://moodle.org/) and Sakai (http://sakaiproject.org/). Moodle and Sakai are open course management systems.
- *Blogging tools* help you create and write content to a blog or weblog. Popular blog service providers include Wordpress (http://wordpress.org/) and Blogger (http://www.blogger.com/).
- *Wiki tools* allow users to add and edit content collectively online. Examples include Wikipedia (http://en.wikipedia.org/), Wikispace (http://www.wikispaces.com/), Mediawiki (http://www.mediawiki.org/wiki/MediaWiki), and Google Docs and Spreadsheets: http://docs.google.com/.

The synchronous and asynchronous characterizations of the above technologies depend on the users. The synchronous tools can be used asynchronously and vice versa depending on the time between receipt and action of the receiver.

Content Creation Technologies

- *Microsoft Office Suite* (http://www.microsoft.com) helps create desktop content (e.g., Word, Excel, PowerPoint, Access, Publisher).
- *Adobe Macromedia programs* (http://www.adobe.com/) create Web-based content (e.g., Photoshop, Dreamweaver, Flash, Contribute, Fireworks, Captivate).
- *Media editor* creates and edits video clips. Examples include Movie Maker (http://www.microsoft.com), Adobe Premiere (http://www.adobe.com), QuickTime Player Pro (http://www.apple.com/quicktime/), Camtasia (http://www.techsmith.com), and Final Cut Pro (http://www.apple.com).
- *Open Office* (http://www.openoffice.org/) is a free multiplatform office productivity suite, including key desktop applications such as a word processor, spreadsheet, presentation manager, and drawing program, with a user interface and feature set similar to other office suites.

CHAPTER SUMMARY

Telling it like it is, the voice of participants and teacher researchers are represented in many forms—from formal reports to multimedia presentations to performances. The audiences are as varied as the issues involved—parents, school boards, local school councils, professional development groups, professional education associations, business groups, faculty, advisory councils, or city councils. Wherever teacher voices need to be heard, there are teachers who will speak.

SECTION SUMMARY

We have discussed two of the most important ingredients of action research in this section—the acts of *writing,* and of *sharing,* that is, of *making one's work public.* Both writing and sharing are key to critical practice. They, as we, are not neutral. In action research we observe, write, and speak from a point of view and a value system; and part of the presentation of our work is to make those perspectives known, to facilitate discussion with colleagues and others who have similar and differing points of view. The quality of what we open to discussion and critique is shaped by our observations and interpretations. As we shape our stories and continue to critique our own and others' action research, we stretch our capacities and fuel our scholarly communities; and not surprisingly, our ideas, practices, and professions grow. Our inner and outer worlds become more obviously part of the same world. From our evolving perspectives we find that Oz has much in common with Kansas and Kent.

In "Exploring the Forest" you are invited to get started with writing up your report. The exercises are designed to help you get started, often the most difficult part of the action research journey. And then in the final section of the book, *Lessons from Oz,* we conclude our journey . . . for the time being.

Exploring the Forest

Portraying and Communicating

To get a feel for different ways to portray your work, we have put together several explorations and exercises for you to try. You might think of yourselves as artists and craftpersons who are trying out different kinds of media. The more media you try out, the larger your repertoire can become and the more choices you will have to render your work.

1. The four parts of this exercise will quickly take you into major aspects of your study:
   - Without taking much time to think about it, come up with an incident, finding, or quotation that might introduce your study to the reader. Write it up as a vignette for the beginning of your report. Now think about an incident, finding, or quotation and write it up as a vignette that will conclude your study. What, if anything, do these suggest for what comes in the middle?
   - Free-write. What *issue* or issues undergird your study? What have you learned in relationship to this issue from your research? What *actions* did you take in your study related to this issue?
   - In two paragraphs tell the story of *how* you studied what you studied.
   - In one paragraph, tell the "so what" of your study. What did you find out from what you did, and what does it mean?
2. In this exercise, we want you to try out four conventions for report writing identified by John Van Maanen (1988). We won't write an entire report using one convention, but we will write up sections of our reports using different conventions to see how each might work with our studies.
   a. Write the preface (or introduction) to your report, using *experiential authority.* This means that you will establish your credibility as the

      researcher in this first part. Speak from your own point of view and in first person.

   b. Select one or two stories that you find to be most interesting within the material to be reported, some of the "parts" you studied, and write it (them) in a richly detailed vignette that could be used in your report. Write them up in a *documentary style.*

   c. Select a person who participated in your study and write a portrait of this person, incorporating his or her language, thoughts, experience, and behavior. Although you put this material together, do not put yourself into the portrait directly—do not include your interpretations (although they will be part of what you select to tell). Keep the portrait brief, and try to portray the *culture member's point of view.*

   d. Write up the "so what" of your study in a manner that conveys your *interpretive omnipotence.* This is a no-nonsense, no waffling, no humility, and no hint of insecurity kind of writing. Tell it as you see it—from your data and analysis.

   e. Now, cut and paste each of these together as a report. What do you need to add? How do these different parts and styles fit together? Which of the four conventions did you most enjoy using? Why? Which did you least enjoy using? Why? What did you learn about report writing from these different kinds of portrayal?

3. Work with a colleague or small group of colleagues. Take several issues of a respected journal in your area of interest. Locate at least three articles with literature reviews. Read these literature reviews with your partner(s). For each literature review, *read as a writer* and describe the review. How was it set up? How would you describe it? Did the author arrange it chronologically, by a raging controversy, or by several logically chunked subheadings? Compare your descriptions with others. No doubt, you will note that there are many ways to write a literature review. Perhaps you will find one that suits your study. Pay special attention to how the authors integrated many studies into a brief review.

4. After you complete a draft section of your report, invite a small group (three to four) of critical colleagues to read it, listen to it, or do both. Invite impressions and questions. Ask for written and verbal feedback. Each can yield valuable results. With written feedback, you get each person's perspective without the influence of one person on another. One person doesn't dominate and influence others' responses. Follow up on pertinent responses. However, if you would like to have their responses act as catalysts for group discussion, reading your work to them without the benefit of their having the written form might be more effective. Or, give them copies before you meet as a group, and ask for their responses so that when you meet as a group, each person can put forward her or his considered responses. To what would you like to have responses? What observations do they offer? Do they hear or see what you intended to convey? What else, if anything, do they

hear or see? If you raise an issue, is it clear? Do they offer any suggestions? Note your thoughts as you begin sharing and after the process is completed.

5. Plan a presentation to a group in your school or institution.

   a. Decide on the group and why you would like to present your work. (Is it to inform, engage in discussion, help to bring about change, invite other perspectives?) State this as your aim. When you present your work, tell the group of your aim.

   b. What three points would you like to convey?

   c. Now, think "outside the box." How can you take these three points and invite others to ponder them? Think of three ways you could present or engage your group with them.

   d. Mine your data—and your report. Where is the gold? What is hot, and what is not? Sift through your report. What attracts your energy? Go with it. Then think about why it attracts your energy. (What has the greatest potential to engage others in such a way that change is made possible?) Is there part of the insider story that you would like to tell?

   e. Now, think about the bookends: How will you get the presentation off the ground? How might you conclude it?

   f. Enjoy presenting your work. Now that you have ideas, use them to get started.

   g. After you have "done it," what worked well and what were the results in terms of your aims? What else happened? What were the surprises? What did you learn? Where is your thinking related to your project now?

Lessons from Oz

66 But you have not yet told me how to get back to Kansas."

"Your silver shoes will carry you over the desert," replied Glinda. "If you had known their power you could have gone back to your Aunt Em the very first day you came to this country."

"But then I should not have had my wonderful brains!" cried the Scarecrow.

"And I should not have had my lovely heart," said the Tin Woodman.

"And I could have lived a coward forever," declared the Lion.

"This is all true," said Dorothy, "and I am glad I was of use to these good friends. But now that each of them has had what he most desired, and each is happy in having a kingdom to rule beside, I think I should like to go back to Kansas. 99

The Wonderful Wizard of Oz
L. Frank Baum (1900)

Are you ready to go now?

Dorothy: Almost. Here I am at the end of the journey. I have traveled the Yellow Brick Road, weathered flying monkeys and wicked witches, and found my way through apple-hurling trees, poppy fields, and hourglasses not in my favor—to the Emerald City, only to discover that the Wizard is a scam artist who couldn't answer my questions! And Glinda reveals that I have always had the power to get home! I need to think about all this. There are so many riddles.

Scarecrow: And puzzling paradoxes! But, you know, I think I'm beginning to understand. The journey itself, with all its riddles and paradoxes, was important, not just the destination.

Tin Man: My, that sounds erudite! And, it's true. I feel different. I guess it's like . . . development . . . or *transformation*.

Lion: Yup. Now, I can take on *anything* that comes my way! After all those poppies, monkeys, and witches, I'm rrrrready to stand by my values and act on their behalf no matter the obstacles. I'll grab those apples and use 'em, not just dodge 'em! I'll climb those apple trees and get to the bottom of my questions. No matter where my curiosity takes me and where I have to meddle, I'll go and I'll meddle!

It sounds as if we've all learned some valuable lessons. Let's follow up on some of those riddles and paradoxes you refer to. We can wander over to those tree stumps by the gates to the Emerald City and ponder our journey. Take a few minutes to come up with a riddle or paradox and we will come back to them soon.

Riddles, Paradoxes, and Contradictions

Most of us formally study teaching in a college or university, and after we begin a career, we realize that we have just *started* to learn the complex art of teaching. We find we have a continuous stream of questions about students, teaching, learning, education, and social issues. And we search for answers—from books, articles, courses, colleagues, and the Web. These questions fuel our professional development and suggest more questions. We "finish" to "begin"! This is a paradox about becoming scholars.

Teaching presents a continuing stream of riddles and paradoxes necessitating the scholar's eye. Few things about teaching and learning are certain, predictable, or tidy. As we look for answers we find more questions. We want to help our students find answers, but only through helping them raise meaningful questions. The more we continue to learn, the more we question what we do. When we recognize, accept, and even celebrate this complexity, we are taking the scholar's journey.

The more we study our students and their learning, the more we can learn about *ourselves.* Teaching requires us to constantly examine ourselves as human beings committed to *teaching and learning.* If we paid attention to what we already know (in our hearts, minds, and souls), and what our colleagues help us to understand, we would not have to journey far and wide to make teaching and learning better for ourselves and our students. But without that journey, we might not gain the wisdom, passion, and courage that our teaching days require of us. That is one of the riddles that makes teaching and learning so complex and yet so simple. We cannot find our way home until we have gotten a little lost in the process of developing as professionals.

The story of Ruby's democratic classroom illustrates this point well. Her action research journey was taken to find ways to enact strongly held democratic ideals in her social studies classroom. Several students maintained *either-or* thinking and contradicted her plan by enacting their personal agendas. The dislike she began to feel for them reminded her even more of her responsibility to create and sustain democratic ideals in her classroom. She wondered if she had emphasized individual freedom without attending adequately to social responsibility. Had she inadvertently reinforced the belief that democracy could exist without responsibility, that we are EITHER free as individuals OR have social responsibility? For some students, this was a paradox.

As Parker Palmer writes in *The Courage to Teach* (1998), "In certain circumstances, truth is a paradoxical joining of apparent opposites, and if we want to know that truth, we must learn to embrace those opposites as one" (p. 63). Part of teaching is helping others to think beyond what seems obvious and often this means accepting multiple perspectives and opposites. Yet, aspects of our culture work against a more integrated and ecological way of thinking. Where mind is separate from heart, we have cognitive objectives and affective objectives. Where one way of developing is separate from another way of developing we have gifted students and disabled students. Where theory is separate from practice we have experts and teachers. Where we have those who have attained great knowledge and those who are waiting to be filled with that knowledge, we have teachers and learners. Where we have those with power who try to control teaching and learning and those who carry out the will of those more powerful, we have accountability—for teachers only.

This kind of thinking is so embedded in our educational systems that we come to believe in these dichotomies, and base our practice on separation rather than on ecology and integration. The net result is that we typically regard teaching, learning, curriculum development, evaluation, educational research, and professional development as separate and distinct educational processes. But as John Elliott (1991) argues, "Action research unifies processes often regarded as quite disparate . . . teaching is conceived as a form of research aimed at understanding how to translate educational values into concrete forms of practice" (pp. 53–54).

Lessons from Home, Heart, Mind, and Courage

Here are a few lessons that action researchers have shared with us over the years.

Their "lessons" are filled with paradoxes, not unlike those of our Oz travelers. Maureen, for example, wrote, "The most important learning . . . was the realization that I should not want to control the outcome." She concluded:

> When I realized that research meant stepping back and allowing changes
> to take place without my input, I allowed myself to relax, let things flow,
> and wait. When I relaxed, I could almost hear a collective sigh from my
> students, and they began to make choices and decisions on their own
> which contributed to the results of my research. When I became aware of
> my apprehension about this, the true research began.

Maureen expresses one of the paradoxes many action researchers face. Part of becoming the teacher you want to be is achieved by stepping back and inviting students to take the lead. By empowering students, we empower ourselves. The process of stepping back and letting go can be difficult. Yet, when we do, we find that we give up control, and we gain control. We give away power and we become powerful.

This theme of *power* can be manifested in expressions of confidence. As Maureen and Chris expressed it, respectively: "My view of myself has changed. I am more confident. . . ." and ". . . the teacher as researcher process empowers me to be a better teacher and learner . . . I am using these skills in developing a new program."

Patricia found that confidence can lead to courage: "I learned never to be content with the status quo." Similarly, Vicki resolved "not to be afraid of experimenting and trying something new and different. I have already made my research project part of my curriculum."

Leann, a math teacher, wrote about the seeming contradiction that in order to understand matters of the mind, it takes *heart:* "I have learned the importance of research. In order to successfully teach and understand an educational concept, you need to get to the root of it. The only way that can be achieved is through heartfelt research."

We (Wendy, Joanne, and Mary Lou) worked through contradictions and paradoxes with this book and learned our own lessons in the process. For example, how might two seemingly opposing processes live within one person and project the importance of, and need for, curiosity, imagination, creativity, and intuition *as well as* the systematic skills, techniques, and research methods necessary to a scholar? "Either-or" is easy; "Both" and "what-when" are harder to describe. How could we weave the elements of AR into a tapestry that would begin to do justice to this rich and evolving structure for educational transformation? On the one hand we emphasized the need to be open and receptive to affective dimensions of the research process, and on the other hand, to adopt and cultivate specific and systematic rule-governed processes, where there is little or no room for creativity. We learned as we wrote and discussed our work. We found out how very different our experiences and perceptions were, one from another. We learned where our writing varied from the values we espoused. And now, it's time to get back to our riddles.

The Riddles of Oz

Authors: Are you ready to share your riddles?

Dorothy: I came all this way, through a land far away, and now I understand home in new ways. I see it differently. It's me, becoming confident, comfortable with uncertainty, skeptical, and committed.

Lion: If I don't take action and face risks how will I develop courage? Courage doesn't come to us when we are sitting on the side of the road. Courage is **acting** on our beliefs, and when we do, we feel powerful. When we work with others that's real power!

Tin Man: I looked to the Wizard for a heart, as if it were a prize that he could give me. He couldn't give me one, but he could help me to see what I already had. I see my heart grow as it is challenged, and I find it reflected back to me by good friends like you.

Scarecrow: I looked for answers only to find more questions. Now I know what it means to have a brain—not only for finding answers, but for asking thoughtful questions, exploring and creating responses, and reflecting critically on them.

Wizard: Ah, my scholarly friends, while it's been said that necessity—whether for heart, courage, brain, home, or democratic classroom—is the mother of invention, let it also be a catalyst for that most splendid of the action researcher's resources, imagination. Let your stories evolve, and as you expand them, they "will become mirror and window both—reflecting back knowledge and understanding . . . for a widening circle . . . opening possibilities for all" (Ayers, 1992, p. 265).

Authors: Hmmm . . . "mirror and window both," wish we'd have said that. Put on those ruby sneakers. You will need them as we conclude our journey by . . .

Exploring the Forest

Constructing Lessons from Oz in a Portfolio

The learning community that we have talked about throughout our time together is fueled by communication, and what better time to communicate than when you have something meaningful to say. This is what we will do together in our concluding exploration: We will reflect on our journey, we will decide what is most meaningful to say, and we will say it in a form that others can appreciate. This is how the knowledge base evolves. We continue to create new conversations and keep the structure for sustaining transformation alive through action research and the cycles of reflective practice with our colleagues.

Reflecting on the Research Process

We offer several suggestions for reflecting on our journey, and, as is true of any party, you can accept the invitation or not! Select what suits you and come up with your own ideas.

1. Ask yourself: What were the *key aspects* of this journey for me? What were the *highlights* of the research process? What were the greatest *challenges?* What were the greatest *lessons* and *turning points* in the process? What were the *riddles* and the *paradoxes?* At what points did you call on your *imagination?* Free-write about these.
2. Look back over your journal and the explorations and exercises you selected to complete. Skim them all. Now, write about what stands out in your mind about what you have completed. Free-write; don't think too much about it.

Envision the whole and the parts within, but do not get caught up in the parts (that's another adventure). Now that the wicked witch has finally been dissolved, and the monkeys are free from her control, they can offer assistance. Our purpose here is to bring the end into sight with the flying monkeys *helping* us to look down over the entire landscape we have traversed. Flying too low in any area could mean getting lost in its details. The monkeys can help to keep us at a safe distance.

3. If you were presenting a step-by-step story of your journey (from "What is AR?" to doing it, and completing the cycle), with a key aspect for each step, how would you describe the process? Take a few minutes to write about it.

4. Ask yourself the following questions. You may want to include your responses in the reflection section of your AR report.
   - What are the *consequences of my actions* for my students, my situation, my teaching, myself?
   - What have I *learned about my students?* (How do they learn? How is their learning, individually and collectively, linked to the social, cultural, political, and economic contexts that frame their lives?)
   - What have I *learned about myself and my values?* (What have I learned about myself as a person, as a professional? In what ways have I grown? In what ways have my new understandings influenced others? What has happened to my convictions? In what ways have I modified my positions? In what ways has my thinking become more inclusive, more complex, more differentiated?)
   - What have I *learned about my situation?* (What power do I have to influence my situation? What are the social, cultural, political, and economic factors that shape the context in which I teach?)

   The ways in which we address these questions will help us to consider the next question:
   - What are the *implications* of what I have learned (about the consequences of my actions) for what I will do next and in the future?

5. Finally, reflect on the *action research process itself.* We conceptualize teaching as a cycle of acting, observing, and reflecting—the work of scholars, best done with the help of critical colleagues. What lessons have we learned about the scholarship of teaching and learning?
   - What have I learned about *documenting my work?*
   - What have I learned about *analyzing and interpreting data, verifying data, and portraying* what I have learned?
   - What have I learned about *working and learning with critical colleague(s)?* How might we continue our work together? What structures can support continuing conversations?
   - What has been the most valuable part of this process? The least? The most difficult or challenging for me?
   - What lessons have I learned for future action research studies?
   - What will I need to do to continue this study or to start another one? In what ways has critical reflection become a part of my everyday practice?

Let's take one last look at a few of Shawn's, Jon and Terry's, Ruby's, and Roberto's reflections on their work. Shawn's study had a major impact on her professional development and teaching career: "I am going to pursue certification in teaching English as a Second Language. I have spoken to the current ESL teacher in my district, and she has directed me in what I need to do." About the researcher log, Shawn writes:

> [It] was a valuable tool. I often went back and read what had gone on in the past week. I was . . . able to note some things about my teaching, for example, lessons that worked and those that did not. I made entries at least four times a week. This seemed to keep me focused on the project.

Jon and Terry reflect on the collaborative nature of their learning:

> Two heads are definitely better than one. Our strengths and weaknesses complemented each other. . . . We had discussed the pros and cons of working together on this project at length before undertaking the study. This is not for everyone. . . . Sharing a common philosophy of education has also made working together possible. . . . Just as the students keep learning, so do we.

Ruby writes about what she might have done: "I should have paid more attention to the results of the Citizenship Survey. Had I done so, I might have spent more time at the beginning of the class creating a common ground of the concrete details about what citizenship and a democratic community entailed." She also reflects on what she will do next:

> "I will . . . use some of the methods of documentation that I learned in action research. No matter what my teaching responsibilities might be . . . documenting the action and my thoughts and feelings . . . will help me to be more responsive to my students and more clear in my thinking." She goes on: "As far as tempering my 'savior' spirit, I'll keep reminding myself (with a little help from my friends) . . . my journal will be my life-long teaching companion."

Roberto concludes his study with a narrative that shows the importance of his study and the direction it will take in the future:

Student: "Hey, are you going to do that club again this year?" a smiling eighth grader asks.

Roberto: "Yes, as soon as I have my class up and running. Do you want to be involved?"

Student: "Oh yes," she states. "And my friends do too!"

Roberto: I chuckled for this is my third conversation like this today.

Kelly, another teacher, reflected on the process of AR, noting that "looking at all the data on one student was like opening a gift; I did not know what I was going to receive. I may have gotten some hints, but until all the data was assembled, I could only guess. . . . I do not need constant tangible proof (a test, a work sheet, or discussion) that learning is taking place. I need to trust the process. Some of the superfluous proof I desired put brakes on my students. I am taking those brakes off. . . ." Finally, Kelly learned that "perhaps my biggest revelation during the study is that my students and I are more similar than I thought."

The Researcher's Story of the Journey

Having reflected on the AR process, we will wrap up our journey by constructing a portfolio. Revisit "Exploring the Forest" in Chapter 2 for the portfolio section if you think this might be helpful. The portfolios we advocate here are narrated and illustrated. The portfolio is narrated by you, the researcher, and illustrated with examples. Engage readers; draw them into the story. Although you can prepare an action researcher portfolio for many different reasons (and from many different points of view), here we will pose questions for a general, simple, and straightforward portfolio.

You have been telling your story all along the way: to yourself, your colleagues and friends, and to your journal where you may have completed "Exploring the Forest" sections throughout the book. Having completed a few of the reflective explorations on previous pages, to get a picture of the "whole"of the journey and of some of the important aspects of the process and the results (at least some of which are processes), we are ready to construct a portfolio whose purpose is to tell the researcher's story of the journey.

- The journey, simply put, can be narrated by the author in a straightforward way, as the newspaper reporter or the historian might move through time, narrating the experiences of *doing the research* and of the *products of the doing.* It can be told from any of the perspectives we discussed in Chapter 7, as well as any others you may create and develop.
- Another way to reconstruct the journey is to find a theme or a few key aspects of the study and follow it or them through, not necessarily in chronological order. Incorporate the story and highlights of the study.
- How about selecting and even writing some vignettes and narrating them for the reader? Do you have any photographs? Take some of the responses you made to selected questions above, and use them to illustrate and tell your researcher's story. How does the tale begin? Where and how does it end? Or does it end? At least one author we know of, Walker Percy, ended his novel *The Last Gentleman* with a blank page! There you are, reading along, and as you turn the page . . . nothing! If you want to make your readers think, try something unusual.

So, there you have it. Truth be known, we are all Wizards. We *are* the colors of the rainbow. The portfolio brings together our developing and evolving insights just as this book, a portfolio of sorts, has done for us. While the magic builds inside, the portfolio brings it outside, and the conversation continues.

Glossary

Action research   (AR) A form of teaching; a form of reflective practice and professional learning founded on an ethical commitment to improving practice and realizing educational values. AR involves individuals and groups identifying areas for improvement, generating ideas, and testing these ideas in practice. AR is characterized by cyclical, critical reflection and action, and collaboration. As research, it is systematic, self-critical inquiry made public (after Stenhouse, 1975). According to John Elliott (1991), AR develops the capacity of teachers to be discriminating; to make informed decisions about their educational aspirations and means of bringing these aspirations and practice together.

Applied research   Research that uses principles and theories but supplements them with informal discovery methods for the purpose of generating practical results.

Autobiographical inquiry   Inquiry into one's own history with the intent to grow as a person and as a professional.

Autopilot   Act of doing something without thinking about it, often out of habit.

Basic research   A type of research in which knowledge is conceived of as separate from practice and can be discovered through the application of rigorous, experimental research methods. The goal of this type of research is the development of theories through the discovery of broad generalizations and principles. An example is Einstein's theory of relativity.

Bias   A point of view, as used in research, generally for the purposes of making results come out in a preconceived or deceptive way. Examples include studying a spelling program but only selecting good spellers for the study; a group of physicians study a promising new heart medicine but only use men in the sample; a state department of education wants its schools to look bad so only includes test scores of districts where many children do not speak fluent English yet and blames test score declines on teachers and administrators.

CARN   Collaborative Action Research Network is an international network of people who practice action research—this includes teachers, teacher educators, administrators, and others involved in education and social change. It has been active since the 1960s under the leadership of John Elliott, from the Centre for Applied Research in Education, University of East Anglia, Norwich, England. Publishers of the *Educational Action Research Journal (EARJ)*.

Central tendency   Sometimes in an array of scores on tests or results of other kinds of assessments, a researcher wants to know how the average or typical learner or case fared. Three measures of central tendency give this information: mean (arithmetic average); median (score which half are above and half below); and mode (the most popular or most frequent score).

Glossary

Classroom action research   Action research that takes place within and is focused on life and practices (teaching and learning) within classrooms and schools.

Classroom research   Any kind of research undertaken by a teacher, teachers, or others, in and about classrooms.

Cognitive development   The term *cognitive* means "come to know." It incorporates all the various ways we come to know, including all the senses.

Collaboration   Willing joint labor toward the same end by two or more people.

Collaborative action research   Action research undertaken by individuals or groups in concert with other individuals or groups.

Community   John Dewey described *community* as a group of like-minded people who come together around the things they hold in common. These may include aims, values, beliefs, aspirations, and commitment to specific actions.

Conceptual development   The developmental journey starts where a person is and moves toward greater complexity and simplicity, creates a larger repertoire from which to draw, and develops problem solving, research abilities and capacities, and reflective processes.

Constructivism   In essence, constructivism means that persons (and systems) constitute and construct their own reality. We are meaning-making beings. Learning is understood as a self-regulatory process of resolving inner conflicts that often become apparent through concrete experience, collaborative discourse, and reflection (Brooks and Brooks, 1993). A philosophical perspective, derived from the work of Immanuel Kant, that views reality as existing mainly in the mind, constructed or interpreted in terms of one's own perceptions. In this perspective, an individual's prior experiences, mental structures, and beliefs bear upon how experiences are interpreted. Constructivism focuses on the process of how knowledge is built rather than on its product or object (Harris and Hodges, 1995). The name most often associated with the study of how children and youth construct knowledge is Jean Piaget and his theory of cognitive development.

Correlation   A correlation indicates the strength and direction of the relationship between two variables. Determined by a statistical test, such as a Pearson Correlation, an example would be: Is there a relationship between the test scores on students in a particular school district and the salaries of the teachers in that district? Is there a relationship between how much television is watched by students and the number or hours they read? Correlations can be positive (there is a positive relationship between student test scores and teacher salaries) or negative (the more television watched, the less at-home reading that occurs). Correlations never prove causation. The resulting number from the test, which is a number up to 1 (as in .78 as a good correlation, .95 as a strong correlation, -.89 as a strong negative correlation) is called the coefficient. Generally speaking, numbers less that .5 are not indicative of a promising relationship.

Critical methods, critical reflection, critical thinking, critical colleagues   Although the term *critical* is often used to mean "finding fault," it is used here to mean holding an emancipatory orientation to the world, and exercising reasoned and careful judgment for socially constructive purposes. *Critical methods* are those methods that enable the researcher to examine false consciousness and to become aware of the dominant forces that have shaped us. Autobiographical and biographical inquiries are vehicles for reflection that can enable some of these forces to be identified and exposed. *Critical reflection* means the act of looking beneath the surfaces, asking questions, raising issues, exercising and judging merit based on an articulated value of social justice. Through *critical thinking* we question the social structures and practices that place people into their present circumstances, often in unequal and exploitative positions. A *critical colleague* is a person who presents a different perspective; one who helps us to question those things taken for granted, and who helps us to view educationally related phenomena through socially and historically critical lenses.

Cycle of reflective practice   A continuous cycle of acting, observing, and reflecting that characterizes action research.

Dependent variable   This is what has been manipulated in order to study the outcome of something in a research study, such as how did the students fare who were being taught phonics in isolation as compared to those who were learning phonics in context. Or how the students regularly exposed to disabilities differ in attitudes from those who have had little experience with disabilities when their attitudes and dispositions are measured.

Descriptive research   This term applies to research designed to study, explain, and illuminate a phenomenon such as public attitudes toward education, or what adolescents think about global warming.

Developmentalism   Development is change over time. As Kegan (1982) explains, "Organic systems evolve through qualitatively different eras according to regular principles of stability and change" (pp. 13–14). Although each individual is unique and varies from other individuals in her or his growth, and each is influenced by earlier environments and experiences, there are predictable patterns to development that can be useful for teaching and curriculum development. For example, what is appropriate for a 6-year-old may not be for a 9-year-old. Development is movement toward more complex, differentiated, and inclusive perspectives.

Diary   Sometimes referred to as a *calendar;* a diary is a book in which personal descriptions, observations, and interpretations are written for one's own benefit and are rarely, if ever, for the eyes of outside observers. Diary-type writing is often a stream-of-consciousness type of writing; it can be creative, expressive, cathartic, and therapeutic. As noted in Section V on designing and planning an action research study, a diary is "a personal, unedited record of transactions and incidents."

Domains of professional development   Development is movement toward more complex, differentiated, and inclusive perspectives. Domains of professional development are the broad areas within which these take place.

Educational learning Learning that increases the capacity and desire for further learning toward socially worthwhile goals. For example, growing individual plants in the classroom leads to a community garden and environmental stewardship.

Educational research A research experience that is educational in and of itself. It must, in John Dewey's terms, lead to further learning and democratic life.

Ethical commitment A commitment to professional practice and to the democratic principles that undergird, and thus, support the foundation for any educational action research project.

Ethical, moral, and social development Deepening consciousness and awareness, respect for diversity, and understanding of others. It promotes collaboration, community, and valuing others.

Evocative forms of telling stories A term used by Laurel Richardson (1998) to describe newer forms of writing to portray one's scholarship, which include narrative of the self, ethnographic fictional representations, poetic representations, ethnographic drama, and mixed genres.

Experimental research and methods; quantitative research and methods The terms *experimental* and *quantitative* are often used synonymously and have much in common, although research using quantitative methods of analysis is often not experimental. The principal methods of quantitative research are those that enable the researcher to quantify data and to manipulate these data for analysis. The researcher is looking for quantitative relationships in the data. The experimental researcher begins with hypotheses to be tested and controls variables in the hope of learning the effects of variables and generalizing these to similar phenomena. Experimental and quantitative research presume objectivity in the researcher. They are normally associated with basic research and with a technical and empirical orientation to research in which researchers use various methods of experimentation and observation of the empirical world. Hypotheses are tested, and variables are manipulated.

Free-writing Writing freely, spontaneously, without forethought or labor. Unedited.

Frequency distribution The array of scores on a test or instrument given to a group with a listing of all scores and how many people or cases earned each score. For example, if you gave students a 20-question quiz, how many students scored 20? 19? 18? 17? etc. on the quiz? Preparing a table of the scores and the number of people getting each score would be a frequency distribution.

General domains of development Development is movement toward more complex, differentiated, and inclusive perspectives. Domains of development are the broad areas within which this development occurs.

Generalizability Typically in action research, we address issues and questions of a local nature, specific to our professional needs and curiosities. Therefore, we don't typically generalize our results to other teachers or groups. In experimental research, and qualitative research done on a larger scale, we hope that the results of our work will inform others and suggest outcomes others can benefit from learning. The act of this suggesting is generalizing. Under the right conditions if research was constructed with sufficient rigor and numbers or depth, generalizing is reasonable. Studies cannot have any threats to external or internal validity if generalizing is to occur.

Histogram   A basic bar graph made from data. Histograms or bar graphs can be constructed using computer programs such as Microsoft Works and Microsoft Excel.

Independent variable   The input in an experimental study, such as age, gender, prior test scores, etc. These are givens in the research design prior to the study.

Inquiry   Process by which a person follows one's curiosity until the mystery is solved or abandoned. According to Lawrence Stenhouse, inquiry can develop into research if it becomes systematic and self-critical and is made public.

In-service   A word descriptive of all those activities and processes that contribute to professional growth and practice. Traditionally, these activities are referred to as *in-service training*, as though something was *done to* teachers; more recently it is referred to as *in-service education* or professional development, in which teachers are perceived to be *active agents* in the learning process.

In-service teacher   A term used to denote any teacher actively teaching (as opposed to those retired or preservice—preparing to become a teacher).

Interquartile range   Often a researcher wants to know how most students or cases fared in an assessment or ranking of some kind. The interquartile range is the spread that includes the middle 50 percent of all the cases or students. This is similar to standard deviation, which measures how approximately two-thirds or one-third of all the cases fared, depending on which standard deviation formula is applied.

Interviews   Obtaining structured or open-ended responses from people. They can be described as discussions with a purpose. Purpose varies from open-ended conversation to highly structured and sequential questions asked of the interviewed person or persons.

I-search   A method of inquiry and a type of scholarship created by Ken Macrorie (1980): "Contrary to most school research papers, the I-Search comes out of a student's life and answers a need in it. . . . The paper is alive, not borrowedly inert. . . . [The I-Search is unlike traditional research papers where] the expert is up there and they [the students] are down there taking notes" (preface). The I-Search can be described as a way "to tell the story of what you did in your search, in the order in which everything happened . . . 1. What I knew . . . 2. Why I'm writing this paper . . . 3. The Search (story of the hunt) . . . 4. What I learned . . ." (p. 64).

Journal—professional journal   An evolving professional document that serves as a continuing professional dialogue and discussion with oneself (selves) on matters related to one's own practice. It serves as a vehicle for praxis (see *praxis* definition), and for synthesis and analysis of one's work and professional life. It can contain log, diary, and other types of expressive and analytical writing. The author is the sole owner and may choose to share snippets or sections with others.

Kidwatching   A term coined by reading educator Yetta Goodman in an article by the same name that appeared in the *National Elementary School Principal* in 1978. As an alternative to school testing, Goodman advocates teacher observation, intuition, and knowledge of students as invaluable sources for assessment and evaluation.

Learning communities   Communities by virtue of their aim and ability to learn, together and as individuals, for socially constructive purposes. Often referred to as communities of practice, each member has unique contributions to the community, and leadership and facilitation shift with focus and need.

Life span development   An approach to studying development from a life-cycle perspective; Erik Erikson's theory of psychosocial development in which he proposes a framework that enables one to contemplate developmental patterns, not only in different periods of life, but also as life continues through time from birth to death. The foundations for each period of development can be seen in the periods preceding it.

Literature circles   Peer-led, heterogeneous groups that focus on reading a common novel or nonfiction selection. Literature circles are part of a reading program under a holistic philosophy in which high-quality trade books— picture books, novels, or informational books—become the teacher- and student-selected materials for learning. In student-led heterogeneous groups of three to five readers, students read literature aloud, write journal responses, and hold student-led discussions until the book is completed. Students plan and execute a culminating presentation, which they perform or present to their classmates, that expresses what the book or story meant to them, without giving away the story essentials (Kasten, 1995). Literature circles are executed in classrooms in a variety of ways that suit the teacher's style and time frame. Sometimes specific roles, such as discussion leader, are assigned to group members (Daniels, 1994). Literature circles can also be called *book clubs* or other terms invented by students and teachers.

Literature review   Both a process of studying and critically reviewing literature pertinent to one's research topic and area, and the product of such review, usually included in a formal proposal, and/or report, or article. More than a listing or presentation, literature reviews provide analysis and synthesis of key studies and present these in such a way that the reader learns more about the literature as a whole than about any of its constituent studies and reviews.

Log   Both a verb—to log one's activities or observations—and a noun—a record or a logbook. Activities and observations are often recorded without interpretive text; theoretically, anyone would record the same observations ("the math lesson lasted 45 minutes").

Metaphor   According to the *Merriam-Webster Dictionary* (1974), "a figure of speech in which a word denoting one subject is used in place of another to suggest a likeness between them" (p. 439). Metaphor can be used more globally as well, such as the journey to Oz as a metaphor for action research.

Middle school   An organizational structure for the education of early adolescents ages 9 to 15, based on a philosophy of developmentalism, social equity, and academic excellence. Its key organizational features include interdisciplinary teaching, flexible scheduling, block scheduling, teacher as advisor, and exploratory and integrated curriculum. It is grounded in the ideas of John Dewey.

Mis-educational learning   John Dewey's term to describe further learning on the topic that is either sidetracked or subverted. An example is that picking apart poems to analyze parts of speech in a poem can extinguish the desire to read poetry.

Modernity   A paradigm and time period when certain beliefs, values, and assumptions are held in common, and these permeate artistic, cultural, social, educational, psychological, economic, and political contexts and practices. Modernity is based on the notion that the world is objectively knowable (Havel, 1992). Certainty, progress, universality, and regularity are hallmarks of modernity and have shaped many of the rational and assembly-line practices in schools, such as use of time and space and instructional practices or delivery of content *to* students, as receptacles, all needing the same treatment.

Multiply handicapped   Descriptive of a person with more than one physical, mental, or social disability (Harris and Hodges, 1995).

Narrative; narrative writing   "[A]ny form of written or spoken presentation" (Polkinghorne, 1988, p. 13). In this book we refer to *narrative* as the process of narration and its product, the narrative. *Narrative writing* refers to the researcher telling the research story in words and presentation.

Naturalistic research and methods; qualitative research and methods   The terms *naturalistic* and *qualitative* are often used interchangeably and have much in common. Researchers using naturalistic and qualitative methods are not interested in controlling and manipulating the environment, although they are often interested in trying out ideas and observing the results in natural settings. There are few entirely "natural" settings in the sense that there is no intervention into what happens within it, but researchers from this orientation formulate descriptions based on careful observation in as unobtrusive a way as possible. Qualitative research comes from the social sciences and is hypothesis-generating, and the researcher does not presume objectivity. Anthropologists, for example, use qualitative (ethnographic) methods to observe in natural (cultural) settings. Many researchers use quantitative and qualitative methods, referred to as *mixed methods*. For example, biologists go into natural settings and make observations under different environmental conditions, sometimes manipulating the environment to study its effects.

Noneducational learning   John Dewey's term to describe learning that doesn't change anything. For example, cramming for a test and forgetting everything 2 days later.

Norms   When a test is made for widespread use, it is tested on a group of people first. This is called the norming group, and test makers get the scores to be used later from this norming group. If the norming group are demographically similar to those later given the test, then the scores are more credible. If the norming group is dissimilar to those taking the test, the resulting scores are less credible. Test makers continually renorm their tests as populations are rarely static.

Paradigm   A world view or model ascribed to a group of people who hold certain beliefs, knowledge, and understandings in common. It is said that we are moving from a modern paradigm (or era) to a postmodern paradigm (or era). Part of the turmoil in such a process is because both paradigms are in existence and conflict; we have a foot in the past and a foot in the future, and today can seem chaotic. Whereas certainty has provided comfort in modern times, today's postmodernists cultivate—and even celebrate—uncertainty.

Philosophy of teaching   According to the *Merriam-Webster Dictionary* (1974), a philosophy is "a critical study of fundamental beliefs and the grounds for them" (p. 522). A teaching philosophy may include beliefs about the purposes of schooling; how children learn; and the roles and responsibilities of teachers, students, and the community. We can use this as a foundation for our thinking about many issues (testing, approaches to discipline, for example) confronting teachers today.

Physical and motor development   Changes related to physical development such as height, weight, muscle, and motor development; for example, dexterity in fine and large muscle control. Marked changes in this domain (sometimes referred to as growth spurts) are noted in early childhood and early adolescence.

Portfolio   A carefully selected, constructed, and narrated collection of work pertaining to a special topic. It comes from an 18th-century Italian term, *porto folio*, literally meaning "portare," to carry, and "fogli," leaves or sheets of paper. Current developments in educational portfolios include *teaching portfolios* (pertaining to one's teaching and containing many narrated examples) and *course portfolios* (pertaining to a specific course). A form of scholarship in which one analyzes, synthesizes, and narrates one's work for oneself and to share publicly with others. The portfolio can be autobiographical as in the examples cited, biographical, or project-oriented; often used as a form of evaluation.

Portraits; portrayal; portraiture   A *portrait* is a likeness of a person, place, event, or circumstance. *Portrayal* is the way of rendering the likeness. *Portraiture* is now considered to be a "genre of inquiry and representation that seeks to join art and science . . . [it] is a method of qualitative research that blurs the boundaries of aesthetics and empiricism in an effort to capture the complexity, dynamics, and subtlety of human experience" (Lawrence-Lightfoot and Davis, 1997, p. xv).

Postmodernity   In contrast to modernity (see *modernity* definition), a period characterized by difference, particularity, and irregularity. The world is not objectively knowable, nor can one "absolutely generalize" to other situations and people. *Context* matters. Open classrooms based on constructivist principles and flexible and evolving curricula, and some alternative schools are more akin with the postmodern paradigm: Children, adolescents, and adults cannot be *absolutely* characterized as categories of learners, just as individuals within each group cannot be absolutely characterized. Each person is unique and socially constructed. Multiple voices and texts are the "rules" in this anti-rule-oriented paradigm.

Praxis   The critically reflective dialogue that takes place continuously between the professional and her or his practice. In action research this results in new actions and a continuance of the cycle of reflective practice. This process is necessary to continuing the relationship between theoretical understanding and critique of society and its institutions, and the actions necessary to transform individuals and the environments within which they live and grow.

Preservice teacher   A teacher education student who engages in teaching experiences (internships, student teaching, and other teaching experiences) before graduation and employment as a practicing teacher.

Primary data sources   Firsthand sources of information.

Problematize   To explore a topic or phenomenon from a critical stance; to dissect or interrogate in order to uncover underlying causes and/or assumptions; to become skeptical of familiar territory. To question historical, social, economic, political, and cultural phenomena from the perspectives of individuals and groups.

Professional development   Anything that contributes to lifelong learning of a teacher, including preservice education, workshops, seminars, professional meetings and conferences, self-initiated and school-sponsored projects and in-service education sessions, professional reading, and graduate study, to name a few. Action research is one of the most potent forms of professional development.

Professional learning   Educational learning that focuses on the integration of three processes necessary to pedagogical success: human development, curriculum development, and teaching, within a value system of social democracy and environmental advocacy.

Professional routines   The often taken-for-granted practices that structure life in classrooms, such as lesson planning, 40-minute classes, grade-level organization, homework, grouping of students by "ability," standardized testing.

Psychological and emotional development   Movement from more closed, protective, defensive, rigid positions to more open, creative, and inclusive perspectives; toward higher self-esteem; and toward increasing capacity and ability to nurture these characteristics in others.

Range   Sometimes it is useful to know the entire range of scores on some instrument. The entire variability is the range. For example, if you gave a

20-question quiz, and the highest score was 19, and the lowest score was 2, then your range is 2 to 19.

Reliability   A test or instrument is called reliable when it works similarly each time it is used. The same kinds of results can be expected in subsequent uses of the same instrument.

Report formats   Different ways in which to tell one's research story. Action researchers can use or create a growing number of ways to organize and arrange their research stories. These include traditional, scientific, case studies, and newer forms such as evocative forms (see *evocative forms* definition).

Research   According to Lawrence Stenhouse, research consists of systematic, self-critical, inquiry made public. Research is what scholars *do*. The attitude they take toward research and its conduct is scholarly.

Sampling   The decision of what people or cases are to be used in a larger experimental study. *Random sampling* is like pulling names from a hat as to who will be tested or surveyed. *Stratified sampling* would be to pull names from a hat (although calculators and computers can do this for us) but only from a particular group, such as special education students, teachers with more than 10 years of experience, or administrators only. *Purposeful sampling* is the term often used when a researcher studies the cases or individuals that need to be studied to address a particular issue (such as the 10 autistic students in the school).

Scattergram or scatterplot   When, for the purposes of determining possible relationships between two features, a graph is constructed using an X axis (horizontal) and a Y axis (vertical) with points being placed on the two continua. The clusterings of the data points can show a direction or progression looking at the resulting picture, or by conducting appropriate tests on the data. For a direct relationship, the slope goes up. For a negative relationship, the slope goes down.

Scholarship   Simply put, professional learning. Scholars are learned and tenaciously inquisitive people. Scholarship is the evolving learning and related knowledge that scholars undertake and "own." It is a curious, skeptical, and inquisitive attitude toward the world and our human places within that world. Research is what scholars *do*. Research is part of scholarship, a way in which scholarship evolves.

Secondary data sources   Sources that are dependent on something else (primary data sources); sources that build on, quote, and use other people's research.

Social and emotional development   Movement from reflexes and relatively undifferentiated feelings in the earliest stages of life to being able to distinguish between tears of laughter and sorrow and to engage in increasingly more sophisticated social relationships.

Story   A narrative, a reporting, a recounting of one's experience or history; a statement or chronicle.

Teacher action research   Action research by a teacher or teachers.

Teacher research   Any kind of research undertaken by a teacher or a group of teachers and others.

Teaching self (and related **self-talk)**   The notion that each of us is not a single, self-contained, monolithic, and congruent "self" who teaches. We are complex beings and have many selves and minds (what Robert Ornstein, 1991, calls "multi-minds" that "wheel-in" on cue) that talk to us and in fact *are* us. We teach with the advice of these "subpersonalities" (Ferrucci, 1982). Self-talk is *listening* to the chorus within and guiding the discussion and outcomes where warranted and possible.

Theory, theorize, theoretical   A *theory* is a systematically organized body of knowledge used to explain a phenomenon; a theory can be *public*, as in Piaget's theory of cognitive development, or *private*, as in our theories of how people learn. Private theories are usually implicit and not articulated consciously, even to ourselves. Scholarship, however, makes it necessary for us to articulate our theories; *praxis* is a method for so doing. To *theorize* is to conjecture, to put forward possible explanations for a phenomenon, and to see if you can gather evidence both pro and con to your conjecture. "If I ask Bridget about her new baby sister, I can probably gauge her feelings on the matter. I think she is upset over the attention she has lost." *Theoretical* refers to a public theory and is used as a basis for conjecturing: "Theoretically, according to Piaget, children cannot learn if they are forced to accommodate more information than they are developmentally able." Often we can test a theory with our own observations.

Transformation, transformational experience   Change is often associated with the outside: doing something more, better, or faster, not necessarily different. Transformation has to do with external and internal conditions—what begins "outside" becomes and is changed by what happens internally. Biologically, there is a bridge between the front cortex and the back cortex (Zull, 2002). Transformative experience (Kolb, 1983) signals transformation in three parts (1) from past to future (ability to take past and create future), (2) transforming the source of knowledge from outside to inside, and (3) transformation of power from dependence to independence.

t **score**   These scores enable a researcher to compare scores from a group with those of the norming group that was used in preparation of the test. Typically *t* scores have a mean of 50 and a standard deviation of 10 from the norm group on which the test was standardized.

t **test**   In a study, when you have two sets of means (such as a pretest and posttest) and you want to consider whether these results can be generalized to other similar groups, and if you want to show that the differences that have been noted are not merely the result of chance, then a researcher may conduct a *t* test (computer software is available for these tests). What the *t* test shows is the extent to which the differences on the means are likely significant and not the result of chance. The resulting value is expressed with the letter "p" on a table. The lower the probability that it is a result of chance (such as below .05) suggests the number is significant. A probability of >.001

is more powerful than one of .01 for example. The level of desired significance can be changed depending on the nature of the study and the degree to which researchers need to be more certain of the results. One wants a stronger significance (such as .001) for a cure for a deadly disease than on comparing two different spelling programs (.05).

Validity   The consideration of whether or not a test or instrument or study is measuring or assessing what it claims to be measuring or assessing. There are factors that can threaten the validity of a study. For example, if one class taking a test has been given precise items from the test in advance, or if items on a test do not adequately reflect the meaning of the concepts the test is to measure, then the results are not valid.

Variability   The extent to which a data set varies in scores from the highest to lowest, and the predictable variations determined by a test on the *standard deviation* or the *interquartile range*.

Vignette   Representation of life on paper or another literary, visual, aural, or composite form that makes comprehension possible; usually brief.

Whole teacher   The person in her or his entirety; social, emotional, physical, motor, and cognitive development and the interaction of these. This is in contrast to singling out cognitive or intellectual growth without reference to how this interacts and is related to other domains.

Writer's perspectives   The points of view assumed by the author.

Writing down, writing up, and writing about   Terms used in this book to call attention to three interrelated processes and functions of writing in action research. *Writing down* refers to developing the art of observation and data collection, capturing rich, detailed information. *Writing up* refers to analyzing and synthesizing the results of our observations and data in writing, to rendering our considered observation in written form (portraits, case studies, research reports). *Writing about* is the process of taking our reports and creating products from these to share, usually moving beyond the report to rendering it in other forms (presentations, articles).

Travelers' Notes **A**

Problematizing the Honor Roll in Your School

Finding problems where we don't see any isn't easy—especially when the topic is a common and taken-for-granted practice. Here we will take a common practice, the honor roll, and work through several questions to problematize this practice.

Imagine that discussions are underway in your school to determine whether or not to continue this practice. Perhaps these discussions were instigated by a student, a colleague, a parent, or a community member. Our goal here is to make our way through these questions as objectively and as logically as we can. We reserve adding our personal feelings until the last question.

What Do I Already Know About This Topic or Question?

Take time to think about this, perhaps putting it in writing.

You may have had some experience with honor rolls from your own school days or those of your children, friends, or colleagues. Perhaps you noticed that the same type of students are generally on the honor roll. Perhaps students have made disparaging comments about the honor roll. Gather any information or knowledge you already have.

What Are the Assumptions in the Topic or Practice or Question?

Assumptions underlie all beliefs and practices. They are subtle and usually unquestioned. Once identified, assumptions can be addressed in light of our aspirations.

We may assume that an honor roll acts as an incentive to students to achieve in order to gain that recognition. We may assume that rewarding student excellence is beneficial in some way. We assume, as a result, that it's a good thing. Is there research or evidence to support or refute this assumption?

What Are the Cultural and Historical Contexts?

Is this a case of: "We've always done it this way"? Is it an entrenched "policy" or "common practice"?

It may be safe to say that the practice has been around for a long time. How long has the practice been in effect? Practices like this may be typically situated in mainstream, middle class, white communities where most people are of Western European origin. The practice is an implicit form of competition; it is a practice that is valued in some cultures and communities and completely taboo in others.

Who Is Well Served if Things Remain as They Are?
Who Is Poorly Served with Things as They Are?

Does this practice privilege one group over another? Does someone gain prestige or wealth? These can be difficult questions because they force us to come to grips with issues of social justice.

One might identify higher achieving students as those who are well served and students who are lower achieving to be poorly served. Generally, when something in education serves a group of students well, it also well serves their parents and families. Parents of honor roll students may enjoy the publicity of their child's achievement.

How Does the Construct of Time Enter into This Question or Issue?

Various cultures have different views of *time*. Mainstream American culture—the one which dominates schools—treats *time* as a *commodity*. We talk among ourselves when we travel as "making good time" and when we work as "using time wisely," or "spending time" (like money). When we do something special with our students we "make time" for them. If we are in a hurry, we say we are "losing time" or "wasting time." Looking at time from a *developmental* perspective is important when we are addressing growth and learning.

Are students who are typically developing time-wise more likely to be rewarded by the honor roll than those who are more atypical in their development? What are the long-term effects on all students, especially if we do not take developmental differences into account?

How Does My Topic Compare to Something Else?

Finding an analogy in another profession or context can illuminate a question. For example, what would my question look like if this were a company, a battalion, a hospital, a business, or a courtroom?

Let's try a medical comparison. If schools are like hospitals, teachers are like doctors and nurses, and students are like patients, would it make sense to have a patient honor roll for those who recovered most quickly from a surgery? Or those who made the most gains recovering from a disease? What would be accomplished with such an honor roll? What would be the consequences for students/patients?

What Are the Possible Unintended Consequences of Change? What Have Been the Unintended Consequences of the Policy, Practice, or Issue as It Is?

Often an idea sounds good on paper. Even with study and projections, all those involved agree on a decision and some change is made. For example, a region rids itself of unwanted bugs by spraying to improve the quality of outdoor life and, in turn, the water supply becomes contaminated and wildlife dies. Our world is full of the effects of unintended consequences. Although we can never anticipate all consequences, there are times we must try. The term "the law of unintended consequences" was first coined by a sociologist at Columbia University named Robert K. Merton who was later awarded the National Medal of Science by President Bill Clinton for his work. So, what are the unintended consequences of an honor roll?

Some schools have reconsidered honor rolls, and discovered that the honor roll can cause schisms among their students. Students who don't believe they have a chance do not put forth effort; and many students have no chance of ever making it. The unintended consequences are apathetic, dispirited students and a schism within the school community.

What Forces Are Supportive of Change? Resistant to Change?

Roadblocks can be human resistance, economic, environmental, or practical considerations. Selected groups support a change; others vehemently oppose the same change.

In the honor roll case, parents whose children are high achievers could become an obstacle to changing the honor roll to include more students, such as those in special education, while parents of students who never have a chance to make the honor roll may become forces for change.

Can You Visualize Things After a Change?

What could a school be like in which students chose their courses, everyone treated each other with respect, there were no ability groupings, or no honor roll? Visualizing can help you to plot the course for change and to anticipate *unintended consequences*. Visualize five to ten years after the potential change.

How could things be different without the honor roll? In what ways could life be and feel differently for students, teachers, and parents? What is the imagined future?

What Are My Feelings and Biases?

How did the honor roll affect you as a student? Have you taken a position on this issue or question in the past? How do you feel now about that position?

Since people who choose teaching as a profession often thrived in school, you may have valued the honor roll. Perhaps you believe it motivated you. If so, this may be an especially good topic for you to unpack—or as we've explored here—to problematize.

Travelers' Notes B

Increasing Social Interaction Between Students with Multiple Handicaps and Their Typical Peers: An Action Research Proposal

Roberto Diaz

What Is My Research Interest?

Roberto

I am interested in the interactions between typical middle school students and students with multiple handicaps. My questions are, What are the attitudes of regular education students about students with handicapping conditions?, and How can I increase the interactions between typical middle school students and those with multiple handicaps?

Why Am I Interested?

My students in the multiple-handicapped (MH) program are placed in integrated classes for part of their school day. The rationale for this inclusion is for the MH students to gain acceptance from peers and to attain social skills needed to build friendships. I also believe that all students should have access to the rich experiences offered by my middle school. I am not seeing this happen, and I wonder if there are other ways to accomplish these worthwhile goals.

What Do I Already Know? What Do Others Know?

Only limited conversation is occurring inside and outside the inclusion classroom. Occasionally, students pass individuals from my class and say "Hi," but dialogue never grows beyond that point. There was a time when one of the regular education students did not even talk to her own cousin who was integrated into her home economics class. I have observed typical students move from a table where their peers with disabilities were eating lunch. Somehow the relationships that inclusion is supposed to foster are just not happening. The research on peer interactions in special education indicates that the relationships cannot be conjured up at will (Van der Klift and Kunc, 1994). The potential benefits of increased and specialized socialization for

311

Increasing Social Interaction Between Students with Multiple Handicaps

students with multiple handicaps are a decrease in their stereotypical behaviors (SoHyun and Odom, 1996) and encouragement of age-appropriate interactions (Janney and Snell, 1996). Typical students believed that they benefited in terms of improved self-concept, increased tolerance, and reduced fear of human difference (Peck, 1990). Some possible solutions found in the research suggested that teacher facilitation increased the interactions between students (Hunt et al., 1996).

What Do I Expect to Find?

I expect that I will have a few interested typical students in the seventh and eighth grades who might be willing to spend time with their peers with disabilities, but I do not anticipate a long-range commitment from them. It is not unusual for middle school students to lose focus when they are asked to participate in an activity.

What Will I Try Out?
Who?

The participants attend a middle school in a suburban area located near a mid-sized university. The students are mixed culturally and economically due to the influence of the university and its employees and students whose children attend the public schools. Subsidized housing throughout the city affects the social and economic status of the group. Approximately 800 students are housed in the sixth, seventh, and eighth grades' heterogeneous teams. The 16 students in the two MH classes are diagnosed with Down's syndrome, cerebral palsy, language disorders, vision impairments, and autism. Also involved in this study will be the school principal, regular education teaching staff, and special education staff.

What?

I could formulate a "Buddy Club," and students could come into my classroom to act as tutors in academic classes. Another option is to develop a "Lunchmate" program in which members will be assigned to a student in my class, and they could eat together. The final option is to initiate a "Peer Club" that would resemble an extracurricular club. Students can sign up and participate in organized social events with their partners from the MH classes. The sole purpose of this club is to increase the time these students get for social interactions. I think I will choose the last option because I feel it will bridge the gap between students better. The group will be called the S.T.A.R. (Students and Teachers Advancing Relationships) Club, and interested students can sign up to be paired with peers with special needs. I think the key to success is to have the nonhandicapped students join the project with their own friends. Several existing friends can be paired with a student from the MH program in the hopes that these friends will feel more comfortable together. This peer club may be very time-consuming for me, but will work within the time constraints of the school day. I need to consider students' busy after-school schedules and maximize their availability during class time. Success will be measured through the students' responsiveness to the club, increased positive feelings of regular education students toward their peers with disabilities, commitment to the activities, and the carryover to other school settings.

When? How Often?

The preliminary work to organize this club should be done during the first semester of the year. All the planning and locating of the peers and staff support will take some time in order to succeed. During the second semester, activities will occur for the club members, and they will participate in informational meetings. There should be at least one planned activity per month. Seventh- and eighth-grade students should be recruited for the club because their schedules replicate the schedules of my students more closely.

Where?

The students will fill out forms to state their interest in membership in a club within their classrooms. I plan to have social activities throughout the school building, and students are always welcome in my classroom.

How Will I Document the Process? What Evidence Will I Collect to Show the Consequences of My Actions?

I will keep a journal of my observations of the existing conditions and how those observations change throughout the process of my project. I will recall what I see happening and my feelings along the way. Conversations and information from other professionals will also be noted. A focus group of selected eighth graders can allow me the opportunity to gather data on their feelings about individuals with handicaps. I will also rely on my 15 years of experience teaching students with special needs. Another data collection method includes reading articles from professional publications that both support and refute peer groups as an effective way to improve interactions. Triangulation of the evidence may occur between the surveys completed by students, my observations noted in my journal, and the student responses during the focus group.

How Will I Verify That My Judgments Are Trustworthy and Credible?

Since I work closely in team-teaching situations with another special education teacher, I know he will offer critique. His perspectives are usually valuable, and he frequently acts as my mentor. The teachers I plan to have in my advisory group also can lend their perspectives and observations. Students who partici-pate in the club will give me feedback about their relationships with the students and their experiences. I shall continually test my emerging hypothesis that this close exposure between the students will branch out to other settings and increase social interactions. Throughout this project, I will need to check for dis-confirming data.

How Will I Interpret the Data?

I will interpret the data by looking at my journal, surveys, and focus group comments for categories and patterns. There may be responses that lead to ideas about what makes socialization work for my students. I will categorize the surveys by placing them in piles and highlighting emerging categories in different-color markers so I can note patterns. The focus group comments and journal entries should have a distinct marking to show positive and negative impressions of integration. I will write my feelings about my experiences in my journal as I go through the process of developing this club. I will go back and forth between my own thoughts and what I am reading in professional jour-nals. Some individuals feel that friendship clubs cannot foster true relation-ships. Others have found that a supportive environment in which the teacher acts as a facilitator is best. Under these circumstances, interactions between the students increased.

How Will I Portray What I Have Learned and Make It Public?

I will share my project with my fellow classmates in my action research course. Also, I will show my results to administrators, staff, parents, and students in my school building. My plans also include presenting my project at an upcoming fac-ulty meeting.

How Will These Actions Make Life Better? And What Will I Do Next?

It is my hope that this project changes how my students are included in their school. It would be rewarding to see other middle school students talk to them and greet them by name in the hallways. This project could be a springboard for other activities possibly after school and in the community. I would like to continue the S.T.A.R. Club and potentially pair activities with student council.

Who Will Be My Critical Colleagues?

My special education team partner will be my critical colleague.

What Permissions Do I Need to Gain?

I will secure written permission from the parents of my special education students and from those students who volunteer to be members of S.T.A.R. Club. I will also explain to all these students what my project entails and will gain their verbal permission to use their journals as evidence. I will then have them read over any quotes of theirs that I might use, and I will gain their written permission to use the quotes in my report to my university class.

References

Hunt, P., Allwell, M., & Goetz, L. (1996). Creating socially supportive environments for fully included students who experience multiple disabilities. *Journal of the Association for Persons with Severe Handicaps, 21*(2), 53–71.

Janney, R. E., & Snell, M. E. (1996). How teachers use peer interactions to include students with moderate and severe disabilities in elementary general education classes. *Journal of the Association for Persons with Severe Handicaps, 21*(2), 72–80.

Peck, C. (1990). Some benefits non-handicapped adolescents perceive for themselves from their social relationships with peers who have severe handicaps. *Journal of the Association for Persons with Severe Handicaps, 15*(4), 241–249.

SoHuyn, L., & Odom, S. L. (1996). The relationships between stereotypic behavior and peer social interaction for children with severe disabilities. *Journal of the Association for Persons with Severe Handicaps, 21*(2), 88–95.

Van der Klift, E., & Kunc, N. (1994). *Creativity and collaborative learning: A practical guide to empowering students and teachers.* Baltimore: Paul Brookes.

Travelers' Notes C

Organizing and Visually Displaying Data

We have devoted an entire section to organizing and visually displaying data in order to offer possibilities for ways to think about processing data. We will provide examples for both quantitative and qualitative data. In these pages you may find inspiration for your own creative ideas.

Quantitative Data

Quantitative data typically consist of numerical values that are analyzed statistically. Raw data need to be organized and displayed so that they begin to make sense. Organizing quantitative data in lists is a simple way to show what data you have. Figure C.1 shows how student scores on a mathematics test can be arrayed in order from highest score to lowest score. Figure C.2 shows how scores can be organized by range.

Displaying numerical values in a graph helps the researcher to see and discuss results. Graphs can be used to compare scores and groups, show trends in data, show relationships between variables, and describe parts of the whole. The

FIGURE C.1 *Student percentages on mathematics test*

Student Name	Percentage
Mary	100
Tom	96
Craig	92
Lou	89
Jeff	88
Sam	86
Tabatha	86
Freddie	79
Anne	77
Wil	70

Organizing and Visually Displaying Data

FIGURE C.2 *Tally and frequency of scores on mathematics test*

Percentages	Tally	Frequency
90–100	|||	3
80–89	||||	4
70–79	||	3

FIGURE C.3 *Bar graph showing frequency of test scores*

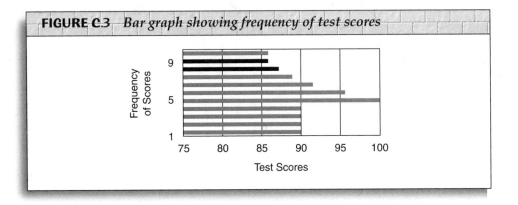

following are examples of types of graphic displays that are commonly used by action researchers.

Bar graph. A *bar graph* compares values across categories. Frequencies are indicated on the vertical axis, and lowest to highest rank-ordered scores are depicted on the horizontal axis. Figure C.3 illustrates the test scores of students on the horizontal axis and frequency of those scores on the vertical axis.

Line graph. A *line graph* is a line with markers displayed at each data value. It is similar to a bar graph. Figure C.4 illustrates the number of children enrolled in after-school activities in four different grade levels. Line graphs are especially appropriate for data over a specific time period.

Scatter plot. A *scatter plot* compares pairs of values and shows the relationship between two variables. The vertical, or *y*, axis indicates performance on one variable. The horizontal, or *x*, axis indicates performance on another variable. Each point is the intersection of two scores for each individual. Figure C.5 shows the relationship of students' scores on an examination and the number of hours they studied. The scatter plot in Figure C.5 indicates a positive relationship between the variables: students who studied longer had higher test scores.

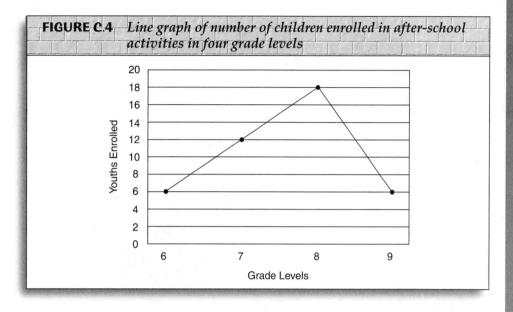

FIGURE C.4 *Line graph of number of children enrolled in after-school activities in four grade levels*

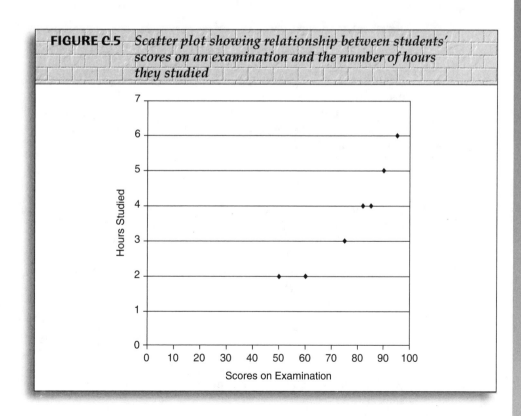

FIGURE C.5 *Scatter plot showing relationship between students' scores on an examination and the number of hours they studied*

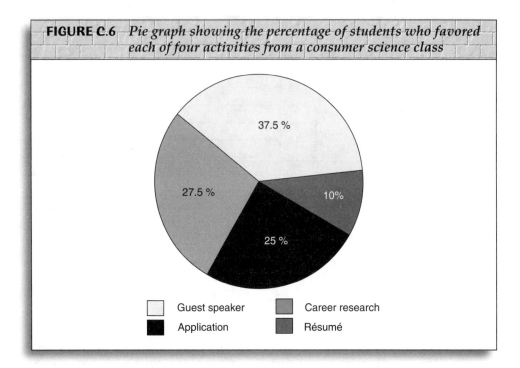

FIGURE C.6 *Pie graph showing the percentage of students who favored each of four activities from a consumer science class*

Pie graph. A *pie graph* displays the contribution of each value to a total and is used to describe the parts of a whole in percent or the equivalent. Figure C.6 shows the percentage of students who favored each of four activities from a consumer science class. Using software, pie graphs can become three dimensional; they can "explode" in form with the segments moving out from the base.

Descriptive Statistics

When we want to summarize data (not generalize from them), we describe the data using the mean, median, mode, range, and standard deviation or interquartile range. Each of these calculations is briefly described.

Mean. The *mean* is the average, and it is computed by summing all scores and dividing by the number of scores.

Median. The *median* is the midpoint in a series of scores. Fifty percent of the cases lie above the median, and 50 percent lie below the median.

Mode. The *mode* is the most frequently occurring score.

Figure C.7 illustrates the computation for the mean, median, and mode for a sample data set.

FIGURE C.7 *Computation of mean, median, and mode for a sample data set*

Raw data:	2, 4, 4, 6, 6, 6, 8, 8, 9
Mean:	2 + 4 + 4 + 6 + 6 + 6 + 8 + 8 + 9 = 5.9
Median:	2 4 4 6 6 6 8 8 9 = 6
Mode:	2 4 4 6 6 6 8 8 9 = 6

FIGURE C.8 *Citizenship Survey: Means for student ratings of importance of characteristics of citizenship*

Characteristic of Citizenship	Number of Students (N)	Mean (X)
Knowledge of current events	17	3.6
Participation in community or school events	17	4.2
Performance of duties	17	5.0
Concern for others	17	5.3
Acceptance of authority	17	4.3
Ability to make wise decisions	17	5.7
Knowledge of government	17	4.0
Patriotism	17	4.2
Moral and ethical behavior	17	6.0

Range. The *range* is the span between the lowest score and the highest score. It is useful in summarizing the variability of scores. For example, using the raw data set from Figure C.7, we subtract 2 (the lowest value) from 9 (the highest value) and determine that the range is 7.

Standard deviation. The *standard deviation* is another measure of variability. It is the difference between a single score in a data set and the mean for the data set.

All the graphs and summary statistics described here can be easily calculated, displayed, and inserted into the body of your text by using spreadsheets that are included in most computer software packages. Displaying these summary statistics in a table makes it easy to see what is going on. Figure C.8 displays data from Ruby's Democratic Classroom Study in a table that shows the mean responses of students on the Citizenship Survey. You can also graph the data by hand on graph paper to understand in what area of the array 1/3, 2/3, or 1/2 (interquartile range) occur.

Choosing a Random Sample

When a researcher is studying an entire class, several classes, a team, a grade level, a time period, or multiage grouping, hundreds of pieces of student work may be generated. It is not always necessary to analyze *every* item. By choosing a *random sample* of the data, the researcher can obtain results that are comparable to analyzing the entire data set.

For example, suppose an action researcher wants to know if portfolios in her science classes are a viable alternative to giving students a final examination. While a rubric keyed to standards, concepts, or competencies can be used to assess student learning, as demonstrated in all the portfolios, it may be impossible to do an in-depth analysis of each. Instead of analyzing *all* of them, a mentor can help you select a representative number from each class or group. But the question then becomes, Which ones to select? A fair way to select them may be *random selection*.

If, for example, you want to select 25 portfolios from the 200 completed in all your five classes, you begin by giving a number to each portfolio. Then you can use a scientific calculator or any number of computer programs to enter the number needed (25) and the set from which to draw (200); and the computer or calculator will print the numbers of the items to select. (If you saved that instruction booklet that came with your calculator, you'll be pleased now!) In the absence of technology, you can use the paper-in-the-hat method (a very technical system). Simply place the numbers of items into a hat, and draw out 25 numbers. No cheating—you can't put back the ones you don't like!

Qualitative Data

Qualitative data consist of the interview notes, descriptive observations written in your journal, and documents and artifacts that have been collected throughout a study. There are fewer restrictions on how these data are displayed and organized for analysis, and we will offer a few ideas to get things started.

Tables with words.   Creating tables with words or concepts instead of numbers can be a useful way to begin analyzing and interpreting data. Figure C.9 presents excerpts from Lauren's journal, which contained her observations and comments from teacher colleagues about the relative benefits of semitraditional groups (classroom divided in half and students in rows, each half facing the other half) versus cooperative groups (small, heterogeneous groups of students that are flexible depending on the nature of the task) in two sections of Spanish. She separated the data into positive and negative aspects. Lauren, a student teacher, decided that a flexible, heterogeneously mixed grouping of students was the optimal physical classroom arrangement for increasing student speaking in the target language.

Concept mapping.   Concept mapping is useful for showing relationships. In Figure C.10 we include a concept map by Lori, another student teacher, who wanted to understand student views of strategies she used to help them perform

FIGURE C.9 *Comparison of semitraditional and cooperative groups in a foreign language classroom*

	Semitraditional Groups	Cooperative Groups
Positive Aspects	More controlled	Positive energy
	Quieter	More student talk
	Better for quizzes	Students take an active role
	Can cover more material	Increased student interaction
	Easy to transition to other activities	Less downtime during oral assessments
	Students are on task	Opportunities for peer teaching
Negative Aspects	More teacher talk	Noise
	Students tune out	Requires more planning
	Boring	Students don't always use target language
	Students can be passive observers	Bad for test taking
	More teacher-centered	Students distracted by others

better on tests in her honors chemistry class. She also interviewed teachers to find out what they thought of the tests and students' performance on them. In both cases, she quoted what the students and her teachers said.

Lori concluded that students viewed different strategies differently and that she would have to accommodate different needs over the course of the term to ensure each student's success.

Thematic organizer. After analyzing his data related to when it was most appropriate to use teacher-directed and student-directed teaching, Matt used quotes from students, his mentor, and the professional literature to illustrate two themes that emerged. (See Figure C.11 for an excerpt of his analysis.)

Snake chart. Andrew wanted to show how he went about his action research project and what he learned along the way. He did this by mapping the progress of his study of cooperative learning groups in his social studies classroom from start to finish. (See Figure C.12.)

To summarize the steps she took in her study of helping students to learn the scientific method, Trish created a snake chart that showed the problems she introduced to her science students, what her students learned and did not learn, and what steps she took in her teaching to address the issues that arose. (See Figure C.13.)

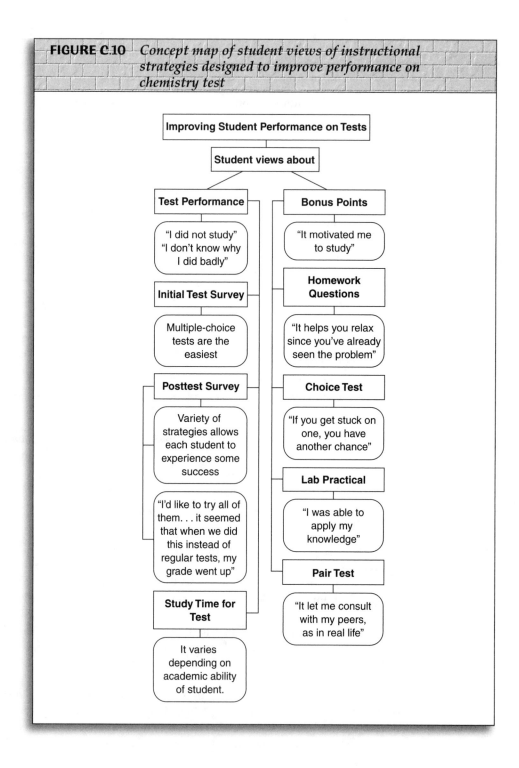

FIGURE C.10 *Concept map of student views of instructional strategies designed to improve performance on chemistry test*

FIGURE C.11 *Thematic organizer showing when it is most appropriate to use teacher-directed and student-directed teaching*

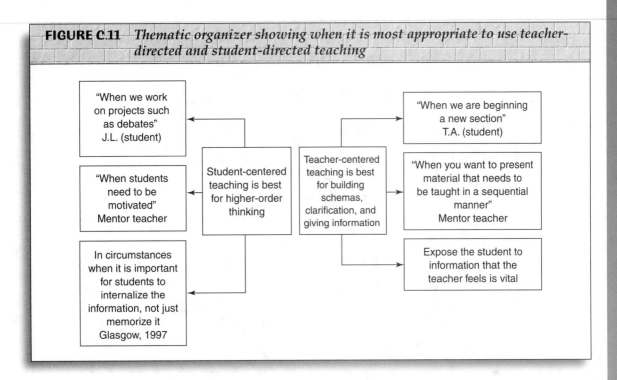

Both Andrew's and Trish's snake charts were used in presenting their study to other student teachers at the end of the term.

Other ways to organize data and show relationships include classification, cause-effect, and sorting. Several sources may be helpful in visually displaying data: Miles and Huberman (1994), *Qualitative Data Analysis,* and Hyerle (1996), *Visual Tools for Constructing Knowledge.*

FIGURE C.12 *Andrew's snake chart showing the development of his cooperative learning study*

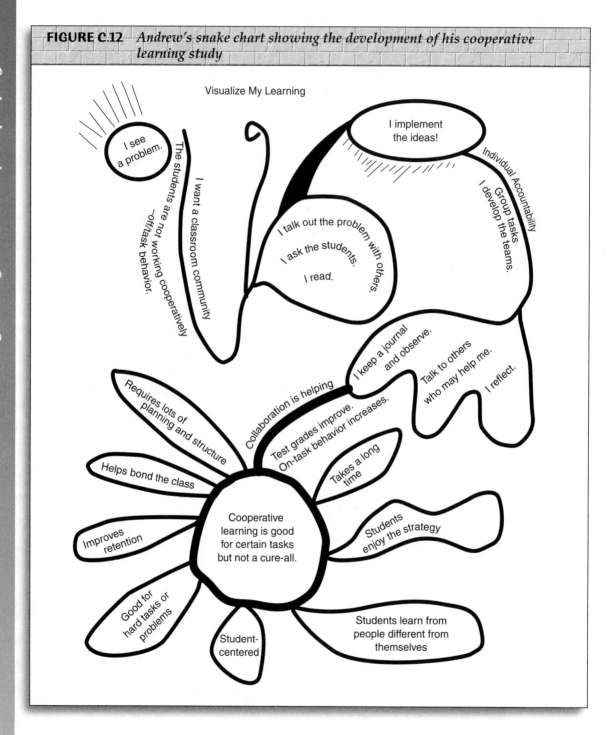

FIGURE C.13 *Trish's snake chart of teaching the scientific method*

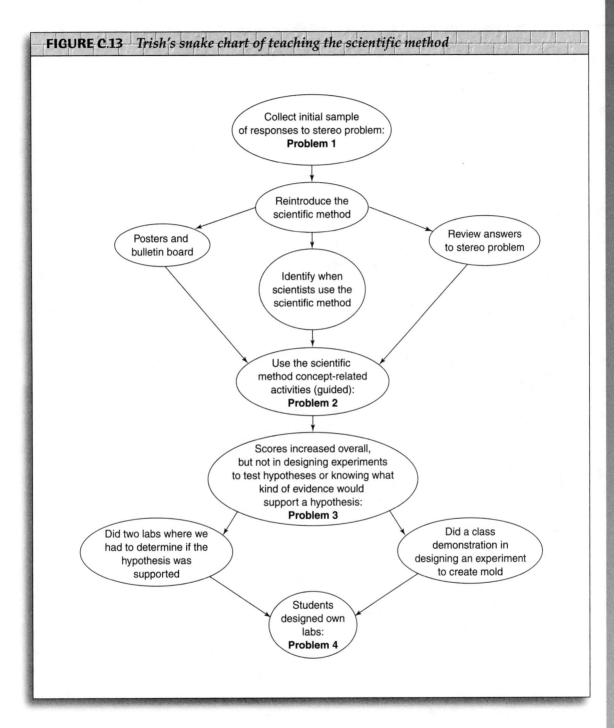

Travelers' Notes D

Analyzing Student Writing and Mathematical Data

Because of the emphasis in education on assessing writing and mathematics, we include specific analytical procedures that may be used to interpret student writing and mathematical understanding. Keep in mind that these are just examples of the ways in which teacher action researchers can approach analyzing student work in these two areas.

Analyzing Student Writing

Written student work may take many forms: responses to an open-ended question, journals, stories, reports, essays, and so on. How you analyze student-written artifacts depends on what your questions are and what you want to find out. You might analyze for spelling development, increased skill in narrative or expository writing, syntactic complexity and maturity, quantity of writing, or use of varied vocabulary. Or you may want to examine student writing for what it reveals about what they are learning in a specific content area, such as social studies. We will make suggestions for each.

Quantity of written work. Keeping in mind that quantity isn't the same as quality, sometimes action researchers are simply curious to see whether students respond to use of a particular teaching strategy by doing more writing. We can find this out by counting words within an entry (such as a journal) or assignment (such as a weekly essay or story). Of course, counting words is not as easy as it sounds. Young students might write as one word what is conventionally several words (e.g., *Onceuponatime*). Some students may break a compound word into two words (e.g., *logger head* for *loggerhead*). As the researcher, you make the decision about how to count such words, keeping in mind that consistency is important.

To help visualize changes over time, teachers might graph the length of written work. Or to compare the length of written work of two classes, a teacher might graph the average length of written work for two classes. This "playing with data" may or may not reveal anything interesting. But the insights it provides may be worth the effort.

Typically when action researchers graph the length of written work of particular students over several months, they learn that the length varies. Some topics are interesting to particular students, while others are not. Sometimes on a given day, a student has more to say than at other times (which is true for adults as well).

One teacher, in doing this, saw that all students wrote a great deal more on one particular day than other days. When she cross-checked that date with her researcher log, she noticed it was the day *she* began writing while her children were writing. She felt certain the effect was due to her modeling.

Sometimes graphing entries or assignments of a student over time will only appear as an up-and-down pattern on a line or bar graph. However, if the work is segmented by week, by month, by grading period, or by first half or second half of the study, and *then* averages are calculated for each segment, changes may show up that otherwise would not. We call this process of segmenting data *disaggregating* the data. This, too, is what we mean by "playing with data."

Quality of written work.   The criteria for narrative or expository writing are more complex than simply counting words. Narrative writing, for example, is judged by the presence and quality of well-developed characters, plot, and setting. Expository texts are judged on specific features of the genre. For example, journalistic newspaper articles present critical information (who, what, when, where, why) up front, prior to any elaboration. Persuasive writing sequences points of argument, often presenting the most powerful reason at the end. Each type of writing has qualities that merit attention by writers. A review of the literature will often provide rubrics or guidelines that teachers can use. Additionally, because many states and provinces now require mandatory testing of writing, rubrics used to evaluate student writing are widely published.

Once you know what you are looking for in writing, you may want to apply the rubric or other guidelines to all student writing over the period; or you may wish to focus on particular students, such as those who are the least-developed writers, or a combination of more and less proficient writers. Or you may want to randomly select students to represent the larger group.

The development of new or young writers.   Many action researchers follow the development of the writing of young children (ages 5 to 9), some learning a new language, such as Jen. Others are interested in adults coming into literacy for the first time. A review of the literature on the development of writing will provide much description of appropriate expectations for these different kinds of students at different stages in their development. The early stages of young children's writing, for example, have been described by some as *pre-phonetic, phonetic, transitional, invented,* and *conventional.*

Simple forms of analysis may involve keeping track of words the child has conventionalized (by giving an identical spelling test of common words multiple times), by counting the number of words in their connected discourse and then counting those spelled conventionally. This finding can be expressed in a simple percentage by placing the number of words spelled conventionally over the total number, obtaining a percentage of words expressed in conventional spelling. These findings may be graphed for individuals or groups.

Analyzing Student Writing and Mathematical Data

The development of more fluent writers.   Once writers are more or less fluent in the writing of connected discourse, you may want to know about syntactic complexity by comparing the writing of students in two classes over time, or by comparing classes that have had writing instruction consistently with those that have not. One way to examine writing complexity is to look at the scope and breadth of the *vocabulary* being used by the writers. One action researcher tracked all words used by one class of students who wrote frequently and compared them to a class where writing instruction was more limited. By first counting the words in student writing samples (called a token word count) and then counting the different words in the student writing (called a unique word count), action researchers have sometimes noted some interesting patterns. In other words, if a student writes a story in which *the* appears 12 times, *of* appears 3 times, and *friend* appears twice, each of those only counts as one word. Consequently, in a piece of connected discourse that consisted of 50 words, some students might have used only 26 different words by being repetitive, while others might have written with more than 42 different words. The latter shows greater scope in vocabulary and also demonstrates that the writer is willing to take risks to try words that are their first choice as opposed to sticking with words that are easier to spell.

With this type of analysis, it would not be valid to analyze only a single piece of writing from a student as representative of that student's writing. A more logical analysis would be to analyze a range of student writing from an individual or group and compute the average unique word count in a group. By taking the unique count in a group of stories for a class, one might gain some insights about the writers and the curriculum.

A secondary foreign language teacher used an analysis similar to this in a study of French I students who kept dialogue journals. Students wrote freely, without prompts, in their newly developing foreign language. The action researcher responded regularly to the students, writing back, noting incorrect grammar or spelling, and attempting to model conventional grammar and spelling in the responses without ever drawing attention to student errors. The researcher then tracked the journals for *token word counts, unique word counts,* and specific incidents where her modeling influenced the student and resulted in a correction in a subsequent entry. The unique word count became most interesting when words showed up in the count that she had not yet presented in class or had not yet been covered in course materials.

In cases where action researchers have an interest in syntactic complexity, *t-unit analysis,* pioneered by Kellogg Hunt (1965), has been used successfully in many studies. T-unit analysis puts text into an analyzable unit, since sentences are not a helpful unit of measure because they vary too greatly. A t-unit is the main clause and any dependent clauses that go with it. For example, the sentence "I went to the store" is simply a main-clause sentence, and one t-unit. But if the sentence is "I went to the store and then I went to the movies," the sentence contains two main clauses and hence two t-units. But a sentence such as "I went to the store and stopped off on the way home at the dry cleaners" is all one t-unit, but has two clauses.

Writing that has a 1:1 ratio of sentences and t-units is considered undeveloped, choppy writing. Writing that has a somewhat higher ratio of t-units to sentences demonstrates more mature writing. Syntactic complexity has limits, however, and sources such as Hunt should be consulted for this type of analysis. For example, while one can easily say that writing with a series of sentences with one or two t-unit ratio might be considered repetitive and boring, one cannot assume that writing with five t-units per sentence will win any prizes. In fact, such writing would likely be cumbersome and difficult to read. For the purposes of analyzing student-connected discourse, simply demonstrating that there is complexity and not all one-to-one correspondences is generally sufficient.

First, the researcher counts the number of sentences in a piece of student writing. Next, the researcher counts the number of t-units and then the number of clauses. This analysis should be double-checked by a knowledgeable colleague for agreement. Some unusual sentences will be harder to analyze than others and will need some discussion to come to agreement. Simply calculating the number of clauses and dividing by the number of sentences, and the number of t-units over the number of sentences (simple division), will yield some possibly interesting profiles.

Writing in the content areas.   Many researchers working in music, math, science, social studies, literature, or foreign language have sought evidence in student writing that certain types of learning have taken place. One researcher hoped to see evidence of scientific logic in student learning logs. Another looked for evidence of critical thinking about issues such as prejudice in her social studies classes.

These researchers began their process of analysis by reading and rereading the student work. By identifying the most desirable qualities as well as the least desired ones, rubrics can be created to assess student writing. For example, in a science log, making an observation may be the lowest level of a desired response. Making the observation with added details might be slightly more desirable. Observations with details and evidence of thinking about why might be more desirable still. And the most desired response might include all those features mentioned and the added element of raising questions about "what if" something were done slightly differently.

Using these criteria, we can create a rubric that assigns a point value (say, 1 to 4) to each type of response. As in all analyses of this type, evaluations should be checked by another colleague with similar expertise. Most rubrics can benefit from refinement and revision once tried out in practice, thereby increasing the effectiveness of evaluation.

Analyzing Mathematical Data

The *teaching experiment* is a formal research method that can be used by the teacher action researcher. Using initial tasks designed to establish the child's level of understanding, the researcher questions, assesses, reflects, analyzes, and then designs additional tasks to move the child in the direction of more sophisticated thinking.

The purpose of this research is to build a model of the mental operations the child employs while constructing meaning for different mathematical content. This model then becomes critical information for teachers in designing lessons in their own constructivist classrooms.

To illustrate this more clearly, let's look at an informal teaching experiment conducted by Judie Mellilo (1999) as part of her doctoral dissertation in mathematics education. Finding the average is typically taught as following the rule. Judie knows that most students develop computational proficiency and never really have an opportunity to extend their thinking beyond the "add them up and divide" procedure. Judie's goal was for her middle school students to develop a more powerful understanding of the arithmetic mean. First, she read research in the area of mathematics education that discussed students' conceptions for the average; what was problematic as they worked with a variety of average-type problems; and what one could expect students to make sense of as they moved away from using the rule and toward applying their understanding of what that rule does to novel problems.

In constructivist research, designing the instructional tasks requires much forethought on the part of the teacher. The task must be structured in such a way that one can assess students' understandings as they move through it. However, the task must be flexible enough to be altered at any moment to accommodate questioning by the teacher, interaction between the students, and whole-group discussion where each child has the responsibility to share and justify her or his thinking.

Judie sequenced the tasks so that the first group of problems acted as her initial assessment. The second group of problems supplied information about how students thought about and were able to discuss the average. The third set of problems moved students away from the use of the rule and toward the decomposition (breaking apart and examining the parts) of the procedure for finding the average. The fourth group of problems provided students with the opportunity to examine and discuss the relationships in the procedure at a more abstract level. The sessions were videotaped, and Judie took notes and collected students' solutions to the problems. Each night, Judie analyzed and reflected on the tapes and the students' written work. Her reflections on what the students were able to understand and do led to new action—new sequencing of problems for the next day, when the process was repeated.

Let's look in on one day of Judie's research. The question she asked of her students was, Can you find five different numbers whose average is 20? Students had to really think about their conception of the average and their understanding of the procedure in order to construct the data set. The following are some of the students' solutions:

MM: [Wrote five 20s on her paper] Take 2 off the first 20, that gives you 18. Give 2 to the next 20, that gives you 22. Now take 3 off this one, 17, and give it [3] to the fourth, making it a 23. Oh, you have a 20 left. We'll take 4 off the 23, make it a 19, and give the 4 to the last 20, making it a 24.

T: So what is your data set?

MM: 18, 22, 17, 19, and 24.

Another two students working together tried guessing five numbers and then used the average procedure to see how close they came to an average of 20. They then made a better guess. Their method was not working, and DM was becoming frustrated. Then suddenly DM had a breakthrough.

DM: Oh! All you have to do is get 100. Once you get 100, you can do it . . . just work backward. 5 times 20 is 100.

T: Can you think of five numbers that add up to 100?

BR: [DM's partner] 50, 25, 5, 10, and 10.

T: Are those the only five numbers that add up to 100?

DM: No, there are lots.

Reflecting on what happened, Judie noted that MM sidestepped the procedure and used mental model-based reasoning to construct the data set. MM saw the average as a leveler, turning everything in the data set into the same number. MM manipulated her mental model of a data set where all the five numbers were the average, 20, to produce the five different numbers.

DM and BR used the procedure but to no avail. Judie noted that they had not abstracted the procedure sufficiently to decompose it into parts and isolate the sum. The breakthrough came after many failed attempts to guess five numbers. Once DM paid attention to the fact that the only way to get an average of 20 when there are 5 numbers is to divide the 5 into 100, because 20 times 5 is 100; DM describes this as working backward. Judie describes it as decomposing the procedure into components, analyzing the components, and reassembling the components to solve nontypical problems such as this. While this type of mathematical research requires thoughtfulness, time, and energy on the part of the action researcher, the results of studies such as this may lead to teaching and learning that are much deeper than traditional "apply the rule" methods.

Travelers' Notes E

Creating a Democratic Classroom: An Action Research Study

Ruby Jones
Research in Secondary Education
Kent State University
Instructor: Dr. Joanne Arhar

It is a contradiction to envision a democratic society when its inheritors, the kids, are forced to live under conditions of unrelieved subordination.

S. Aronowitz and H. Giroux
Education Under Siege

Free speech is important, not for the words that we like, but rather for the words that we hate.

Senator Bob Kerry
Massachusetts

What Is My Research Interest?

Ruby

Everywhere people bemoan the state of U.S. society and the destruction of democracy. Pundits argue that civility has declined, aggression has increased, and U.S. citizens grow more cynical of the political process. Fewer and fewer people register to vote; not all those who register actually vote. Fewer and fewer people write letters to the editor, wear campaign buttons, try to convince others about an issue or a candidate, or donate money to a cause. Those who are concerned about these developments say that people are too willing to give up control over the decisions that affect their lives, thereby giving too much power to too few and leaving the citizenry vulnerable to manipulation.

335

How does this become the problem of the classroom? I believe that rehabilitating democracy requires citizens to challenge the status quo. As William Greider (1991) states in his critique of democracy, this "insurgency" must begin with "ordinary people who find the will to engage themselves with their surrounding reality and to question the conflict between what they are told and what they see and experience" (p. 410). This political will begins in human conversation built on mutual respect, among people who have learned to question the evidence provided by those in authority and who have learned to listen to the voices that are usually silenced. Such a people can be nurtured in truly democratic classrooms.

Yet, research has shown that social studies classes are those in which democracy is studied but not practiced (Engle and Ochoa, 1988; Radz, 1983). For example, it is essential that citizens know how to verify the truth of what they are being told in order to be socially responsible and to vote intelligently. In class, however, students are concerned primarily with developing the skills necessary to retrieve and remember decontextualized discrete bits of information, rather than constructing their own knowledge in a way that connects their past knowledge with the course content to create new knowledge. They learn how others have made decisions rather than how to use their knowledge to make their own decisions and participate in the implementation of those decisions. Citizens need to balance their rights and interests with their responsibility to others and to society in general, but students are rarely required to examine controversial issues in light of the common good and weigh both the benefits and the dangers of a given policy. Such classrooms are not democratic and cannot create a commitment to democracy that extends beyond lip service.

In the semester before student teaching, my mentor and I noted that the students in civics classes rarely participated in class discussion. Further, a few students tended to dominate discussion, opinions were rarely supported by reference to evidence, and there was little interest in civics as a course of study. Students complained that civics was "boring" and had nothing to do with "real life." I administered a Citizenship Survey to the students in one class in order to discover which characteristics of citizenship they identified as most important. Results from this survey are presented in Table E.1.

Even though the students in this class identified the ability to make wise decisions as the *second* most important characteristic, they identified participation in community or school events, knowledge of government, and knowledge of current events as the three *least* important characteristics, thus demonstrating the lack of connection between knowledge and behavior. Thus my research question became, How can I create a democratic classroom in which students would begin to develop the knowledge, skills, and characteristics necessary for active involved citizens living in a democracy?

What Did I Try Out in Order to Improve My Practice?

Participants and setting.   In this study I chose to focus on three ninth-grade, required, college-preparatory civics classes. Of the 86 students in these classes, the majority were middle- to upper-middle-class and white. In my eighth-period class,

TABLE E.1 *Citizenship Survey: Summary of responses and means for various characteristics of citizenship*

| | | Least Important | | | | Most Important | | |
| | | 1 | 2 | 3 | 4 | 5 | 6 | 7 |
Characteristic of Citizenship	**Means** $n = 17$				Number of Responses			
Knowledge of current events	3.6	3	2	1	6	2	3	0
Participation in community or school events	4.2	2	1	3	3	3	3	2
Performance of duties	5.0	2	1	1	0	5	3	5
Concern for others	5.3	2	0	0	1	4	6	4
Acceptance of authority	4.3	0	3	1	6	3	2	2
Ability to question ideas	5.0	2	0	0	3	4	4	4
Ability to make wise decisions	5.7	1	0	0	1	4	5	6
Knowledge of government	4.0	1	2	1	10	0	1	0
Patriotism	4.2	3	1	1	1	9	0	2
Moral and ethical behavior	6.0	0	0	2	1	2	2	10

two students were of Hispanic ancestry, one was Japanese, and one was Indian. In fourth period, there were 21 females and 8 males; in fifth period there were 14 females and 14 males; in eighth period there were 18 females and 11 males. The study took place during spring term during my student teaching. The school is a large comprehensive high school located in a predominantly white, middle-class suburb between a major university and a mid-sized metropolitan area in northeast Ohio.

The action. I decided to focus my study on building a classroom community by establishing a collaborative ethos. As one who has long been committed to a more democratic, egalitarian, and just U.S. society, I am also committed to the kind of teaching that develops habits of the heart and mind that make democratic life possible, that asks what it really means to be human, and that finds the answer in listening to each and every voice. In creating a democratic classroom, I wanted to ensure that everyone had the opportunity to participate, that the dignity of individuals was protected by making them feel safe and respected when expressing opinions, that student choice was a primary element of the classroom, that students learned to evaluate carefully the information that we gathered, and that the students and teacher developed a feeling of community within the classroom. I also hoped they would develop empathy for the perspectives of others.

Creating a Democratic Classroom: An Action Research Study

Based on the work of Hutchison (1994), I selected two aspects of collaboration: teacher–student collaboration and student–student collaboration as means of developing a democratic classroom environment. The activities I chose included small cooperative group work; reflection dialogue journals; student choice in assignments, group members, and readings; a classroom compact; a Bill of Rights project; a variety of community-building exercises; and discussions of controversial issues. These activities were also designed to help students construct their own understandings of democratic life.

How Did I Document the Process?

I developed a chart to help me think through my data collection process. I listed the classroom strategies that I planned to use, the data collection methods I could use to document the consequences of my actions, and some ideas about what I would look for when I examined the data (see Figure E.1).

I adapted the Classroom Community Survey developed by Schaps et al. (1996) and had the students complete it at both the beginning and the end of student teaching. I have included it in Figure E.2.

FIGURE E.1 *Data collection plan*

Strategies	Data Collection Methods	What Will I Look for in the Data?
Reflective activities	Student journal written in twice a week and collected weekly	Student ideas about how to create a classroom community and their attitudes about collaborative work
Classroom compact	Student compacts	Evidence of respect for one another; ability to work together and make collaborative decisions
Discussion of controversial issues	Observations recorded in my journal; student journal	Evidence of ability to understand the perspectives of others
Teacher–student collaboration	"Before" and "after" Community Survey	Evidence of student decision making
Student–student collaboration	Community Survey	Evidence of problem solving and respect

FIGURE E.2   *Classroom Community Survey*

Directions:

1. Please do not put your name anywhere on this sheet.

2. Please use marker or pen.

Note: Thank you for taking this survey. It is part of the research project that I am required to do during my student teaching. You will not be graded on this survey. It is designed to let us know how you feel about this particular class right now. Please answer these questions by yourself, as honestly as you can. I appreciate your help.

For this set of questions, use this scale:

1 = disagree a lot, 2 = disagree a little, 3 = don't agree or disagree, 4 = agree a little, 5 = agree a lot

_____ Students in my class are willing to go out of their way to help someone.

_____ My classmates care about my work just as much as their own.

_____ My class is like a family.

_____ The students in my class don't really care about one another.

_____ A lot of students in my class like to put others down.

_____ Students in my class help one another learn.

_____ Students in my class help one another, even if they are not friends.

_____ Students in my class don't get along very well.

_____ Students in my class just look out for themselves.

_____ Students in my class are mean to one another.

_____ When I'm having trouble with my work, at least one classmate will try to help.

_____ Students in my class treat one another with respect.

_____ Students in my class work together to solve problems.

_____ When someone in my class does well, everyone in the class feels good.

_____ The teacher cares about how well we are doing on our work.

_____ The teacher cares about what we think.

Use this scale for the next set of questions: 1 = never, 2 = hardly ever, 3 = sometimes, 4 = often, 5 = always

_____ Students have a say in deciding what goes on.

_____ The teacher lets us do our work our own way.

_____ The teacher is the only one who decides on the class rules.

_____ The teacher lets me choose the kinds of things that I will work on.

_____ The teacher and students together plan what we will do.

_____ Students in my class can get a class rule changed if they think it is unfair.

_____ The teacher asks the students to help decide what the class should do.

_____ Students in my class get to help plan what they will do.

_____ The teacher and the students decide together what the class rules will be.

_____ I get to do things that I want to do.

Adapted from E. Schaps, C. Lewis, and M. Watson. Building community in school. *Principal, 76*(2), 29–31. Copyright 1996, National Association of Elementary School Principals. All rights reserved.

How Did I Verify That My Judgments Are Trustworthy, Credible, and Respectful?

I realized that I would have to verify any judgments I would make to my peers, advisor, and mentor, so I triangulated the data. I used multiple sources of data: (1) interviews of students (journals, Citizenship Survey, Classroom Community Survey); (2) observations of group work, class projects, etc., recorded in my journal and log; (3) actual artifacts (classroom compacts, personal-values project, Bill of Rights project); and (4) documents (student journals and other written work). Throughout the study, I also consulted with my mentor, several of my peers and friends, and my university action research supervisor.

How Did I Interpret the Data?

In this section, I will show how I analyzed my data and how I interpreted and verified what I was learning. I will also show the changes that I made in my action during the study in response to what I was learning from my data.

The following items from the Classroom Community Survey were particularly relevant to teacher–student collaboration and student–student collaboration. I numbered them 1 to 5 to make it easy to analyze and calculated the mean scores for each item.

1. Students make decisions about what is going on (teacher–student collaboration).
2. Teacher involves students in decision making (teacher–student collaboration).
3. Students in my class work together on solving problems (student–student collaboration).
4. A lot of students in my class like to put others down (student–student collaboration).
5. Students in my class treat one another with respect (student–student collaboration).

Table E.2 presents the mean scores for each item for each of my three classes in what I call the *before* survey.

TABLE E.2 *Mean scores for selected items on the "before" Classroom Community Survey*

Class Period	Question 1	Question 2	Question 3	Question 4	Question 5
Fourth	3.2	2.7	3.6	1.9	3.8
Fifth	3.1	2.2	2.9	3.5	2.7
Eighth	3.0	2.5	3.3	3.0	3.0

What I learned by finding the mean scores for each item was that students in my fifth-period class perceived that they had less input into decisions, were less cooperative in group problem solving, and were less respectful of one another than students in my other classes. My own observations recorded in my journal suggested that this was the case.

> Students are laughing when other students debate controversial issues.
> Students are making comments about clothing, hairstyles, and jewelry,
> calling students who have different clothing styles the "dirties." I decided
> to increase the number of reflective activities and discussion that centered
> on the principles of respect, responsibility, and tolerance.
>
> *Journal, March 15*

With a few weeks left in my student teaching, I decided to administer the same survey again and called it my *after* survey. By comparing the students' mean scores before and after implementation of many of the reflective activities, group activities, and exercises designed to increase collaboration and community, I was able to look again at how my students felt about collaboration. I was particularly interested in fifth period because I had given those students more focused attention after the before survey. Table E.3 compares the means of all three classes on the three items.

While the responses to questions 1, 2, and 3 indicated that students sensed an increase in teacher–student collaboration, responses to questions 4 and 5 indicated that there was an increase in disrespect in all classes, and particularly in fifth period. At this point, I wrote in my journal:

> I wonder if I am cut out for teaching.
>
> *Journal, April 25*

I really thought that I might quit student teaching. I had many discussions with friends, peers, and my university action research adviser who convinced me that I should continue.

In addition to the classroom compact, which I had planned to do next, I added some new activities to address this disrespect, one of which was the Personal-Values Project. So that you can see the changes that I made in my teaching, I have

TABLE E.3   *A comparison of means on the "before" and "after" Classroom Community Survey*

Class Period	Question 1		Question 2		Question 3		Question 4		Question 5	
	Before	After	Before	After	Before	After	Before	After	Before	After
Fourth	3.2	3.5	2.7	3.7	3.6	4.0	1.9	2.5	3.8	3.5
Fifth	3.1	3.5	2.2	3.1	2.9	3.5	3.5	4.0	2.7	2.1
Eighth	3.0	3.6	2.5	3.5	3.3	3.7	3.0	3.4	3.0	2.7

Creating a Democratic Classroom: An Action Research Study

Creating a Democratic Classroom: An Action Research Study

made two flowcharts (see Figures E.3 and E.4). Let me first tell you what happened when I assigned the classroom compact.

The classroom compact activity exacerbated an already difficult situation in fifth period. In small groups, students were to develop a classroom compact based on the personal values each had already outlined in her or his journal. Two of the groups (all boys) developed compacts that put down the dirties. I have included one of the boys' compacts to illustrate the situation (see Figure E.5).

I noticed that the other students were visibly upset when this compact was posted. When the boys in these two groups each voted for their own compact (rather than vote as a block for one of theirs), they were outvoted by the rest of the class, who chose a compact that reflected a more inclusive and respectful attitude.

The final activity was the Personal-Values Project. Students were to create or select an artistic work which represented a value related to democracy (equality, freedom, etc.) or a value of personal importance. They presented their project to

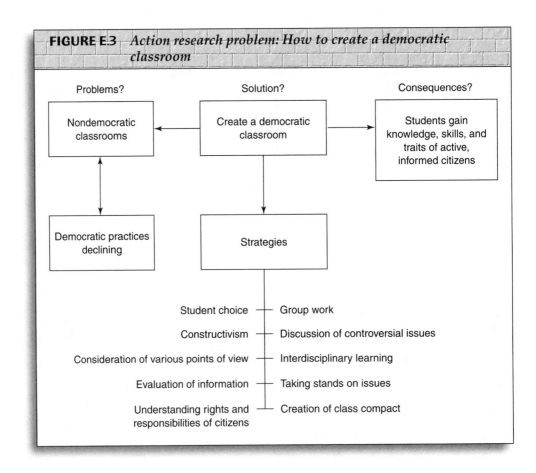

FIGURE E.3 *Action research problem: How to create a democratic classroom*

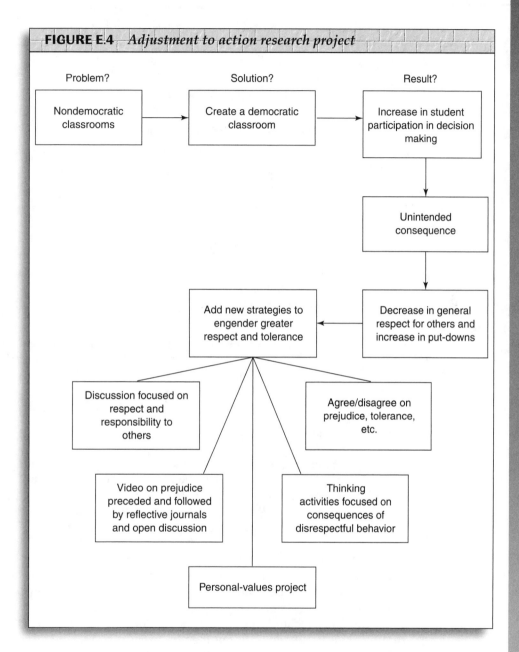

FIGURE E.4 *Adjustment to action research project*

Problem?

Nondemocratic classrooms

Solution?

Create a democratic classroom

Result?

Increase in student participation in decision making

Unintended consequence

Decrease in general respect for others and increase in put-downs

Add new strategies to engender greater respect and tolerance

Discussion focused on respect and responsibility to others

Agree/disagree on prejudice, tolerance, etc.

Video on prejudice preceded and followed by reflective journals and open discussion

Thinking activities focused on consequences of disrespectful behavior

Personal-values project

Creating a Democratic Classroom: An Action Research Study

FIGURE E.5 *Classroom compact of one group of boys in fifth period*

We the clean people of room 2000 have agreed upon these following rules to make our classroom a better place—

> No DIRTY attire—no jackets, chains, animal collars, ripped and stained clothing.

> Students can pick where they want to sit.

> No people are allowed to stand outside and look in to see their friends.

> Must have a signed note by parent saying that you've washed yourself the night before.

the class. One of the "dirties" acted out a poem by Howard Rollins in which the narrator sees himself in the suffering of another.

At the end of that day, I recorded in my journal what happened after she read her poem:

> Then she quietly showed them a painting of a girl, all in black,
> who uses words that describe her good qualities as a shield against
> the cruel comments of others. There was silence in the classroom
> when she finished. The entire class erupted in applause. She
> taught them more in 5 minutes about prejudice than I had all
> semester.

Journal, May 20

I tried to make sense out of what had happened. I reread their journals and carefully analyzed one in which I asked them to write about how *they* would create a sense of community in their classroom. To analyze this particular set of entries, I read over all the students' writings, looked for categories that emerged, and clustered them into what became a pattern of student thinking (see Table E.4).

What I found was that students thought of community as concrete activities such as working together in groups, more so than intangibles such as respect for one another and participation, terms used in the citizenship survey that they rated as least important to citizenship.

I compared what each source of data told me and talked over the evidence that I had accumulated with my mentor, friends, peers, and advisor. I thought back on what I had learned in political science courses about democratic processes and reflected on my own experiences as an activist during the 1960s. I was trying to put all this into a broader context to explain how my good intentions and efforts could have gone so wrong.

TABLE E.4 *Reflective journal 2: Fifth-period student responses*	
What Can We Do in This Class to Create a Sense of Community?	**Number of Students Responding**
Work together, share work, group work.	11
Help others, take care of those who fall behind.	12
Respect others.	6
Listen to others, make sure everyone has a chance to talk.	4
Other	1
Total (there are 28 students in class; some students had more than one response)	34

What Have I Learned About My Students, My Situation, Myself, and the Action Research Process?

I made the assumption that a democratic classroom would create a caring community. I assumed that if I gave students the opportunity to participate equally, they would treat one another as equals. But what I found was that the more opinionated, more arrogant, louder, and less thoughtful people who never questioned their own judgments were the ones who participated. It happened early in my student teaching, so I had to change my strategies. It was not good enough to just encourage participation. I had to push for respect to save the class because some students were really wounded by the classroom compact and the teasing. I couldn't figure out how to deal with those assertive students and make them want to become part of my classroom. My own experiences in politics and my understanding of the Bill of Rights should have warned me that a democracy that relies too heavily on rights cannot create a safe community.

I also learned something about my own prejudices. When the students responded to my democratic classroom in a way that I had not anticipated, I became angry and depressed. Although I resisted the urge to lash out at them, I blamed them for their feelings; I saw the problem as belonging entirely to the students and not the result of any mistakes that I might have made. I was shocked at the depth of my dislike for certain students. I am going to have to deal with these feelings.

Finally, a close friend with whom I communicated throughout the study helped me to deal with the extreme anxiety that I felt when my actions seemed to ironically turn themselves back on my good intentions. I have always been a type of "savior," wanting to stop the war in Vietnam, wanting to reverse the ills of society in the civil rights movement, and now trying to create a type of classroom that championed the rights of students. To temper my emotional response to what I consider to be injustice so that I can still feel empathy for my students, but not at the expense of my own ability to teach, will be a lifelong struggle.

As for the process of action research, I learned that even though it seemed overwhelming at first, it really kept me focused on my students as well as myself. I could have easily gotten so involved in my own plans and activities, and emotional feelings of inadequacy and anger, that I might have forgotten to remember that these are young people who were perhaps testing me and my ideals. The project forced me to keep a journal, which served as therapy for me and forced me to closely observe what I was seeing in my classroom. Finally, the process heightened my commitment to my ideals. My belief in classroom community is even stronger now than it was before. What I have done is to sharpen those ideals and expand them to include the field of education.

What Will I Do Next and How Will This Make Life Better?

I should have paid more attention to the results of the Citizenship Survey. Had I done so, I might have spent more time at the beginning of the class creating a common ground of the concrete details about what citizenship and a democratic community entailed. For example, I would create a classroom compact earlier on, at the beginning of a class. Then, when students act in disrespectful ways, I could bring them back to the compact and remind them of what agreements they had made.

I will also use some of the methods of documentation that I learned in action research. No matter what my teaching responsibilities might be, from teaching a class to monitoring a study hall, I think that documenting the action and my thoughts and feelings about what is going on will help me to be more responsive to my students and clearer in my thinking.

As far as tempering my savior spirit, I'll keep reminding myself (with a little help from my friends) that I can easily burn out as a teacher if I take everything too seriously. I think that my journal will be my lifelong teaching companion.

References

Aronowitz, S., & Giroux, H. (1985). *Education under siege: The conservative, liberal, and radical debate over schooling.* South Hadley, MA: Bergin & Garvey.

Engle, S. H., & Ochoa, A. S. (1988). *Education for democratic citizenship: Decision making in the social studies.* New York: Teachers College Press.

Greider, W. (1991). *Who will tell the people? The betrayal of American democracy.* New York: Touchstone.

Hutchinson, J. (1994). Creating a classroom community. In J. G. Henderson (Ed.), *Reflective teaching: The study of your constructivist practices* (pp. 133–145). Upper Saddle River, N.J.: Merrill.

Radz, M. A. (1983). Promoting a democratic school climate. In M. A. Hepburn (Ed.), *Democratic education in schools and classrooms* (pp. 67–87). Washington, DC: National Council for Social Studies.

Schaps, E., Lewis, C., & Watson, M. (1996). Building community in school. *Principal, 76*(2), 29–31.

Travelers' Notes F

Writing the Literature Review

What follows here is an exercise that anyone can use to learn to write a literature review. Literature reviews are part of most research studies and most manuscripts, articles, or chapters that report a research study. You can do this exercise alone or with a colleague, in a class or a place where you study.

1. *Selecting sample research journals.* From your favorite research journal, take two or three issues and find the literature review in several articles. Usually literature reviews are near the beginning of a manuscript; often a subheading labels it. If it's difficult to locate, look for parts where there are many parentheses with names and dates.

2. *Determining the organization of the literature review.* Read several literature reviews (for this purpose, no need to read the entire article or chapter) and be prepared to describe to a colleague how it was organized. In other words, tell your colleague how the review starts, how it proceeds, and how it ends. Here are some typical ways of organizing a literature review. See whether the ones you selected fit these examples.

   a. A chronology of what has been known or has been done to date on the topic or issue, over a period of years, working toward the current state of the issue or topic.

   b. A statement of a controversy with some space given to each point of view.

   c. An attempt to persuade the reader as to the importance, urgency, or need for something that is going to be addressed.

   d. A presentation of the main themes within the literature review.

   e. An argument that makes a case for something.

   f. A presentation going from more general issues toward more specific ones.

3. *Understanding the writing style of the literature review.* If you own the journals or are working from your own photocopies, consider using a pencil or highlighter for what we are going to do here.

   a. Identify the topic sentence of each of approximately seven consecutive paragraphs. Underline or highlight these, if possible, or copy the sentence (or the essence of the sentence) onto a piece of paper. Notice how each paragraph is concise with only one main idea. Notice the order in which the main ideas begin to form logic in their organization. You can choose to continue this process for the entire literature review if you believe it will help you in your writing.

    b. Locate an instance where more than one study (whether they are sole authored or co-authored) share the same parenthesis.

       i. In what order are the studies presented?

      ii. How did multiple studies end up in the same parenthesis? This is how academic writers integrate and synthesize what they have learned in their reading before they write their literature review.

     iii. Locate the bibliography at the end of the article or chapter. Find the complete citations for what you have located in the literature review. Do the citations come from a book? Article? Chapter in a book? Notice how each is written in those "Selected References."

     iv. While you are in the bibliography, look for examples of different kinds of citations. In addition to those mentioned, notice how dissertations, government reports, ERIC documents, or Web sites might be written.

4. *Preparing for your literature review.* Before you return any sources to the library, ensure that you have taken good notes on each article, book part, or chapter you have decided informs your literature review. Using a different index card or piece of paper for each source enables you to sort and arrange them later as needed. Be sure to note the entire citation in APA style (or whatever style you've been directed to use) and all the page numbers needed. If you copy something verbatim you think you may quote, put it in quotation marks and note the page numbers. If you jot down ideas that are not verbatim, don't use quotes (so you can distinguish in your notes later as needed), but jot the page numbers anyhow in case you need to find that material again. Once you have the needed array of sources you have been directed to use, or made the decision to use, then the next step is to plan how you will present your review.

    a. Reread your notes a few times. Notice patterns in the sources. For example, maybe two different sources talk about why your topic is a *good idea*. Maybe three sources (different or overlapping) present the *benefits* of your topic for teaching. Maybe two other sources issue *cautions*. As you continue to read and think, some of these patterns may become subheadings in your literature review.

    b. As you see patterns and decide on some subtopics for subheadings or sections, consider color coding them or noting them in some way that makes sense. Some action researchers put colored Post-it notes on different cards to be able to retrieve the cards when writing a section. For example, maybe you placed a yellow Post-it note on each card that talked about *good idea*, a pink Post-it note on all the cards that talked about *benefits*, and a blue Post-it note on places where *cautions* were addressed. You may want to consider using highlighters to also highlight precisely the part you want to remember for later. Thus you could have a card or page that has a green and pink Post-it note on it, and you have further color coded where the notes are that go with the blue Post-it note and where the notes are that go with the pink Post-it note.

Writing the Literature Review

   c. Many writers benefit from making an outline on paper, on a large poster-sized piece of paper, or even on a whiteboard or chalk board; some may even draw an outline using drawing tools on a computer.

5. *Writing your literature review.* Many action researchers report that writing a literature review is a "brain drain." Knowing your working style best, plan your writing accordingly. For example, do you need an immense amount of quiet in order to proceed? Do you need to take breaks in this process? Do what works for you.

   a. Using your outline, gather up the pages or cards that apply to the beginning of your literature review. Decide how to begin. Often an advanced organizer is a good start. For example, *"In this literature review, I first present the reasons for teaching vocabulary in social studies, followed by strategies for teaching vocabulary, and finally by some final thoughts to ensure success teaching vocabulary in a content area class."* Starting with an advanced organizer keeps you on track, informs your reader about what to expect, and makes for a tidy organizational plan.

   b. Gather up the cards that apply to the next section of your presentation, and repeat this step until you feel you have completed the literature review.

   c. Remember not to present your sources one by one. A literature review is not a laundry line with one source at a time pinned on in some order. A literature review is an integrated synthesis of your learning.

6. *Understanding the integrated synthesis for your literature review.* Recall earlier how you saw multiple sources presented in the same parenthesis. Earlier you chunked or clustered your sources logically. Now try synthesizing in this example before you try out your own. What follows here are some real sources for a review on multiage education. Read and reread these sources. Color code them if you like. Decide on some sources that are saying something similar that can be presented together. Here are two example sentences created from the cards below that could result from synthesizing these cards. Read these over and try out some of your own. Consider doing this with a colleague. Sections might begin with general statements as in the two examples. Find as many ways as you can to link these cards with each other and practice writing a small section of this review.

Example 1
Multiage classes can be beneficial to the academic development of students (Brody, 1970; Decotis, 1993; Halliwell, 1963; Milburn, 1981).

   Note on "cards" highlighted areas that contribute to this statement. Then the writer might go on to describe more about that achievement, together or specifically to one or more of these studies, citing them as needed.

Example 2
Students in multiage classes have some advantages in social development (Decotis, 1993; Gartner, Kohler, & Riessman, 1971; Goldman, 1981).

   Note underlined areas on cards that contribute to this statement. You may then decide to elaborate on these, citing ones that are most interesting.

Brody, E. (1970). Achievement of the first and second year pupils in graded and nongraded classrooms. *Elementary School Journal,* **70(7), 391–394.**

High-ability groups will show increased benefits of nongrading the longer they are in the program.

Pupils in nongraded schools usually perform better on standardized tests.

362 boys and girls in first and second year nongraded schools vs. control students in regularly grouped classes in same district were grouped for analysis according to IQ scores. Stanford achievement tests were given. The group in the first year with the lowest IQ scores benefited most from nongrading. Second year pupils with high IQ scores benefited the most.

Bunting, J. R. (1974). *Egocentrism: The effects of social interaction through multiage grouping.* **Unpublished doctoral dissertation, State University of New York, Buffalo.**

Findings:

Mixed age groups excelled in cooperative communication.

Children allowed to work in groups that allow interaction and cognitive conflict produced significantly more gains in reducing spatial egocentrism and increasing cooperative communications than isolated age subjects.

Carbone, R. (1961). Comparison of graded and non-graded elementary schools. *Elementary School Journal,* **62(2), 82–88.**

Compared schools in fourth, fifth, and sixth year sampling of 122 nongraded and 122 graded pupils; graded pupils scored higher in 1 of 5 mental health factors.

Connell, D. R. (1987). The first 30 years were the fairest: Notes from the kindergarten ungraded primary (K-1-2). *Young Children,* **42(5), 30–68.**

K/1 curriculum between 1920 and 1950 was more developmentally appropriate than the later "back to basics" movement. The push to make K/1 more demanding after Sputnik made far more K/1 failures. Recommends changing the structure of primary instead of changing the curriculum toward more academics.

British created family grouping after WWII to nurture traumatized children.

Children in multiage one-room schoolhouse created by authors were generally above average in standardized tests.

Cushman, K. (1990). The whys and hows of the multiage primary classroom. *American Educator,* **Summer, 28–32, 39.**

p. 30

Piaget and Bruner theories support mental age that differs in chronological age by 4 years.

"By creating a model that expects diversity rather than uniformity among kids, many problems in a single grade class lose their destructive grip over teachers and students both." p. 30

"In classes that stay with the same teacher for more than one year, proponents say, the teacher–student relationship becomes so personal that both academic and discipline problems diminish." p. 30

Decotis, J. D. (1993). *The effects of continuous progress nongraded primary school programs on student performances and attitudes towards learning.* Unpublished doctoral dissertation. University of Georgia, Athens.

Study used Survey of School Attitudes, Georgia Kindergarten Assessment Program, local report cards, and an attitude assessment toward reading, science, social studies, and math.

First year nongraded compared with Ks in traditional class; second year nongraded pupils compared with first graders in traditional class.

Students in nongraded continuous progress showed more positive attitudes toward schoolwork than those in traditional classes on language arts and science. Traditional students were more positive in math and social studies. Achievement levels higher in nongraded classes in 5 of 8 report card grades. An assessment of citizenship favored kids in nongraded classes.

Doise, W., & Mugny, G. (1984). *The social development of the intellect.* Elmsford, NY: Pergamon Press.

"We subscribe to the idea that social interaction can produce new cognitive coordinations." p. 25

"Most of our experiments demonstrate that participation in certain forms of social interaction leads to cognitive development. They thus lend substance to Vygotsky's claim." p. 27

"In interacting either with adults or among themselves, children not only demonstrate more advanced forms of cognitive organization than those they are capable of alone prior to interaction, but also are able to produce by themselves more advanced forms of the interaction. It is these very abilities that then allow them to take part in more complex interactions and in this way progress up the spiraling developmental path which characterizes the interacting effects of social activity and cognitive development." p. 27

"Improvements in performance often derive not from copying a correct model but from the confrontation of opposed centrations that are socially produced." p. 29

Gartner, A., Kohler, M. C., & Riessman, F. (1971). *Children teach children: Learning by teaching.* New York: Harper & Row.

"Children learn more from teaching other children." p. 1

Writing the Literature Review

-has big socialization impact on children because of responsibility taken by older peer and the opportunity to work through problems at a safe emotional distance with siblings and peers. p. 17
Tutoring peer learns the significance of their knowledge. p. 19

Goldman, J. A. (1981). Social participation of preschool children in same versus mixed age groups. *Child Development, 52*(2), 644–650.

Study of 3- and 4-year-olds in mixed-age and same aged groups to study kinds of play and interaction. Four-year-olds in mixed-age groups spent more time in solitary play (a higher developmental behavior); spent less time in parallel play (a less mature developmental behavior); 3-year-olds also spent less time in parallel play if they were from the mixed-age group.
Lower frequency of negative interactions in mixed-age classes.

Goodlad, J., & Anderson, R. H. (1987). *The nongraded elementary school.* New York: Teachers College Press.

"Our central problem, then, emerges out of the conflict between long established graded structure on one hand, and increasing awareness of variation in children's abilities and attainments on the other. Our graded structure and parent-teacher-pupil expectations are long established; they represent a certain antique respectability. Our insight into individual differences as a phenomenon to be accounted for is not generally shared, however. The problem is effectively relating individual differences and school structures is of such formidable dimensions that a simple exposition of our dilemma will not dispel it." p. 4
Individual children's achievement patterns differ markedly from learning area to learning area. p. 27
"At all grade levels, promoted low achievers generally do better in school work than their non-promoted counterparts." p. 35

Halliwell, J. W. (1963). A comparison of pupil achievement in graded and nongraded primary classrooms. *Journal of Experimental Education, 32*(1), 59–66.

Nongraded pupils scored better on most subjects. Effects were more dramatic for first graders than for second and third graders, except in math where third graders were significant.

Milburn, D. (1981). A study of multiage or family grouped classrooms. *Phi Delta Kappan, 62*(7), 513–514.

Studies two schools of five multiage classes each, 25 students per class, age ranges varied (6–8; 7–9; 8–10; 9–11; similar SES, both schools in British Columbia. Compared children on two academic standard tests, two self-concept and attitude instruments.
Nongraded kids scored higher in vocabulary. Youngest kids in each age group of the multiage classes scored better than comparison groups. In multiage school, children had more positive attitudes toward school and schoolwork.

Travelers' Notes G

E-folios: Motivating Our Students to Speak More

Martha Pero

Rebecca Wiehe

Action Research in the Classroom

Hudson High School

Submitted to Dr. Joanne Arhar

An important goal of a foreign language classroom is for students to be able to communicate orally, yet it is often the most infrequently practiced skill in the curriculum. We changed that in our classes this year through the use of E-folios, which included a concentration on authentic speaking and listening practice as well as reflective learning activities. With the addition of computer technology and with the use of software such as Audacity and Skype, students were able to record their own speech, listen to their peers' recordings, as well as conduct videoconferencing with native speakers. Through our data analysis and reflection, we found three areas of learning: (1) student willingness to speak as an indicator of improved attitude toward oral communication, as well as an improved perception of their speaking abilities; (2) an improvement in oral communication abilities as evidenced by informal observation by teachers and student self-evaluations; and (3) self-reflection as teachers has helped to improve classroom practices.

What Is Our Research Interest?
What Is Our Question?

The lack of speaking skills for authentic communication is a major concern for our students. Speaking the target language leads to student anxiety. The fear of embarrassment in front of their peers causes students to shy away from opportunities to practice speaking in the second language. It is often difficult, due to large class sizes, to give students ample practice in class to ease their insecurities. Motivating students to stay on-task and to practice speaking becomes a

E-folios: Motivating Our Students to Speak More

challenge for the instructor. We have tried many strategies in our classes to encourage student participation and improve student speaking proficiency such as class presentations, storytelling, small-group discussions, question-and-answer activities with visual cues and/or picture sequences, video creations, and other alternative assessment type of speaking activities and projects, but we are still encountering student resistance when it comes to speaking Spanish in class. We have varying levels of experience with technology and wondered whether there were ways that we could use technology to help students with their speaking proficiency. When the Ohio Department of Education's eTech Ohio sent out a request for proposals for integrating technology into teaching to improve student learning, we decided to submit a proposal. Our research question became How can we improve our students' speaking abilities through the use of technology? We were awarded a grant and the story of our action research journey began.

Why Are We Interested?

We are interested in improving our students' oral communication skills because we want them to be able to communicate with native speakers whether they are on the job or on vacation. In the past, the focus in second-language learning has been more on writing and reading. We wanted to minimize stress and fear for the students. It is also difficult having students speak every day in large classes.

We have had many discussions about our teaching philosophies, and we have found that we complement each other rather well. We both have similar classroom environments, and we establish an easygoing rapport with our students. Our classes are structured so that students have a lot of freedom to experience growth. We both challenge our students with our expectations. We use humor and are genuinely interested in our students' lives. With regard to the curriculum, we do have some different philosophies about teaching strategies, but we enjoy experimenting with each other's ideas. These variations help us to improve our practice as we step outside of our comfort zones and try new approaches to teaching Spanish. We work very well together and are both equally concerned about our students' speaking abilities.

What Do We Already Know?

Our experience in the classroom has taught us that when students are motivated, they retain what they learn and are able to use the information in context. This past year, our students wrote letters to students in a neighboring district, and we found their level of Spanish rose because they wanted to impress their new friends. We believe that providing them with a more authentic use of Spanish will result in them wanting to improve their speech as well. Throughout the process, we had to be careful not to fall back on the more traditional methods of teaching that we have been doing for years and are comfortable for us. This new type of teaching forces us to be prepared well in advance, be organized, and above all be flexible as technological problems arise. The more successful students in the traditional sense, the ones who like bookwork, often struggle with different approaches.

What Do Others Know?

In reviewing the literature on oral communication skills in the foreign language classroom, we found that Tomlin and Douglas (1989) conducted a research study through which they created a computer-based software program to assist students in developing their listening comprehension skills. The program involved the students in simulated real-world problems, and through their understanding of the oral language provided by the computer, the students were able to solve the problem posed. Tomlin and Douglas (1989) wrote, "Oral communication skills—the ability to comprehend and produce oral discourse—are crucial in nearly every educational, business, and scientific setting of language use. Yet the development of oral communication skills remains a difficult theoretical and practical problem, and traditional language teaching approaches regularly fail to help many learners" (p. 4). Although Tomlin and Douglas found success in their computer-based software, it was mainly a one-way process in which the students listened to the computer-generated prompts and followed the directions.

Mark Warschauer (1996) tested the effect of electronic discussion in the second-language classroom. Through his research, he concluded that computer-mediated communication resulted in a strong equalizing effect among students, with more speakers sharing the floor, rather than one or two students dominating the topic and the discussion time. In addition, he found that those students who were typically quieter and less likely to participate were more willing to contribute. Jalongo (as cited in Geiss and Mayer, 1998) stressed the importance of speaker variety in developing skill at oral communication, suggesting that students should hear each other speak as much as the teacher, so as to train their ears to the different pronunciations of the second language. In our classrooms, we have worked to provide the same opportunity for our students. With this grant, however, we will be able to go beyond what those researchers have proposed and include a variety of native speakers of the language as well, not just the class members. This involvement of native speakers by way of computer technology will allow our students to further understand the dialectical difference among Spanish speakers and to enhance their comprehension of both the language and the different cultures of those who speak it.

Other researchers have stressed the importance of reflective practice in second-language learning. Geiss and Mayer (1998) suggest that the students keep a "listening journal" in which they reflect on their experiences as oral communicators. Little (as cited in Lamy, 1999) claims that language proficiency is based on "conscious language learning" and that students must be aware of their success and difficulties in order to improve as users of the second language. With this study, we will have the students create e-folios of their work with a component of those portfolios being oral reflections about their interactions with their Spanish-speaking peers, both native speakers and their classmates. These reflection pieces will encourage the students to analyze their own learning experiences as well as give them additional practice in speaking the target language. As far as we are aware, this idea of e-folios with an emphasis on oral reflection is a new area in second-language research.

What Do We Expect to Find?

We expect that through the creation of e-folios as well as with the emphasis on practicing and improving their listening and speaking abilities, our students will be able to converse with a native speaker with relative ease. Last fall, we administered a proficiency test including writing, reading, speaking, and listening. As expected, overall, the students' scores were low in the speaking and listening sections. Next year, we expect to see an increase in those scores. One of our biases is that all students are going to like and appreciate these new methods. We must be cognizant that they have been learning and receiving grades in a different manner for 3 years, and we need to be respectful of the huge changes we are making.

What Did We Try Out?

Why?

We chose to focus on audio recordings of the students' speech, podcasting for listening comprehension skills, and videoconferencing with native speakers. We chose to use the computer for the audio recordings because many students are familiar with the computer and how it works, and they enjoy working on it. The podcasting was a new technique for us this year, and we chose it as a means to allow our students to practice their speaking and listening comprehension skills outside of the classroom. Typically we have done all of the practice for this skill during class time. As part of our study, the computers helped us expand students' use of the language beyond our walls and beyond the school day. The videoconferencing was our third strategy because it allowed our students to come face-to-face with native speakers. They had the opportunity to hear native speech as well as practice their own speech and learn about the culture of those from other countries directly from the people who live and speak it. This interaction has the potential for bringing a true purpose for improving their communication skills. We believed that students would strengthen their skills and become better Spanish speakers and listeners if they were motivated to learn.

Who?

We tested our theories with four sections of Spanish 4 students at Hudson High School. There were 76 total students. The majority of the students were juniors, 16 or 17 years of age, who began studying Spanish as a second language in seventh grade. They took Spanish level one over two school years (seventh grade was two and a half 42-minute periods per week and eighth grade was five 42-minute periods per week), so while they are in level four this year, it is actually their fifth year of language study. These students have chosen to take Spanish 4 for a variety of reasons, including parental influence, personal interest in the language and/or the culture, and future academic plans. Overall, they were well motivated academically and could be described as genuinely "good kids." We chose to work with this group for several reasons. First, we are the only ones in the department teaching this level, which allowed us to offer the new methodology to all of the students enrolled. Second, Spanish 4 has a lot of flexibility in its curriculum. The focus is more on how to use the language and less on the rigid learning of grammar rules and specific vocabulary lists. Third, as previously mentioned, the students are motivated.

What/How?

We had already begun to collect preliminary data for our study. Last May, we administered a proficiency test provided by the Ohio State University to all of our Spanish 3 and 4 students. It was called the Collaborative Articulation and Assessment Project (CAAP). We administered a facsimile of this test in October and also plan to administer next year's test to compare the scoring of the students on the listening and speaking portions.

We began our action plan the third week of school. We wanted the students to become accustomed to the new way we were conducting class. Most of them adapted quickly to having the computer included as a daily part of their instruction. We began with the audio recordings by scaffolding them into the process with pair practice before the initial recording. As time passed, we increased the difficulty of the speaking prompts as well as had them work together to record dialogues rather than simple monologues. The podcastings were one of the first recordings we did and published on the school Web page. They introduced themselves but did not provide their names. The students then listened to the podcasts and guessed who their classmates were. The videoconferencing was the most difficult activity for the students. They spoke with native speakers from the Kent State University translation program using Skype (free downloadable video/audio Internet communication software at http://www.skype.com/download/skype/windows/downloading.html). One speaker was from Venezuela and the other from Ecuador. We prepared the students by having them develop questions at home of things they would like to ask a native speaker. Although they were nervous, the students quickly found value and excitement in the activity. The native speakers complimented them on how well they negotiated meaning. Figure G.1 summarizes our action plan.

Where?

This research study took place in our classrooms in Hudson High School. This year we moved with our department into a newly constructed wing of the building. Our classrooms were designed to manage nine computers. Our tech and media coordinator were very helpful in setting up stations. Our project was fully supported by our district.

E-folios: Motivating Our Students to Speak More

E-folios: Motivating Our Students to Speak More

FIGURE G.1 *Action plan*

Date to Start	What?	For How Long? How Often?	Who?
May 2006	CAAP testing	90 minutes	Spanish 3 & 4
Aug. 2006–June 2007	All written and audio files recorded on the key drives creating the Cyber-folios	Daily/weekly/monthly	Spanish 4
Aug. 2006	LinguaFolio/Attitude scale	Ongoing reflective journal	Spanish 4
Sept. 2006–June 2007	Audio recordings	Once per week	Spanish 4
Sept. 2006–June 2007	Podcasting	Once per week	Spanish 4
Sept. 2006–June 2007	Videoconferencing	As situations become available	Spanish 4
Nov. 2006	CAAP (or comparable exam) testing	90 minutes	Spanish 4
Jan. 2007 (midterm)	LinguaFolio update	Ongoing reflective journal	Spanish 4
May 2007	CAAP testing	90 minutes	Spanish 4
June 2007	LinguaFolio update	Ongoing reflective journal	Spanish 4

How Did We Document This Process?

Since reflection is a major portion of action research, we decided to document our observations in a dialogue journal. We set up a blog online so both of us could access it at any time to add information when we had the time. This also gave us a written record of our thoughts. We also noted students' attitudes toward speaking Spanish and their self-perception of their ability to do so by having them complete a written attitude/perception survey. We had them rate themselves from one to five (one as the lowest score) on the following questions: How would you rate your attitude toward speaking Spanish at this point in Spanish 4? How would you rate your ability to speak Spanish at this point in Spanish 4? We also had them answer the following questions in narrative form the second time that they took the survey: If your attitude has changed, to what do you owe the change? If your ability has changed, to what do you owe the change? What activities have you enjoyed and/or found beneficial this year in Spanish 4? Explain. What activities have you disliked and/or found difficult this year in Spanish 4? Explain.

In addition to the attitude/perception survey, we asked the students to evaluate in writing their experiences after specific activities, such as when they spoke with native speakers, using the following questions: What did you talk about? What was hard for you to express? What new vocabulary words did you learn? What is one thing you would like to share with the class about your conversation? Also, on a scale of one to five, how comfortable did you feel speaking in Spanish? Finally, we gathered information from our students through informal student interviews during class time. We recorded this information, along with our own thoughts, on our blog.

One of our common values was that we care about student attitudes and would like them to reflect more on what they are doing and how they are learning. So, we also used the LinguaFolio, which is intended to promote autonomous learning and the ability to assess one's skills, to serve as a tool to assess language learning, and to set personal language learning objectives for the students. The LinguaFolio consists of three separate pieces: Language Passport, Language Biography, and Dossier. It was designed in Europe to help employers of foreign workers know the language abilities of their prospective employees. It is currently being adapted in the United States for the same purposes. Students have a list of "I can" statements (e.g., I can understand short and simple conversations on familiar topics live or recorded). They self-assess by answering "I can do this easily" or "This is one of my goals." The students also keep a log of any language experience they have, including summer trips. Perhaps they already speak another language. This is all contained in one document. For more information on the LinguaFolio, see http://www.pen.k12.va.us/linguafolio/. Our students self-assessed in August before we began our project and have had two more opportunities to reassess where they are and how much they have accomplished.

After some initial technical problems were solved, our students recorded audio files once a week on the computers using Audacity (free recording software found at http://audacity.sourceforge.net/). They were required to buy a key drive on which they saved their files as well as on the computers so we were able to access the files and provide feedback using the American Council for the Teaching of Foreign Language (ACTFL) guidelines (see Appendix A). We had a baseline for them from the CAAP test they took last year at the end of the year. Figure G.2 summarizes our data collection strategies.

FIGURE G.2 *Data collection strategies*

Observing	Interviewing	Examining Documents and Other Data Sources
• Teacher blog of class observations	• Informal student interviews	• Electronic portfolio entries
	• Attitude/Perception survey	• CAAP test
	• Student-written evaluations of specific activities	• LinguaFolio
	• LinguaFolio	

How Did We Ensure That Ethical Procedures Were in Place?

Our grant proposal was read and approved by both the district technology coordinator and the district curriculum director. We have also presented our project to the school board and the district curriculum council. All parties have honored our work and pledged support. According to the Hudson school board policy, research projects that are conducted with students must be explained to both students and parents, and written consent must be obtained.

We created a consent form to obtain student and parental permission for our study (see Appendix B). We were available through e-mail, telephone conversations, or face-to-face meetings for any parents with further questions or concerns about how we will be working with their students. We discussed our project with parents at the school's open house in early September. Although the students and parents were given the option of withdrawing from participation in the class activities, no one chose that option. In addition, throughout the study, we have kept the privacy and confidentiality of the students by using their Spanish names keyed to student numbers as a reference to their work. In regard to the safety and welfare of our students, we strictly monitored the use of the electronic equipment, especially the use of the Internet and the webcams, so that at all times students were conducting themselves in educational activities. Our school also maintains strict firewalls for students.

How Did We Interpret the Data?

To analyze our data in this study, we set time aside to focus on it for an extended period of time. We focused on all 76 students. In our analysis, we were looking for signs of improvement in student attitude toward oral communication and in student oral communicative ability.

We created charts to show changes in the quantitative components of our study (attitude surveys, CAAP test results, and in-class student evaluations). These tools allowed us to better demonstrate the patterns we found in our data. They gave us a visual representation of our findings. In regard to the qualitative data, the cyber-portfolio entries, we looked for student speech samples that showed improvement. These samples were then compared to our quantitative findings. Upon creation of charts and/or graphs and the selection of student work samples, we began to develop assertions about our study that would describe what we had learned with regard to our research question. We also planned for future action with regard to our study and our work in our classrooms.

How Have We Verified That Our Judgments Are Trustworthy and Credible?

We triangulated our observations, the rubric scores, and the documents and files the students produced. By doing so, we were able to add validity to our judgments about the students' improvement or lack of improvement in attitudes and their oral communication skills with evidence from all three sources. Additionally, we cross checked our data from last year and made reasonable assumptions about our students' progress. Since some of our data was provided by an outside source, The Ohio State University, we feel confident that our assertions are more objective. By involving the students directly in the planning process and in the reflection of the class activities, we were also able to member-check our data as well, as we progressed through the study.

What Have We Learned?

Through our data analysis and reflection, we found three areas of learning: (1) student willingness to speak, as an indicator of attitude toward oral communication, as well as self-perception of their speaking abilities; (2) whereas the overall scores on the postassessment of student oral communication abilities did not greatly improve over the original CAAP scores, our informal observations and student self-evaluations indicate there was improvement; and (3) our self-reflection as teachers has helped us to improve our classroom practices.

First, the students' attitude toward speaking has greatly improved. They are willing to record their speech, talk to a native speaker, and speak Spanish in class and in front of their peers. In mid-October we collected data from the students through attitude surveys regarding their perception about their ability to speak Spanish and their attitude toward speaking and compared it to the results of the same survey conducted in August. See Figures G.3 and G.4.

In August, after completing Spanish 3, 54% of the students had a positive attitude toward speaking Spanish. In November 2006, after 6 weeks in Spanish 4, the number increased to 62%. The greatest improvement, however, was in their perception of their ability to speak. In Spanish 3, 18% felt they had a very good or excellent rating on ability. After 6 weeks in Spanish 4, 58% felt they were very good or excellent. This is a 40% increase in their perception of their skills. Overall students' comments were positive about their attitudes and abilities. The following are examples of their feelings: "We speak more often and since everyone makes mistakes and speaks, it becomes less embarrassing when you screw up."

FIGURE G.3 *Attitude toward speaking Spanish*

	Negative or Neutral Attitude			Positive Attitude	
	1–very poor	2–poor	3–neutral	4–good	5–excellent
August 2006	2 2.6%	9 11.8%	24 31.5%	36 47.3%	5 6.5%
November 2006	2 2.6%	4 5.2%	23 30.2%	42 55.2%	5 6.5%
N=76					

FIGURE G.4 *Self-perception of ability to speak Spanish*

| | Negative or Neutral Attitude | | | Positive Attitude | |
	1–very poor	2–poor	3–neutral	4–good	5–excellent
August 2006	2 2.6%	4 5.2%	46 60.5%	11 14.4%	3 3.9%
November 2006	0 0%	3 3.9	29 38.1%	38 50%	6 7.8%
N=76					

"Due to speaking and recording without a lot of preparation, I have become more confident and fluent when speaking Spanish." "I am understanding Spanish more this year. Last year we were taught more about grammar and vocabulary. This year we are applying it to speaking and it is a challenge." "I think speaking it more makes it more fun so you want to learn it." Since we have had technical difficulties with videoconferencing, we invited a native Spanish speaker to converse with our students in small groups. They completed an evaluation after their experience:

- 94% of the students felt their ability to communicate even if the grammar was not perfect was very good or excellent.
- 69% indicated they felt comfortable speaking Spanish.
- 90% of the students wanted to speak with a native speaker in the future.

Although the score for ease of speaking Spanish is only 69%, it is encouraging to know that 90% are very willing and eager to continue working with native speakers because the more practice they have the better speakers they will become. They are taking a risk and learning from it.

Our second area of learning was with regard to the students' abilities to communicate orally as measured with the CAAP test and our postassessment. We administered the CAAP test last June to our level three students. Our posttest was administered in November to the level four students.

The CAAP scores did not improve greatly overall: 55% received the same overall score, 33% improved, and 11% scored lower. Of the 33% who did improve, 22.2% improved by only .25 of a point, 7.4% improved by .5 of a point, and 3.7% improved by 1 point.

Although there was not marked improvement in the overall scores, after listening to the students' responses, we did feel that there were some differences in the subcategories in which they were improving and declining. (See Appendix A for a list of the subcategories.) For example, many of the students appeared to have improved fluency and thoroughness and sufficiency of detail. We believe that the improvement is due to the increased amount of oral speaking practice that the students have had during the class thus far this school year in Spanish 4. Several students also seemed to improve intonation and pronunciation, and we believe that it is once again due to the increased amount of speaking practice as well as the opportunities to listen to other students and native speakers. The students have overwhelmingly expressed more comfort with speaking in Spanish (as shown by our attitude surveys mentioned previously), and we believe that this level of comfort has led to their marked improvement in the ease with which they currently speak.

In addition to improving in several subcategories, we noticed that the students declined in others. For example, in the subcategories of "complicated grammar structures" and "use of idiomatic expressions," the students seemed to score lower than they did when they took the test at the end of their Spanish 3 class. We believe that this is due to the grammar and vocabulary lessons of each respective class at the time of the test. In Spanish 3, at the end of the school year when the CAAP test was administered, we were working with very high level grammar and vocabulary structures, having progressed to that point throughout the school year. The students were using these structures in their grammar text, in their reading activities, and in their writing activities. These same structures then transferred easily into their speech. At the beginning of Spanish 4, however, the grammar and vocabulary lessons were not at the same level of difficulty. Due to the lapse of practice during the summer, we begin each year with a review of basic grammar and vocabulary and then advance to more difficult structures. At the time we administered the posttest, we were still focusing on more basic structures, and we believe that this caused the students to rely more on those grammar and vocabulary constructions than the more difficult ones used in the first test. As we continue to increase the difficulty of lessons in Spanish 4, we expect to see the scores in those subcategories rise once again.

Also, once the students reach the "Clearly Demonstrates Proficiency" level, it takes a lot of practice to climb to the "Demonstrates High Proficiency" level. It does not occur in one year. It is an accumulation of many years of study. We were also using the ACTFL guidelines to assess, and when you are at an upper level, it is very difficult to improve your number score to meet the highest criteria. Perhaps we should have used an assessment tool that would have pinpointed the growth or lack of growth in a more precise manner. The combination of the rise in several subcategories counterbalanced by a decline in others, the use of an assessment tool that lacks precision, and the difficulty in moving from "Clearly Demonstrates Proficiency" to "Demonstrates High Proficiency" are factors contributing to only modest gains of fewer students than we had hoped for.

Our more informal assessments of their speaking ability show a different picture. We found evidence in our field notes that the students have improved in their daily speech and on assignments not recorded in class. They did a project in which they were divided into four groups in which each group wrote a mystery scenario including a fake crime, suspects, and testimonies. They also wrote a newspaper article to explain the logistics of the crime and then presented their testimonies to the class. The other groups in the class had the opportunity to question the "suspects" and to vote on who they believed was guilty of committing the crime. Overall, the students' performance was excellent. The majority of students willingly asked several questions of each group and were truly interested in solving the mystery. There was little hesitation in speech, all of which was spontaneous

E-folios: Motivating Our Students to Speak More

since the students had to create and answer questions in the moment. The students also felt it was good experience. In their project evaluations several students wrote comments such as the following: "The interrogation was fun and made us listen, write, and talk!" "I found the trial difficult yet helpful to work on my language skills." We attribute this to the greatly increased amount of time they are speaking via technology as well as the availability to speak with native speakers in real-time conversations. We have also increased the amount and detail of the feedback we can provide to our students because we are able to listen to our students' audio files instead of making quick, less-detailed assessments during class time.

Our third area of learning was in our own individual improvement as teachers through self, peer, and student reflection. We found most obvious that we were overzealous in our planning and did not anticipate the amount of technical difficulty that we encountered. We had planned for two recordings per week, which did not happen. When we started, the headphones were not compatible with our computers, and we did not realize that for 2 weeks. We made many attempts to correct the problem and now know that 4 OLM headphones are not compatible with our computers. Until we remedied this situation, we were recording all of our students on two laptops. We are now pretty consistent with one recording per week. We also had planned as a motivator the videoconferencing with native speakers. We continued to have technical issues using Skype with Kent State. State universities, in an effort to keep their band width open, slow access to Skype, which creates problems viewing and speaking at the same time. We expressed our frustrations in our blogs and field notes. Rebecca wrote, "I feel more frustrated during class, because I constantly feel one day behind. Not having the headphones for the computers functioning has made it very difficult. We have done a lot of juggling and stretching of time." Martha also wrote, "The tech problems have exhausted my brain. The learning curve has been incredible. The bottom line is we are doing it, and I for one, am proud of our efforts." Overall, we have learned to be more flexible both in our planning and in our daily classroom and interactions with our students. Allowing the students more freedom and giving up some of the control over each moment in the class period has proven to be a difficult challenge, but one with great dividends. Our students have become more empowered in their own learning, and in doing so have become more responsible and involved in the class.

Technology has been the most important part of our students' improvement in both attitude and ability. Our students are recording every week on the computers and at times twice a week. They are reflecting on their work and that of their peers. In past years, our students have not had the time to speak in class because of sheer numbers, nor did they have the feedback we are now able to provide them by listening to their recordings. They have never felt an urgent need to speak correctly, and though we do not have specific data on the use of Skype and videoconferencing in our classroom, we were recently able to connect with a student from Uruguay, who is studying at Kent State University. Early indications are that our students are excited and cannot wait until the next time they get to speak with her and inquire more about her life and country. Recording every week and speaking with native speakers is having a noticeable change in their attitude, fluency, and ability.

How Have These Actions Made Life Better? What Will We Do Next?

Our study is truly not complete. We plan to continue monitoring the progress of our students throughout the rest of the school year. When we introduce more complex grammar and vocabulary structures, we expect that our students will improve in their overall CAAP scores, which we will administer in May. We will videoconference again in the near future. We expect to see more improvement in student ability and attitude with this component. We would also like to take it one step further and examine the students' written work for increased proficiency.

Life will be better not only for our students but for us as well. Our students have already received compliments on their speaking abilities from the visiting native speaker and the Kent State students from Ecuador and Venezuela. They are all impressed that these students are in a public school system and speaking at such a high level. Since we value the use of Spanish in authentic situations, we believe our practice has come more in line with our values. We have carefully thought through our work. Our goal has always been communication. In the past, our students' reading and writing gave evidence of that, and we believe that we now have found a way to help students improve speaking and listening skills. We are much more cognizant of what and how we are teaching. We have learned a lot about technology, collaboration, and reflection. We are passionate about sharing our experience and to date have had two articles written about our study in professional educational publications. We have also presented at three conferences in an effort to share our work with others. We have been asked to return next year to share our work again. Many teachers have e-mailed us and are currently using our ideas in their classrooms. Martha has been contracted by eTech Ohio to develop an online virtual Spanish 1 course. We see ourselves as teacher leaders in our district. By sharing our work with our colleagues we hope to model our teamwork. Through our writing, presentations, and conversations with others, we hope to inspire the use of technology in teaching.

References

Geiss, P., & Mayer, R. (1998). *Improving listening skills.* Master's Action Research Project. St. Xavier University. (ERIC Document Reproduction Service No. ED426613)

Lamy, M. (1999). "Reflective conversation" in the virtual language classroom. *Language Learning & Technology, 2*(2), 43–61.

Tomlin, R., & Douglas, S. (1989). *Beginning second-language instruction: Computer-based curriculum improvements* (FIPSE Grant Report No. G008541129). University of Oregon. (ERIC Document Reproduction Service No. ED362020)

Warschauer, M. (1996). Comparing face-to-face and electronic discussion in the second language classroom. *CALICO Journal, 13*(2), 7–26.

Appendix A

ACTFL Speaking Guidelines

The following is the rubric used for the two CAAP tests administered.
CAAP Scoring Rubric for Speaking Assessment

9-8   DEMONSTRATES HIGH PROFICIENCY
             Excellent command of the language:
             Few or no grammatical errors
             Strong attempts at more complicated structures
             Extensive use of vocabulary, including idiomatic expressions
             Articulate, flowing speech
             Good intonation and largely accurate pronunciation with slight accent
             Thorough response with interesting and pertinent detail

7-6   CLEARLY DEMONSTRATES PROFICIENCY
             Good command of the language:
             Minor grammatical errors
             Some attempts at more complicated structures
             Adequate use of vocabulary and idiomatic expressions
             Some gaps in fluency
             Acceptable intonation and pronunciation with distinctive accent
             Thorough response with sufficient detail

5-4   DEMONSTRATES PROGRESS TOWARD PROFICIENCY
             Comprehensible expression:
             Some serious grammatical errors
             Reliance on simple structures
             Limited vocabulary marked with some anglicisms
             Unnatural hesitations
             Errors in intonation and pronunciation with heavy accent
             Some detail, but not sufficient

3-2   DEMONSTRATES STRONG NEED FOR INTERVENTION

Limited command of the language:

Serious grammatical errors

Limited grammatical structures

Limited vocabulary marked by frequent anglicisms that force interpretation by the listener

Errors in intonation and pronunciation that interfere with listener's comprehension

General, narrow response

1   UNACCEPTABLE

Response falls below the above descriptions or is inappropriate

Appendix B

Dear Students and Parents,

Sra. Pero and I have recently been awarded grant money from eTech Ohio to do a study on how to help you improve your speaking and listening skills in Spanish. As a result, we have nine new computers, two webcams, one video camera, and a printer available in each classroom to conduct our study. In addition, the Dodie Snyder Endowment Fund has granted us money to provide software, head-phones, and tripods for the project. We want to do this to help you feel more comfortable and be more proficient in your Spanish language usage.

You will be asked to keep an oral portfolio journal on a computer and will also be communicating through videoconferencing with native speakers who are gradu-ate students attending Kent State University. We will also attempt to set up a videoconference project with a school in Mexico.

Through this process, we believe you will become much more proficient in speak-ing and listening to native speakers. Ultimately, your oral skills will be on par with your writing and reading skills.

You will be asked to record your thoughts and feelings about your language learn-ing in a LinguaFolio during this time. We will also ask you to take a CAAP profi-ciency test provided by The Ohio State University at the end of the year to mea-sure the success of our study. All data collected will be anonymous because you will be using your Spanish names on all collected work. If you do not want your work publicized, you may speak with us, and we will omit it from our study.

If you have any questions, please set up a time to speak with us or e-mail us at perom@hudson.edu (Mrs. Pero) or wieher@hudson.edu (Mrs. Wiehe).

I _____(name) agree to take part in this project. I know that my work will be included anonymously at conferences and on the eTech Web site.

_____   _____
Signature   Date

I _____(guardian name) agree to allow my student to take part in this project. I know that his/her work will be included anonymously at conferences and on the eTech Web site.

_____   _____
Signature   Date

References

Adelman, C. (1993). Kurt Lewin and the origins of action research. *Educational Action Research, 1*(1), 7–22.

Alvermann, D. E., Young, J. P., Weaver, D. E., Hinchman, K. A., Moore, D. W., Phelps, S. F., Thrash, E. C., & Zalewski, P. (1996). Middle and high school students' perceptions of how they experience text-based discussions: A multicase study. *Reading Research Quarterly, 31*(3), 244–267.

American Psychological Association. (2001). *Publication manual of the American Psychological Association* (5th ed.). Washington, DC: Author.

Archambault, R. D. (1964). *John Dewey on education*. New York: Modern Library.

Arendt, H. (1958). *The human condition*. Chicago: University of Chicago Press.

Arieti, S. (1976). *Creativity: The magic synthesis*. New York: Basic Books.

Aronowitz, S., & Giroux, H. (1985). *Education under siege: The conservative, liberal, and radical debate over schooling*. South Hadley, MA: Bergin & Garvey.

Ashton-Warner, S. (1963). *Teacher*. New York: Simon & Schuster.

Atweh, B., Kemmis, S., & Weeks, P. (Eds.). (1998). *Action research in practice: Partnership for social justice in education*. New York: Routledge.

Ayers, W. (1992). Disturbances from the field: Recovering the voice of the early childhood teacher. In S. A. Kessler and B. B. Swadner (Eds.), *Reconceptualizing early childhood: Beginning the dialogue*. New York: Teachers College Press. 256–266.

Barr, R., & Tagg, J. (1995). From teaching to learning: A new paradigm for undergraduate education. *Change, 27*, 12–25.

Barrell, J. (1995). *Teaching for thoughtfulness: Classroom strategies to enhance intellectual development* (2nd ed.). White Plains, NY: Longman.

Baum, L. F. (1900). *The wonderful wizard of Oz*. New York: Dover.

Bell, B., Gaventa, J., & Peters, J. (1990). *We make the road by walking: Conversations on education and social change/Myles Horton & Paulo Freire*. Philadelphia: Temple University Press.

Blase, K. (1988). The teachers' political orientation vis-à-vis the principal: The micropolitics of the school. *Politics of education association yearbook*. Washington, DC: Falmer Press.

Bloome, D., & Katz, L. (1997). Literacy as social practice and classroom chronotypes. *Reading and Writing Quarterly: Overcoming Learning Difficulties, 13*(3), 205–226.

Bogdan, R. C., & Biklen, S. K. (1992). *Qualitative research for education: An introduction to theory and methods*. Boston: Allyn & Bacon.

Borich, G. D. (1999). *Observation skills for effective teaching* (3rd ed.). Columbus, OH: Merrill.

Brady, I. (Ed.). (1991). Introduction. *Anthropological poetics*. Savage, MD: Rowman & Littlefield.

Brennan, M., & Noffke, S. E. (1997). Uses of data in action research. In T. Carson & D. J. Sumara (Eds.), *Action research as a living practice*. New York: P. Lang.

Brookfield, S. (1984). *Adult learners, adult education, and the community*. New York: Teachers College Press.

Brookfield, S. (1995). *Becoming a critically reflective teacher*. San Francisco, CA: Jossey-Bass.

Brooks, J. G., & Brooks, M. G. (1993). *The case for constructivist classrooms*. Alexandria, VA: Association for Supervision and Curriculum Development.

Bullough, R. V., Jr., & Gitlin, A. (1995). *Becoming a student of teaching: Methodologies for exploring self and school context*. New York: Garland.

Carini, P. (1986). *Prospect's documentary processes*. Bennington, VT: Prospect School Center.

Carr, W., & Kemmis, S. (1986). *Becoming critical: Education, knowledge, and action research*. Lewes, Sussex: Falmer Press.

Carr, W. (2003). Remarks at the "Simpos: Internacional: The educational researcher as an agent of educational change." W Facultat de CC. de I'Educacio, Universitat Autonoma de Barcelona, Barcelona, Spain.

Carson, T. (1990). What kind of knowing is critical action research? *Theory into Practice*, 9 (Summer '90). Columbus, Ohio: Ohio State University (pp. 167–173).

Carson, T. R., & Sumara, D. J. (Eds.). (1997). *Action research as living practice*. New York: P. Lang.

Carspecken, P. F. (1996). *Critical ethnography in educational research: A theoretical and practical guide*. New York: Routledge.

The Chicago manual of style. (1993). Chicago: University of Chicago Press.

Cisneros, S. (1991). *The house on Mango Street*. New York: Vintage.

Clandinin, D. J., & Connelly, F. M. (1998). Personal experience methods. In N. K. Denzin & Y. S. Lincoln (Eds.), *Collecting and interpreting qualitative materials*. Thousand Oaks, CA: Sage.

Clough, P. T. (1992). *The ends of ethnography: From realism to social criticism*. Newbury Park, CA: Sage.

Cochran-Smith, M., & Lytle, S. L. (1999). Relationships of knowledge and practice: Teacher learning in communities. In A. Iran-Nejad & P. D. Pearson (Eds.), *Review of research in education* (pp. 249–305). Washington, DC: American Educational Research Association.

Coles, R. (1967). *Children of crisis: A study of courage and fear*. Boston: Little, Brown.

Coles, R. (1986). *The political life of children*. Boston: Atlantic Monthly Press.

Coles, R. (1989). *The call of stories*. Boston: Houghton Mifflin.

Coles, R., & Coles, J. H. (1980). *Women of crisis: Lives of struggle and hope*. New York: Delecorte.

Combs, A., & Snygg, D. (1959). *Individual behaviour: A perceptual approach*. New York: Harper & Row.

Connelly, F. M., & Clandinin, D. J. (1988). *Teachers as curriculum planners: Narratives of experience*. New York: Teachers College Press.

Creswell, J. W. (2003). *Research design: Qualitative, quantitative, and mixed methods approaches* (2nd ed.). Thousand Oaks, CA: Sage.

Daniels, H. (1994). *Literature circles*. York, ME: Stenhouse.

Delpit, L. (1995). *Other people's children: Cultural conflict in the classroom.* New York: New Press.

Denzin, N. K. (2003). The call to performance. *Symbolic interaction, 26*(1), 187–207.

Denzin, N. K., & Lincoln, Y. S. (Eds.). (2003). *Collecting and interpreting qualitative materials.* Thousand Oaks, CA: Sage.

Denzin, N. K., & Lincoln, Y. S. (1998). Entering the field of qualitative research. In N. K. Denzin & Y. S. Lincoln (Eds.), *Collecting and interpreting qualitative materials* (pp. 1–34). Thousand Oaks, CA: Sage.

Dewey, J. (1916). *Democracy and education.* New York: Macmillan.

Drucker Kanevsky, R. (1993). Descriptive review of a child: A way of knowing about teaching and learning. In M. Cochran-Smith, & S. L. Lytle (Eds.), *Inside/outside: Teacher research and knowledge.* New York: Teachers College Press.

Dunning, S., Lueders, E., & Smith, H. (1966). *Reflections on a watermelon pickle.* Glenville, IL: Scott Foresman.

Ebbutt, D. (1985). Educational action research: Some general concerns and specific quibbles. In R. Burgess (Ed.), *Issues in educational research.* London: Falmer Press.

Eisner, E. (2001). *The educational imagination: On the design and evaluation of school programs.* Upper Saddle River, NJ: Prentice-Hall.

Eisner, E. W. (1985). *The educational imagination: On the design and evaluation of school programs* (2nd ed.). New York: Macmillan.

Eisner, E. W. (1991). *The enlightened eye: Qualitative inquiry and the enhancement of educational practice.* New York: Macmillan.

Elbow, P. (1973). *Writing without teachers.* New York: Oxford University Press.

Elkind, D. (1997). Schooling and family in the postmodern world. In A. Hargreaves (Ed.), *Rethinking educational change with heart and mind: ASCD year book* (pp. 27–42). Alexandria, VA: Association for Supervision and Curriculum Development.

Elliott, J. (1991). *Action research for educational change.* Milton Keynes, Philadelphia, PA: Open University Press.

Elliott, J. (2003). The struggle to redefine the relationship between knowledge and action in the academy: Some reflections on action research. Doctor Honoris Causa John Elliott Address, Universitat Autonoma de Barcelona, Barcelona, Spain.

Emig, J. (1977). Writing as a mode of learning. *College Composition and Communication, 28*(2), 122–128.

Emig, J. (1982). Inquiry paradigms and writing. *College Composition and Communication, 33,* 64–73.

Engle, S. H., & Ochoa, A. S. (1988). *Education for democratic citizenship: Decision making in the social studies.* New York: Teachers College Press.

Erickson, F., & Shultz, J. (1992). Students' experiences of the curriculum. In P. W. Jackson (Ed.), *Handbook of research on curriculum* (pp. 465–485). New York: Macmillan.

Erikson, E. (1950). *Childhood and society.* New York: Norton.

Ferrucci, P. (1982). *What we may be*. New York: Putnam.

Fine, A., & Sandstrom, K. L. (1988). *Knowing children: Participant observation with minors*. Thousand Oaks, CA: Sage.

Flower, L. (1981). Writer-based prose: A cognitive base for problems in writing. In G. S. Tate & E. P. J. Corbett, (Eds.), *The writing teacher's sourcebook* (pp. 269–293). New York: Oxford University Press.

Flower, L., & Hayes, J. R. (1980). Writing as problem solving. *Visible Language, 14*, 388–399.

Flower, L., & Hayes, J. R. (1981). A cognitive process theory of writing. *College Composition and Communication, 32*(4), 365–387.

Fouts, J. T., & Myers, R. E. (1992). Classroom environments and middle school students' views of science. *Journal of Educational Research, 85*(6), 356–361.

Freeman, M. (1997). *Listen to this: Developing an ear for expository*. Gainsville, FL: Maupin House.

Freire, P. (1970). *Pedagogy of the oppressed* (M. B. Ramos, Trans.). New York: Herder & Herder.

Fuller, F. (1969). Concerns of teachers: A developmental characterization. *American Educational Research Journal, 6*(2), 207–226.

Fulwiler, T. (1987). *The journal book*. Portsmouth, NH: Heinemann/Boynton Cook.

Gardner, H. (1993). *Multiple intelligences: The theory in practice*. New York: HarperCollins.

Giroux, H., & McLaren, P. (1986). Teacher education and the politics of engagement: The case for democratic schooling. *Harvard Educational Review, 56*(3), 213–238.

Goldberg, N. (1990). *Wild mind: living the writer's life*. New York. Bantam Books.

Goldberg, N. (1986). *Writing down the bones: Freeing the writer within*. Boston: Shambhala Press [New York].

Goodlad, J. I. (1984). *A place called school*. New York: McGraw-Hill.

Goodman, Y. M. (1978 & 1991). Kidwatching: An alternative to testing. *National Elementary Principal, 57*, 41–45.

Greider, W. (1991). *Who will tell the people? The betrayal of American democracy*. New York: Touchstone.

Grumet, M. (1990). Retrospective: Autobiography and the analysis of educational experience. *Cambridge Journal of Education, 20*(3), 321–326.

Guba, E. G., & Lincoln, Y. S. (1994). Competing paradigm in qualitative research. In D. K. Denzin & Y. S. Lincoln (Eds.), *Handbook of qualitative research* (pp. 105–117). Thousand Oaks, CA: Sage.

Habermas, J. (1972). *Knowledge and human interests*. Boston: Beacon Press.

Hall, E. T. (1976). *Beyond culture*. New York: Doubleday.

Hargreaves, A., Earl, L., & Ryan, J. (1996). *Schooling for change: Reinventing education for early adolescents*. Washington, DC: Falmer Press.

Harris, T. L., & Hodges, R. E. (Eds.). (1995). *The literacy dictionary*. Newark, DE: International Reading Association.

Havel, V. (1992, March 1). The end of the modern era. *New York Times*.

Heath, S. B. (1983). *Ways with words: Language, life, and work in communities and classrooms.* New York: Cambridge University Press.

Henk, W., & Melnick, S. (1995). The reader self-perception scale (RSPS): A new tool for measuring how children feel about themselves as readers. *The Reading Teacher, 48,* 470–482.

Herr, K., & Anderson, G. L. (2005). *The action research dissertation: A guide for students and faculty.* Thousand Oaks, CA: Sage.

Hiebert, J., Gallimore, R., & Stigler, J. W. (2002). A knowledge base for the teaching profession: What would it look like and how can we get one? *Educational Researcher, 31*(5), 3–15.

Hodder, I. (1998). The interpretation of documents and material culture. In N. K. Denzin & Y. S. Lincoln (Eds.), *Collecting and interpreting qualitative materials* (pp. 110–129). Thousand Oaks, CA: Sage.

Holly, M. L. (1989). *Writing to grow: Keeping a personal-professional journal.* Portsmouth, NH: Heinemann.

Holmevick, J. R., & Haynes, C. (2000). Lingua MOO. Retrieved November 11, 2003, from http://www.dartmouth.edu/~webteach/cases/linguamoo.html

Hopkins, C., & Antes, J. (1985). *Classroom measurement and evaluation.* Itasca, IL: Peacock.

Hopkins, D. (2002). *A teacher's guide to classroom research* (3rd ed.). Philadelphia: Open University Press.

Horton, M. (1993). *The long haul: An autobiography.* New York: Teachers College Columbia.

Hubbard, R. S., & Power, B. M. (1993). *The art of classroom inquiry: A handbook for teacher-researchers.* Portsmouth, NH: Heinemann.

Hubbard, R. S., & Power, B. M. (1999). *Living the questions: A guide for teacher researchers.* York, ME: Stenhouse.

Hunt, K. (1965). *Grammatical structures written at three grade levels.* Urbana, IL: National Council of Teachers of English.

Hunt, P., Allwell, M., & Goetz, L. (1996). Creating socially supportive environments for fully included students who experience multiple disabilities. *Journal of the Association for Persons with Severe Handicaps, 21*(2), 53–71.

Hutchinson, J. (1994). Creating a classroom community. In J. G. Henderson (Ed.), *Reflective teaching: The study of your constructivist practices* (pp. 133–145). Englewood Cliffs, NJ: Merrill.

Hyerle, D. (1996). *Visual tools for constructing knowledge.* Alexandria, VA: Association for Supervision and Curriculum Development.

Janney, R. E., & Snell, M. E. (1996). How teachers use peer interactions to include students with moderate and severe disabilities in elementary general education classes. *Journal of the Association for Persons with Severe Handicaps, 21*(2), 72–80.

Kasten, W. C. (1991). Books beget books. In K. S. Goodman, L. B. Bird, & Y. M. Goodman (Eds.), *The whole language catalog.* Santa Rosa, CA: American School.

Kasten, W. C. (1995). Literature circles for the teaching of literature based reading. In M. C. Radencich & L. J. McKay (Eds.), *Flexible grouping for literacy in the elementary grades*. Needham Heights, MA: Allyn & Bacon.

Kegan, R. (1994). *In over our heads: The mental demands of modern life*. Cambridge, MA: Harvard University Press.

Kegan, R. (1982). *The evolving self*. Cambridge, MA: Harvard University Press.

Kemmis, S., & McTaggert, R. (1988). *The action research planner* (3rd ed.). Geelong, Victoria, Australia: Deakin University Press.

Kent State University Human Subject Review Board. *Application to use human subjects in research*. Unpublished document. Kent, OH: Kent State University.

Kolb, D. (1983). *Experiential learning*. New York: Simon & Schuster.

Kotter, J. P. (1996). *Leading change*. Boston: Harvard Business School Press.

Kuhn, T. (1970). *The structure of scientific revolutions*. Chicago: University of Chicago Press.

Lambert, J. (2006). *Digital storytelling: Capturing lives, creating community*. Berkeley, CA: Digital Dinner Press.

Lawrence-Lightfoot, S. (1983). *The good high school: Portraits of character and culture*. New York: Basic Books.

Lawrence-Lightfoot, S., & Davis, J. H. (1997). *The art and science of portraiture*. San Francisco: Jossey-Bass.

LeDoux, J. (1996). *The emotional brain: The mysterious underpinnings of emotional life*. New York: Simon & Schuster.

LeDoux, J. (2002). *The synaptic self: How our brains become who we are*. New York: Penguin Putnam Inc.

Leistyna, P., Woodrum, A., & Sherblom, S. A. (1996). *Breaking free: The transformative power of critical pedagogy*. Reprint Series No. 27. Cambridge, MA: Harvard Educational Review.

Lincoln, Y. (1997). What constitutes quality in interpretive research. In C. K. Kinzer, K. A. Hinchman, & D. J. Leu (Eds.), *Inquiries in literacy theory and practice*. Forty-sixth Yearbook of the National Reading Conference. Chicago, IL: National Reading Conference.

Lippitt, R. (1949). *Training in community relations: A research exploration toward new group skills*. New York: Harper.

Lortie, D. C. (1975). *School teacher: A sociological study*. Chicago: University of Chicago Press.

Macrorie, K. (1980). *Telling writing* (3rd ed.). Rochelle Park, NJ: Hayden Book.

Mallon, T. (1984). *A book of one's own: People and their diaries*. New York: Ticknor & Fields.

Maroufi, C. (1989). A study of student attitude toward traditional and generative models of instruction. *Adolescence, 24*(93), 65–72.

Marshall, C., & Rossman, G. B. (1999). *Designing qualitative research* (3rd ed.). Thousand Oaks, CA: Sage.

Maxwell, J. A. (2005). *Qualitative research design: An interactive approach*. Thousand Oaks, CA: Sage.

McCabe, N. (1995). Twelve high school 11th grade students examine their best teachers. *Peabody Journal of Education, 70*(2), 117–126.

McDowell, E. E., & McDowell, C. E. (1986). *A study of high school students' expectations of the teaching style of male, female, English and science instructors.* (ERIC Document Reproduction Service No. ED 278 074)

McKernan, J. (1996). *Curriculum action research: A handbook of methods and resources for the reflective practitioner* (2nd ed.). London: Kogan Page.

McLaren, P. (1992). Collisions with otherness: "Traveling" theory, post-colonial criticism, and the politics of ethnographic practice—The mission of the wounded ethnographer. *The International Journal of Qualitative Studies in Education, 5*(1), 77–92.

McNiff, J. (1993). *Teaching as learning: An action research approach.* New York: Routledge.

McNiff, J., Lomax, P., & Whitehead, J. (1996). *You and your action research project.* London: Routledge.

McTaggart, R. (1991). *Action research: A short modern history.* Geelong, Australia: Deakin University Press.

McTaggart, R. (1997). *Participatory action research: International contexts and consequences.* Albany: State University of New York Press.

Mead, M. (1934). *Mind, self, and society: From the standpoint of a social behaviorist.* Chicago: University of Chicago Press.

Melillo, J. A. (1999). *An analysis of students' transition from arithmetic to algebraic thinking.* Unpublished doctoral dissertation, Kent State University, Kent, OH.

Mezirow, J. (1981). A critical theory of adult learning. *Studies in Adult Education, 32*(1), 3–24.

Miles, M. B., & Huberman, A. M. (1994). *Qualitative data analysis* (2nd ed.). Thousand Oaks, CA: Sage.

Moffit, J. (1966). To look at any thing. In S. Dunning, E. Lueders, & H. Smith (Eds.), *Reflections on a watermelon pickle* (p. 21). Glenville, IL: Scott, Foresman.

Montagu, A. (1989). *Growing young* (2nd ed.). Granby, MA: Bergin & Garvey.

National Forum to Accelerate Middle Grades Reform. Retrieved on November 11, 2003, from http://www.mgforum.org

Oakes, J. (1985). *Keeping track.* New Haven, CT: Yale University Press.

Oakley, A. (1981). Interviewing women: A contradiction in terms. In H. Roberts (Ed.), *Doing feminist research.* London: Routledge & Kegan Paul.

Oja, S. (1989). Teachers: Ages and stages of adult development. In M. L. Holly & C. S. McLoughlin (Eds.), *Perspectives on teacher professional development.* London: Falmer Press.

Oliver, M. (1995). *Blue pastures.* New York: Harcourt, Brace.

Ornstein, R. (1991). *The evolution of consciousness: Of Darwin, Freud, and cranial fire—The origins of the way we think.* New York: Prentice Hall.

Ornstein, R. (1995). *The roots of the self: Unraveling the mystery of who we are.* New York: HarperCollins.

Ornstein, R., & Ehrlich, P. (1989). *New world new mind.* New York: Simon & Schuster.

Oxford English Dictionary. (1979). *The compact edition of the Oxford English Dictionary*. Vol. II. P–Z. Oxford, England: Oxford University Press.

Palmer P. (1998). *The courage to teach: Exploring the inner landscape of a teacher's life.* San Francisco, CA: Jossey-Bass.

Peck, C. (1990). Some benefits non-handicapped adolescents perceive for themselves from their social relationships with peers who have severe handicaps. *Journal of the Association for Persons with Severe Handicaps, 15*(4), 241–249.

Perl, S. (1980). Understanding composing. *College Composition and Communication, 31*, 363–369.

Perl, S. (1981). Creativity and the composing process: Making thoughts visible. (ERIC Document Reproduction No. 202025)

Piaget, J. (1926). *The language and thought of the child.* New York: Harcourt, Brace, and World.

Polkinghorne, D. (1988). *Narrative knowing and the human sciences.* New York: State University of New York Press.

Power, B. M. (1996). *Taking note: Improving your observational note taking.* York, ME: Stenhouse.

Radz, M. A. (1983). Promoting a democratic school climate. In M. A. Hepburn (Ed.), *Democratic education in schools and classrooms* (pp. 67–87). Washington, DC: National Council for Social Studies.

The Random House Dictionary of the English Language (unabridged ed.). (1967). New York: Random House.

Richardson, L. (1998). Writing: A mode of inquiry. In N. K. Denzin & Y. S. Lincoln (Eds.), *Collecting and interpreting qualitative materials* (pp. 345–371). Thousand Oaks, CA: Sage.

Rilke, R. M. (1987). *Letters to a young poet.* New York: Random House.

Roget, P. (1980). *Roget's thesaurus of English words and phrases.* New York: St. Martin's Press.

Rowan, T. E., & Bourne, B. (1994). *Thinking like mathematicians: Putting the K–4 NCTM standards into practice.* Portsmouth, NH: Heinemann.

Schaps, E., Lewis, C., & Watson, M. (1996). Building community in school. *Principal, 76*(2), 29–31.

Schram, T. H. (2006). *Conceptualizing and proposing qualitative research.* Upper Saddle River, NJ: Pearson Merrill Prentice Hall.

Selfe, C. L. (2008). *Multimodal composition: Resources for teachers.* Cresskill, NJ: Hampton Press.

Shug, M. C., Todd, R. J., & Beery, R. (1984). Why kids don't like social studies. *Social Education, 48*, 382–387.

Slavin, R. (1988). Synthesis on research on grouping in elementary and secondary schools. *Educational Leadership, 46*(1), 67–77.

Smith, F. (1988). *Joining the literacy club.* Portsmouth, NH: Heinemann.

SoHuyn, L., & Odom, S. L. (1996). The relationships between stereotypic behavior and peer social interaction for children with severe disabilities. *Journal of the Association for Persons with Severe Handicaps, 21*(2), 88–95.

Spradley, J. P. (1980). *Participant observation*. New York: Holt.

Spradley, J. P. (1979). *The ethnographic interview*. New York: Holt.

Stake, R. E. (1995). *The art of case study research*. Thousand Oaks, CA: Sage.

Stake, R. (1988). Case study methods in educational research: Seeking sweet water. In R. M. Jaeger (Ed.), *Complementary methods for research in education* (pp. 253–278). Washington, DC: American Educational Research Association.

Stenhouse, L. (1975). *An introduction to curriculum research and development*. London: Heinemann.

Stenhouse, L. (1981). What counts as research? *British Journal of Educational Studies 29*, 2.

Strauss, A., & Corbin, J. (1990). *The basics of qualitative research: Grounded theory procedures and techniques*. Newbury Park, CA: Sage.

Stringer, E. T. (1996). *Action research: A handbook for practitioners*. Thousands Oaks, CA: Sage.

Stringer, E. T. (2004). *Action research in education*. Upper Saddle River, NJ: Pearson.

Tagg, J. (2003). *The learning paradigm college*. Boston: Anker Publishing.

Taylor, K., & Roselli, H. (1993). *Results of student survey: Thomas E. Weightman Middle School—Florida*. Unpublished report.

Taylor, W. (1984). Metaphors of educational discourse. In W. Taylor (Ed.), *Metaphors in education* (pp. 4–20). London: Heinemann.

Tom, A. R. (1997). *Redesigning teacher education*. Albany: State University of New York Press.

Tripp, D. (1990). Socially critical action research. *Theory into Practice, 29*(3), 158–166.

Tripp, D. (1993). *Critical incidents in teaching: Developing professional judgements*. New York: London: Routledge.

Tripp, D. (1996) *The SCOPE Program*. Perth: Western Australia: Murdoch University Center for Curriculum and Professional Development (http://murdock.edu.au/scope/)

Van der Klift, E., & Kunc, N. (1994). *Creativity and collaborative learning: A practical guide to empowering students and teachers*. Baltimore: Paul Brookes.

Van Maanen, J. (1988). *Tales of the field: On writing ethnography*. Chicago: University of Chicago Press.

Wasserman, P. (1995). What middle schoolers say about their schoolwork. *Educational Leadership, 53*(1), 41–43.

Webb, E., Campbell, D., Schwartz, R., & Sechrest, L. (1966). *Unobtrusive measures: Non-reactive research in the social sciences*. Chicago: Rand McNally.

Wenger, E., McDermott, R., & Snyder, W. M. (2002). *Cultivating communities of practice*. Boston, MA: Harvard Business School Press.

Wheelock, A. (1994). *Alternatives to tracking and ability grouping*. Arlington, VA: American Association of School Administrators.

Whitehead, J. (1996). Reconceptualizing policy on in-service teacher education. In R. McBride (Ed.), *Teacher education policy: Some issues arising from research practice*. London: Falmer Press.

Wolcott, H. F. (1992). Posturing in qualitative inquiry. In M. D. Le Compte, W. L. Millroy, & J. Preissle (Eds.), *Handbook of qualitative research in education* (pp. 3–52). San Diego, CA: Academic Press.

Wolcott, H. F. (1994). *Transforming qualitative data.* Thousand Oaks, CA: Sage.

Zeni, J. (1998). A guide to ethical issues and action research. *Educational Action Researcher, 6*(1), 9–19.

Zeni, J. (1999, June 21). Ethics data [e-mail correspondence related to *How to approach ethical issues in teacher research, presentation at the International Conference on Teacher Research*, Magog, Quebec, Canada, April 23, 1999].

Zull, J. (2002). *The art of changing the brain.* Sterling, VA: Stylus Press.

Index

About the Authors

Joanne M. Arhar

Kent State University

Joanne M. Arhar is a professor and associate dean in the College of Education, Health, and Human Services at Kent State University. She started her career as a high school English teacher in the Cleveland area, where she established the first interdisciplinary team teaching program at the school. She then moved into administration, supporting teachers in curriculum development, professional development, interdisciplinary teaming, and school reorganization from a traditional junior high school to a middle school. During her doctoral program at the University of Cincinnati, she studied the ways in which teams in schools as well as industry developed and supported a more collaborative and productive work and learning environment. Following graduate school, Joanne took a faculty position in the Department of Educational Leadership at the University of South Florida and in 1994 became a faculty member in the Department of Teaching, Leadership, and Curriculum Studies at Kent State University, where she coordinated the Middle Childhood Education program and taught action research courses to teachers. In her current role as associate dean, Joanne oversees student services, undergraduate education, and teacher education. She also teaches an online action research course for the Ohio Department of Education.

Mary Louise Holly

Kent State University

Mary Louise Holly is a professor in the department of Teaching, Leadership, and Curriculum Studies, and director of Kent State University's Faculty Professional Development Center. Her career began in 1968 as an elementary school art consultant. She became a classroom teacher of young children, and later a professor of curriculum and teaching. Her study of professional development led her as a visiting scholar to the Centre for Applied Research in Education at the University of East Anglia in England, and the School of Education at Deakin University in Australia. Early in her career Mary Lou began documenting and learning from teaching using artistic and qualitative methods. This led her to action research and laid a foundation for later work with adults using life history and biographical methods. Related works include: *Writing to Grow: Keeping a Personal-Professional Journal* (Heinemann, 1989) and *Perspectives on Teacher Professional Development* with Caven McLoughlin (Falmer Press, 1989).

Wendy C. Kasten

Kent State University

Wendy C. Kasten is a professor of Curriculum and Instruction in Literacy at Kent State University, teaching the action research course for the graduate program in reading specialization. At KSU since 1995, Kasten has taught elementary school in Maine, and higher education at the University of South Florida, University of Maine, and at Deakin University in Australia. She earned her PhD degree from the University of Arizona's program in Language and Literacy in 1984, where she was a graduate teaching and research assistant. Kasten is active in the International Reading Association, the National Council of Teachers of English, the National Reading Conference and the Whole Language Umbrella. She is the 1997–2001 President of the Center for the Expansion of Language and Thinking (CELT), an invitation-only collective of literacy educators in multiple countries who share holistic and constructivist views of learning. She is co-author of *Living Literature: Using Children's Literature to Support Reading and Language Arts* (with J. V. Kristo and A. A. McClure, 2005, Pearson) and many chapters and articles on literacy topics. Kasten is also an associate editor of the *Reading and Writing Quarterly* and is extensively involved in international education projects.